GW00507309

The life and times of Sir Frederick Hamilton

13.9.2013

To Dolores,

The life and times of
Sir Frederick Hamilton
1590–1647
'The Bragger'

Dominic Rooney

With very best wishes
& happy memories of
the 'olden' days in manor Hamilton.

Dominic

FOUR COURTS PRESS

Typeset in 10.5 pt on 13.5 pt AGaramondPro by
Carrigboy Typesetting Services for
FOUR COURTS PRESS LTD
7 Malpas Street, Dublin 8, Ireland
www.fourcourtspress.ie
and in North America for
FOUR COURTS PRESS
c/o ISBS, 920 NE 58th Avenue, Suite 300, Portland, OR 97213.

© the author and Four Courts Press 2013

A catalogue record for this title is available
from the British Library.

ISBN 978–1–84682–396–1 hbk
978–1–84682–424–1 pbk

All rights reserved.
Without limiting the rights under copyright
reserved alone, no part of this publication may be
reproduced, stored in or introduced into a retrieval system,
or transmitted, in any form or by any means (electronic, mechanical,
photocopying, recording or otherwise), without the prior
written permission of both the copyright owner and
publisher of this book.

SPECIAL ACKNOWLEDGMENT

This publication has been made possible by financial assistance from the Marc Fitch Fund for Research
and Publication (established by Marcus Felix Brudenell Fitch CBE DLitt HonFBA FSA in 1956)
and Leitrim Development Company Rural Development Programme, which is financed by the Irish
Government under the Rural Development Programme Ireland 2007–13 and by the European
Agricultural Fund for Rural Development: Europe Investing in Rural Areas.

MARC FITCH FUND

Printed in England
by CPI Antony Rowe, Chippenham, Wilts.

In memory of my parents,
Paddy and Maureen Rooney,
who inspired me with a love of my native place

Contents

Abbreviations

AIT	Athlone Institute of Technology
AOSB	Axel Oxenstiernas Skrifter och Brefvexling, manuscript collection in SRA
Bodl.	Bodleian Library, Oxford
BL	British Library, London
CBK	Committee of Both Kingdoms
comp.	compiler/compiled by
CPRI	*Calendar of the patent and close rolls of chancery in Ireland, 1514–1633*, ed. J. Morrin (3 vols, Dublin, 1861–3)
CSPD	*Calendar of state papers, domestic, Charles I*, vols xii–xxii, *1637–49* (London, 1869–97)
CSPI	*Calendar of state papers, Ireland: 1603–25*, ed. C.W. Russell and J.P. Prendergast (5 vols, London, 1872–80); *1625–60*, ed. R.P. Mahaffy (4 vols, London, 1900–4); *1660–70, addenda, 1625–70*, ed. R.P. Mahaffy (London, 1910)
HMC	Historical Manuscripts Commission (merged with PRO to form TNA in 2003)
IHS	*Irish Historical Studies: the Joint Journal of the Irish Historical Society and the Ulster Society for Irish Historical Studies* (Dublin, 1938–)
JRSAI	*Journal of the Royal Society of Antiquaries of Ireland* (Dublin, 1892–)
Marsh	Marsh's Library, Dublin
NAI	National Archives of Ireland [includes former PROI], Dublin
NLI	National Library of Ireland
NRS	National Records of Scotland [formerly National Archives of Scotland], Edinburgh
NUIG	National University of Ireland
ODNB	*Oxford dictionary of national biography*
OS	Ordnance Survey
PA	Parliamentary Archives [formerly House of Lords Records Office], London
PRIA	*Proceedings of the Royal Irish Academy* (Dublin, 1836–)
PRO	Public Record Office [merged with HMC to form TNA in 2003]
PRONI	Public Records Office of Northern Ireland
QUB	Queens University Belfast
RAOSB	*Rikskansleren Axel Oxenstiernas Skrifter och Brefvexling* (1st ser., 15 vols, Stockholm, 1888–; 2nd ser., 14 vols, 1888–)

repr.   reprint/reprinted
RIA   Royal Irish Academy
RPCS   *Register of the Privy Council of Scotland*, 2nd ser., v (1630–2), ed. P.
             Hume Brown (Edinburgh, 1902)
ser.   series
SO   Signet Office
SRA   Swedish Riksarkivet [the National Archives of Sweden]
SSNE   Scotland, Scandinavia and northern European biographical database,
             published online at http://www.st-andrews.ac.uk/history/ssne/
TCD   Trinity College Dublin
TNA   The National Archives of the United Kingdom [formerly PRO], London
UCD   University College Dublin

Acknowledgments

As a youngster growing up in the shadow of Hamilton's castle and hearing stories of dungeons, scaffolds, banquet murders and escape tunnels, I was always fascinated by what lay behind those tall ivy-clad bawn or courtyard walls. The answers I received to my many questions were, however, usually based on legend and folklore.

Then in the mid-1960s I read with great interest Fr Daniel Gallogly's authoritative and substantial article on Sir Frederick Hamilton in the historical journal *Breifne*. Using Gallogly's footnotes as a starting point, I gradually began to acquire copies of the various documents upon which he had based his study. I have spent the last twenty years in particular greatly expanding my research into all aspects of the life and times of the colourful and complex Hamilton.

I am indebted to many scholars who either transcribed copies of seventeenth-century documents relating to Hamilton into modern English or who translated relevant material from Latin, Swedish and mid-seventeenth-century Scots. Chief among these was the late Gearóid Mac Niocaill, of the Department of History at NUIG, for his painstaking transcription of lengthy documents – a few of which were almost illegible. John A. Madden, of the Department of Classics at the same university, translated from Latin the Hamilton correspondence that came from the Swedish Riksarkivet, while Louise Yeoman, Manuscripts Department, National Library of Scotland, deciphered Sir Frederick's testament dative and inventar from Old Scots. PhD students from St Andrews and NUIG – Siobhan Talbott, Adam Marks, Adam Carr, Björn Nordgren and Jerry Lidwill – carried out further transcriptions and translations.

I received much help along the way from many individuals. I would like to thank in particular Steve Murdoch, Professor of History at St Andrews University, for his patience and unfailing courtesy when responding to my endless questions relating to the Thirty Years War in general and to Hamilton's campaign in particular. He also generously provided me with relevant material from his personal research and writings on the Scots' involvement in the armies of northern European powers in the seventeenth century. In addition, I have made extensive use of his and Alexia Grosjean's *Scotland, Scandinavia and northern Europe* (*SSNE*) biographical database of some eight thousand of the military, naval, diplomatic, intellectual, mercantile and social elite from the British Isles who migrated to or worked in Denmark-Norway, Sweden and the Baltic countries between 1580 and 1707.

Robin Greenwood and Alex Forbes also very kindly made available to me their research on Alexander, Master of Forbes, who had collaborated with Sir Frederick Hamilton in raising troops for Swedish service in Germany in 1631. I benefited greatly from our three-way correspondence over several years as we sought to explore the intricacies of that mission. Robin alerted me as well to several other important sources of relevant information.

The following also provided information, advice or help at various times during my research: David Stevenson, Professor Emeritus of Scottish History at St Andrews University; Edward Furgol, Curator, Naval Historical Center, Washington DC; Roger Stalley, TCD; Raymond Gillespie, NUI Maynooth, who was encouraging and supportive from the start, but particularly at the publication stage; Alastair Cherry, Assistant Keeper, National Library of Scotland, whose assistance and personal interest in the Hamilton story were much appreciated; the late Bob Hunter, University of Ulster, who made freely available to me much of his research on Sir William Cole; Rolf Loeber, University of Pittsburgh; Harmon Murtagh, AIT; Eddie McParland, Department of History of Art, TCD; Mary O'Dowd, QUB; Ronald Hutton, Professor of British History, University of Bristol, Alex Ward, Assistant Keeper, Art and Industrial Division, National Museum of Ireland at Collins Barracks; Damien McGarry, Rathfarnham Castle; Bríd McGrath, TCD; Robert Armstrong, TCD; Kevin McKenny; Anthony and Maura Daly, who allowed me to consult the Clements' House deeds of Manorhamilton Castle and the Cottage; Winifred Molloy; the dukes of Abercorn and of Hamilton; Viscount Boyne; Philip McHugh, who provided archival material on the Tottenham estate; Robert H. Bonar, assistant secretary, Presbyterian Historical Society of Ireland; Gabriel Miney, former district engineer, Leitrim County Council; William Roulston, Research Director, Ulster Historical Foundation; Kevin and Aoife Rooney, who explained archaic legal terminology used in some of the court cases in which Sir Frederick was involved; Barry Bradfield; Fr Padraig O'Connor; James Molloy, who provided me with a photograph of Hamilton's Castle; Rory Fitzgerald, Ruth Hegarty and Ian Hilder.

I am grateful to the staff of the following archives and libraries for their assistance and courtesy: the Riksarkivet in Stockholm (esp. Helmut Backhaus and the late Per-Gunnar Ottosson), the Swedish Military Archives (esp. Bo Lundström), the British Library, Bodleian Library in Oxford, National Archives in Kew, Parliamentary Archives, National Records of Scotland, National Library of Scotland, Hamilton Library, Paisley Library, Kinneil Museum in Falkirk, Public Record Office of Northern Ireland, Central Library in Derry, Linen Hall Library, Tower Museum, Derry City Council, Derry Genealogy Centre, St Columb's Cathedral, Derry (especially Ian Bartlett, tour guide), Western

Education and Library Board, Omagh Library, Enniskillen Library, TCD Library (esp. Martin Whelan and Paul Ferguson), TCD Alumni Office, Marsh's Library (esp. Maria O'Shea), National Library of Ireland (esp. Colette O'Flaherty and Gráinne Mac Loughlainn), Royal Irish Academy, Leitrim County Library (esp. Seán Ó Suilleabhain, Gabrielle Flynn and Mary Conefrey), Sligo County Library, Cavan County Library, and NUIG Library (esp. Marie Boran and Margaret Hughes).

I wish to express my sincere thanks to those who read all or part of the text. Their valuable suggestions for improvement were very much appreciated and saved me from many errors. I am particularly grateful to Joe Clarke, who proofread, and made a critical analysis of, the draft of each chapter as it appeared and then reviewed the completed manuscript at the end. The comments and advice of Raymond Gillespie, Steve Murdoch, Brian Mac Cuarta, director, Archivium Romanum Societatis Jesu, Rome, and the external reviewers from Four Courts Press were also much valued, as were those of Prin Duignan, Eamonn Gunn, Margaret Connolly, Anthony Daly and John Grigg. Needless to say, any mistakes that remain are entirely my own.

I received much help along the way from Róisín, Maureen and Maria at I-Supply, Quay Street, Galway. Special thanks must go to Pádraig, who designed and produced all the maps.

I am very grateful to the editorial staff of Four Courts Press – especially Michael Potterton – for their support and commitment to the project.

I would like to acknowledge the strong backing and practical help I received from the Manorhamilton and District Historical Society and I am especially indebted to the Leitrim Development Company Rural Development Programme and the trustees of the Marc Fitch Fund for their financial assistance.

Finally, I would like to thank my wife Mary for her tolerance of, and patience with, the unseen but very pervasive presence in our home of Sir Frederick Hamilton over many years. Without her support and encouragement, I could not have undertaken and accomplished the task of researching the life of 'the Bragger'.

A NOTE ON DATES AND CURRENCY

Dates throughout are given according to the Old Style (Julian) calendar, which was used in Britain and Ireland during the seventeenth century. This calendar was ten days behind the New Style (Gregorian) one, which was then used on the Continent. I have, however, taken the New Year to begin on 1 January, not on 25 March as reckoned by most of those who followed the Julian calendar. The £ sterling was worth £12 Scots in the seventeenth century.

Introduction

One of the most salient of Sir Frederick Hamilton's character traits was his tendency to exaggerate both his own importance and his achievements, especially when seeking favours from a higher authority. He was, in other words, a 'bragger' – one who boasts loudly or exaggeratedly. This feature of his personality became especially evident in his 'humble' petitions, remonstrances and information addressed to the English parliament and the Committee of Both Kingdoms (CBK) during the mid 1640s when he was seeking a regimental command in the army in Ireland, joint presidency of Connacht, governorship of Derry and Sligo and compensation for his losses during the rebellion.

In his so-called diary, which was written up by one of his clerks or clergymen, he boasted about the 'particular' or exceptional services performed by his troop of horse and company of foot at Manorhamilton. These included the killing of sixty of the enemy, with the loss of only two his own men in an engagement with rebels from Leitrim and Sligo who outnumbered the soldiers in his garrison by more than ten-to-one in February 1642. The following month he claimed to have routed an insurgent force from Sligo that was five times larger than his own, killing many of them, while sustaining no casualties himself. Again, in November of that year, he insisted that a hundred of his soldiers defeated one thousand rebels from Cavan and Fermanagh. In other pamphlets to Westminster he boasted that he had maintained his castle at Manorhamilton in the midst of many enemies from Connacht and Ulster, without any aid or relief. His small handful of horse and foot had killed hundreds of insurgents, including many experienced Irish soldiers who had returned from fighting for Spain in the Thirty Years War. His service in Leitrim was so successful that 'it hath been a terrour to the powerfulest of those bloody rebels'. Not surprisingly, he proclaimed that the 'wonderfull things God hath done for us, and with us, is not unknown to my greatest enemies'.

On one occasion in 1643 he even pressurized one of his English prisoners, Robert Parke from Newtown, into writing to his father-in-law, Sir Edward Povey, who was then seeking his release, that Sir Frederick's record of service to the state 'even with a very few men and with so small losse of them, is not to be paralleled in any kingdom ... and the whole relation whereof would take up a volum to be written'. He also gave such a glowing account of his achievements to the sub-committee for Irish affairs in London that it concluded that 'no one man in that kingdom ... with so small a force as he hath had, can possibly pretend to more satisfaction from the state than himself' on account of his bravery, perseverance and success against the rebels. Unfortunately, however, the lack of corroborating evidence makes it difficult to establish the veracity of some of Hamilton's assertions.

In February 1644 he also claimed to have been successful 'beyond expectation' in persuading most of the Scots army in Ulster (which was allied with the English parliament) not to abandon the northern province and return to its homeland, despite its impoverished condition. He further maintained that the Presbyterian ministers who were sent from Scotland to administer the Covenant to all the British in Ulster two months later, would not have succeeded in their mission in Derry were it not for his involvement and assistance.

Hamilton had similarly tried to impress Queen Kristina and the senate of Sweden in 1637 with claims of his own importance when he was seeking redress over the unfair disbandment of his regiment by the Swedish authorities in Germany five years earlier. He alleged that he could not travel to Sweden in the meantime because he was employed in certain 'special' services at the English court. He also declared that King Gustavus Adolphus of Sweden had, in 1632, commended him to Charles I of Britain and had personally given him several princely tokens of his favour when sending him back to England to recruit more soldiers for Swedish service in the Thirty Years War.

Hamilton was, however, far from being a one-dimensional character. He was also a complex mix of many other personality traits. For example, he was accused by the lord lieutenant, the marquis of Ormond, of denigrating many of the Ulster British commanders in 1644, in an attempt to ingratiate himself with the English parliament. On other occasions, he appeared both oversensitive and hot-tempered, especially whenever his honour was called into question. His deadly duel with his fellow countryman, Sir Arthur Forbes, in Germany in 1632 bears out this fact. Hamilton frequently found himself in conflict with authority, as is evidenced by his numerous quarrels with Lord Deputy Wentworth and Viscount Ranelagh, president of Connacht. He was also in dispute with several of his neighbouring British settlers over title to land. Moreover, he was unable to take no for an answer, frequently appealing court decrees which were not to his liking and making repeated requests to the English principal secretary of state, Sir John Coke, to be allowed to travel over to England, despite Wentworth's prohibition. And he certainly showed signs of moodiness or sulking when Bishop Bedell refused to accept his offer of hospitality in Manorhamilton Castle in 1638.

On the other hand, he had the ability to commit himself totally to any project that he undertook. Wentworth sarcastically remarked once that 'the violence and assurance of Sir Frederick in his own particular appetites ... shew their earnestness and metal equally, be the cause good or bad'. Hamilton was also a very demanding but capable commander who maintained high standards of training and discipline among his garrison, which resulted in some instances of desertion among his soldiers to the more lax routine that prevailed in Sir William Cole's Enniskillen. Nobody disputed the fact that Sir Frederick was a brave and courageous colonel who personally led his men in many engagements with the rebels. On one occasion, in the course of a rebel ambush, he emerged unscathed despite having been knocked from his horse three times by 'rogues playing hard upon him'.

Perhaps the most conspicuous of all of Hamilton's attributes – and one the memory of which has lived on in folklore down to the present day – was his cruelty. There are many instances in his own writings of his men killing and beheading numerous rebels. There is also his fire and sword policy, whereby civilians were put to the sword because they were suspected of aiding and abetting those in arms. Their lands were laid waste, their animals driven off and their cabins destroyed. It is important to remember, though, that such unjustified slaughter of the general population was a feature of war at the time, practised by both British and Irish commanders alike.

Sir Frederick's career was both colourful and significant. Capitalizing on his noble birth and wealthy background, as well as his position at the court of James I, he embarked on a lifelong quest for power and military adventure. He began by more than quadrupling the size of his original plantation grant in Leitrim. He then raised a regiment of 1,200 men to fight for the Swedish commander, Gustavus Adolphus, during the Thirty Years War in Germany. On his return to Ireland, he succeeded in being appointed a member of the army council of war. Hamilton had an active involvement on the royalist side in the First and Second Bishops' Wars. During the 1641 rebellion and early Confederate War in Ireland, he suppressed the rebels' revolt in Leitrim and Sligo. In 1644 he switched his allegiance from the king to the covenanters and then canvassed the CBK (which was made up of both covenanters and their allies, the English parliament) for the presidency of Connacht and the governorship of Sligo and Derry. And when these petitions ultimately proved unsuccessful, he retired to Scotland to take command of his horse regiment in the Army of the Solemn League and Covenant against royalist forces there.

Finally, two of Hamilton's pamphlets in particular – his diary and *The information of Sir Frederick Hammilton* – lift the lid on the underlying tensions that existed between him and Sir William Cole, at a time when both men were involved in a desperate struggle with the Irish. Their differences are exposed in minute detail in the latter pamphlet, which Hamilton submitted in evidence to an English House of Commons parliamentary enquiry in 1645 into the various allegations of the two men. As well as providing fascinating insights into the complexities of the British response to the rebellion in Leitrim, Fermanagh and the surrounding counties, it especially assists us in our understanding of the character and mindset of Sir Frederick Hamilton himself.

CHAPTER ONE

Family background and life at court

Frederick Hamilton wrote in 1645 that his enemies called him a 'bragger'. He could, however, legitimately boast of having a very distinguished pedigree. The Hamiltons not only belonged to the Scottish nobility, but were also closely related to the royal house of Stewart/Stuart itself and had been at the nerve-centre of Scottish affairs for well over a century before Frederick was born. The family could trace its origins back to a Walter FitzGilbert Hamilton of Lanarkshire in the thirteenth century, but it really came to prominence in 1474 when James, first Lord Hamilton, married Princess Mary, sister of James Stewart III, king of Scotland (fig. 1). The union generally ensured the Hamiltons' loyal support of the monarchy for many years afterwards, even if at times it seemed that various members of the family might actually challenge the Stewarts for the crown.[1]

By the sixteenth century, the Hamiltons were one of the most influential families in Scotland, owning over two hundred estates in Lanarkshire, Ayrshire, Dumfriesshire, West Lothian and Aberdeenshire, and holding the highest offices in church and state. James Hamilton, second earl of Arran and later duke of Châtelherault (fig. 2), was regent of Scotland and heir presumptive to the crown during the early minority of Mary Queen of Scots from 1543 to 1554, and would have become king had Mary died childless. Meanwhile, his half-brother John Hamilton was installed as archbishop of St Andrews and primate of the Scottish Roman Catholic church in 1547.[2]

The period during which the Hamilton brothers were at the height of their powers was one of great political unrest and even crisis in Scotland. Both England and France wished to gain control of the country through a marriage with the young Mary Queen of Scots. Moreover, a great movement of religious change coincided, and became interlinked, with this time of political upheaval. The reform movement that was developing along radical lines in Scotland was supported by many of the country's most powerful noblemen, including the duke of Châtelherault. They resented the growing French Catholic influence and military presence in their country following the marriage of their young queen to

---

1 *The humble remonstrance of Sir Frederick Hammilton, knight and colonell, to the right honourable the Committee of Both Kingdoms* (London, 1645), p. 2.   2 M. Lynch (ed.), *The Oxford companion to Scottish*

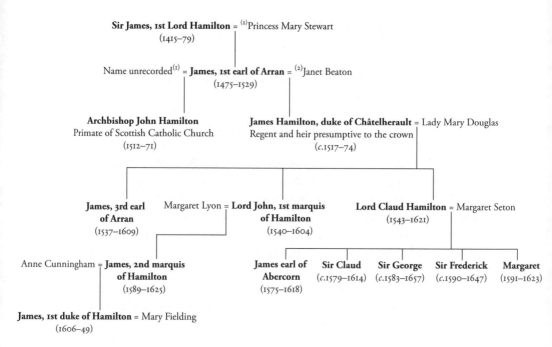

1 Frederick Hamilton's genealogy.

the French dauphin. These nobles, who were supported by Queen Elizabeth of England, emerged victorious and Scotland became a Protestant kingdom.[3]

Following her young husband's death in France in 1560, Mary Queen of Scots returned to her native land as its Catholic queen and represented a serious threat to the new Protestant establishment there. In 1565 she married her Catholic cousin, Lord Darnley, and after his assassination, she married the earl of Bothwell, but was soon forced by Protestant nobles to abdicate in favour of her infant son James VI. She then raised an army of six thousand men, which included lords John and Claud Hamilton, sons of Châtelherault, in an attempt to recover the throne. Following her defeat at the Battle of Langside, she fled to England, where she was imprisoned by her cousin Elizabeth I.[4]

A period of civil war ensued in Scotland between the supporters of Mary and those of James VI. John and Claud Hamilton remained loyal to the queen. However, the forces of James prevailed, and the Hamilton estates were forfeited. Both John and Claud fled to England, where Claud spent several years at the court of Elizabeth I.[5]

history (Oxford, 2001), p. 283. **3** G. Donaldson, *Scotland: the shaping of a nation* (Nairn, 1993), pp 42–5. **4** Ibid., 45–6. **5** J.C. Lees, *The abbey of Paisley, 1163–1878* (Paisley, 1878), pp 231–4; Sir J. Balfour Paul, *The Scots peerage* (9 vols, Edinburgh, 1904), i, pp 38–9.

James Hamilton, Earl of Arran,
Duke of Chatelherault.

From the original of Ketel, in the Collection of

His Grace, The Duke of Hamilton.

Drawn by Wᵐ Hilton. R. A. & Engraved (with Permission) by W. Holl.

London, Published July 1.1819. by Lackington, Hughes, Harding, Mavor & Jones, and Longman, Hurst, Rees, Orme & Brown.

2 James Hamilton, second earl of Arran, by William Holl Sr
(© National Portrait Gallery, London).

In 1586 lords John and Claud were restored to their former possessions and became members of a new privy council that was appointed by James VI in an attempt to achieve national unity in Scotland. Claud retained his position on the council in spite of the fact that he had sought intervention from Spain on behalf of Mary Queen of Scots prior to her execution by Queen Elizabeth on a charge of treason in 1587. He was even still plotting in 1588 (the year of the Armada) with other Catholic nobles for a Spanish invasion of England and Scotland, which they hoped would be followed by James VI's conversion to Catholicism. James put up with their conspiracies and dealt quite leniently with them – as he also did with the extreme Protestant lords – playing off one group against the other, and thus breaking the political threat of each. At the same time, he remained loyal to an earlier alliance with England, which he had concluded in the hope of succeeding Queen Elizabeth. By the year 1600, revolts and feuds were over and James was in total control in Scotland. His position was further enhanced when he ascended the throne of England on the death of Elizabeth in 1603. He was to maintain this control over Scotland for the next twenty-two years as an absentee monarch, and even boasted that he ruled his native land by the pen (rather than the sword) from England.[6]

Lords John and Claud Hamilton both continued to play a part in Scottish politics during the 1590s. John, who had disassociated himself from the Spanish plots in the previous decade, became a favourite of the king and was created first marquis of Hamilton in 1599. Claud had already been made a peer of parliament, with the title Lord Paisley, in 1587. King James shrewdly used the granting of such hereditary lordships and titles as a means of ensuring the loyalty and support of recipient nobles.[7]

Just as Archbishop John Hamilton and his half-brother Châtelherault had divergent attitudes towards the reformed religion in the 1550s and 1560s, so too had lords John and Claud in the decades that followed. By now, the Scottish Roman Catholic church was in serious decline. Many Catholics, including clergy, had transferred to the reformed faith. Protestantism had been adopted by the Scottish parliament as the state religion, and pressure was put on nobles and lords to conform. James VI, who was a staunch Protestant himself, promoted the reformed religion, although he did have a certain sympathy for Catholics. Lord John Hamilton had been a member of the 1560 parliament that outlawed the Roman Catholic faith, whereas there is much circumstantial evidence to suggest that his younger brother Claud remained a papist. In 1574 he married Margaret, daughter of Lord Seton, a practising Catholic. Claud may have conformed

6 Donaldson, *Scotland: the shaping of a nation*, pp 79–80.   7 www.hamiltongensociety.org/history.php, accessed 2 May 2005.

outwardly, especially after his time at the court of Queen Elizabeth in England, but it is doubtful if he ever became a Protestant. In 1588 he was reported as being a receiver of Jesuits, although this may have been in connection with the Spanish invasion plots. It is suggested that he retained a Catholic chaplain – a former monk of Paisley Abbey (pl. 1) – right up to the end of his life. His daughter Margaret married William, first marquis of Douglas, in 1601. The groom's father is said to have proposed the match because he wished his son to grow up with Roman Catholic associates.[8]

Lord John Hamilton, who died in 1604, was succeeded by his eldest son James, second marquis of Hamilton. This man later became the king's Scottish favourite at the English court. He was appointed a gentleman of the bedchamber in 1620, and lord high commissioner to Scotland the following year. He died from a fever in 1625, leaving a young son who was later to become third marquis and first duke of Hamilton.[9]

Lord Claud retired from public life in 1598 and his eldest son James was chosen to replace him on the Scottish privy council. In the same year, James became a gentleman of the Scottish bedchamber. In 1603 he was created a peer with the title of lord of Abercorn and three years later was given the hereditary earldom of Abercorn. James was able to use his influence with the king to become one of the principal beneficiaries in the Ulster Plantation in 1610. He was initially granted three thousand acres in Co. Tyrone, but had doubled the size of his holding and built a large castle, a school and a church in Strabane by 1614. Lord Claud, who lived on until 1621, had three other sons – Claud, George and Frederick. Claud and George were also awarded sizeable grants of land in Co. Tyrone in 1610. Frederick, the youngest son, would have to wait another decade before benefiting from the Hamilton family's close ties with the Stuart monarchy.[10]

AT THE COURT OF JAMES I

Frederick Hamilton of Paisley Abbey (pl. 1) was born about the year 1590. Nothing is known about his early life, but it is certain that he received a good education. The Reformation had given a great impetus to education in Scotland, as the reformers strove for the ideal of a well-instructed ministry and laity who would advance their cause. There were grammar (that is, Latin) schools in many

8 Sir H. Maxwell, *A history of the house of Douglas* (2 vols, London, 1902), ii, pp 185–6. **9** N. Cuddy, 'The revival of the entourage: the bedchamber of James I, 1603–1625' in D. Starkey (ed.), *The English court: from the Wars of the Roses to the Civil War* (Harlow, 1987), p. 220. **10** Balfour Paul, *The Scots peerage*, i, pp 46–7.

towns by the 1570s. Larger centres of population had colleges where logic, rhetoric and languages were taught. For those with ability and who could afford it, four universities – St Andrews, Glasgow, Aberdeen and Edinburgh (from 1583 onwards) – offered courses in languages, arts, sciences and divinity. By the mid-sixteenth century, nobles were able to both read and write. When the political situation stabilized towards the close of the century, nobles' children were tutored privately at home. There is evidence from Frederick Hamilton's later writings that he studied Latin, logic, rhetoric and divinity – including Old and New Testament. Indeed, his letter in Latin to Queen Kristina and her Swedish regency in 1637 shows a high degree of competence in that language. It is possible that Frederick attended the University of Glasgow, although his name does not appear on its matriculation rolls. There is no record of him either at any of the other three Scottish universities – or indeed at Oxford or Cambridge, where several of his Scottish contemporaries studied. However, he could have still attended one of these universities without officially enrolling or graduating, as procedures were much less formal then.[11]

On reaching his mid-twenties, Frederick was given a position at the court of James I (pl. 3) in England. His older brother, Claud, who had served in the privy chamber there, died in October 1614, so Frederick, through his father's influence, was sworn in as his successor in that department the following year. The origins of the English court can be traced back to the fifteenth century, coinciding with the emergence of a powerful Tudor monarchy. It was in the reign of Henry VII that the king's household began to become known as the 'court' and members of the royal entourage as courtiers. These courtiers consisted of loyal and powerful nobles and gentry who helped provide a ceremonial setting for the king at his royal palaces. The court became the centre of power, pomp and splendour in England. James I's court was a world of fashion and magnificence, with young men showing off the latest French 'cringes' and lords living in perfumed lodges. Here, king and courtiers wore gold. The royal court thus became the natural goal for any man with ambitions for personal or political advancement.[12]

Each monarch, depending on his or her particular personality, brought in a new style of court. Queen Elizabeth had been distant and aloof from her courtiers and granted audiences sparingly. James on the other hand, in a fashion reminiscent of Henry VIII, was extrovert and sociable and liked to participate fully in court life. This meant that courtiers had easy access to the king. They were able to present

11 G. Donaldson, *Scotland: James V to James VII* (Edinburgh, 1965), pp 262–8; SRA, AOSB E619, Frederick Hamilton's petition to the queen and senate of Sweden, *c*.end 1637. **12** *The humble remonstrance*, p. 1; see D. Starkey (ed.), *The English court*, pp 1–3; N. Cuddy, 'Reinventing a monarchy: the changing structure and political function on the Stuart court, 1603–88' in E. Cruickshanks (ed.), *The Stuart courts* (Stroud, 2000), p. 78.

their requests for favour directly to the monarch himself. This placed them in a most advantageous position because not only could they enrich themselves personally, but they could also work for the advancement of their family, friends and 'clients'.[13]

James' claim to rule by Divine Right implied that he was chosen by God, and that all his decisions had to be respected. He was head of both church and state, and the source of all power in the kingdom. He dictated policy and chose his privy council – his official advisory body – as well as his prelates and courtiers. All were dependent on him for position and advancement. Only he could reward or punish, elevate or demote. It was therefore important for courtiers and others to have the skills and talents to win royal favour. Not surprisingly, the court became a world of intrigue where men vied with each other for the rewards on offer. No one could be trusted, especially if competing for the same prize. Cliques were formed, power struggles ensued and insecurity became a fact of life.[14]

There was also a notable deterioration in standards of behaviour and morality in the court of James I as his reign progressed. James' alleged affair with George Villiers, duke of Buckingham, and the latter's extensive abuse of power at court and in the administration of the country, brought the court generally into disrepute. There were other scandals too involving people closely associated with the king. The earl of Somerset and his wife, Lady Frances Howard, were both convicted of murder in 1616. Somerset's father-in-law, Lord Treasurer Suffolk, and his wife were convicted of large-scale embezzlement of funds three years later. Other courtiers were also imprisoned in the Tower of London for sexual or financial offences. Such scandals were responsible for the public image of the court falling to a low ebb towards the end of James' life.[15]

The court of James I was made up of three components or departments – the household, the bedchamber and the privy chamber. All three accompanied the king whether he resided in one of his palaces such as Whitehall, Theobalds or Hampton Court, or at a royal deer-hunting lodge such as Royston or Newmarket. James had a passion for hunting and spent a lot of time at these lodges. Here, he divided his time between the sport and state business. The latter was managed through regular correspondence with his privy council, especially Principal Secretary Cecil and Lord Treasurer Howard back in London.

The household section of the court, which dealt with accounting and household management, was run by the lord steward. He oversaw about twenty service departments such as kitchen, larder, buttery, pantry etc., which employed approximately five hundred servants who provided and prepared the food. James'

13 D.L. Smith, *A history of the modern British Isles, 1603–1707* (Oxford, 1998), p. 40. **14** See Starkey (ed.), *The English court*, pp 12–13. **15** See Smith, *A history of the modern British Isles*, pp 44, 50.

court practised, at huge expense to the state, royal hospitality on a grand scale, and provided lavish free feasting for his officers and guests at about fifty communal tables. James believed that hospitality was part of genteel behaviour, so he exhorted his nobles and gentry on several occasions to practise it in their own castles also.[16]

The bedchamber was a network of the king's private apartments, or an inner court, to which only James' closest entourage had access. The twelve gentlemen of the bedchamber, who also lodged in the private apartments, performed the rather menial role of dressing, feeding and constantly attending the king by day, while one gentleman slept at the foot of the royal bed by night. The attractions of the job, however, lay in the fact that these were the only courtiers who were authorized to have close and constant access to the monarch. Everybody else had to request permission for an audience. Since all power rested solely with the king, service in the inner court was one of the most important routes to advancement of any kind. The bedchambermen were perfectly positioned to avail of the large amounts of royal patronage on offer. From the beginning of his reign, the king had even used the bedchamber as an alternative to the privy council in the government of the country. In his later years, two bedchamber favourites, Somerset (1611–15) and Buckingham (1615–28), were controlling the administration of the kingdom.[17]

Buckingham in particular became notorious for the way he took advantage of the confidence and affection of James I – and later of his son, Charles I – in order to gain a controlling influence over patronage and the formation of policy. He was instrumental in the removal from office of such powerful figures as Lord Chancellor Bacon and Lord Treasurer Cranfield. He himself acquired immense power, and with his large family profited in no small way when honours, pensions and court benefits were being distributed. He built up a 'connection' of important officials in Ireland including Lord Deputy St John, Surveyor General Parsons and Vice Treasurer Blundell. These men owed their position and allegiance to Buckingham, and all benefited from the plantation policy that they had promoted. The perks for Buckingham included a grant of the extensive O'Rourke estate of Dromahair during the plantation of Leitrim in the 1620s.[18]

The privy chamber was the outer circle of the king's court, and this was the department to which Frederick Hamilton belonged. It was responsible for formal

16 See Cuddy, 'Reinventing a monarchy' in Cruickshanks (ed.), *The Stuart courts*, pp 63–6. 17 See K. Sharpe, 'The image of virtue: the court and household of Charles I, 1624–1642' in D. Starkey (ed.), *The English court*, pp 249–50. 18 A year after Buckingham's death, Frederick Hamilton wished to purchase this estate from Buckingham's half-brother, Sir William Villiers in 1629, but the latter also died before the deal could be concluded. Frederick appealed the matter to the then monarch, Charles I, but he, still favouring the Buckingham family, would not allow Villiers' widow to be pressurized into a deal against her will. *CSPI, Charles I, 1625–32*, pp 309, 474, 478, 479; see V. Treadwell, *Buckingham and Ireland, 1616– 1628: a study in Anglo-Irish politics* (Dublin, 1998), pp 47–70 for membership of the elaborate web of

and ceremonial service. James used the gentlemen of the privy chamber to provide company for himself when he was receiving visiting dignitaries such as ambassadors or secretaries of state. The gentlemen were therefore required to have linguistic skills in order to be able to communicate with foreign officials. They might also occasionally be sent on diplomatic missions to other countries. More routinely, however, they attended the king 'in his going to chappell, or any other publique place, [and] upon all occasions of devocions, solemnitie or recreation'. Charles I required that they be capable horsemen and used them in a special regiment of horse that accompanied him on his Scottish tour in June 1633. They also acted as his bodyguards during the First Bishops' War in the summer of 1639. Frederick Hamilton was at his master's side on both of these occasions.[19]

When Frederick was appointed to the privy chamber in 1615, the department consisted of thirty-two gentlemen, half of them English and half Scots, who waited in quarterly shifts of eight. The position was therefore not a full-time career and explains why much of Frederick's life was spent away from court. The Scots contingent was usually more important than their English counterparts, as many of them came from Scottish noble families. Regardless of their nationality, however, the heads of families wishing to secure a place for a member in the chamber had to pay for the privilege. And although the gentlemen were lodged and maintained within the state departments, they were generally not recompensed for their service.[20]

Even though the gentlemen of the privy chamber did not enjoy regular intimate access to the king, they were presented with many opportunities for informal contact with the monarch, such as when members of both chambers joined James on hunting trips at his lodges. Three royal letters written in 1623 all indicate James' personal acquaintance with, and appreciation of, the young Frederick Hamilton. In the first letter to Viscount Falkland, the king requested his lord deputy in Ireland to ensure that Frederick, who was going to inspect his recent acquisition of Valentia Island in Co. Kerry, 'may have justice and all possible expedition, and whatsoever good shall result unto him thereby by your furtherance, will be very acceptable to us, as being done unto one whom we value and wish well to'.[21]

The second letter is addressed to the earl of Thomond, president of Munster, recommending Frederick to him as 'our servant whom wee esteeme extra-

Buckingham's Irish connection.   **19** N. Carlisle, *An enquiry into the place and quality of the gentlemen of His Majesty's most honourable privy chamber* (London, 1829), pp 26, 111; *CSPD, 1638–9*, p. 378; Bodl., Wood MS F33, fos 69, 70, a list of the king's servants appointed to attend his majestie into Scotland, 11 May 1633; Parliamentary Archives, HL/PO/JO/10/1/47, petition of Sir Frederick to House of Lords, 14 Jan. 1641.   **20** BL, Add. MSS 64,911, letter from Sir Frederick to Sir John Coke, sec. of state, 3 Dec. 1635; Sir Frederick, in *The humble remonstrance*, p. 1, stated that he had served in the privy chamber for nearly thirty years without pension or monopoly.   **21** TNA, SP63, vol. 237, 47B.

ordinarily, as also all such courses of his'. The final letter is from the king at Theobalds Palace to the Commissioners for Irish Causes. It relates to Frederick's earlier petition to the king to surrender all his lands and have them regranted into one entire manor called Manorhamilton. James asks the commissioners to let him know how he may satisfy Frederick's request, observing that he wishes to grant him 'extraordinary favour in these particulars, not intending that the same shall be a precedent for anyone else, and that if he may be satisfied it will be a great ease to His Majesty, and also it should be dispatched with all possible expedition'.[22]

Some six years earlier, Frederick must also have felt very honoured by the king. In the summer of 1617, James I returned to his native Scotland for the first time since ascending the English throne in 1603. He was accompanied as usual by his bed and privy chambermen, among them the recently appointed Frederick. On 24 July, the king and his entourage paid a visit to the then elderly Lord Claud Hamilton and his eldest son James, earl of Abercorn, at Paisley Abbey (pl. 1). The visit may even have been suggested by Frederick. In any case, the future looked bright for the privy chamberman in view of the high regard in which his family was held by the king. Lord Claud had invested wisely in securing a place at court for his youngest son. The rest was up to the young courtier's ability and ambition. And, as we shall see, Frederick Hamilton lacked neither of these attributes.[23]

COURT INFLUENCES ON FREDERICK'S LIFE

Frederick's sense of identity was coloured by several aspects of court life. King James' policy of uniting Scotland and England into one single state – the Kingdom of Great Britain – certainly made an impression on him. The court was one of the prime locations in which James tried to implement his plan. He laboured to establish and preserve harmonious relations between his Scottish and English courtiers. To this end, he was careful to strike a balance in the representation of both countries among his privy chambermen right from the beginning of his reign and in the bedchamber by 1620. With the same aim in mind, a marriage was arranged between the son of the Scottish favourite, James, second marquis of Hamilton (Frederick's first cousin) and a niece of Buckingham, the English favourite. Again, when the Irish plantation process was being implemented in Ulster, Wexford, Longford and Leitrim, half of the British grantees, including many with court connections, were Scots. Frederick, who was

---

22 Ibid., 47; *CSPI, James I, 1615–25*, p. 431.   **23** See Lees, *The abbey of Paisley*, pp 234–7 for an account of the visit.

one of these British courtier grantees, was himself mindful to choose a combination of English and Scottish tenants on his Leitrim estates over the next twenty years or so.[24]

This same notion of 'Britishness' was also promoted by James I – and later, to a certain extent, by Charles I – among contingents of Scottish, English, Welsh and Irish soldiers who fought on the Protestant side in the Thirty Years War. Frederick Hamilton was one of the colonels who commanded a 'British' regiment, made up of Scots and Irish troops, for this war in Germany during 1631 and 1632. Even though he and his men were seconded to a Swedish army when they arrived in Germany, they had originally been intended for service in a six-thousand-strong British force under the command of his cousin's son, the third marquis (and later first duke) of Hamilton. This man, then a rising star at the English court, described himself as a 'British subject' in a petition to King Charles I. Frederick was a partisan of the marquis and, like him, strove to support the idea of a British identity.[25]

It was quite common in the 1640s for English and Scottish settlers in Ireland to be called British. Frederick therefore was in no way unusual when he described the English and Scottish residents of Sligo town, which was besieged by the rebels in December 1641, as 'poore Brittishe soules'. Similarly, in a letter to the lords justices and council of Ireland, written from Manorhamilton Castle on 6 July 1643, Frederick mentions 'me, mine and all the other distressed Brittish subjects who hath this long sheltered themselves within my castle from the butcherous cruelty of the bloody rebels'. However, when he wrote to the CBK two years later that although 'he was of the Scottish nation … he was long incorporated with the English by marriage and otherwise, and had always hated and abhorred nationall difference betwixt these two kingdoms', his sentiments show that his idea of being British went far deeper than just the conventional meaning of the term. His former master, James I, had he still been alive, would certainly have been pleased with the way his privy chamberman had embraced the ideal of Britishness. James' son, Charles I, was by then, however, far less impressed by Frederick's change of political affiliations since his days at court. Hamilton was now colonel of a regiment in the Army of the Solemn League and Covenant, and no longer sought his favours from the king, but from the English and Scottish parliaments through their coordinating body, the CBK.[26]

24 *Another extract of severall letters from Ireland … As also, an exact relation of the good service of Sir Frederick Hammilton since the rebellion begun* (London, 1643), p. 18.   **25** For a comprehensive treatment of the various attempts at developing a British identity among English and Scottish soldiers in the several phases of this war, see S. Murdoch, 'James VI and the formation of a Scottish-British military identity' in S. Murdoch and A. Mackillop (eds), *Fighting for identity: Scottish military experience, c.1550–1900* (Leiden, 2002), pp 3–31.   **26** Parliamentary Archives, HL/PO/JO/10/1/198, petition of Sir Frederick to House of

Frederick was also influenced for many years by the prevailing Anglican Church ambience at court. He had been born into a family that was Catholic, or at least nominally so. His older brother, George, remained staunchly Catholic throughout his life. However, like his eldest brother James, first earl of Abercorn, who had spent many years at the Scottish court before James Stuart ascended the English throne, Frederick adopted the reformed religion. It is quite likely that he was also influenced by his Protestant first cousin, James, second marquis of Hamilton, the king's Scottish favourite at the English court. Frederick's religious convictions were sufficiently strong to be at least partially responsible for his engagement, under the Protestant Gustavus Adolphus, in the Thirty Years War. But the court can hardly be held accountable for his extreme anti-Catholic views that emerged during the 1641 Irish Rebellion and Confederate War, when he described the Irish as 'idolatrous rebels whose religion teacheth them to be wholly addicted unto treacheries and perfidiousnesse'. In fact, this latter conviction became so great that he 'vowed and swore in the presence of Almighty God [that he would never negotiate with] such traitors to God [even if his own sons were held captive by them, but would] rather instead that they should die gloriously for the cause of Christ'. Frederick was by then beginning to take his religious inspiration from the radical Covenanting movement, which had established a Presbyterian controlled state in Scotland following its military successes in the 1639–40 Bishops' Wars against Charles I.[27]

Frederick also acquired a heightened sense of his own importance from his membership of the privy chamber. It was, after all, a very useful mark of distinction for any nobleman to boast of. Had he not been abroad in Sweden in January 1638, it is very likely that he would have lent his support to his fellow privy chambermen who petitioned the king to restore some of the privileges of the chamber, which had lapsed in previous years. He actually made mention of his office when striving to impress potential benefactors such as Queen Kristina and the Swedish senate at the time and, surprisingly, the CBK in 1645. Furthermore, he never hesitated to appeal to a supreme authority whenever favours were required. To this end, he petitioned directly James I, Charles I, Gustavus Adolphus and Kristina. On other occasions, he directed his 'humble' remonstrances to the lords justices and council of Ireland, the lord chancellor of Scotland, the English houses of Lords and Commons, as well as the CBK.[28]

Lords that he not be made subject to the new governor of Connacht, c.June 1645; *The information of Sir Frederick Hammilton, knight and colonell, given to the committee of both kingdoms, concerning Sir William Cole, knight, and colonell; with the scandalous answer of the said Sir William Cole, knight …* (London, 1645), pp 58, 65. **27** *The information of Sir Frederick Hammilton*, pp 39, 43; *Another extract of severall letters*, p. 57. **28** SRA, AOSB E619; *The humble remonstrance*, p. 1; *CSPD, 1637–8*, p. 216.

It was surely this sense of his own importance that led him to model his castle in Manorhamilton on Rathfarnham Castle in Dublin, the impressive residence of a former archbishop of Dublin and lord chancellor of Ireland. It is tempting to speculate also that his elevated self-image and his recollections of court splendour would have influenced his choice of attire even at the height of the 1641 rebellion in Ireland. He was then 'well knowne [to the rebels] by his horse and habit'. Attributes such as his appetite for power and wealth, and his natural instinct for self preservation, may also have been significantly sharpened at court. Frederick was, after all, a gentleman of the privy chamber for over a quarter of a century. It would be quite extraordinary had not such a significant institution impacted deeply on his attitudes and lifestyle – and perhaps even given him cause to brag a little.[29]

29 *Another extract of severall letters*, p. 31.

CHAPTER TWO

The plantation of Leitrim, 1620

When James VI extended the power of central government to certain Gaelic areas of Scotland, he reinforced his authority there by planting the territories with colonies of loyal subjects. Kintyre and the Island of Lewis were thus planted with Lowlanders in the early seventeenth century. As James I of England, he repeated this policy of plantation in various parts of Ireland. Loyal British subjects from England and Scotland were awarded grants of land in Ulster, Wexford, the midlands and Leitrim. Many of the grantees were courtiers, or state officials and army officers already based in Ireland. The young nobleman and courtier, Frederick Hamilton, was allocated a substantial grant of land in the plantation of Leitrim in 1622. His membership of the privy chamber was beginning to pay dividends.

BACKGROUND TO THE LEITRIM PLANTATION

The O'Rourke clan (fig. 3) had ruled over Breifne, comprising the present counties of Leitrim and Cavan, since the tenth century. It provided four provincial kings of Connacht over the following two hundred years. By the middle of the thirteenth century, however, the clan's advancement was checked when its own sub-chiefs, the O'Reillys, rose to power and forced the splitting of the territory between both septs. The O'Rourkes retained west Breifne (modern Co. Leitrim), while the O'Reillys assumed control of east Breifne (Co. Cavan).[1]

In 1583 Brian O'Rourke of the Ramparts, chief of O'Rourke's country – as west Breifne was then known – submitted to the lord deputy, and his territory was designated the county of Leitrim. The new county was sub-divided into six baronies representing the traditional lands of Brian O'Rourke, his kinsmen and his principal sub-lords, the MacClancys and the MacRannalls (Reynolds). Dromahair (O'Rourke), Carre or Car (O'Rourke) and Rosclogher (MacClancy) were located in the north of the county, while Carrigallen (O'Rourke), Leitrim (Reynolds) and Mohill (Reynolds) were in the south.[2]

1 Domhnall Mac an Ghallóglaigh, 'Breifne and its chieftains, 940–1300', *Breifne*, 7:26 (1988), 524, 546–51. 2 See Daniel Gallogly, 'Brian of the Ramparts O'Rourke (1566–1591)', *Breifne*, 2:5 (1962), 50–9; Mac an Ghallóglaigh, 'Leitrim, 1600–1641', *Breifne*, 4:14 (1971), 229–31.

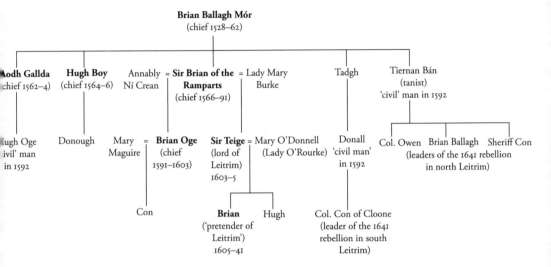

Brian Ballagh Mór
(chief 1528–62)

Aodh Gallda (chief 1562–4) — Hugh Boy (chief 1564–6) — Annably Ní Crean = **Sir Brian of the Ramparts** (chief 1566–91) = Lady Mary Burke — Tadgh — Tiernan Bán (tanist) 'civil' man in 1592

Hugh Oge 'civil' man in 1592 — Donough — Mary Maguire = **Brian Oge** (chief 1591–1603) — **Sir Teige** (lord of Leitrim) 1603–5 = Mary O'Donnell (Lady O'Rourke) — Donall 'civil man' in 1592 — Col. Owen, Brian Ballagh, Sheriff Con (leaders of the 1641 rebellion in north Leitrim)

Con — **Brian** ('pretender of Leitrim') 1605–41 — Hugh — Col. Con of Cloone (leader of the 1641 rebellion in south Leitrim)

3 The O'Rourkes of Dromahair: chieftains of west Breifne/lords of Leitrim.

Two years later, Brian O'Rourke, in conjunction with the other native chieftains of the province, concluded an agreement called the Composition of Connacht with Lord Deputy Sir John Perrott. They would henceforth hold their lands by secure tenure under the crown, with succession rights going to their eldest sons, in return for abandoning the Irish system of elective chieftainship, foregoing other customary Gaelic rights and observing English common law. Brian O'Rourke soon revolted again, however, and was driven out of Leitrim in 1590 by Sir Richard Bingham, president of Connacht, and hanged the following year in London.[3]

Brian's eldest son, the Oxford-educated Brian Oge, then claimed his father's estate and fought alongside the northern chiefs in the Nine Years War against the English. When he returned to Leitrim, after the Battle of Kinsale, he was opposed by his English-supported half-brother Teige. Brian Oge was forced to flee the county and died of a fever while awaiting transport to the Continent in January 1604.[4]

3 B. Cunningham, 'The composition of Connacht in the lordships of Clanricard and Thomond, 1577–1641', *Irish Historical Studies*, 24:93 (1984), 1–14; M. O'Dowd, *Power, politics and land: early modern Sligo, 1568–1688* (Belfast, 1991), pp 32–40; G.A. Hayes-McCoy, 'The completion of the Tudor conquest and the advance of the Counter-Reformation, 1571–1603' in T.W. Moody, F.X. Martin, F.J. Byrne (eds), *A new history of Ireland, iii: early modern Ireland, 1534–1691* (Oxford, 1976), pp 109–15. 4 For a general account of the life of Brian Oge, see Mac an Ghallóglaigh, 'Brian Oge O'Rourke and the Nine Years War', *Breifne*, 2:6 (1963), 171–203; B. Mac Dermot, *O Ruairc of Breifne* (Manorhamilton, 1990), pp 84–118.

Teige's untimely death twelve months later at the age of twenty-nine led to speculation that Leitrim should revert to being a crown possession since he had allegedly no male heirs according to English law. Teige was in fact married to Mary, sister of Red Hugh O'Donnell, and had two sons by her, but she had formerly wed Sir Donal O'Cahan of Derry and there were serious doubts as to whether that marriage had ever been legally dissolved. In 1613 Lord Deputy Sir Arthur Chichester wrote that Leitrim had by then become a 'secure den of many ... outlaws [from] Ulster and Connacht ... [and was] the most unreformed county in the whole realm'. Strategically situated on the north-eastern flank of Connacht, bordering the recently planted Ulster counties of Donegal, Fermanagh and Cavan, it was quite inaccessible from an English point of view on account of its mountainous terrain and partially wooded valleys. It was also relatively distant from the Connacht governor's base in Athlone and had only one small English garrison within its boundaries. The lord deputy recommended, therefore, that the power of the O'Rourkes should be broken once and for all by planting the county with English settlers.[5]

Chichester's successor, Sir Oliver St John, also strongly favoured the plantation model as being the best method of ensuring a loyal and peaceful Leitrim. He presided over a 'corruptly assembled' jury in Carrigallen, which found the O'Rourke heirs to be illegitimate because of Teige's unlawful marriage to Mary O'Donnell.[6] Teige's eldest son, Brian, had earlier, as a royal ward, been sent by the authorities to complete his education in England. In reality, the main purpose in removing him from his territory was to facilitate the plantation of Leitrim. To make matters worse for the young O'Rourke, an incident occurred on the eve of St Patrick's Day 1619 in London that would alter his life completely. He became involved in a dispute with a group of Englishmen and was charged with assault. He was found guilty, heavily fined and, because he was unable to pay, committed to prison.

With the issue of illegitimacy decided and the pretended heir to the county held in confinement, the plantation lobby pressed ahead with their final preparations. The Irish surveyor general, Sir William Parsons, measured the amount of profitable and unprofitable land in the county early in the summer of

---

5 J. Casway, 'The last lords of Leitrim: the sons of Sir Teige O'Rourke', *Breifne*, 7:26 (1998), 559–62; Chichester to Sir Humphrey May, 20 Feb. 1613: R.D. Edwards (ed.), 'Letter book of Sir Arthur Chichester, 1612–14', *Analecta Hibernica*, 8 (1938), 89–90. A small fort was built at Carrick-on-Shannon about the year 1610 with Captain Maurice Griffith in charge of the garrison of ten men: *CPRI, 10 James I*, p. 238: another small fort, situated on an island in the River Bonet near Dromahair, was granted to Lieutenant Walter Harrison on 25 Nov. 1612, but there was no mention of a garrison there. **6** MS C.iv.1 (RIA) quoted in MacDermot, *O Ruairc of Breifne*, p. 213; the members of this jury would, no doubt, be hoping to benefit from any subsequent redistribution of O'Rourke's land. Interestingly, Carrigallen is situated in the southern part of Co. Leitrim, almost thirty miles from Sir Teige's stronghold and estate of Dromahair; Casway, 'The last lords of Leitrim', 564–5.

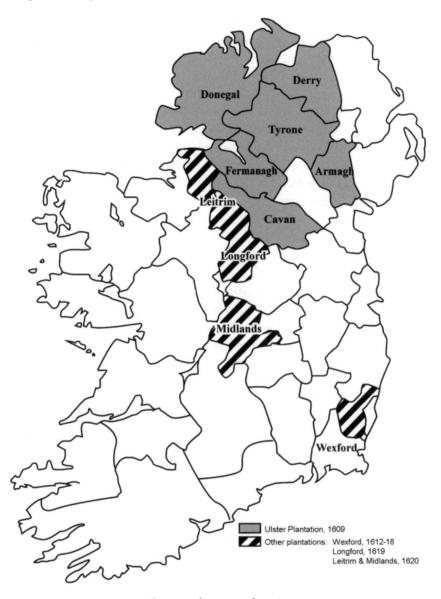

Ulster Plantation, 1609

Other plantations: Wexford, 1612-18
Longford, 1619
Leitrim & Midlands, 1620

4 Seventeenth-century plantations.

1620. Shortly afterwards, Lord Deputy St John and Parsons secured the backing of the most powerful man – after the king – in England for their plantation plans. This was George Villiers, marquis and later duke of Buckingham, the king's favourite and chief advisor. He had already been involved behind the scenes in a minor way in the Longford and Ely O'Carroll plantations (fig. 4). In 1620 he married Lady Katherine Manners, daughter of the earl of Rutland, and purchased a huge estate in Leicestershire for £28,000. But he still needed to acquire further substantial land banks – preferably at little or no cost – both to reflect his own personal status and to reward his growing 'connection' of supporters. Irish plantation land seemed to fit the bill perfectly.[7]

Parsons and Buckingham used the summer break at court away from London to persuade the king that plantation would be the most effective means of imposing English civility and the Protestant religion on the troublesome county of Leitrim. Although Parsons was unable to produce the royal title to the county, the privy council was induced to sanction the project at a meeting in Hampton Court Palace on 30 September 1620.[8]

A fortnight later, Lord Deputy St John was authorized to accept surrenders of the estates of all freeholders in Leitrim. In return, the owners would receive new patents for their lands, after a portion had been taken away for the king. Anybody who refused to surrender would forfeit his whole estate. By Christmas, some two hundred Leitrim and midland owners had 'freely' surrendered their lands. This was the word cleverly inserted by the lord deputy in a letter to the privy council. He reassuringly added that the Leitrim natives were glad to 'relinquish the old and insolent and overgrown title of the O'Rourkes'.[9]

When Brian O'Rourke, who was still in prison, refused to renounce his claim to Leitrim in March 1621, crown lawyers set about reconstituting the royal title from old Norman claims. This procedure was complete by August of that year, and, within a matter of weeks, the apportioning of lands commenced. Brian was transferred to the Tower of London in February 1623 and, despite having paid his debts, remained there until his death in January 1641.[10]

PLANTATION INSTRUCTIONS AND GRANTEES

The territories to be planted, according to the instructions dawn up at Theobalds Palace on 2 October 1620, were the entire county of Leitrim, which was reckoned to contain 182,536 acres, as well as a group of smaller lots in the midlands amounting to 125,946 acres. The land in Co. Leitrim was to be allocated in the following manner. First of all, the 'unprofitable mountain, wood and bogg' were to be temporarily taken out of the equation. According to the recent measurement of the county, this amounted to 92,000 acres, or about half the total area. Secondly, the 15,000 acres that had belonged to the Catholic Church was now

7 Treadwell, *Buckingham and Ireland*, pp 135–6. **8** B. Mac Cuarta, 'The plantation of Leitrim, 1620–41', *IHS*, 32:127 (2001), 307–8. **9** St John to lords of the council, 31 Dec. 1620, *CSPI, 1615–25*, p. 310; lord deputy and council to privy council, 6 Feb. 1621, *CSPI, 1615–25*, p. 313. **10** Casway, 'The last lords of

transferred to the Church of Ireland bishops of Kilmore and Ardagh, parts of whose dioceses lay within the county. Then almost 5,000 acres were set aside as glebe lands for the upkeep of Protestant ministers in the sixteen parishes of the county. Finally, six hundred acres in total were to be reserved for the site of an administrative town and the construction of a fort in the county. There then remained about 70,000 acres of good land and profitable woodland. Half of this was to be planted with British undertakers and the rest regranted to natives who had surrendered their lands to St John in December 1620. The allocation of 50 per cent of Leitrim's profitable land to undertakers was in stark contrast to the 25 per cent of profitable land that undertakers received in the smaller midland territories of Offaly, Leix and Westmeath. The plantation instructions justified the increased percentage in Leitrim on the grounds that the crown was promising life pensions to both Brian and Hugh O'Rourke, sons of the late Sir Teige, and also because the Leitrim natives were in need of greater civilization than the midlanders. In conjunction with the portion of good land that they were granted in the Leitrim plantation, British undertakers and natives alike were also given a larger amount of mountain, bog and wasteland.[11]

Apart from 'some few men of especiall qualitie' who received very large grants, the principal undertakers in the Leitrim plantation, as those in Longford, were given one thousand acres of profitable land. These persons were to hold their grants by knight's service, which involved military obligations, and were to be responsible for the security of the general planter community. They were required to build strong castles, surrounded by a high defensive bawn or courtyard wall. Their estates were usually strategically positioned alongside barony or county boundaries, creating a sort of buffer zone between natives from one territory and another. Apart from this restriction, all undertakers were allowed to live interspersed among the native population, as there had been continuous peace and prosperity in Ireland for the previous fifteen years. This dispersal of planters among the natives was quite a progression from the pattern in Ulster some ten years earlier, when settlers were grouped together in secure clusters for mutual protection. To achieve the goal of civilizing the Leitrim population, grantees were

Leitrim', 567–9. **11** The midland lots were made up of lands in three different counties: the large west-Offaly section of 90,869 acres comprised the baronies of Ballyboy, Ballycowen and Eglish belonging to the O'Molloy clan, the barony of Garrycastle belonging to the MacCoughlans, and the Kilcoursey area ruled over by the Fox clan. The Co. Leix barony of Tinnahinch, containing 27,405 acres belonging to the O'Dunnes, was included. Finally, 7,672 acres of the barony of Kilcolman, which belonged to the O'Melaghlins, in Westmeath was also planted; Brian O'Rourke's pension, described as 'liberal', amounted to £400 per annum. Apparently, it soon fell into arrears as the king was short of money. Hugh was allocated a pension of £100 a year: 'Royal instructions for the plantation of Leitrim', 1620, nos 2, 3, 4, 5, 29, 37 in B. Mac Cuarta (ed.), 'Leitrim plantation papers', *Breifne*, 9:35 (1999), 116,117, 122, 123; Mac an Ghallóglaigh, 'Leitrim, 1600–1641', 240; Mac Cuarta, 'The plantation of Leitrim', 300.

required to accommodate up to five British freeholders on their estates, depending on their extent. The lands of the principal undertakers were also to be formed into a manor, giving them the right to hold manorial courts, which enforced the payment of services due to themselves and dealt with debts, trespasses or disputes between tenants. Smaller estates, ranging in size from eight hundred down to two hundred acres, were granted to less favoured undertakers who had fewer privileges and obligations.[12]

All undertakers, regardless of the size of their grants, were bound to observe the following stipulations: they were to take the Oath of Supremacy, acknowledging the king as supreme head of the church. None could sell land to another without a special licence. They were compelled to reside on their estates and could only be absent with the permission of the king or the lord deputy. Before a grant received the royal seal, the grantee had to pay a surety of £500 for every thousand acres he received that he would fulfil all the conditions of the plantation within three years. Moderate rents of three pence an acre had to be paid to the king for profitable land received, and a fraction of this for waste land. They were also obliged to pay fines at the rate of £100 per thousand acres, within five years, for the construction of a wall around the new administrative town of Jamestown. Finally, they were to encourage their tenants to build together in clusters.[13] As in the case of the undertakers, a handful of privileged or favoured natives were also to be given large grants of land in the plantation. These were the leading ladies and gentlemen of the O'Rourke, MacClancy and Reynolds clans – excluding Brian and Hugh O'Rourke, who had been promised pensions instead. Some received grants of over one thousand acres of profitable land, with the rest being allocated between seven hundred and eight hundred acres. The intention here was to treat these 'civill men [and women]' very favourably, in the hope that they would keep the less important freeholders from venting their anger and resentment against the English authorities and the British undertakers.[14]

Those natives to be kept in check fell into two groups. Firstly, there were the freeholders who, before the plantation, owned medium-sized estates. These were now regranted land that amounted to 25 per cent less than the size of their original holding. Their new estates ranged from five hundred down to sixty acres of profitable land. The second group was made up of former small freeholders who had owned less than a hundred acres. These lost everything, and were now reduced to becoming tenants of either the undertakers or native grantees. It was hoped that these 'inferior natives' who, before the plantation, had tended to be both semi-nomads, who moved seasonally with their cattle, and potential

---

12 'Royal instructions for the plantation of Leitrim', 1620, nos 6, 12, 14, 16, 17, 18, 19, 21 in Mac Cuarta (ed.), 'Leitrim plantation papers'. **13** Ibid., nos 13, 26, 32, 33, 34, 35, 43. **14** Ibid., no. 11.

5 George Villiers, first duke of Buckingham, by Michiel Jansz. van Mierevelt (© National Portrait Gallery, London).

trouble-makers, would now be more easily controlled and civilized by becoming long-term tenants in fixed locations. But the loss of property and status led to deep feelings of unrest among both of these groups, which explains the crown's reliance on the privileged natives to dampen any stirrings of protest on the part of their unfortunate countrymen.[15]

All native landowners who received estates were subject to particular conditions that aimed at ensuring discipline and loyalty within the local population from the top down. To prevent a resurgence of the O'Rourke dynasty, no one could sell, without permission, a portion of his estate to another native. Any who rebelled

15 Ibid., nos 23, 36, 38.

against the crown or assisted the O'Rourkes in setting themselves up as native lords again would lose their estates. One incentive offered by way of reward to cooperative individuals related to the holding of four weekly markets and nine annual or biannual fairs throughout the county. These were to be held mainly on the estates of British undertakers, but also on a few belonging to privileged natives. A rent was payable to the crown by such estate owners in return.[16]

A total of forty-eight grantees shared the 35,000 acres of profitable land that were allocated to British undertakers in the plantation of Leitrim. 16,000 acres went to the principal promoter of the plantation, George Villiers, marquis of Buckingham (fig. 5), and to members of his 'connection'. This was a network of family, friends and supporters, whom Buckingham assembled in Britain and Ireland, on account of the favours he was able to bestow, due to his influence with the all-powerful James I. The greatest beneficiary was Buckingham himself, who received 6,500 acres of what had been the former estate of Sir Teige O'Rourke at Dromahair. Buckingham did not wish to draw attention to himself on account of his acquiring this prized asset, so he arranged that the former O'Rourke lands would be nominally allocated to two Scottish courtier brothers, Sir Robert and James Maxwell, for the time being. The Maxwell brothers were part of the Villiers connection. The more important members of the connection were expected, both by the marquis and even by the king himself, to marry into Buckingham's extended family in order to solidify their support for their patron. Sir Robert had duly married Elizabeth Beaumont, a cousin of Buckingham's, in 1619. The following year, he was allocated five thousand acres of the Dromahair estate, and his brother, James, an adjoining 1,500 acres. Both were rewarded for becoming Buckingham's proxies. Robert was created earl of Nithsdale in Scotland, while James was compensated with the sale of two Irish peerages. The enterprise achieved its purpose. It was only in January 1627, following many more secretive manoeuvres, that Buckingham's letters patent for the Dromahair estate were finally sealed, and his grant became public knowledge.[17]

The Villiers connection included nearly all of the major officers of state in Ireland, which allowed Buckingham to exert such control over the allocation of land in the Leitrim plantation. The principal officer of the Irish administration was Lord Deputy Sir Oliver St John, and it was he that Buckingham used to cloak a gift of almost four thousand acres of land in the barony of Leitrim, for William, son and heir of one of his half-brothers, Sir Edward Villiers. This was a

16 Ibid., nos 22, 23, 27, 30.   **17** See Treadwell, *Buckingham and Ireland*, p. 139; The Maxwell brothers were Catholic, and King James I sent Sir Robert to Rome in 1624 to obtain a papal dispensation for the young Prince Charles to marry Henrietta-Maria of France: see A. Grosjean and S. Murdoch, *SSNE Database*, www.st-andrews.ac.uk/history/ssne ID:531 Robert Maxwell; N. Cuddy, 'Reinventing a

mutually satisfactory arrangement for Buckingham and St John, as the lord deputy's niece, Barbara, was Sir Edward Villiers' wife. So St John was a great-uncle of the young William Villiers. But St John was also rewarded in 1621 when he was created Viscount Grandison of Limerick. And the following year he was given a seat in the English privy council, shortly after having been replaced as lord deputy by another member of the Villiers connection, Lord Falkland.[18]

Another major beneficiary of the Leitrim plantation was Sir Francis Blundell, the king's secretary for Irish business, who had drafted the royal instructions in the summer of 1620. He was also a member of the connection, and like his patron, managed initially to hide his grant of 1,635 acres in the barony of Leitrim, by having it originally allocated to Sir James Balfour, a Scottish courtier and Ulster planter. Sir William Parsons, the Irish surveyor general, who surveyed Leitrim in May 1620, had come into the Villiers fold shortly beforehand. He and Buckingham later worked together advising the king on how the various grants should be allocated. Not surprisingly, Sir William and his brother, Fenton, an admiralty judge in Munster, were awarded a total of 1,400 acres in the barony of Carrigallen. Other Villiers' supporters to receive estates were St John's nephews, George and Richard St George, who had both worked in the customs adminis-tration in Ireland. George, later appointed commander of Carrick-on-Shannon fort, now got four hundred acres and Richard two hundred acres in Leitrim barony. Sir Thomas Rotheram, a member of the planting lobby, was allocated seven hundred acres. Sir Charles Coote, acting president of Connacht, who became contractor and first sovereign of Jamestown in 1622, later received a grant of 1,300 acres in various parts of the county. Thus, through his recruitment of St John, Parsons and Blundell, key personnel at court or in the Irish administration, Buckingham was able to siphon off almost 50 per cent of the land available to undertakers in the Leitrim plantation for his own benefit and that of his cronies.[19]

One of the most substantial beneficiaries of the plantation, outside of the Buckingham connection, was Frederick Hamilton. As noted in chapter one, Frederick had been at court as a gentleman of the privy chamber since 1615. He was therefore in a very favourable position to present his request for an estate in Leitrim directly to the king himself. Undoubtedly he also had the backing of his first cousin, James, second marquis of Hamilton, the king's Scottish favourite, who had become a gentleman of the bedchamber a few months before the plantation instructions were drawn up. Frederick was awarded 1,568 acres of profitable land and almost four thousand acres of mountain, wood and bog in two separate lots in the barony of Dromahair, north-east of the Villiers estate.

monarchy', p. 73. **18** Mac Cuarta (ed.), 'Leitrim plantation papers', 130. For a detailed account of the Villiers connection in Ireland, see Treadwell, *Buckingham and Ireland*, pp 47–59. **19** Mac Cuarta (ed.),

The first lot lay alongside the border with Co. Fermanagh, and just south of the barony of Rosclogher, in the area called Glenfarne. The second lot, which centred on what was later to become the town of Manorhamilton, also lay adjacent to the Rosclogher barony. In return for his grant, Frederick had to pay an annual rent of £25 18s. 10¾d. to the crown, as well as a one-off payment of £150 when his grant was officially confirmed by royal patent. As one of the principal undertakers in the plantation, he was to be responsible for the military security of his estate, and to this end he was required to build, within three years, a thirty feet long by twenty feet wide by twenty-five feet high castle, surrounded by a bawn wall, three hundred feet in circumference and fourteen feet in height. His whole estate was created into the manor of Hamilton, entitling him to hold a manor court, with rights of local jurisdiction over his tenants. He was to retain at least four hundred acres as a demesne for his own personal use. Three hundred acres of the remainder had to be assigned to two British freeholders, and the rest could be leased out to either British or Irish tenants. Frederick was also granted permission, for a fee of £1 per annum, to hold a weekly Tuesday market, and two fairs on 21 January and 22 September, at a settlement called Dewellishe on the Glenfarne portion of his estate. He, in turn, could charge his tenants tolls and customs on the sale of produce and animals at these markets and fairs.[20]

Apart from the Maxwell brothers and Frederick Hamilton, four other Scots received sizeable grants of land in the Leitrim plantation. This was in line with James I's policy of treating his Scottish and English subjects with equal favour, in the hope of promoting a sense of harmony and 'Britishness' among both nationalities. The estates of three of these Scots – James Creighton, John Waldron and the privy chamberman, Sir William Irwin – lay in close proximity to that of Hamilton, and he was to have differences with all three, or their successors, in the years to come. The estate of the fourth Scot, Sir Arthur Forbes, was situated in the barony of Mohill, nearly forty miles to the south. Frederick would also cross swords, literally, with this man ten years later during the Thirty Years War in Germany. The remaining undertakers in the Leitrim plantation included other courtiers, royal servants and Irish officials, as well as a dozen or so junior army

---

'Leitrim plantation papers', 130–1. **20** Marsh, MS Z4.2.6, king to lords justices, 12 Jan. 1630. In this document, a figure of 1,568 acres of arable land is given as the size of Frederick Hamilton's original grant; the 1622 survey of the Leitrim plantation (cited in Mac Cuarta (ed.), 'Leitrim plantation papers', 130) credits him with having been allocated 1,500 acres only; see *CPRI, James I*, p. 539 for Frederick's grant in full, although here his acreage is given as just 1,333 acres. The following townlands made up the Glenfarne portion of his estate: Lacoon, Loughros, Laghty Barr, Meenagh, Carrickrevagh, Ardmoneen and Moneyduff. Those in the Manorhamilton area were Tullyskeherny, Tawnymanus, Cloonclare, Ramooney, Ross, Carrickleitrim, Cornastauk, Manorhamilton, Skreeny, Donaghmore and Donaghbeg. I have had to make an educated guess in a few cases, as the names of some townlands changed during the mid-seventeenth century, and others in the nineteenth century during the Ordnance Survey in 1835/6.

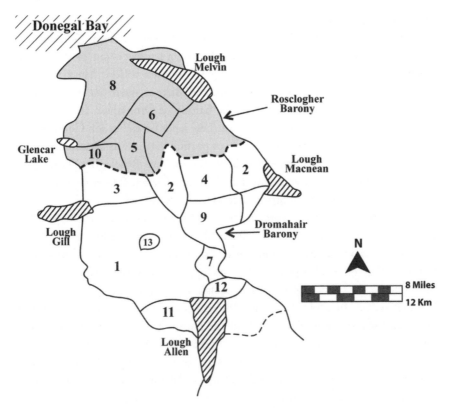

6 Principal grantees of the plantation in north Leitrim. British: 1. Buckingham; 2. Sir Frederick Hamilton; 3. Sir William Irwin; 4. Capt. Faithful Fortescue; 5. James Creighton; 6. John Waldron; 7. Walter Harrison. Irish: 8. Elizabeth Clancy and co.; 9. Lady O'Rourke; 10. Tiernan MacOwen O'Rourke; 11. Mary Maguire; 12. Mulmory Mac Ternan; 13. Bryan Ballagh O'Rourke (sources: Calendar of patent rolls (James I) and Royal instructions for the plantation of Leitrim, 1620).

officers in Ireland. Many of these were men who were owed favours by the crown, or who had missed out on being granted estates during previous plantations.[21]

The main beneficiaries among the cohort of 151 native grantees were the widows of Sir Teige O'Rourke and his half-brother Brian Oge, as well as the daughter and heiress of Cahir MacClancy of Rosclogher (fig. 6). Sir Teige's widow, Mary O'Donnell, whose marriage Lord Deputy St John had been so insistent on proving invalid, was given a grant of 1,600 acres of profitable land and 3,414 of mountain and bog. Her estate was situated in Glenboy, towards the eastern end of the barony of Dromahair, and a dozen miles from the former

---

21 *CPRI, James I*, pp 543, 577; Mac Cuarta, 'The plantation of Leitrim', 306–7. Creighton's estate was in Lurganboy in Rosclogher barony. Waldron's was in Mullies in the same barony, just north of Hamilton's lands. Irwin's estate bordered Buckingham's in Dromahair barony.

O'Rourke lands. She was assigned the lands only for the duration of her own life. The grant would revert on her death to Nicolas Preston, Viscount Gormanston, and John Rochford of Kilbride, who had made a similar claim to that of the crown to the title of Leitrim. Brian Oge O'Rourke's widow, Mary Maguire, received a grant of 711 profitable acres and 823 of waste in the parish of Inishmagrath at the southern end of the barony of Dromahair. In contrast to Mary O'Donnell, she was allowed to pass these lands on to her son Conn. A very substantial grant of four thousand acres of profitable land was allocated to three ladies who were related to the MacClancy sublords of Rosclogher. These were Elizabeth Dubh, daughter and heiress of Cahir MacClancy, Catherine MacClancy (née O'Rourke) and Mary Crofton (née MacClancy).[22]

Four leading gentlemen, representative of all three branches of the O'Rourkes, were allocated substantial acreages. Shane Oge (1,258 acres), Donell Mac Tadhg (800) and Owen Oge (752) got estates in Carrigallen barony, while Tiernan Mac Owen of Car received 798 acres in Rosclogher. A few significant gentlemen belonging to the other important native clan in the county, the Reynolds, were also well looked after. John Reynolds of Lough Scur, who was sheriff of Leitrim in 1613, and whose anglicized branch of the family had long resented the over-lordship of the O'Rourkes, received 787 acres. William Reynolds, his brother, who was MP for Co. Leitrim from 1613 to 1634, got 708 acres. Charles Reynolds, John's son, was awarded 793 acres. All three Reynolds' grants were located in the barony of Leitrim.[23]

In the category of those who forfeited one quarter of the size of their original holding, were thirty-four O'Rourkes, thirty-six Reynolds and five MacClancys. They received holdings ranging from five hundred down to sixty acres, although many of these estates were at the lower end of the scale. Other natives allocated similar sized estates were members of the MacLoughlin, MacTernan, MacMorrow, MacKeegan, MacShanley, Forde (MacConsnamha), O'Duignan, O'Heslin and O'Mulvey families.[24]

---

22 *CPRI, Charles I*, pp 439, 612; *Down Survey*, Co. Leitrim (RIA); see also Casway, 'The last lords of Leitrim', 573–4. Sometime after Sir Teige's death, Mary O'Donnell married Gerald Nugent, who was elected MP for Leitrim in the 1613 Irish parliament. Gerald's brother, Richard, earl of Westmeath, got 733 acres in Carrigallen barony in the Leitrim plantation. After Gerald's death, Mary married David Bourke, son of Viscount Mayo. By 1641, she owned 2,400 profitable acres of land. Mary died in 1662, having survived all her husbands and children; Elizabeth Dubh MacClancy later bought out her two co-grantees, and with her son Ross, extended her estate to 4,400 acres.   23 Humphrey Reynolds, another son of John of Lough Scur, was sheriff of Leitrim in 1620, 1621, 1623, and MP for the county in 1640. He was allocated 112 acres in the plantation, also in Leitrim barony: see A. Harrison (compiler), 'County of Leitrim: a roll of all gentlemen who filled the offices of high sheriff, sub-sheriff, foreman of grand jury, lieutenant of county, members of parliament for the county, with the date of office, from the year 1600 to 1868' (unpublished document, 1869).   24 See Mac Cuarta (ed.), 'Leitrim plantation papers', 132–6.

The Leitrim plantation instructions of 1620 directed how the former lands of the O'Rourkes and their sublords were to be reallocated to British undertakers and compliant natives. Special conditions were laid down according to which both groups were to hold their grants. An important requirement for undertakers was that they were to reside permanently on their estates. Natives would forfeit their grants if they ever rebelled against the crown. Undertakers were subdivided into principal and lesser grantees, with the former having responsibility for the overall military security of the county. Large grants were also given to privileged natives who were then expected to keep in check their less favoured countrymen who had lost a part or all of their land in the scheme. The instructions specifically attempted to ensure that the power of the O'Rourkes was crushed once and for all. The pretended heirs to the title were allocated pensions rather than land in the plantation. Steps were also taken to dissuade other natives from ever backing an O'Rourke return to prominence. The grant of the large estate of Dromahair to Buckingham could be interpreted as a confirmation of the demise of the once-prominent clan.

THE 1622 SURVEY OF THE PLANTATION IN LEITRIM

Early in 1622, the English lord treasurer, Sir Lionel Cranfield, first earl of Middlesex, pressed for the setting up a commission to enquire into all aspects of the Irish administration. These included the courts of justice, the army, finance, trade, the Church of Ireland and the recent plantations. Cranfield felt that abusive government practices in Ireland were proving to be a drain on English resources, and he was determined to make Ireland self-sufficient. The investigation by the commissioners into the plantation in Leitrim, although coming only nine months after the first grantees had been offered their estates, does provide a progress report on the early days of the plantation. It illustrates the limitations of the scheme, the abusive practices of some undertakers and the plight of many natives. Importantly for this study, it positions Frederick Hamilton already on his Leitrim estate by August 1622.[25]

The commission of enquiry sat in Dublin Castle from April to November 1622. It publicized its purpose and scope through the provincial presidents, the archbishops and the county sheriffs, and issued invitations to anyone who had information or complaints to bring these to the commissioners' attention in Dublin. There followed a flood of complaints from aggrieved individuals in the

---

25 Ibid., 131; for a thorough account of the Irish commission of 1622, see Treadwell, *Buckingham and Ireland*, pp 186–211.

counties affected by the recent plantations. The only Irish-speaking member of the commission, Richard Hadsor, a lawyer originally from the Pale, but who was then crown counsel for Irish affairs, was appointed to hear those who had no knowledge of the English language. Several Leitrim natives who had owned quite substantial estates before the plantation now alleged that they had been deprived of as much as two thirds of their former lands, instead of the specified one quarter. Other natives with smaller holdings, but which were still above a hundred acres, stated that they had lost all their land, contrary to the plantation instructions. A number of former landowners complained that the plantation surveyors had used false measurements. They deliberately marked down the size of native holdings, so that the owners would lose their lands, and later readjusted the acreage when the confiscated lands were being redistributed to undertakers. It is also likely, however, that some of the more important native gentlemen, who were appointed to oversee the distribution of land to lesser natives, also managed to allocate extra land to themselves, at the expense of their unfortunate neighbours. A few natives complained that they were given poorer quality land than they had originally owned. In other cases, the new holding was made up of several small parcels of land in different places, instead of the one compact entity that they had owned before the plantation. All of these injustices led to frustration, discontentment and social disruption among the poorer classes of the native population, as the new lord deputy, Viscount Falkland, acknowledged in a letter to the English privy council later in 1622.[26]

Hadsor was only able to promise the natives that their grievances would be investigated and that the king would be informed about those that proved to be legitimate. Furthermore, they were told that commissioners would visit each planted area to assess the situation on the ground, presumably with a view to checking and remedying any abuses. As promised, three commissioners were appointed in late July to view the progress of the plantation in Leitrim. Two of the trio were Lord Wilmot, president of Connacht, and Sir Dudley Norton, secretary of state for Ireland. Astonishingly, the third member was Sir Francis Blundell, formerly king's secretary for Irish business, drafter of the plantation instructions and third largest beneficiary of the scheme. He was now Irish vice treasurer. However, their subsequent report was far more concerned about the lack of progress in the Leitrim plantation in general, the non-compliance of many of the British undertakers with the plantation instructions and the consequent

26 See TCD, MS 672, 149r–162v, Leitrim material in the schedule of native complaints, noted by Richard Hadsor in May 1622, printed in Mac Cuarta (ed.), 'Leitrim plantation papers', 138–9; Bodl., MS Carte 30, fo. 131, Lord Deputy Falkland and council to English privy council, 1 Oct. 1622, quoted in Mac Cuarta, 'The plantation of Leitrim', 314.

loss of revenue for the crown, than about the plight of the natives who had been deprived of their land.[27]

The commissioners were in fact dismayed that there was almost no evidence of 'anie thing like a plantac[i]on' in Leitrim. Only twenty-three of the forty-eight British undertakers had bothered to go to the trouble and expense of procuring letters patent for their grants. The king was not benefiting financially from the land rents of the other twenty-five, as these were going towards the cost of building the walls of Jamestown, the new county town. Of the twenty-three who did pass their patents, only four were resident in the county, and only one of these four – Frederick Hamilton – was a newcomer. The other three had already been living in Leitrim for at least a decade. Sir Maurice Griffith was appointed captain of the garrison at Carrick-on-Shannon around 1610. Henry Crofton acquired the priory of Mohill in 1612 and Lieutenant Walter Harrison was granted an island fort in the River Bonet near Dromahair in the same year. Harrison bought the adjacent disused abbey of Creevelea in Dromahair in 1615. He later roofed part of the building and charged fees for burials within the grounds. He also got a licence to run a tavern nearby in 1618. But there were no British freeholders or tenants on the estates of any of these four resident undertakers by 1622. None of them had as yet built a castle or substantial house. Jamestown had only six or seven houses, and no start had been made on the walls of the new town. The commissioners also found that, contrary to the plantation instructions, British undertakers were buying out some fellow grantees, without having got the requisite permission. One of the guilty parties named in this respect was Frederick Hamilton, who had already acquired the neighbouring estates of William Nesbitt and William Sidney.[28]

There were also one or two other practices, which were not in accordance with the plantation instructions, that the commissioners conveniently failed to notice or examine. For example, several Englishmen were classified as natives, and in addition to their grants as British undertakers, were also given some of the land intended for the native freeholders. These included Griffith, Crofton and Harrison, who had been living in the county for some years prior to the plantation. Then there was the question of the real ownership of some of the larger grants. Commissioners Wilmot and Norton made no effort to discover the true beneficiaries of the grants made out to the Maxwell brothers and Lord Balfour. Of course, their colleague Blundell had no intention of enlightening them. His own and Buckingham's grants were to remain hidden, at least for the time being.

---

27 Mac Cuarta, 'The plantation of Leitrim', 308–11. **28** See *CPRI, James I*, pp 238, 292, 389. Lieutenant Walter Harrison also became sheriff of Sligo in 1616.

Buckingham was, in fact, working behind the scenes for the duration of the 1622 commission of enquiry to protect his own and his connection's interests in Ireland. He was able to ensure that the commissioners did not have access to Lord Deputy St John's private papers. Wilmot and Norton were warned off from meddling in the question of land ownership in the Leitrim plantation. Buckingham also worked successfully at court to delay the return of the commissioners and their reports to England until the end of November 1622, in order to allow time for his various projects in Ireland to be implemented. He later escaped any privy council investigation into his affairs, as he had left for Spain in February 1623 to try to negotiate a marriage between Prince Charles and the daughter of the king of Spain. He had thus succeeded in furtively promoting, manipulating and benefiting hugely from the Leitrim plantation, as well as from several other projects in Ireland, while at the same time continually frustrating the commissioners' investigations into his intrigues.[29]

There were several other grantees outside of the Villiers connection who also left their mark on the plantation. Foremost among these was certainly Frederick Hamilton. In terms of overall grant size, according to the 1622 survey, he ranked fourth after Buckingham, St John and Blundell. Unlike the other three, he had decided from the beginning to become a resident undertaker. Within a matter of months of receiving his grant in March 1622, he had passed his patent and taken possession of his estate. By mid-summer, he had already begun a process of expansion through the purchase of seven hundred acres of good land and 3,225 of waste from neighbouring planters. This was to be the start of a vigorous and sustained policy of land acquisition on his part, primarily in north Leitrim, but also in places as far apart as Kerry, Derry, Mayo and Donegal. The plum Villiers estate of Dromahair became a prime target of his in the late 1620s after Buckingham's death, until the king intervened to ensure that it remained in the Villiers family. This desire for more and more land would bring him into conflict with other British settlers and natives alike.

The plantation tradition, involving confiscation of Irish land and its redistribution among English settlers, extended back to the 1550s. Initially, it followed the suppression of a rebellion by native chieftains. By 1620, when the Leitrim scheme was set in motion, there had developed a policy of almost continuous plantation in an attempt to 'civilize' more and more areas of the country – even those with no history of recent revolts. The power of the O'Rourke lordship was on the wane, and the territory of west Breifne was undergoing a gradual process

---

29 For details of Buckingham's other Irish schemes, such as the plantation in Upper Ossory, the establishment of an Irish court of wards, with Sir William Parsons as its master, and the reimposition of fines on Irish squatters in Ulster, see Treadwell, *Buckingham and Ireland*, pp 143–4, 205–11.

of anglicization well before 1620. But the plantation itself, pushed through by Buckingham and other self-seeking officials, gave the coup de grâce to the once-powerful Gaelic dynasty. It gradually introduced a network of British landlords into the lands of O'Rourke and those of his sublords, while the pretender to the title was confined in the Tower of London. Buckingham and his connection cherry-picked almost half of the acreage allocated to undertakers. The remainder was granted to British courtiers, Irish officials and army officers. Leading 'civil' members of the O'Rourkes, Reynolds and MacClancys received substantial grants in order to create a satisfied and loyal body of natives. These were then expected to show little sympathy to their less important fellow countrymen who lost some or all of their holdings. As a result, the plantation seems to have been largely non-violent, with British settlers complaining more about the inhospitable terrain than about hostile natives.

The 1622 survey indicated that the Leitrim plantation made very little progress in the first year of its operation. There were few physical signs of new settlements and undertakers were flaunting regulations. But the survey commissioners paid scant attention to the complaints of disposed natives, who, with Brian and Hugh O'Rourke, were the big losers in the plantation.

CHAPTER THREE

The 1620s: a decade of expansion

Frederick Hamilton's first significant career move had occurred in 1615 when he left his native Scotland at the age of twenty-five to become a gentleman of the privy chamber at the court of James I in England. Another major milestone in his life was his move from the court to his newly acquired estate in the north-west of Ireland seven years later. He did not completely forsake the court, since his privy chamberman's oath bound him, at least in theory, to attend the king for three months every year. Frederick succeeded at first in regularly fulfilling this obligation, although difficulties arose at a later stage in getting a licence from the lord deputy to cross over to England. Despite his many travels, both within Ireland and across the Irish Sea, the main focus of his attention during the 1620s was his new base in Leitrim where he would set about rearing his young family, expanding his estate and maintaining a company of foot in the standing army in Ireland.

DEVELOPMENTS IN FREDERICK HAMILTON'S PERSONAL LIFE

The years leading up to 1622 had been both a period of huge career advancement, but also a time of significant personal sadness for Frederick Hamilton. His elevation at court and his award of a large estate in the plantation of Leitrim were put somewhat into perspective by five close family bereavements. The first to die was his older brother, Claud, who had been a gentleman of the English privy chamber and a member of the privy council in Ireland. He had been allotted two thousand acres in the barony of Strabane, Co. Tyrone, in the Ulster Plantation, but had only begun to reside on his estate a year or so before his death in Dublin in October 1614 at the age of thirty-seven. Frederick's sadness would have been tempered by the fact that he himself was admitted to the privy chamber in his brother's place the following year.[1]

In 1616, Frederick's mother Margaret, daughter of George, fifth Lord Seton, passed away at her home in Paisley. Two years later, Frederick's eldest brother James, earl of Abercorn, gentleman of the Scottish bedchamber and Scottish privy councillor, died aged forty-three, also at Paisley. James had been one of the

1 Balfour Paul, *The Scots peerage*, i, pp 40–1.

principal undertakers in the Ulster Plantation, having been allotted three thousand acres at Strabane. He was a committed planter from the beginning and had soon doubled the size of his estate. Frederick's father, Lord Claud Hamilton, passed away at the advanced age of seventy-eight in 1621, again at Paisley Abbey (pl. 1). Finally, Frederick's youngest sister, Margaret, who was married to William, first marquis of Douglas, died two years later at the age of thirty-two.[2]

Frederick experienced another significant, if less personal, bereavement a few years later when his first cousin, James, second marquis of Hamilton, died aged thirty-six in March 1625. James had been a close friend of King James I, a gentleman of the English privy chamber and a member of both the English and Scottish privy councils. He was thus a very powerful ally and patron whom Frederick had relied on when seeking royal favours. The marquis' son, James, third marquis (and later duke) of Hamilton, then aged nineteen, succeeded to his father's titles that same year, but really only came to prominence in 1628 when he was appointed a gentleman of the bedchamber by Charles I. For the next fourteen years, Frederick would rely on this man's influence at court in times of need.[3]

The early 1620s also brought much happiness and personal fulfilment to Frederick Hamilton. It was during these years that he met his future wife Sidney, eldest daughter and heiress of Sir John Vaughan. Of Welsh extraction, Vaughan was a captain in the army of Sir Henry Docwra, who had been sent over to Ireland in 1600 to quell the unrest in Ulster towards the end of the Nine Years War. Vaughan was awarded a grant of land in Co. Donegal during the Ulster Plantation and represented that county in the Irish parliaments of 1613 and 1634. He gave advice on the construction of the walls of Derry in 1612 and four years later became governor of that city and a member of the Irish privy council. During the early 1620s, Vaughan became controller of Prince Charles' household and was based at the English court. It was probably here that Frederick and Sidney met and married about the year 1622. Sidney joined her husband on his new Leitrim estate almost at the beginning. She was to prove a true frontier woman who ran the estate during her husband's frequent absences. She would also be at his side during the 1641 rebellion and its aftermath. The couple's three eldest children, Frederick (*c.*1624), James (*c.*1626) and Christina (*c.*1629) were born in Leitrim before the end of the decade.[4]

2 Lees, *The abbey of Paisley*, p. 237; Maxwell, *A history of the house of Douglas*, ii, pp 186, 193. **3** G.E. Cokayne, *The complete peerage of England, Scotland, Ireland, Great Britain and the United Kingdom, extant, extinct or dormant* (new ed., 13 vols in 14, 1910–59; repr. in 6 vols, Gloucester, 2000), vi, pp 258–60. **4** R. Loeber, 'A biographical dictionary of engineers in Ireland, 1600–1700', *Irish Sword*, 8:53 (1979), 310–11; V. Treadwell, *Buckingham and Ireland*, pp 56, 57, 111; A. Young, *Three hundred years in Innishowen* (Belfast, 1929), pp 50–1; TNA, SP63, vol. 237, fo. 119, petition of Sir Frederick Hamilton to the king, 3

Although Frederick Hamilton was a nobleman by virtue of the fact that his father, Lord Claud, had been raised to the peerage in 1587, he felt the need to acquire another title of honour before setting out for Ireland to take over his estate. He therefore set about procuring for himself a knighthood in the late spring of 1622. This honour was probably conferred by James I in court, and would have cost Frederick in the region of £100. The king had, since his accession to the English throne, substantially increased not only the number of knights, but also that of the peerage – dukes, marquises, earls, viscounts and barons – as a means of raising funds for the crown. However, Frederick would have considered the expense well worthwhile, since a knighthood was then considered to be an important badge of British 'civility' in Ireland. Furthermore, two of his older brothers, Claud and George, had already been conferred with the title. With this latest honour, Sir Frederick was now ready to take possession of his Leitrim estate.[5]

LEITRIM IN THE LATE SIXTEENTH AND EARLY SEVENTEENTH CENTURY

The contrast between the glittering English court and the rural north Leitrim environment could not have been greater. In a petition to the king, written one year after his arrival in the county, Sir Frederick describes it as 'that most barbarous place'. He was, no doubt, referring to the inhospitable, rugged landscape of mountains and partially wooded valleys (fig. 7), but probably also to the local inhabitants whose lifestyle and living conditions would have differed so much from what he had been accustomed to. Leitrim in 1623 was largely untouched by outside influence. A small English settlement had indeed grown up around the fort of Carrickdrumrusk (Carrick-on-Shannon) and a new county walled town was beginning to develop at nearby Jamestown. However, both of these settlements were in the south of the county, and were more than thirty miles from Hamilton's estate.[6]

The lives and conditions of the native Irish in Leitrim were well described by a Spanish sea captain who spent over three months in the north of the county after his Armada galleon had been shipwrecked off the nearby Sligo coast in September 1588. Things had probably changed very little by the time Sir Frederick arrived there over thirty years later. Francisco de Cuellar wrote that the followers of his host and protector, Teige MacClancy of Rosclogher, sub-lord of Brian of the Ramparts O'Rourke, lived 'as the brute beasts among the mountains which are very rugged in that part of Ireland'. They were accustomed to hard work, active as the roe deer,

Oct. 1623.   **5** B. Mac Cuarta (ed.), 'Leitrim plantation papers', 130–1; Treadwell, *Buckingham and Ireland*, pp 104–6.   **6** TNA, SP63, vol. 237, fo. 119.

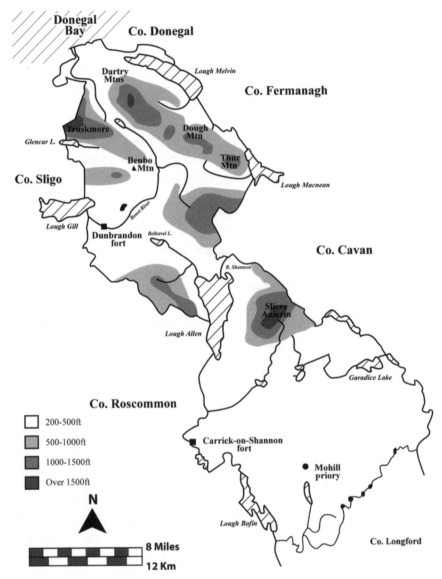

7 Topographical map of Co. Leitrim, also showing pre-plantation British settlements within the county.

and great walkers. They lived in villages of thatched huts or cabins and slept on beds of rushes or straw. They had no other property apart from their cattle, and retired to the mountains with their women, children and cattle in times of danger.[7]

7 H. Allingham (ed.), *Captain Cuellar's adventures in Connacht and Ulster, AD1588* (London, 1897), repr. under the title *The Spanish Armada: Captain Cuellar's adventures in Connacht and Ulster, AD1588* (Sligo,

The men were described as being 'all large-bodied and of handsome features and limbs, and wear their hair down to their eyes. They clothe themselves … in tight trousers and short loose coats of very coarse goat's hair … and cover themselves with blankets'. De Cuellar found the women generally to be 'very beautiful, but badly dressed. They do not wear more than a chemise, and a blanket with which they cover themselves, and a linen cloth much doubled over the head and tied in front. They are also great workers and housekeepers, after their fashion'. The people ate just once a day in the evening. Their diet consisted of buttered oaten bread and sour milk. On feast days, they ate some half-cooked meat, without bread or salt. Some of them were well educated and had a knowledge of Latin.[8]

MacClancy (who lived with his family in a tower house on an island in Lough Melvin) and his people were constantly at war with the English, whom they hated, and endeavoured to prevent from entering their territory of Rosclogher. Although de Cuellar records many acts of kindness and assistance to himself and other shipwrecked Spaniards during their sojourn in north Leitrim, he added that 'the chief inclination of these people is to be robbers and to plunder each other, so that not one day passes without a call to arms among them'. They would thus attack neighbouring villages at night and take away their cattle. They were armed and would kill one another during these escapades. 'In short', the Spaniard concluded, 'there is neither justice nor right in this kingdom, and everyone does as he pleases'.[9]

De Cuellar's description of the Leitrim natives and their customs mirrors fairly closely the impressions that English officials and planters gave of the Irish in various parts of the country in the late sixteenth and early seventeenth centuries. For example, the poet and planter Edmund Spenser wrote in 1596 that the areas inhabited by the native Irish seemed wild, wooded and forbidding, and 'full of narrow corners and glannes under the mountaines foote, in which they lurked'.[10] Cattle were considered the only valuable property, and people seemed to live with their cattle, whether the herd was being brought to upland areas for summer grazing or whether the owners needed to flee to the mountains for protection against the English.

Irish huts or cabins were often windowless and chimneyless, quickly erected temporary structures made of wattle, daub and thatch. Sir John Davies (James I's attorney general in Ireland) wrote in 1606 that 'the habitations of this people are so wild and transitory as there is not one fixed village in all this country

1988), pp 61–2. **8** Ibid. **9** Ibid. **10** E. Spenser, 'A view of the state of Ireland [1596]' in James Ware (ed.), *Ancient Irish histories: the works of Spenser, Campion, Hanmer and Marleburrough* (2 vols, Dublin, 1809), i, p. 23; M. Elliott, *The Catholics of Ulster* (London, 2000), pp 30, 35.

[Fermanagh]'. The bardic poets had often satirized as effeminate and unmanly those who slept in feather beds and cropped their hair. Not surprisingly, therefore, one Tudor visitor remarked that the Irish 'care not for pot, pan, kettil nor for mattrys, fether bed'. The blanket to which de Cuellar referred was the Irish mantle, rug or cloak worn by both men and women, which acted as both clothing and bedding.[11]

It is no wonder that Leitrim seemed a barbarous place to Sir Frederick Hamilton when he first arrived there in 1622. The rugged, untamed landscape as well as the living conditions and customs of the Irish natives were totally alien to what he had been used to at the English court. He was, however, a resolute planter who would not be easily deflected from the enterprise he had undertaken – that of expanding and developing his estate and harnessing its resources. He would, in the process, have worked towards the 'civilization' of the natives through the promotion of more formal and finer attire, the building of stone houses in permanent villages and the advancement of tillage as an alternative to cattle herding.

ESTATE EXPANSION

Just as in Ulster some ten years earlier, a process of consolidation took place in Leitrim in the 1620s and 1630s. The more progressive British planters bought out those who never arrived to take possession of their estates, as well as those who failed to make a success of their ventures. They also acquired land from native Irish grantees, a substantial number of whom had fallen into debt in their efforts to try and meet the demands of the new British lifestyle, which involved paying fixed annual fees and rent charges, using the legal system and adopting English fashions. As a result, they were often forced to either sell or mortgage their land to acquire the necessary cash. The end result was often the same, as borrowers frequently failed to redeem a mortgage and the property was eventually acquired by the mortgagor. Henry Crofton of Mohill, for example, had increased his estate from the original one thousand to almost two thousand acres through both mortgaging and purchase by 1641. Similarly, Robert Parke, who had bought Sir William Irwin's estate of 1,500 acres at Newtown, near Dromahair in 1628 and built a castle there on the site of an old O'Rourke fortress, also held 953 acres in mortgage from Con O'Rourke of Castle Car, which in total was worth £1,000 per annum in the 1630s.[12]

11 Sir J. Davies, 'A discovery of the true causes why Ireland was never entirely subdued' in H. Morley (ed.), *Ireland under Elizabeth and James I* (London, 1890), i, p. 374, cited in L.M. Cullen, *Life in Ireland* (London, 1979), p. 46. 12 See O'Dowd, *Power, politics and land*, pp 80–94; Books of Survey and

Sir Frederick Hamilton, who was the first of the new Leitrim planters to take possession of his estate in the summer of 1622, immediately set about enlarging his holding through the purchase of land from both British and Irish grantees. His main aim would seem to have been to acquire all the land that lay between both sections of his original grant, but he was also interested in picking up any other portions that became available within, and sometimes even beyond, the county boundaries. Not all of his attempts proved successful, but this did not deter him from trying whenever the opportunity arose. By August 1622, he had bought out the strategically situated estates of William Nesbitt and William Sidney, amounting to seven hundred acres of profitable land and 3,225 acres of bog and wood. These properties in the townlands of Boleyboy, Lissinagroath, Loughaphonta and Glenkeel, although situated in the barony of Rosclogher, lay just to the north of his own estate.[13]

Next on Hamilton's list was an army officer named Captain Faithful Fortescue who had been granted 1,500 acres in the Leitrim plantation. On inspecting his estate, Fortescue had complained that his lands 'are of so poor and bad condition that they are not worth his undertaking'. Sir Frederick thought otherwise, as they were also situated between his own two parcels of land, just to the south of those of Nesbitt and Sidney. Accordingly, they were speedily acquired early in 1623.[14]

By the summer of that year, Hamilton had purchased the island of Valentia in Co. Kerry from Sir John Ayres, whom he had probably met at court. Before setting out from London to inspect his latest acquisition, he procured two letters from the king, dated 6 August 1623. One was addressed to Lord Deputy Falkland and the other to Donogh O'Brien, fourth earl of Thomond and then president of Munster, requesting both officials to assist Sir Frederick in every way possible in his new business venture in Munster, 'that he may have justice and all possible expedition'. Even though Valentia Island was over two hundred miles from his Leitrim base, Hamilton still retained his holding there right up to the 1641 rebellion.[15]

Recognizing that these recent acquisitions of land were contrary to the terms of the Leitrim plantation, whereby 'noe undertakers shall aliene their lands to one another without speciall lycence', Sir Frederick soon took steps to rectify the situation. In September 1623, he requested the king to instruct the lord deputy to accept a surrender of his original grant and to issue a new one, which would incorporate his already substantially enlarged holding. The request was indeed referred by the king to the new Commission for Irish Affairs on 3 October, with

Distribution for Co. Leitrim (NAI); Down Survey, Co. Leitrim (RIA).   **13** *CPRI, 19 James I*, p. 539; B. Mac Cuarta (ed.), 'Leitrim plantation papers', 131.   **14** Bodl. MS Carte 30, fo. 117, Sir Dudley Digges to Buckingham, 19 Apr. 1622. Fortescue was a nephew of the former lord deputy, Sir Arthur Chichester, and had also been granted lands in the Wexford plantation.   **15** TNA, SP63, vol. 237, 47A and B.

a strong recommendation that a new grant be drawn up. However, the critical reports of the 1622 survey of the recent plantations led the commissioners to advise that no new patents should be issued until rents and tenures had been approved by the privy council. So, despite royal backing, Hamilton's request was thwarted, and he did not renew it until the end of the decade, when new grants were once again being issued more liberally.[16]

Not all of Sir Frederick's attempts at acquiring more land for himself were successful. He failed on two occasions in the 1620s to significantly expand his estate in north Leitrim and across the county boundary in Sligo. The first of these ventures concerned 2,500 acres at Ballintogher in Co. Sligo. These lands, originally part of west Breifne, had been in dispute between O'Rourke and O'Connor Sligo during the sixteenth century. The Composition of Connacht in 1585 failed to rule on the issue and included the territory in both counties, Leitrim and Sligo. In the early seventeenth century, William Taaffe of Ballymote, the largest landowner in Co. Sligo, claimed to have acquired the land, but the occupying family, the MacKeons, disputed his assertion, and furthermore recognized the O'Rourkes as their overlords. Despite their protests, Taaffe was formally granted the lands, which were created into the manor of Ballintogher in 1616. However, when Taaffe returned to his birthplace in Co. Louth four years later, the MacKeons tried in the provincial court to get title to the estate. Around the same time, Mary O'Donnell, Sir Teige O'Rourke's widow, also claimed the lands, which she maintained were part of her dowry from her husband. The court accepted Lady O'Rourke's claim and granted her the estate. Taaffe then brought the case to the Dublin courts and got letters patent for the lands. In 1621, the MacKeons agreed to rent from him. The following year, shortly after his arrival in Leitrim, Sir Frederick Hamilton became involved in the dispute. The MacKeons now agreed to share the lands with Hamilton if he could gain possession of the estate. The attempt failed, however, and in 1625 Taaffe secured a chancery decree regranting the lands to him, on condition that he lease them to the MacKeons for a term of three lives. The Ballintogher estate would have been a valuable asset to Sir Frederick as it contained one of the finest natural woods in Co. Sligo, which supplied the then flourishing export timber trade in Sligo town.[17]

Some years later, Sir Frederick was again unsuccessful in an attempt to quadruple the size of his original estate. This time he cast his eye on the former O'Rourke lands of Dromahair, amounting to 6,500 acres of profitable land, which had been granted to George Villiers, duke of Buckingham, through his

---

16 B. Mac Cuarta (ed.), 'Leitrim plantation papers', 131. **17** A.M. Freeman (trans.), *The compossicion booke of Conought* (Dublin, 1936), p. 144. The lands of Ballintogher contained 22 quarters, with a quarter reckoned at 120 acres; M. O'Dowd, 'Landownership in the Sligo area 1585–1641' (PhD, UCD, 1979), pp 321–7.

Scottish proxies, the Maxwell brothers. Having survived an attempt by the English parliament in 1626 to impeach him on the basis of his secret acquisitions of Irish land, and of defrauding the royal revenue through the sale of honours and offices for his own personal gain, Buckingham decided to gift his Dromahair estate to his half-brother, Sir William Villiers of Brokesby. King Charles sanctioned the transfer on 13 February 1628. As Sir William had no intention of personally residing in Leitrim, he was granted permission by the king to put an agent there in his place.[18]

Within a few months, Hamilton had approached Sir William with a view to purchasing his newly acquired estate. At their first meeting, Villiers agreed in writing to sell for £4,000. Later, a more legal form of agreement was drawn up by Sir Frederick's lawyer. Villiers refused to accept this contract unless Sir Frederick's own lands were included as a surety for the payment. This time Hamilton disagreed. Villiers then offered him £100 to be released from the deal, but Hamilton demanded £1,000. He then brought a legal action in the Court of Chancery in Ireland against Villiers for breach of contract. However, the king intervened on 8 January 1629 and directed Lord Chancellor Adam Loftus to stop the case as Sir William had fallen ill and could not travel over to Ireland. The king assured Sir Frederick at the same time that he would receive justice.[19]

Sir William died in June of that year. Hamilton then requested of the king that the Dromahair estate be entrusted to him during the minority of Sir William's son and heir, George (fig. 8). He also sought an assurance that he would get title to the estate when George reached adulthood. In return, Sir Frederick offered to pay the £4,000 originally agreed. However, in early August, King Charles referred the matter to Sir Thomas Coventry, the lord keeper, recommending that he persuade both parties and their lawyers to come to some mutually acceptable agreement. If this proved impossible, Coventry, as head of the judiciary, was to give a formal decision on the dispute himself. A week later, the king directed Sir William Parsons, master of the Court of Wards in Ireland, not to grant the Dromahair estate to Sir Frederick until the lord keeper had made his adjudication. Coventry's report at the end of August stated that young George Villiers had legally inherited the estate and could therefore not be deprived of the lands. Although this was unfortunate for Hamilton, he could have no claim on them. Sir Frederick was thus thwarted in his efforts to acquire the county's prime estate, which remained a Villiers possession.[20]

---

18 *CSPI, 1625–32*, p. 309. **19** Ibid., p. 420; see also D. Mac an Ghallóglaigh, 'Sir Frederick Hamilton', *Breifne*, 3:9 (1966), 61–2. **20** TNA, SP63, vol. 249, fo.127RH: petition of Sir Frederick Hamilton to the king, and the king's referral to the lord keeper, 7 Aug. 1629; TNA, SP63, vol. 249, fo. 178RM: king to master of the wards, 14 Aug. 1629; *CSPI, 1625–32*, p. 478: lord keeper to the king, 25 Aug. 1629.

8 Petition by Sir Frederick Hamilton to the king for Villiers' Dromahair estate and the king's referral of the matter to the lord keeper, 7 Aug. 1629 (TNA SP63/249 F127RH, courtesy of the National Archives, London).

The Ballintogher and Dromahair failures by no means signalled the end of Sir Frederick's land acquisitions. He purchased a strategic six hundred acres from the British undertaker, James Fotney (alias Ratrye), who had never bothered to take out a patent for his grant. This land was situated in the barony of Rosclogher, adjoining the western section of Sir Frederick's estate. Hamilton also bought up several small isolated parcels of land from four native Irish grantees – one hundred acres at Laureen, near Lough Melvin from Owen MacMorrow, 326 acres in Glenade from Cahir and Rory MacClancy and seventy-seven acres in Glencar from Tiernan O'Rourke. By 1629, Sir Frederick's estate amounted to almost five thousand acres of profitable land and double that amount of bog and mountain. He now made another attempt to regularize all of his acquisitions in line with the terms of the plantation, by requesting Charles I for permission to unite all his lands into one single grant. He reminded the king that a similar favour had been accorded to the late Sir William Villiers the previous year, when he had been allowed to amalgamate the two portions of the estate transferred from his half-brother, the duke of Buckingham.[21]

The restrictions on the issue of new grants had by now been lifted. Moreover, the king was probably anxious to show some favour to Sir Frederick following the lord keeper's ruling against him in the Villiers estate case. Charles therefore ordered the lords justices in January 1630 to accept Hamilton's surrender of his original estate and to regrant him his greatly enlarged one in its place. The king also directed that Sir Frederick should not be fined for any breaches of the original plantation regulations, provided that he build 'in convenient time one fair castle and one bawn upon the said manor, instead of all other buildings' already there. The actual surrender of the lands took place in Dublin some months later, when Hamilton duly received letters patent for his new manor of Hamilton.[22]

THE ARMY MAN

Even before seeking a substantial grant of land in the plantation of Leitrim, Sir Frederick Hamilton had ambitions for a career in the army. He was not unqualified for such a way of life. Being a privy chamberman, he was already an accomplished horseman, and as part of a liberal education he had also acquired some training in the use of weapons. Perhaps he was influenced by his older brother George, who, in addition to receiving a grant of land in the Ulster Plantation, was also a captain of fifty foot-soldiers in the army in Ireland. In any case, a military background would be an asset for any planter to have. And as a future principal undertaker in the Leitrim plantation, Frederick would hold his grant by knight's service, with responsibility for the security of the general planter community in his area. So, early in 1620 he sought a captaincy from the king, who granted his wish on 8 April of that year. His first trip to Ireland occurred soon afterwards, when he presented to the lord deputy the king's letter, which directed that he be given command of the first company of horse or foot that became available.[23]

There had been a standing or regular army in Ireland since 1474, when a force of 120 archers, forty horsemen and forty pages was established for the defence of the Pale during the reign of Edward IV. Towards the end of Henry VIII's

21 Marsh, MS Z4.2.6, king to lords justices, 12 Jan. 1630; Mac Cuarta (ed.), 'Leitrim plantation papers', 131; see also *CPRI, 19 James I*, pp 535–6 for original grants to these native Irish; *CSPI, 1625–32*, p. 506; *CSPI, Charles I, 1647–60, addenda, 1625–60*, p. 142.   22 Marsh, MS Z4.2.6, king to lords justices, 12 Jan. 1630; *CPRI, Charles I*, pp 540–1.   23 J. Anderson, *Historical and genealogical memoirs of the house of Hamilton* (Edinburgh, 1825), p. 243.

monarchy, the numbers in the army increased to three hundred horse and 160 foot. When Queen Mary was on the throne (1553–8), the military personnel amounted to 1,200 men. During the reign of Elizabeth (1558–1603), the totals varied between 1,500 and 2,000. These figures remained the same during the monarchies of both James I and Charles I. These were peacetime numbers, however. In times of Irish unrest and rebellion, they were considerably greater. A list of the army in Ireland in 1630 shows that it was divided into nine companies of horse and twenty-five companies of foot. Each company contained fifty men and lived either in a garrison generally located on the estate of the commanding officer, or in one of the forts around the country such as Athlone, Carrickfergus, Derry, Culmore or Duncannon. Army numbers were tightly regulated, and a new officer could only be appointed on the death or retirement of an existing one. Hence the statement in James I's letter that Sir Frederick should be allotted the first company that became available.[24]

No vacancy had occurred by December 1621, when the king issued a second letter to Lord Deputy St John, again granting Hamilton the first company of horse or foot that fell vacant in Ireland. However, it was not until June 1623, when Sir Francis Rushe of Rush Hall in Co. Leix (and Dunsink in Co. Dublin) died, that Sir Frederick, who had by then spent a year on his Leitrim estate, succeeded to Rushe's company of foot. Within a very short time, the king ordered Hamilton to hand over the soldiers to Lord Esmond, major general of the army in Ireland, who had requested them for the defence of his fort at Duncannon, Co. Wexford.[25]

Sir Frederick strove to be allocated a replacement company, and in September 1623 he procured a third letter from the king again directing that he should have the very next vacant company. Armed with this letter, he approached the new lord deputy, Viscount Falkland, the following year, pressing strongly for command of the company of foot belonging to the earl of Thomond, who had just died. It would seem as if Hamilton was not the only aspirant who had procured a royal letter that promised a company of foot to the recipient, and so his hopes were dashed once more.[26]

Sir Frederick's turn finally seemed to come in spectacular fashion in February 1625, when the ageing James I allocated him the late Arthur Chichester's troop of horse and company of foot, together with the governorship of Carrickfergus, which post Chichester had held since his retirement as lord deputy in 1615. There was a certain disappointment once again, however, when the king partially changed his mind and transferred Chichester's troop of horse to Henry Power,

Viscount Valentia, and awarded the governorship of Carrickfergus to Chichester's brother, Sir Edward. But, making the best of the situation, Hamilton built a garrison for his newly acquired foot company near his residence in the eastern portion of his estate, at the hamlet called Cloonmullen in the district of Glenfarne.[27]

Sir Frederick's early years as a junior officer in the standing army coincided with a general state of alert in Ireland, occasioned by England's war with Spain (1625–30) and also its later one with France (1627–9). In 1604 James I had brought to a conclusion a previous Anglo-Spanish war, which had dragged on after the Armada attack. Even when Spanish troops invaded the Rhineland Palatinate in Germany, home territory of his son-in-law, Frederick, in November 1620, James, who had always seen himself as a pacifist, was reluctant to declare war on Spain again. But, when the proposed marriage of his son and successor, Charles I, with the Infanta Maria, daughter of Philip III of Spain, collapsed, following Spain's humiliating demands in late 1623, James gave way to the strong anti-Spanish sentiment in Britain. When he died in March 1625, both countries were on the brink of war.

After the failure of the English attack on the port of Cadiz in south-western Spain in October 1625, there was a danger of a Spanish invasion of Ireland. The English feared in particular that Spain would send its Irish regiment in Flanders to Ireland in the hope that disaffected Irish natives at home would join it in open rebellion. Such an invasion never materialized, but the English watched closely all potential native leaders and conspirators. One such man who became identified with popular conspiracy was Hugh O'Rourke, younger son of the late Sir Teige, because of the old O'Rourke ties with Spain at the time of the Armada. By 1624, Lord Deputy Falkland had put the twenty-four-year-old Hugh under surveillance, and found him to be stirring up resistance against the government. Hugh was then living on his mother's estate in Glenboy, next to Sir Frederick Hamilton's lands. It is thus quite likely that the surveillance on O'Rourke was carried out by Sir Frederick. In view of the threat that O'Rourke posed for the authorities, Falkland invited him to Dublin with promises of royal favour and a pension if he would leave the country. Hugh, however, was wary of the lord deputy, since his older brother Brian was then being held in the Tower of London. So, instead of complying with Falkland's request, he went to live with his mother, Lady O'Rourke, who was residing in Co. Mayo with her then husband David Bourke.[28]

CSPI, James I, p. 539: lord deputy and council to privy council, 23 Oct. 1624. **27** Parliamentary Archives, HL/PO/JO/10/1/47, petition of Sir Frederick Hamilton to the House of Lords, 14 Jan. 1641; *The humble remonstrance*, pp 1–2; *CSPI, James I*, p. 573; *CSPI, 1625–32*, p. 54. **28** Casway, 'The last lords of Leitrim', 570.

Hugh returned to Glenboy in June 1625. Falkland was again notified, presumably by Sir Frederick, who by now had his company of foot stationed nearby, that O'Rourke was being visited by a large number of native Irish. Fearing that, if a rebellion or invasion took place, Hugh (who was then described as a figure of great importance) would attract a large following, the lord deputy again encouraged him to go to England with promises of travel expenses, letters of recommendation to the king, and a pension. O'Rourke eventually travelled to Dublin to meet Falkland in May 1626. The lord deputy was impressed with the young man, who conducted himself honourably, and might even, he felt, be persuaded to take the oath of allegiance. Hugh agreed to go to London the following month to avail of the privy council's promises of the king's favour and a £100 pension. However, he soon discovered that the promises were conditional on his residing with the archbishop of Canterbury, as well as resigning his rights and title to his ancestral estate of Dromahair.[29]

On failing to agree to these conditions, Hugh and his cousin, Con MacCaffery O'Donnell (nephew of Rory, earl of Tyrconnell), who had accompanied him from Ireland, were both imprisoned. They later succeeded in escaping with the help of another cousin, Mary Stuart O'Donnell, and fled to Flanders, where Hugh sought a Spanish pension and a command in the Irish regiment there. Hugh's departure from Leitrim reduced the state of alert in the county, at least for the time being, although there were reports of 'a strong knot of rebels in Cavan, Longford and Leitrim' in the autumn of 1626. But the fact that Sir Charles Coote, based in Jamestown, was delegated to suppress these insurgents would seem to indicate that the disturbances occurred in south Leitrim rather than in the northern part of the county, where Sir Frederick Hamilton was situated.[30]

Despite Charles I's marriage to Henrietta Maria, sister of Louis XIII of France, in 1625, and an Anglo-French political alliance formed to counteract the growing power of the Habsburgs, England soon found itself at war with France over the Huguenot situation. The Huguenots had set up what was essentially a state within a state in parts of the south of France. The English felt an affinity with their co-religionists, and in June 1627 an expedition led by the duke of Buckingham set out to relieve the Huguenots, who were then besieged by the French government in the western French sea port of La Rochelle. Four months later, the expedition had proved, no less than Cadiz, an embarrassing and expensive failure. A counter-attack, this time from either France or Spain, was again expected in Ireland. To secure the country against such an invasion,

29 *CSPI, 1615–25*, p. 66: Falkland to Conway, 17 June 1625; *CSPI, 1625–32*, p. 132: Falkland to English privy council, 7 June 1626. It is not clear whether this was the £100 annual pension allocated to Hugh in the Leitrim plantation instructions in October 1620 or whether it was a supplementary payment. **30** B. Jennings (ed.), *Wild Geese in Spanish Flanders, 1582–1700* (Dublin, 1964), pp 210–13; *CSPI, 1625–32*, p. 195.

England had, during the Spanish alert, sent over 2,250 foot soldiers to strengthen the standing army in Ireland. Later reinforcements brought the total number up to five thousand foot and five hundred horse. However, since the English parliament, at odds with the monarch over his policy of ruling by Divine Right, and in particular his marriage to the Catholic Henrietta Maria, had refused to subsidize these troops, money had to be found in Ireland to pay for the country's defence. Charles I began to explore in 1626 the possibility of funding the expanded army through payments from the Old English (Catholic descendants of the Anglo-Norman settlers in Ireland) in return for measures of religious and political reform. The New English (Protestant Tudor and Stuart planters and administrators) agreed to share the burden of payments in 1627 in return for the granting of some of their particular demands. The Graces – a series of royal concessions on religious and land issues – were finally agreed the following year in return for three annual subsidies of £40,000 to meet the cost of supporting the expanded army.[31]

In the summer of 1627, while negotiations were still ongoing, the lord deputy was forced to impose an additional levy of £43,000 to pay for the immediate costs of the army. A list of commissioners, representing both Old and New English, was drawn up in each county, who would be responsible for raising the extra funds. Sir Charles Coote and Sir Frederick Hamilton, head the list of the ten military men and prominent landowners who were given the task of raising £400 in Co. Leitrim.[32]

The army in Ireland had always been a substantial drain on the English exchequer. In the early 1620s, when there was a chronic shortage of cash in Ireland, soldiers were owed substantial arrears of pay and were in a near-mutinous state. At times, they were billeted on the local population and had to live on their wits. A state of the army report in 1623 accuses them of being prone to 'pillage and extort unreasonably from the country peasants as they pass'. The situation deteriorated when army numbers trebled in the mid 1620s, and funding to support the new soldiers was very slow in being raised. Things had become so bad in Co. Leitrim by June 1627 that a commission was given to army officers, such as Sir Charles Coote, Sir Frederick Hamilton, Captain Maurice Griffith and Lieutenant Henry Crofton

> authorizing them to examine and try by martial law, all extortions, mis-
> demeanors, outrages and other offences committed by the 'new supply' of
> fifty foot, under the command of Lord Grandison [former Lord Deputy, St
> John]; and upon their conviction to proceed to judgement and punishment

31 *CSPI, 1625–32*, p. 246.   32 Ibid., pp 250–3; R. Gillespie, *Seventeenth-century Ireland* (Dublin, 2006),

by death or otherwise, according to the nature of the offence and the articles of war.

However, once Britain signed truces with France (in 1629) and Spain (in 1630), the army in Ireland was halved and conditions improved for the personnel who remained in service.[33]

It was not only the ordinary soldier who did not receive his pay during these years of crises. It would seem as if Sir Frederick's request to Charles I for the right to nominate two baronets of Ireland in 1628 was motivated by the non-payment to him of substantial army arrears. English and Irish baronetcies were initially created during the reign of James I to raise money for the defence of the Ulster Plantation and for the upkeep of military forces in Ireland generally. They formed a new hereditary order in the social ladder between non-hereditary knights and hereditary peers, and had seats in the upper houses of parliament. The fee for being conferred with an Irish baronetcy in the 1620s appears to have been about £250. Sir Frederick's request was probably made when he was at court on privy chamberman duties in February 1628. The king, when bestowing the favour on him six months later (fig. 9), was in effect granting him £500. It was not until May 1629 that Hamilton was able to procure the money from his two nominees, John Magrath of Allevollan, Co. Tipperary, and John Wilson of Killenure, Co. Donegal.[34]

As the state of emergency decreased in Ireland towards the end of the decade, Sir Frederick was further remunerated for his army service when the king directed Lords Justices Ely and Cork (who had charge of the administration in Ireland between Lord Deputy Falkland's recall in August 1629 and Sir Thomas Wentworth's appointment as his replacement three years later) to pay full arrears due to him and his brother Sir George. The fact that Sir Frederick was a courtier, as well as having the backing of his cousin, James, third marquis of Hamilton, one of the king's closest attendants, would certainly have helped him secure such entitlements.[35]

CONTINUED LIMITED PLANTATION PROGRESS

The 1622 commissioners who carried out a survey of recent Irish plantations concluded that there was very little evidence at all of a plantation in Co. Leitrim.

p. 76.   **33** G. O'Brien (ed.), *Advertisements for Ireland* [1623] (Dublin, 1923), p. 45; *CPRI, Charles I*, p. 244.   **34** Marsh, MS Z3.2.6, king's letter for Sir Frederick Hamilton to nominate two baronets, 18 Aug. 1628; *CPRI, Charles I*, p. 463: nomination of the two baronets by Sir Frederick, 20 May 1629; *CSPI, 1625–32*, p. 313: king recommends Hamilton to the lord deputy; see also Treadwell, *Buckingham and Ireland*, pp 104–11, on the creation of baronets.   **35** *CPRI, Charles I*, p. 553.

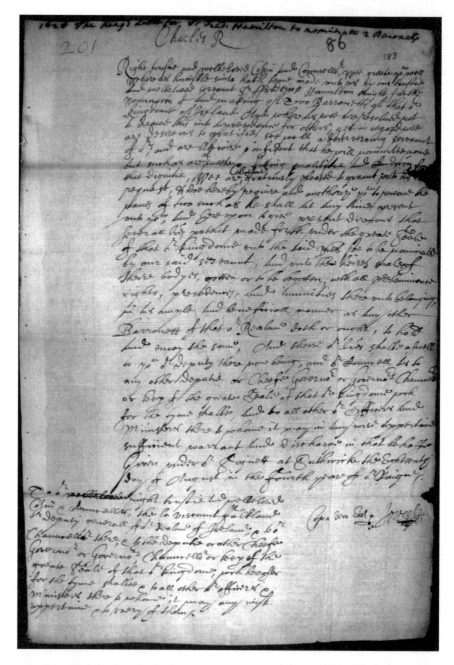

9 The king's letter for Sir Frederick Hamilton to nominate two baronets, 18 Aug. 1628 (Marsh Z3.2.6, by permission of the Governors and Guardians of Marsh's Library, © Marsh's Library).

There were then only four British settlers in the whole county, and three of these had been resident there before the plantation. Sir Frederick was the only new planter to take possession of his estate. The other nineteen British grantees who had by then passed their patent, continued to live in Britain or on their other estates in Ireland, while their agents collected the rents from their Leitrim lands. The situation had changed very little by 1626 when the lord deputy and council were ordered to ensure that undertakers in the plantations of Wexford, Offaly, Longford and Leitrim complied with the conditions of their grants, and be in residence on their estates by the end of September of that year. Two years grace was later given to the planters until 1628, and this had to be further extended again until 1630. Sir Thomas Dutton, Leitrim planter and scoutmaster general of the army in Ireland, bemoaned the absence of resident planters in a letter to the king at this time when he observed that

> the plantations of Wexford, King's County, Longford and Leitrim have been so badly made … that they had much better been left alone. These settlements should be reinforced with English undertakers like those in the north.[36]

The main priority of those settlers who did come to live on their Leitrim estates seems to have been to expand their holdings. Sir Frederick was certainly the prime example in this regard, but others such as Sir Charles Coote, Henry Crofton and George St George in the south of the county, as well as Robert Parke, who replaced William Irwin, Thomas Abercromy, who succeeded James Creighton, and John Waldron in the north, also bought up whatever available land they could afford. Initially, there was little attempt to develop and consolidate the estates in line with plantation regulations, through the importation of British freeholders and the building of castles and strong houses. Apart from work on the construction of the town of Jamestown, the county's administrative capital, there was little evidence of the building of significant settlers' residences surrounded by bawns, by the end of the decade. Planters were also slow to stock their new estates and sought instead an immediate income by letting their land to native Irish tenants at a considerable rent.

A further characteristic of the early British settlers in Leitrim was that many of them were military men. These included Coote, Hamilton, Captain Maurice Griffith, Captain George St George, Lieutenant Henry Crofton and Lieutenant Walter Harrison. Given the constant state of alert and occasional disturbances

---

36 *CSPI, 1625–32*, p. 185: direction to lord deputy and council for settling the civil affairs of Ireland, summer 1626; ibid., pp 334, 499: Sir Thomas Dutton to the king, 20 Dec. 1629.

within the county during the mid- and later 1620s, it would not have been easy for these planters to devote their full time and energy to their estates, even if they had wished to. Furthermore, given the fact that army officers, as well as the ordinary soldier, were so poorly paid during this period, it would have been difficult to generate adequate funds to develop their holdings.[37]

According to the terms of Sir Frederick's original grant, he, as a principal undertaker, was obliged to build within three years a castle surrounded by a bawn, or to forfeit £780. His castle, however, did not materialize until the mid 1630s. Instead, he probably initially built 'a good timber house, after the English fashion', incorporating chimneys, as the English planter, Sir William Cole, had done at Enniskillen, and his brother, Sir George Hamilton, had built near Strabane a decade earlier. Or he may have opted for a stone or brick house with slated roof, which, although more expensive, was still required of even lesser undertakers in the Leitrim plantation. This building was situated in the Glenfarne area, on the eastern portion of his holding. When Sir Frederick was re-granted his new enlarged estate in 1630, he was again required to build 'one fair castle and bawn instead of the other buildings upon the said manor'. However, he was not only excused for having neglected to build it before then, but was even extended the latitude of constructing it at some 'convenient time' in the future. This is probably an example of one of the significant concessions that the New English planters had derived from the 'Graces' two years earlier.[38]

The 1620s had indeed proved to be a period of expansion for Sir Frederick Hamilton and several other progressive Leitrim planters. But it would be the following decade – one of uninterrupted peace in Ireland – before a significant building programme in terms of castles, strong houses and villages with their churches and mills, got underway throughout the county. It would only be then also that these undertakers would set about extensively stocking their lands and exploiting the natural resources on their estates.

37 *CPRI, Charles I*, p. 244. 38 *CPRI, 19 James I*, p. 539; R.J. Hunter, 'Sir William Cole, the town of Enniskillen and plantation County Fermanagh' in E.M. Murphy and W.J. Roulston (eds), *Fermanagh, history and society* (Dublin, 2004), p. 132; M. McCarthy Morrogh, 'The English presence in early seventeenth-century Munster' in Ciaran Brady and Raymond Gillespie (eds), *Natives and newcomers* (Dublin, 1986), pp 182–3; Marsh, MS Z4.2.6, king to lords justices, 12 Jan. 1630.

CHAPTER FOUR

At war in Germany, 1631–2

THE ORIGINS OF THE THIRTY YEARS WAR

The Habsburg dynasty was the greatest power in Europe at the beginning of the seventeenth century. The Austrian branch of the family ruled over the Holy Roman Empire, comprising Austria, Germany and Bohemia, while their cousins the Spanish Habsburgs governed Spain (with its holdings in Italy and colonies in the New World), Portugal, the Netherlands and parts of eastern France (fig. 10). Nevertheless, there were many semi-autonomous princes and rulers within the empire who, over the years, had succeeded in extending their independence and power at the expense of the emperor. A common cause of friction between the Catholic Habsburgs and their subordinates was the reformed religion – Lutheranism and Calvinism – which many of the latter had adopted. The early decades of the seventeenth century were marked by much unrest and a build-up of military strength on the part of princes who wished to protect their interests vis-à-vis the emperor or neighbouring states. It would only take one serious incident to spark a major war.[1]

The catalyst for the Thirty Years War was the rebellion in Bohemia (a state comprising much of the present-day Czech Republic) in May 1618 by Protestant subjects who felt that their Habsburg king, Ferdinand of Styria, was attempting to re-catholicize their state. They deposed Ferdinand and offered the crown to their Calvinist neighbour, Frederick V of the Palatinate. Shortly afterwards, Ferdinand was elected Holy Roman emperor, and in November 1620 imperial troops and their Catholic allies quashed the rebellion. In addition, the Spanish Habsburgs sent an army to invade the Palatinate, forcing Frederick to flee his home territories and become an exile in the Dutch Republic. Some minor German princes and foreign countries and states such as Britain, the Dutch Republic and Denmark did send contingents to help Frederick and the Bohemians. But, in the escalating conflict, the emperor generally maintained the upper hand until the end of the 1620s. However, with the intervention in July 1630 of Gustavus Adolphus of Sweden (fig. 11) – the self-styled 'Protector of

1 C.V. Wedgwood, *The Thirty Years War* (London, 1938), pp 19–24, 41–9; G. Parker et al. (eds), *The Thirty Years War* (Abingdon, 2nd ed., 1997), pp 19–29; H. Livermore, *A history of Spain* (London, 1958), pp 199–200, 227–30; M. Magnusson (ed.), *Chambers biographical dictionary* (Edinburgh, 1990), p. 646.

10 Boundary of the Holy Roman Empire, *c.*1630.

Protestantism' – in the war, the balance of power began to change in favour of the Protestant cause.[2]

COMMISSIONED BY THE SWEDISH KING TO LEVY A REGIMENT

Britain had several reasons for becoming involved in the war. First and foremost of these was the fact that Frederick V of the Palatinate was married to Elizabeth Stuart, daughter of James I. Consequently, attacks by the Habsburgs on Bohemia and the Palatinate were seen by the British as acts of aggression against the House of Stuart. Secondly, as a Protestant nation, Britain sympathized with the cause of

2 P. Čornej and J. Pokorný, *A brief history of the Czech lands to 2004* (Prague, 2003), pp 20–31.

11 Gustavus Adolphus, king of Sweden, by unknown artist (© National Portrait Gallery, London).

its co-religionists in Europe against the Catholic emperor. From 1624 onwards, therefore, King James and his successor, Charles I, began to sanction the levying of increasing numbers of Scottish and English troops for service in Germany. One of these armies, numbering six thousand men, which was raised and commanded by James, marquis of Hamilton (fig. 12), son of Sir Frederick Hamilton's first cousin, fought alongside the Swedes in 1631. Despite suffering from famine and disease, it campaigned along the River Oder and at the siege of Magdeburg, before being eventually disbanded in the autumn of the following year.[3]

Gustavus Adolphus needed as much support as possible from his allies if his campaign in Germany was to be successful. So, shortly after the marquis of Hamilton had agreed in May 1630 to raise his army, the Swedish king issued commissions to several lesser Scottish nobles to levy more troops, which were probably also intended to serve under the marquis. The most important of these nobles was Lord Reay from Sutherland, who was contracted to raise three regiments. Meanwhile, his kinsman, Alexander Master of Forbes from Aberdeen-shire committed himself to recruiting two more. Forbes actually travelled to Germany to secure his commission from Gustavus in person.[4]

Although resident in Ireland for almost a decade, Sir Frederick Hamilton was the third of these Scottish noblemen to receive a commission from the Swedish king. It is not clear if he went, like Forbes, to Germany to draw up the contract or if his commission was arranged for him under the auspices of his cousin the marquis. One way or the other, he was motivated 'by a certain laudable ambition to attach myself to the cause of so glorious and victorious a king' and deeply appreciated the opportunity to fight under Gustavus. Sir Frederick, who was then a captain in the army in Ireland, would probably have seen the war in Germany as an adventure. It would be one in which he, with the added status of colonel, might play a significant role. While the hope of monetary gain may also have been a motivating factor, it was certainly not the primary one. Much more important would have been his desire – like that of many of the other recruiters – to defend the Protestant religion and the claims and honour of Elizabeth Stuart, sister of Charles I.[5]

---

3 S. Murdoch, 'James VI and the formation of a Scottish-British military identity' in S. Murdoch and A. Mackillop (eds), *Fighting for identity*, pp 19–21; www.st-andrews.ac.uk/history/ssne, Andrew Gray, ID: 378, accessed 12 Jan. 2007; S. Schama, *A history of Britain: the British wars, 1603–1776* (London, 2001), pp 57–65; A. Grosjean, *An unofficial alliance: Scotland and Sweden, 1569–1654* (Leiden, 2003), pp 88–91. 4 www.st-andrews.ac.uk/history/ssne, Lord Reay, ID: 93, John Monro of Obsdell, ID: 178, Sir Thomas Conway, ID: 6634 and Alexander Forbes, ID: 1616, accessed 30 Dec. 2004; 'Master of' is a courtesy or honorary title for the heir apparent of a Scottish baron; R. Greenwood, 'Colonel Alexander Master of Forbes' two regiments raised in 1631' (unpublished compendium of events, 2007), pp 25–6, 30, 36–7; SRA, AOSB E601, Forbes correspondence with the Swedish authorities: Alexander Forbes to Chancellor Oxenstierna, 3 Nov. 1633 (recent translation by Alex Forbes, who has collaborated with Robin Greenwood in researching the life of his namesake, Alexander Master of Forbes); the size of a regiment in Gustavus Adolphus' infantry was fixed by the king in 1621 at eight companies, each nominally of 150 men, giving a total of 1,200 men.   5 NRS, GD 406/1/204, Archibald Douglas to Marquis Hamilton, 9 May 1631; SRA, AOSB E619, Hamilton correspondence with the Swedish authorities: Sir Frederick's letter of

12 James Hamilton, first duke of Hamilton, by Robert White
(© National Portrait Gallery, London).

It seems that the marquis recommended in June 1631 that Sir Frederick's regiment and both of those belonging to Forbes should be merged to form two new regiments. This suggestion may have resulted either from a lack of Swedish levy funds or from recruitment difficulties on the part of both commanders. Forbes, for example, would only receive the first half of his levy payments in August 1631, although this had been due the previous March. The second half was never paid. As a result, he had to let go several hundred of his recruits in Scotland. Forbes and Sir Frederick met to consider the recommendation, which included the proposal that Forbes, who had received the first and more important commission, would become the channel through which the Swedish levy funds would be directed for both regiments. Although describing the terms of his agreement with Forbes as 'difficult, unusual and dangerous', Sir Frederick concluded the deal before the end of June 1631, albeit 'contrary to the goodwill of my most loyal and noble friends and against their persuasion'.[6]

The deal, which was to lead to a serious dispute between both parties four months later, seems to have been rather loosely concluded. Sir Frederick, given his own financial input and much greater military experience, understood from the start that he was not only to recruit, but also to be colonel of one of the two regiments. He had been a captain in the army in Ireland since 1625, whereas Forbes was simply a recruiter with little or no military experience. However, Forbes believed that, in virtue of his previous commission and as paymaster of the two regiments, he was to remain sole commander of both.[7]

It would appear as if Charles I was either not aware of, or had no intention of becoming involved in, the finer points of a private deal between two of his subjects. The king, therefore, on the strength of Sir Frederick's original commission from Gustavus Adolphus, instructed the Scottish privy council on 30 June 1631 to issue him with a warrant to both recruit and command a regiment of 1,200 men for Germany. Three weeks later, the British monarch requested the council to grant Forbes a similar warrant to levy two thousand men. These warrants were subsequently issued by the council to both men on 26 August. Commanders often began their recruitment activity while the issue of such warrants was pending. We know that Forbes' captains had begun raising levies as early as 1 March. It is reasonable to assume that Sir Frederick was not slow off the mark either.[8]

grievances to the queen and senate of Sweden, *c*.end 1637. I am very grateful to Steve Murdoch of St Andrews University for this and other Hamilton correspondence; see also Parker et al. (eds), *The Thirty Years War*, p. 174. **6** SRA, AOSB E601, Forbes to Oxenstierna, 3 Nov. 1633; SRA, AOSB E619, Sir Frederick's letter of grievances, *c*.end 1637; *RAOSB*, 2nd ser., 9 (1898), 431: Colonel Alexander Leslie's letter to Oxenstierna, 29 June 1631; Grosjean, *An unofficial alliance*, p. 92, n. 105. **7** SRA, AOSB E601, Forbes to Oxenstierna, 3 Nov. 1633; *RPCS*, 2nd ser., 4, p. 348; Greenwood, 'Colonel Alexander Master of Forbes' two regiments', pp 1, 71–2. **8** SRA, AOSB E601, Forbes to Oxenstierna, 3 Nov. 1633; *RPCS*,

Both men also got warrants from the lords justices in Dublin to recruit men in Ireland. Forbes contracted a distant cousin, Sir Arthur Forbes, a planter in south Leitrim and north Longford, to levy five hundred Irishmen and to bring them to Leith, the port of Edinburgh, by 30 September, from where they would be shipped to Germany. Sir Frederick also recruited several hundred men in Ireland, most likely from among his own tenants in north Leitrim. When he arrived in Germany some months later, his regiment was described as being composed of both 'Scottish and Irish people'.[9]

Due to various difficulties, Reay's, Forbes' and Sir Frederick's regiments all missed out on being part of the marquis' army, which sailed for Germany at the end of July 1631. Reay had run into serious problems in May of that year for his part in exposing an alleged plot against Charles I, whereby the marquis of Hamilton, instead of sailing for Germany, supposedly intended to use his army to invade Scotland and seize the Scottish crown for himself. Reay was confined in the Tower of London for several months and in August asked that troops already raised for his own regiment be given over to Sir Thomas Conway. The latter, who had been recruiting for Reay's second regiment in England throughout the summer, eventually set sail for Germany with one thousand men in October. Reay's third regiment under Colonel John Monro of Obsdell, which was levied over the course of the summer and autumn, was transported piecemeal to the Continent around the same time.[10]

Lack of money, storms in the Baltic Sea and differences between the two colonels were the main reasons for delays in recruiting and shipping the regiments of Forbes and Sir Frederick Hamilton. By 1 October 1631, Forbes' captains in Scotland had raised only six hundred men due to lack of funds, since the second half of the levy money never arrived from Sweden. Forbes also had problems securing contracts from skippers of Scottish vessels to transport both regiments on account of the winter storms then raging in the Baltic. He

2nd ser., 4, pp 317–20; a commission might be defined as a mandate given by a king or leader to an individual to raise troops on his behalf. It was a contractual obligation specifying payment in return for a specific number of recruits delivered. A warrant, on the other hand, was a licence or permit to recruit within a particular jurisdiction. Recruiters were sometimes given warrants for more men than their commissions specified, in order to allow for natural wastage due to illness, death or desertion. **9** NRS, Lord Forbes Papers, GD 52/93, contract between Alexander Master of Forbes, Sir Arthur Forbes and Captain Baillie, 29 July 1631 (cited in Greenwood, 'Colonel Alexander Master of Forbes' two regiments', pp 80–1); *The Swedish intelligencer, the fourth part* (London, 1633), p. 127; W.S. Brockington (ed.), *Monro, his expedition with the worthy Scots regiment called Mac-Keys* (London, 1999), p. 114; *CSPD, 1631–3*, p. 229. This was not the first time that Irishmen were levied for service in anti-imperial armies. For example, several hundred men had been raised in Ireland for the earl of Nithsdale's regiment that fought in the Danish army in Germany in 1627 and 1628. For a comprehensive treatment of such levies in Ireland at this time, see Grosjean and Murdoch, 'Irish participation in Scandinavian armies during the Thirty Years War', *Irish Sword*, 24:97 (2005), 277–87. **10** Greenwood, 'Colonel Alexander Master of Forbes' two

eventually had to pay three times the normal fee to mainly foreign ship-owners to take the regiments to Germany.[11]

By the end of October, both regiments had arrived in Leith with most of their recruitment completed, although Sir Frederick was still awaiting the arrival of some two hundred men from Ireland. A major row between the two colonels erupted over the command, maintenance and transportation of Sir Frederick's regiment, which threatened to destabilize the whole venture. It became so serious that the Scottish privy council was asked to intervene. On 2 November, the council nominated three of its members to call the warring parties together to settle their differences. Both Forbes and Sir Frederick duly appeared before the committee later that day and soon the following terms of agreement were worked out. In the first instance, Forbes accepted Hamilton's right as colonel to appoint officers in his own regiment of 1,200 men. Both colonels agreed, however, that Gustavus Adolphus should have the final say as to whether or not Sir Frederick should retain his command on arrival in Germany. Secondly, Forbes undertook to transport both regiments to Germany. He would take as many companies of Hamilton's regiment as he had place for on his ships at Leith. The one company of 150 men belonging to Sir Frederick, which could not be accommodated, would be looked after by Forbes and shipped from Dundee within a few days. He would also transport from Dundee Hamilton's two hundred Irish recruits, provided they arrived in Scotland by 8 November. Otherwise, Sir Frederick would have to pay the additional subsistence costs of the whole 350 men, as well as the costs of delaying the ships for each day after that. Finally, in return for Forbes' undertaking to transport all of Hamilton's men, Sir Frederick agreed to forego the £400 levy money that Forbes owed him. The whole agreement was then set out by way of contract and registered with the privy council on 3 November.[12]

With their differences settled, the way was now clear for the transportation of the main contingent of the troops to begin. The ten or twelve ships required for the mission set sail over the following few days, perhaps in two convoys, grouped according to regiment. Forbes was able to notify the Scottish privy council on 15 November that he had shipped 1,800 men to Stralsund in northern Germany by that date. These are likely to have been made up of one thousand or so of Forbes' own regiment under his lieutenant colonel, Sir Arthur Forbes, and 750 men in five companies of Sir Frederick's regiment under Hamilton himself.[13]

---

regiments', pp 51, 88–9, 99. **11** SRA, AOSB E601, Forbes to Oxenstierna, 3 Nov. 1633; *RPCS*, 2nd ser., 4, pp 360–1: complaint from the Master of Forbes regarding Scottish sea-captains who were transporting his men to Germany; A. and H. Tayler, *The house of Forbes* (Aberdeen, 1937). **12** *RPCS*, 2nd ser., 4, pp 348–50, 626–7. **13** *The Swedish intelligencer*, p. 127; *RPCS*, 2nd ser., 4, pp 360–1.

The two hundred men from Ireland, whom Sir Frederick was waiting for, seem to have arrived in Leith within the allotted five days. On 8 November, a warrant was issued by the Scottish privy council to a Colonel Baillie to 'receave the mustours of such companies belonging to Sir Frederick Hamiltoun as ar not as yitt delivered to the Maister of Forbes, and to make ane record and roll of the number of men, to the effect the same may be givin to the same Maister of Forbes'. Once again, Forbes had trouble in hiring Scottish ships to transport these levies, which may have been more numerous than had been anticipated. Sir Frederick was later to insist to the Swedish council of state that he had raised his full complement of soldiers, that is, 1,200 men, for his regiment. 750 of these left for Germany with him shortly after 3 November. One hundred and fifty remained behind with Forbes. So there would need to have been three hundred recruits making up the 'certain companies of men from Ireland' that had arrived in Leith and Edinburgh by 8 November.[14]

One week later, the Scottish privy council appointed William Dick, burgess of Edinburgh, to ensure that a fair deal was struck between Forbes and two Scottish skippers regarding the transportation of the remainder of Hamilton's regiment. It is reasonable to assume that the 200–300 Irish, plus the 150 men who had remained behind with Forbes, were all now dispatched together.[15]

Even though Forbes later maintained that he himself sailed for Germany immediately after seeing off both regiments, it seems more likely that he did not set sail for at least another month. There are records of him selling some property on his estate in Aberdeenshire on 21 and 23 November, perhaps to offset expenses occasioned by the extended levy and transportation process. A week later, he was in London visiting Lord Reay, who was still in the Tower pending trial for his part in exposing the marquis of Hamilton's alleged plot. This was not a friendly encounter, and shortly afterwards Forbes prepared a witness statement to be used in the trial against Reay. Forbes may still not have left Britain on 22 December, when the Scottish privy council wrote to Charles I endorsing a petition of Forbes to the king. That very same day, the council also cancelled a contract between Forbes and a Scottish skipper, John Jack, and ordered the latter to repay money to Forbes. With all these details taken care of, Forbes eventually set out at the end of December 1631 to take command of his regiment in Germany.[16]

14 SRA, AOSB E619, Sir Frederick to the queen and senate of Sweden, *c.*end 1637; *RPCS*, 2nd ser., 4, pp 351, 360–1. **15** *RPCS*, 2nd ser., 4, pp 360–1. **16** SRA, AOSB E601, Forbes to Oxenstierna, 3 Nov. 1633; the case of Reay v. Ramsay is covered in T.B. Howell, *A complete collection of state trials and proceedings for high treason and other crimes and misdemeanors from the earliest period to the year 1783* (21 vols, 1816), iii, pp 483–514; NRS, Lord Forbes Papers GD 52/94 deals with Forbes' visit to Reay in London (all three documents are cited and discussed in Greenwood, 'Colonel Alexander Master of Forbes' two regiments', pp 111, 115–25); *RPCS*, 2nd ser., 4, pp 398, 402.

SIR FREDERICK'S CAMPAIGN IN GERMANY
(November 1631–September 1632)(fig. 13)

The winter storms that the Scottish skippers had been reporting in the Baltic in October 1631 continued unabated into November. The North Sea also proved to be a dangerous crossing at that time of year. Sir Frederick later referred to his five companies and himself being 'in great danger of our lives on account of the storms by which we were being tossed on the sea'. As a result, what normally would have taken just a single week's journey to Germany, now took two or three times as long. Perhaps his regiment had to seek shelter in some port along the way. They eventually reached Germany about 27 November, disembarking at the Baltic port of Warnemünde just north of Rostock, in the duchy of Mecklenburg. This was fifty miles to the west of Stralsund, their planned destination.[17]

The survivors of Sir Thomas Conway's regiment, which had sailed from England at the end of October, also docked at Warnemünde around the same time as Sir Frederick. They had also been caught up in the treacherous North Sea storms, but were not as fortunate as Hamilton. Conway himself, his lieutenant colonel, Stewart, and three hundred of his men were all drowned off the coast of Norway on 5 November. The five remaining companies were now commanded by Sergeant-Major Thomas Grove.[18]

The regiment of Alexander Master of Forbes, under the command of Sir Arthur Forbes, seems to have escaped the storms and landed as planned at Stralsund some time earlier than Hamilton's and Grove's men. Sir Frederick's remaining companies – the Irishmen who arrived late in Leith, as well as the 150 men for whom there was no place on the initial sailing – eventually landed somewhere else in northern Germany. They only managed to link up with the main body of their regiment the following summer.[19]

With the arrival of four British regiments – Sir Frederick's, Forbes', Conway's and Monro of Obsdell's – on the German Baltic coast in November 1631, King Gustavus Adolphus had to decide where they were to be deployed. At that very time, he was having discussions, at his winter quarters in Mainz, with the marquis of Hamilton regarding Britain's future role in Germany. The marquis' army, for which these new regiments were originally intended, was by then in poor shape. His troops, wasted by disease, had dwindled from the original 6,000 to 1,500 men. They had ceased to be a stand-alone force and had joined General Banér's Swedish army in the siege of Magdeburg on the middle Elbe, some 150 miles from the Baltic coast.[20]

17 SRA, AOSB E619, Hamilton Correspondence, Frederick Hamilton's petition to the queen and senate of Sweden, *c.*end 1637; *The Swedish intelligencer*, p. 127.   18 *The Swedish intelligencer*, pp 126–7.
19 Ibid., p. 127.   20 Ibid., p. 108; Burnet, *The memoirs of the lives and actions of James and William Dukes*

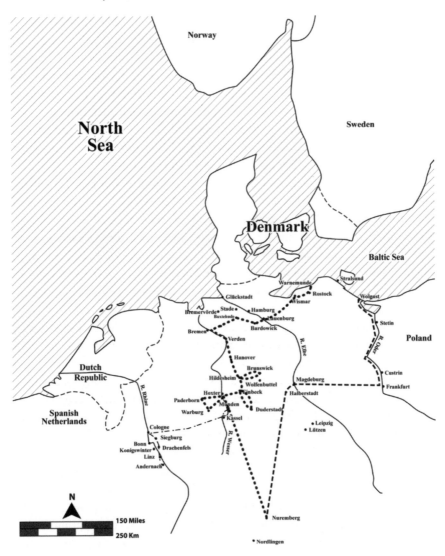

The marquis --- Sir Frederick ••• Sir Frederick's regiment after his departure –·–·

13 The marquis of Hamilton and Sir Frederick in Germany, 1631–2.

Meanwhile, another Swedish army, under the command of Field Marshal Åke Tott, was campaigning in Mecklenburg. Tott had by then overrun most of that duchy, with only a few fortified towns still remaining in imperial hands.

The Swede, who had made a name for himself as an able commander in Mecklenburg, was now planning to advance over the Elbe into Lower Saxony. If he was to continue to be successful, he needed to increase the size of his current four thousand strong army of Swedes and Mecklenburgers. Perhaps it was for this reason that Gustavus Adolphus took the decision in December 1631 to second the newly arrived British regiments to Tott's army, though they may have still remained under the marquis' nominal command. Tott was also joined by two more regiments of Scots under Colonel Robert Leslie and Lieutenant Colonel Robert Stuart, and an English regiment under Colonel Aston.[21]

All these British regiments were ordered to link up with Tott near Lauenburg on the lower Elbe in mid-January 1632. The Swedish army had by then captured the fortified town of Wismar, one of the last remaining imperial strongholds in Mecklenburg, and was about to begin a new campaign in Lower Saxony. After crossing the Elbe, the whole army quartered for two or three weeks in Bardowick, where they were also joined by local German forces belonging to Duke George of Lüneburg. These latest additions brought Tott's numbers up to fourteen thousand men.[22]

Sir Frederick's claim to be colonel of his regiment seems never to have been called into question by the Swedish authorities. Gustavus Adolphus may not even have been aware that he was to decide between the Master of Forbes and Hamilton for the position, once both Scotsmen arrived in Germany. In any case, the Master only reached Germany after his own and Sir Frederick's regiments had joined Tott's army on the Elbe. He was immediately captured by the imperialists between Glückstadt and Hamburg, and was then imprisoned in Wolfenbüttel in the duchy of Brunswick for the following eighteen months. So, in the Master's absence, there was nobody to dispute Hamilton's command of his own regiment.[23]

When Tott's army marched into Lower Saxony, the local imperial forces decided to make a stand in three of the strongest fortified towns in the area – Buxtehude, Stade and Bremervörde. Buxtehude is situated some eight miles west of Hamburg on the small river, Essa. On or about 1 February 1632, an advance

---

21 *The Swedish intelligencer*, pp 126, 127, 134; Grosjean, *An unofficial alliance*, p. 92; Brockington (ed.), *Monro, his expedition*, p. 231; There is no record of the four newly arrived British regiments in the muster rolls of Tott's army (emails from Steve Murdoch, 4 and 31 Oct. 2006). This might imply that they were still counted as part of the marquis' army even though they came under Tott's command. **22** *The Swedish intelligencer*, p. 127; Brockington (ed.), *Monro, his expedition*, p. 231; T.A. Fischer, *The Scots in Germany* (Edinburgh, 1902), pp 89–90: both Monro and Fischer state that many of these British regiments – including Sir Frederick's – had actually taken part in Tott's campaign in Mecklenburg. *The Swedish intelligencer*, however, which was published just a year after the event, maintains that they were only directed to join Tott just before he advanced into Lower Saxony. There are some other small differences among the three sources as to the precise number of British regiments involved, although all three mention Sir Frederick's. **23** *The Swedish intelligencer*, p. 127; SRA, AOSB E601, Forbes Correspondence, Alexander Master of Forbes to Oxenstierna, 3 Nov. 1633.

party, consisting of Sir Frederick's, Forbes' (led by Sir Arthur Forbes) and Grove's regiments, was sent by Tott to set up camp within a mile of the town. Ten days later, they were ordered to advance to the ruins of a twelfth-century Benedictine cloister on the very edge of Buxtehude. While Swedish cannon fired into the town every day, the three British regiments carried out much of the actual siege work. Having heard that many of the British and Irish were poorly armed raw recruits, two hundred of the garrison's horsemen sallied forth one night to attack them. However, two of Tott's companies of horse quickly arrived on the scene and helped repulse the attackers, though not before the Irish had managed 'with their swords and skeynes' to cut down some of the assailants. The siege itself lasted until 4 March, when the imperialist garrison surrendered Buxtehude on condition that it be given safe passage to Stade.[24]

The strong town of Stade, which was ten miles north-west of Buxtehude and had a garrison of four thousand men, was next on Tott's agenda. He blockaded the town on about 10 March, but did not attempt an assault on it due to poor weather and a shortage of manpower. Tott's efforts were further hampered by the fact that the town's garrison made frequent sorties with up to one thousand horsemen and musketeers, who launched lightning attacks on the besiegers before retreating just as quickly back inside their fortifications.[25]

It would appear that Tott did not use either Sir Frederick's or Forbes' regiments in the siege of Stade. Both were left behind in Buxtehude, perhaps to garrison the town. While there, a dispute broke out between both commanders, allegedly over living quarters, but more likely due to a latent animosity between Hamilton and the Forbeses. Some personalized remark by Sir Arthur obviously gave offence to the rather sensitive and excitable Sir Frederick. Believing that his honour was being called into question, he challenged Forbes to a duel on 14 April. Weapons would have comprised pistols and/or long and short swords. Whichever were used, Sir Arthur was slain. He was buried in Buxtehude and later replaced as lieutenant colonel by John Innes, a major in Monro of Obsdell's regiment. There are no firm indications that Hamilton was ever disciplined as a result of his actions. The episode was long remembered and bestowed on Sir Frederick a certain notoriety. Sir Thomas Wentworth, lord deputy of Ireland, pointedly remarked to the English secretary of state in 1634 that there were many complaints against Sir Frederick in Ireland, 'which might pass perhaps in a Swedish army, but I am sure in no civil commonwealth'.[26]

---

24 *The Swedish intelligencer*, pp 127–9; Grosjean, *An unofficial alliance*, p. 93.   25 *The Swedish intelligencer*, pp 130–1.   26 E.S. Shuckburgh (ed.), *Two biographies of William Bedell, bishop of Kilmore* (Cambridge, 1902), pp 34–5, 195; Fischer, *The Scots in Germany*, p. 128; Brockington (ed.), *Monro, his expedition*, p. 115; SSNE Database, Sir Arthur Forbes, ID: 132; W. Knowler (ed.), *Letters and despatches of Thomas, earl of Strafforde* (2 vols, London, 1740), i, pp 280–1; see R. Gillespie, *Seventeenth-century Ireland,*

Stade was still under siege by Tott at the end of April 1632. By then, a regiment of German allies of the Swedes was besieging the town of Bremervörde. Its garrison, although short of food, vowed that it would only submit to the Swedish king's troops. Tott, therefore, sent Sir Frederick's regiment, under the command of Lieutenant Colonel Cunningham, to accept the town's surrender. Hamilton himself may have been wounded in the course of his duel with Forbes, or perhaps he was indeed temporarily under a cloud as a result of the incident. Shortly after Cunningham's arrival at Bremervörde, the garrison entered into surrender negotiations. Before these could be concluded, however, the colonel of the allied German regiment, who had been huffed at being superseded by Cunningham, quietly concluded a more lenient deal with the town's garrison, allowing it to leave the town and march unimpeded to Stade.[27]

No sooner had Cunningham taken over Bremervörde than word reached him that Field Marshal Count Pappenheim, second in command to the imperial General Tilly, was within ten hours' march of the town en route to relieve Stade with an army of fourteen thousand men. Once Tott was made aware of the situation, he ordered Cunningham to return immediately to Buxtehude and leave Bremervörde under the control of the German regiment. Cunningham's men then set off at dusk, and, 'being most Irish and Scots, used to wading and night-marching, came flouncing thorough the bogs and by-places, and recovered safely into Boxtehude; notwithstanding the enemies drummes, were all the night within hearing'. It would appear as if the north Leitrim men in the regiment had lost none of the agility and fleet-footedness that Captain Cuellar had attributed to their ancestors in the 1580s![28]

In the meantime, Pappenheim, known for his boundless energy, had slipped past Tott's blockade and entered Stade even before the Swedes realized what had happened. Once Tott found out, he immediately withdrew most of his army to Buxtehude, although two regiments belonging to Major General Leslie and Monro of Obsdell were trapped by Pappenheim north of Stade. Leslie had been sent to replace Tott some two months earlier, but had been shot in the foot shortly afterwards by the Buxtehude garrison, while he was visiting Sir Frederick's quarters in the Old Cloister, and had to retire temporarily from his position. Now, 1,500 of his own and Obsdell's men were taken prisoner by the imperialists. Many of the Scottish officers were sent into captivity in Minden on the Weser, where they were to remain for the following year and a half.[29]

---

pp 89–90 regarding the importance of the concept of honour in seventeenth-century society.   **27** *The Swedish intelligencer*, p. 131.   **28** Ibid., pp 131–2; H. Allingham (ed.), *Captain Cuellar's adventures*, pp 61–2.   **29** *The Swedish intelligencer*, pp 128, 132; Brockington (ed.), *Monro, his expedition*, p. 137.

Although Pappenheim had relieved the town of Stade, he had in effect got himself into a serious predicament. There was little food in the town, so he could not survive there for very long. Moreover, Tott controlled the surrounding countryside, while two Swedish ships patrolled the Elbe to the north, preventing any supplies that might arrive from Glückstadt or Hamburg. Pappenheim had to try to break through the Swedish net. His first attempt was at Hornburg between Stade and Buxtehude. He eventually succeeded in levelling all its defences with cannon fire, though not before some Scotsmen, notably Captain Gibson of Sir Frederick's regiment, had mounted brave and strong opposition. Once Tott realized that the hamlet could no longer be held, he set it on fire and withdrew all his forces to Buxtehude.[30]

On 3 May 1632, Pappenheim again tried to break through the enemy cordon, laying waste the countryside as he went. This time he reached the outskirts of Buxtehude, but could get no further. Tott, had he wished, might have attempted to confine him to the Old Cloister area of the town, but believed that he had not enough men to take that chance. He was afraid that Pappenheim, 'like a tyed Tyger', would have made desperate attempts to break free. Had he succeeded, Tott's reputation, which he had gained in Mecklenburg, would have been tarnished. So the Swede was content to maintain his defensive position around Buxtehude and Stade, without seeking to press home his advantage.[31]

Pappenheim retired once again to Stade, but was now becoming desperate. So, gathering up all his baggage and ammunition, as well as whatever provisions still remained in the town, his army quietly slipped away on the night of 6 May. Passing quite close to Tott's army in Boxtehude, he then headed south via Rotenburg and Verden into the duchy of Brunswick. Within days of Pappenheim's escape, changes were made in the command structure of the Swedish army in Lower Saxony. Tott was dispatched to Rostock in Mecklenburg, possibly because of his failure to seize the opportunity to defeat the imperial general. He was replaced by Duke George of Lüneburg, who did not join the Swedish army for another month. In the meantime, the newly appointed Lieutenant General von Baudissin assumed overall command. Lüneburg and Baudissin were directed to hunt Pappenheim out of Lower Saxony and clear the Elbe and Weser basins of all imperialists.[32]

Baudissin accordingly set off in pursuit of Pappenheim on 12 May. Marching via Bremen on the Weser, he arrived at Verden, where his army encamped until the end of the month. He dared not advance any further, as he was still not strong enough to confront the enemy in battle. Early in June, the Swedes pushed southwards to Hannover, where they were joined by the duke of Lüneburg with

---

30 *The Swedish intelligencer*, p. 132. **31** Ibid., pp 133–4. **32** Ibid., pp 134–7.

five thousand of his men. He now assumed overall command of the expanded force. While the army was still in Hannover, Gustavus Adolphus sent an Englishman, Sir John Caswell, to be colonel of the late Sir Thomas Conway's regiment, whose numbers had by now dwindled to just three hundred men. Lüneburg then advanced south-eastwards to the town of Hildesheim, which surrendered after a short siege. The citizens there were forced to contribute forty thousand dollars, being the equivalent of a month's pay, to the Swedish army.[33]

Pappenheim in the meantime had left part of his army near Hamelin, west of Hildesheim, while he himself hastened south to Münden, laying waste the countryside and plundering some neighbouring towns. He failed, however, to take the heavily fortified city of Kassel. In the middle of June, he received a message from his second-in-command, the count of Gronsfelt, informing him that the Swedes were beginning to take control of the area around Hildesheim and Brunswick. So, crossing the River Weser north of Höxter, he linked up with Gronsfelt and eventually set up his camp five miles from Hildesheim.[34]

Although the Swedes were expecting Pappenheim to attack at the first opportunity, the imperial general still managed to surprise a Swedish colonel, Laus Cag, who was laying siege to a neighbouring town called Kalenberg. Cag was forced to retreat to Hildesheim. Skirmishes were now occurring on a daily basis between the two armies. Into this arena there arrived unexpectedly Sir Frederick's four companies – at least two of which were Irish – which the Master of Forbes had shipped from Scotland some weeks after the main section of the regiment. They had landed at a different port to Sir Frederick and must have been assigned to one of the other Swedish armies or allied forces in the intervening months. These now brought numbers in Hamilton's regiment up to 880 men.[35]

On 25 June, Lüneburg reorganized his army. Companies that had lost many men were now disbanded and surviving soldiers were assigned to strengthen stronger units. Regiments were also grouped together in brigades. Sir Frederick's and Caswell's men thus became one brigade, which marched together from then on under Sir Frederick's command. In preparation for an enemy attack, the foot regiments of the Swedish army were drawn up in battle formation just south of Hildesheim. Three Swedish brigades formed the vanguard. Behind these were two British brigades, one comprising Forbes', Obsdell's and Robert Leslie's regiments on the right wing, and the other, Hamilton's brigade on the left. The Swedish Colonel Cag commanded the reserve brigade at the rear. Lüneburg's army then numbered over eleven thousand men, including the horse regiments that had not been drawn up in battle formation on that occasion.[36]

33 Ibid., pp 137–8.   34 Ibid., pp 138–41.   35 Ibid., pp 127, 141; W. Guthrie, *Battles of the Thirty Years War from White Mountain to Nördlingen 1618–1635* (Westwood, CT, 2002), pp 250–1.   36 Parliamentary

Pappenheim's army was approaching the town on the night of 21 June when they were spotted by Sir Frederick's brigade which was then on night watch. The imperial attack on the following day came to a rather abrupt end, with Pappenheim firing a mere twenty or thirty cannonballs into the town. The only casualties were two pigs that had been roaming in the town's streets. The attackers, on the other hand, lost up to fifty men in the return fire. It was reported that the poor performance of Pappenheim's men was caused by a mutiny in the camp. In any case, the imperialists withdrew to Kalenberg that evening, although skirmishes continued between both armies for the rest of the week. Pappenheim then led his army on a long march westwards across the River Rhine and the Dutch border to Maastricht after he had received an invitation to relieve that besieged city.[37]

With the departure of Pappenheim, Lüneburg set about regaining the duchy of Brunswick from the enemy. On 12 July, after having left two regiments in Hildesheim, he made a trek southwards to try and take the town of Duderstadt. The siege lasted a full week, with great heroism being displayed by both attackers and defenders. Among those killed was Francis Beton, Sir Frederick's captain lieutenant, who received 'a bullet of a sling peece in the shoulder'. As the Swedish army made ready to storm the town on 24 July, the garrison requested peace talks, which resulted in its surrender. Lüneburg then commandeered all the food, cannon and ammunition from the defenders. He also sent out detachments of soldiers to subdue the surrounding area. Thus, by the end of the month, he had restored order to this southern tip of Brunswick, which Pappenheim had earlier incited to rebellion.[38]

Flushed with success, Lüneburg decided to split his army on 1 August in order to undertake two separate missions simultaneously. He set off northwards with three brigades to take Wolfenbüttel, one of the most important Brunswick towns. His siege, which lasted two months, was eventually to prove unsuccessful. Meanwhile, Baudissin took charge of the other three brigades, which included Sir Frederick's and the entirely Scottish one, made up of Forbes', Obsdell's and Robert Leslie's men. Baudissin initially made an attempt on the town of Einbeck, to the north-west of Duderstadt, before heading sixty miles due west to Paderborn in Westphalia. He laid siege to this town on 13 August. Sir Frederick's brigade

Archives, HL/PO/JO/10/1/47, petition of Sir Frederick Hamilton to the lords assembled in the upper house of parliament, seeking redress against Strafford, 14 Jan. 1641; *To the honourable the knights, citizens and burgesses assembled in the Commons House of Parliament, the several petitions of William Hansard and Sir Frederick Hammiltoun knight and colonel … as also, the several remonstrances of the committee at Grocers Hall for Irish affairs, in the behalf of Sir Frederick Hammiltoun* … (London, 1646), p. 32; *The Swedish intelligencer*, pp 141–2; Guthrie, *Battles of the Thirty Years War*, pp 250–1. **37** *The Swedish intelligencer*, pp 142–3. **38** Ibid., pp 143–4.

was assigned quarters in an old abbey where there was plenty of food and drink to be had. Some Swedish officers, however, sounded an alarm on the first night and tricked Hamilton's men into moving to a less favourable location.[39]

The siege itself was a difficult one, which was further hampered by the wet weather. Baudissin lost almost a thousand men and was forced to call off the offensive after a week on hearing that an imperial force under Gronsfelt was approaching. The Swedish army now withdrew to Warburg, a day and a half's march to the south-east, where they spent some time extorting food and money from the local population. After having been joined by two thousand to three thousand German allies, they now turned northwards once again to Höxter. They forced their way through enemy troops and took possession of the town on 27 August. The next three weeks were spent repairing the town's fortifications in anticipation of an imperial attack.[40]

Within a few days of arriving in Höxter, Baudissin summoned Sir Frederick to discuss the possibility of him going back to Britain to raise further companies of men, and perhaps even a new regiment, for Swedish service. On expressing his agreement, Hamilton was given written direction by Baudissin to get the authorization of Gustavus Adolphus for the venture. The royal army was at that time in Nuremberg, where Gustavus had allowed himself to be semi-besieged, in the hope of enticing Wallenstein, the new imperial supreme commander, to attack him. Sir Frederick undertook the two-hundred-mile trip south to Nuremberg in the early days of September. Gustavus approved of his mission and granted him almost seven months' leave from the army to get the necessary British authorization and then to undertake the recruitment drive. It was also agreed that he would be free to attend to his own personal business during this time. Sir Frederick must have impressed the Swedish monarch, who spoke highly of him in a letter to Charles I and bestowed several 'princely tokens' on him before his departure to England.[41]

Around the same time as Sir Frederick was preparing to go back to Britain to 'enlist new soldiery' for Swedish service, the marquis of Hamilton was also planning his return to London, but for entirely different reasons. His military involvement in the Thirty Years War had ended the previous February, and he had spent the following six months involved in increasingly frustrating

---

39 Ibid., pp 144–6.　**40** Ibid., pp 147–8.　**41** SRA, AOSB E619, Hamilton correspondence, Frederick Hamilton's petition to the queen and senate of Sweden, *c*.end 1637: in this letter, Hamilton mentions that he went from Hildesheim to Nuremberg. This is impossible, since the Swedish army, including Sir Frederick's regiment, left Hildesheim on 12 July, and Baudissin, who sent him to Gustavus, did not become Sir Frederick's commander until 1 August. The mix-up may be accounted for by the fact that the letter was not written until five years after the event: *The humble remonstrance*, p. 2; see also Grosjean, *An unofficial alliance*, p. 91, n. 99: it was quite common for officers of British regiments in Swedish service to

discussions with Gustavus Adolphus regarding his future role in Germany. So, in early September 1632, he decided to return permanently to the British court. The marquis invited his cousin, Sir Frederick, as well as two other Scottish colonels, Sir John Hepburn and Sir James Ramsay 'the Fair', to accompany him on the return journey, and all four took their leave of the Swedish king on 15 September. They arrived safely on 11 October in London, where it was noted that 'the marquess of Hamilton is landed, and hourly expected at court; but I see Mr Frederick Hamilton in town'. This then was the end of Sir Frederick's ten-month personal campaign in the war in Germany. He would never again set foot in that troubled empire or retake command of his regiment. It was by no means, though, the end of his dealings with the Swedish authorities, from whom he would not definitively cut his links for several years more.[42]

'DISBANDMENT' OF SIR FREDERICK'S REGIMENT

General Baudissin had been rebuilding the fortifications of Höxter in anticipation of an imperial attack when Sir Frederick left the Swedish camp for Nuremberg at the beginning of September 1632. On 19 September, when the marquis and his three colonels were already on their way back to Britain, Pappenheim, who had by then returned from Maastricht, appeared before the gates of Höxter with twelve thousand men. The town walls were defended by the Scottish musketeers of Sir Frederick's regiment and one hundred of Forbes' men. Baudissin, who had only half as many troops as the imperialists, was not strong enough to withstand the enemy attack. That very evening his army was forced to retreat southwards towards Münden. Pappenheim's horse regiments actually caught up with the Swedes the following morning while they were still en route. Although Baudissin's army was able to take temporary refuge in a wood, the imperialists continued to attack, picking off all the sick and tired Swedish soldiers. The Swedes did manage to counter-attack, with the result that almost a thousand men were killed on both sides that day.[43]

The following day, Baudissin retreated further south to Kassel and spent the next two weeks criss-crossing the surrounding territory, still hotly pursued by Pappenheim. Eventually, he decided to make the long trek westwards to attack

be given six months' leave to recruit more men in Britain.   **42** Burnet, *The memoirs of the lives and actions of James and William*, pp 30–1; Fischer, *The Scots in Germany*, pp 85–6; T. Birch, *The court and times of Charles I* (2 vols, London, 1848), ii, p. 161 (cited in Greenwood, 'Colonel Alexander Master of Forbes' two regiments', p. 158); see also SRA, AOSB E619, Hamilton correspondence, J. Hamilton to Oxenstierna, *c.*1636, which seems to suggest that the writer, Colonel James Hamilton of Priestfield, did not, as Burnet states, travel home with the marquis in September 1632. His name was probably mistaken for that of Sir Frederick.   **43** *The Swedish intelligencer*, pp 148–50.

the bishopric of Cologne, hoping to force the Catholic elector there to call for assistance from Pappenheim, who might then remove himself from the Weser basin. On 19 October, Baudissin captured the strongly fortified castle of Siegburg, just east of Bonn, and in the weeks that followed, the towns of Linz-on-the-Rhine and Andernach to the south also fell to him. Pappenheim did not respond directly to Baudissin's tactic. Instead, he sent a deputy, the count of Merode, to follow the Swede. He himself pursued Lüneburg to Wolfenbüttel, forcing him to lift the siege of that town. Then, after recapturing Hildesheim, he eventually proceeded eastwards to Electoral Saxony, where he linked up with Wallenstein. It was here that the imperial field marshal was killed at the Battle of Lützen near Leipzig on 16 November 1632, the same day that the Swedes lost their commander-in-chief, King Gustavus Adolphus.[44]

While the Battle of Lützen was taking place, Baudissin's army was still campaigning along the Rhine. In late November, Sir Frederick's regiment captured Drachenfels Castle, which was strategically perched on a one-thousand-feet-high hill overlooking the river. It proved to be a worthwhile conquest as it was well stocked with provisions. Shortly afterwards, on 3 December, the whole army was assembled for inspection at Königswinter, on the opposite bank of the Rhine.[45]

It was at this location one week later that General Baudissin, under orders from Axel Oxenstierna, the Swedish chancellor and regent to Queen Kristina, set about reorganizing some of the regiments in his army. Probably due to falling numbers, it was decided to reduce Sir Frederick's nine companies and Forbes' eight to five strong companies in each regiment. This was done despite the fact that Hamilton's regiment still numbered over six hundred fighting men. In addition, Sir Frederick's lieutenant colonel, Cunningham, was replaced as commander by a junior captain. It has recently been suggested that this junior officer may well have been a Forbes, thus transferring the regiment to the control of the still imprisoned Master of Forbes. If true, this would surely have been an even bitterer pill for Sir Frederick to swallow.[46]

The redundant captains in Forbes' regiment immediately made their way eastwards to Halle, in Electoral Saxony, where Chancellor Oxenstierna was in residence, to seek arrears of pay. Lieutenant Colonel Cunningham and the other officers who lost their positions in Hamilton's regiment may have done likewise, but without success. The only course of action left open to them then was to return to England to seek redress there, with the assistance of Sir Frederick himself. In early February 1633, Hamilton, who was still endeavouring to get a

44 Ibid., pp 150–4.   45 Ibid., p. 150.   46 Ibid.; SRA, AOSB E619, Hamilton correspondence, Sir Frederick's petition to the queen and senate of Sweden, *c.*end 1637. Hamilton states that Baudissin's reorganization took place in January 1633. Speculation by Alex Forbes about the identity of the junior officer in an email dated 17 Nov. 2006.

commission from Charles I to levy more troops for Sweden, met these officers in London 'in the most utter destitution in all things, having no armour or weapons, and afflicted by disaster'. They were very aggrieved at the way they had been treated, after having soldiered continuously for so long in difficult conditions in the Swedish army.[47]

Sir Frederick wasted no time in seeking out Lord John Oxenstierna, son of the Swedish chancellor, who was then in London trying to encourage further British support for the war in Germany. Lord John agreed that the action taken by his father seemed unjust. He advised Hamilton not to make an official complaint to the British authorities or publicize the incident in Britain, but rather to return to Germany and personally make his case to the chancellor. As an expression of his support, he gave Sir Frederick a letter he had written to his father, requesting the latter to either restore Hamilton's officers to their former positions or to compensate financially the colonel and his officers for the offences caused.[48]

Although Sir Frederick did receive a small sum of money by way of compensation from Oxenstierna's commissioner in Hamburg shortly afterwards, he still resolved to go and meet with the Swedish chancellor in person. It did not suit him, however, to undertake a journey to Germany at that time, since preparations were already under way for King Charles' coronation in Scotland in June of that year, and Hamilton did not want to miss out on the chance of being considered for the royal entourage on such a momentous occasion. Nevertheless, he did cease all further attempts at raising any more men for service in Germany. Presumably in view of the way he had been treated, he no longer felt bound by the commitment he had made to the late Gustavus Adolphus some months previously. His contacts with Sweden thus ceased for the time being. The six hundred men of his former regiment continued to serve in Baudissin's army 'until they died fighting bravely in the Nör[d]lingen disaster' in 1634.[49]

DISCHARGE FROM SWEDISH SERVICE, JANUARY 1638

It was Sir Frederick's intention to complain in person to the Swedish chancellor as soon as was practically possible after having discussed the matter of the 'disbandment' of his regiment with Lord John Oxenstierna. However, the new lord deputy of Ireland, Sir Thomas Wentworth, who took up office in July 1633,

47 SRA, AOSB E619, Sir Frederick to the queen and senate of Sweden, *c.*end 1637; SRA, AOSB E601, A. and G. Forbes to Oxenstierna, *c.*Dec. 1632. **48** SRA, AOSB E619, Sir Frederick to the queen and senate of Sweden, *c.*end 1637. **49** Ibid.; *RAOSB*, 2nd ser., vol. 14, *Brev från Johan Adler Salvius*, ed. Per-Gunnar Ottosson and Helmut Backhaus (Stockholm, 2012), p. 135; Salvius to Oxenstierna, Hamburg, 23 Feb. 1633. I am very grateful to Steve Murdoch for this reference.

forced him to put his plans on hold. Wentworth seems to have taken a dislike, almost from the beginning, to Hamilton, who returned to Ireland to rejoin his family and transact some estate business. In 1634 the lord deputy refused, despite the intervention of the English secretary of state, to allow Sir Frederick to leave Ireland, even to attend his quarterly court duties in England. It was more than two years later, when Hamilton threatened to complain the lord deputy to the king, that Wentworth relented and issued Sir Frederick with the necessary licence to leave the country.[50]

In the years 1636 and 1637, many Scottish officers, such as Sir James Hamilton of Priestfield and Lieutenant General James King, who had spent time in Swedish service, began seeking compensation for arrears of pay still owed to them. Now that Sir Frederick's travel restrictions were lifted, he decided to pursue the matter of the 'disbandment' of his regiment with the Swedish authorities in the summer of 1637. As well as outlining his case in writing, he probably also forwarded to the chancellor, who had recently returned from Germany to Sweden, the letter that his son had given him in London some years earlier. In reply, Oxenstierna requested Sir Frederick to make the journey to Sweden as soon as possible if he wished his case to be examined.[51]

Hamilton then set about making various preparations for the trip. The first of these involved the raising of the necessary finance. With the assistance of his brother, Sir George, and a Nicholas Loftus of the city of Dublin, both of whom acted as guarantors, he borrowed £300 on the Cork staple on 3 August 1637. The staple in the thirteenth century had been a regulatory body to govern trade in basic or staple goods such as wool or hides. By the seventeenth century, it had become a means by which loans could be raised and spare capital ventured in relative security. The borrower entered into a bond to pay the creditor double the amount of the loan, if the debt was not repaid with 10 per cent interest in the agreed time. Sir Frederick therefore agreed to repay his creditor, Thomas Skiddy of Cork city, £600 on 4 August 1638 if he had not by then repaid the debt with £30 interest. The staple at the time operated in fourteen of the major towns around the country. It is interesting to speculate why Hamilton chose to borrow on the Cork staple rather than on the much larger Dublin one, which he had already used some two years earlier. Perhaps he could not find a willing creditor in the capital in 1637.[52]

50 Knowler (ed.), *Letters and despatches*, i, pp 280–1, 406; J. Rushworth, *The tryal of Thomas, earl of Strafford* (London, 1680), pp 26–7; BL, Add. MSS 64909, Sir Frederick Hamilton to Sir John Coke, secretary of state, 14 Apr. 1635. **51** SRA, AOSB E619, Sir Frederick to the queen and senate of Sweden, *c*.end 1637; SRA, AOSB E619, Sir James Hamilton of Priestfield to Oxenstierna, *c*.1636; SSNE Database, James King, ID: 2814. **52** D430/142, PRONI: bond of Sir Frederick Hamilton and others to pay Thomas Skiddy of Cork £600, 3 Aug. 1637; J. Ohlmeyer and E. Ó Ciardha (eds), *The Irish statute staple books, 1596–1687* (Dublin, 1998), pp 1–3, 234.

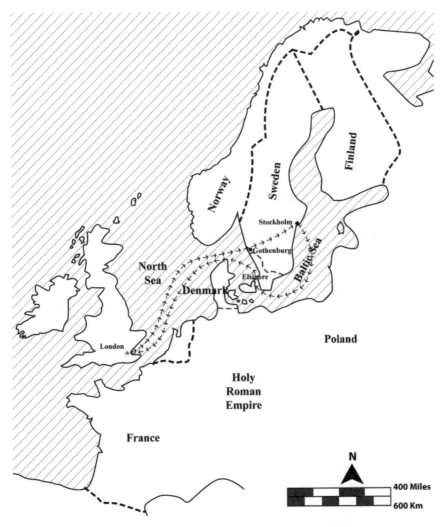

14 Sir Frederick Hamilton's visit to Sweden in 1637–8.

With adequate finance now secured, Sir Frederick made his way to the English court. There, he successfully petitioned the king not only to grant him permission to travel to Sweden (fig. 14), but also to write a letter to the Swedish authorities, explaining that he had been prevented from making the journey sooner due to his duties at court. Sir Frederick also prevailed upon his cousin, James, marquis of Hamilton, to write to Chancellor Oxenstierna on 24 September in support of his mission.[53]

53 SRA, AOSB E619, Sir Frederick to the queen and senate of Sweden, *c*.end 1637; SRA Riksregistraturet, vol. 192, fo. 96v, Oxenstierna to the marquis of Hamilton, 30 Dec. 1637 in which he refers to the marquis'

Sir Frederick then set about putting his travel arrangements in place. He hired a ship called *The Adventure* from Samuel Truelove of Ratcliff, 'for the transportation of himself, his servants and trunks' to Sweden. Before Hamilton's party was ready to sail, a complication arose when the English navy commandeered the ship for the purpose of transporting the king's horses to Charles Louis, son and heir of Frederick V of the Palatinate. Sir Frederick therefore had to secure an order from the English privy council on 29 September directing the officers of the navy to release the ship so that skipper Truelove could fulfil his previous agreement with Hamilton 'who is by His Majesty's command and for his service to repair to Gothenburg'.[54]

On their arrival at the Swedish port towards the end of 1637, Sir Frederick's party undertook the 250-mile overland journey to Stockholm on the Baltic coast. There, Hamilton was asked to present in writing his grievances and petitions to the regency or council of state that administered Sweden during the minority of Queen Kristina from 1632 to 1644. After outlining his motives for raising a regiment for Swedish service and dealing briefly with his campaign in Germany, Sir Frederick highlighted the irregular 'disbandment' of his men while he was on official leave in Britain. He went on to request that his case be heard by a 'publicly and lawfully convoked' war tribunal, so that his name might be cleared and his reputation restored. Otherwise, he feared he would lose out on being offered other honours and positions of responsibility in the future. Finally, he asked for a free discharge from Swedish service and hinted that compensation and arrears of pay were also due to him.[55]

It is very unlikely that Hamilton's appeal for a war tribunal was ever agreed to by Oxenstierna. However, Sir Frederick seems to have been granted a meeting on 18 January 1638 with the Swedish State Council, at which it was decided that only a portion of his claim would be paid, due to the difficult conditions that the Swedes were then experiencing in the war in Germany. He was advised to accept this offer and, if the situation were to change for the better, he could return to Sweden sometime in the future to look for more. The council then presented him with an official discharge from Swedish service, signed by the chancellor and three of the other four council members, which had been drawn up some two weeks earlier (fig. 15). It included a glowing tribute to Sir Frederick's courage, outstanding leadership qualities and loyalty to the Swedish cause. The document

---

letter of the previous September.   **54** TNA, SP16/366–368, privy council to officers of the navy, 29 Sept. 1637.   **55** SRA, AOSB E619, Sir Frederick to the queen and senate of Sweden, *c*.end 1637: although Kristina, who became queen of Sweden on the death of her father, Gustavus Adolphus, in 1632, was a precocious and highly intelligent child, she did not begin attending council meetings until 1640. Up till then, Oxenstierna completely controlled the council, since he, his brother and his cousin made up three of the five-member body.

intentione ac proposito sit continuatura, & Reip. cupidos favore,
regiu fotura. De cætere Ser.te vram Divinæ protectioni paranter
commendamus Dab

Gog. 18tg. cr. Ao. Go8.

Dimissio pro Dño Friderico
Hamiltsonio.

Nos Christina Dei graa Suecorum ppp Constare volumus, quorum
interest poterit, & qui basce visuri sunt, universis & singulis, quod cu præ-
sentium exhibitor Illustris ac Strenuus nobis sincere dilectus D. Frider.
Hamiltsonius Eques auratus & Seren.mi M.Britanniæ interioris cubicu-
li nobilis, sub signis auspiciisque Divi parentis uri gloriosæ recordationis
in Germania meruerit & coi Evagelicorum cææ opam ac servitia
contribuerit, Colonelliq; munere functus eu Suæ Mti fidem ac forti-
tudine comprobarit, ut postulantibus id ipsis & virtutibus & meritis,
Nos eis opa militari libenter uteremur. Ex quo v. cauša, cuius
auctorem se præbuit, legione, occasio ipsi prærepta fuit, nobis
quoque porro coi cææ inserviendi, o potuit quidem, prout tulit aiis
reapse id ipsum præstitisse. Nunc, cum ex Anglia ad nos rediret,
nec condignam virtutibus ipsius locu sub militia nra in Germania
vacuum inveniremus, nec voluntati nræ, nec desiderio ipsius in ad-
iuvanda publica ac coi cææ hac vice satisfieri potuit; quin ferentibus
ita rebus, & requirente id pariter statu ac conditione eius, cum eu denuo
singulari cum graa nra dimissum se reciperet, o potuimus o commendaa
re nra eundem communire, & quo aliis etiam eius merita luculen-
tius innotescerent, hoc ipsi virtutis suæ testimonium clementer elargi-
ri. Proinde ab oibus potestatibus, Regibus, Principibus, Rebus publicis liberis

15 Sir Frederick's discharge from Swedish service, end of December 1637 (Riksregistraturet 1637 (Latin), vol. 192, fo. 96 (by permission of the Swedish Riksarkivet, Stockholm).

concluded by recommending Hamilton to Charles I of Great Britain and to any other state to which he might happen to apply for a position. Oxenstierna repeated the same expressions of praise for Sir Frederick when replying to the letter that the marquis of Hamilton had written to the chancellor on 24 September in favour of his cousin.[56]

Although Sir Frederick expressed his satisfaction with the outcome of his mission to Sweden to some of his relatives in Scotland at the time, he must have been rather disillusioned with his overall treatment by the Swedes. He had indeed secured an honourable discharge and had his reputation restored, but he received only partial compensation for the unjust disbandment of his regiment and there was no mention at all of any arrears of pay. In his letter of grievances and petitions to the Swedish State Council, he had said that he had not undertaken to raise his regiment with 'any hope of gain or private profit' in mind. Nevertheless, he had expected to be paid in accordance with the terms of his original commission. There is no evidence to suggest that he achieved this objective. Despite his disappointment, though, he never lost his admiration for the late Gustavus Adolphus, and named his youngest son, born in Manorhamilton in 1634, after the Swedish king. Meanwhile, his journey home from Sweden took much longer than expected, since he was forced to wait two months at Helsingør (Elsinore) in Denmark 'for a wind and shipping for London'.[57]

Irrespective of how Sir Frederick felt about his former Swedish masters, his campaign in the Thirty Years War impacted significantly on his subsequent military career. The training and combat experience in the most advanced practices of Continental warfare gained in Germany stood him in good stead during the 1641 rebellion and the subsequent civil wars in Britain. But his exposure to the brutality and horrors of the German war, even if only for a period of ten months, also left a harsh and ruthless streak in his character, which became more evident as the years progressed.[58]

56 There are no war court records that refer to Sir Frederick in the Swedish military archives: (email from Bo Lundström, archivist, Swedish Military Archives, 26 May 2005); N.A. Kullberg et al. (eds), *Svenska Riksrådets Protokoll, 1621–1658* (18 vols, Stockholm, 1878–1959), vii, 1637–9, p. 127: Riksråd minute 18 (28) Jan. 1638. Sir Frederick's meeting with the Swedish state council is indexed 'Colonel Hugo (?) Hamilton'. However, it is clear from the question mark that the editor simply guessed at the colonel's first name. Although there was in fact a Colonel Hugo Hamilton in Swedish service at the time, the date and context of the January 1638 meeting suggest that it concerned Sir Frederick rather than Hugo, who did not seek recompense until much later. I wish to thank Steve Murdoch for providing me with this entry from the council records, and also PhD student Björn Nordgren for translating it into English; SRA Riksregistraturet, vol. 192, fo. 96r–v: Swedish royal 'Dimissio' for Sir Frederick, end of Dec. 1637; SRA Riksregistraturet, vol. 192, fo. 96v: Oxenstierna to marquis of Hamilton, 30 Dec. 1637. 57 Balfour Paul, *The Scots peerage* (Edinburgh, 1904), i, p. 45, 58 I. Gentles, 'The civil wars in England' in J. Kenyon and J. Ohlmeyer (eds), *The civil wars: a military history of England, Scotland and Ireland, 1638–1660* (Oxford, 1998), pp 127–30; *The information of Sir Frederick Hammilton*, p. 75: Sir Frederick used drill training with his garrison in Manorhamilton in 1641–3.

CHAPTER FIVE

Progress and development despite the harassment of the lord deputy, 1633–May 1641

Charles I succeeded his father, James I, on 27 March 1625 (pl. 4). At his coronation ceremony in Westminster Abbey the following February, he was crowned king of England, Scotland and Ireland. Since he had been born in Dunfermline in Scotland and had spent the first four years of his life there, it was always intended that he would also have a coronation ceremony in his native country. His visit to Scotland was postponed on a number of occasions, and it was not until the spring of 1633 that Charles announced his intention to travel to Edinburgh for the ceremony. He hoped that his belated coronation there would help cement the relationship between himself and his Scottish subjects.

The king was determined to impress the Scots on this, his first, visit to his native country in almost thirty years. He set out from Whitehall Palace in London on 13 May with a huge entourage of 250 lords and courtiers and almost a thousand servants. The impressive retinue boasted the lord chamberlain, the lord treasurer, the duke of Lennox, the marquis of Hamilton, ten earls, the secretary of state and the bishops of London and Ely. It also included many more obscure court members such as physicians, surgeons, apothecaries, chaplains, choir, musicians and even a barber. A special guard of horsemen drawn from the privy chamber rode alongside the king. Sir Frederick Hamilton was one of the eight men chosen for this honour. His decision to temporarily postpone his trip to Sweden had certainly paid off. But it is also likely that the marquis of Hamilton, with whom he had returned from Germany the previous autumn, helped him secure the position. The marquis had been appointed one of Charles' chief advisors in Scottish affairs early in 1633, and as such played a key role in organizing the king's coronation in Scotland.[1]

The king and his retinue travelled northwards at a leisurely pace, stopping off at several palaces and mansions such as Stamford, Grantham and York along the way. Justices of the peace had been ordered to improve the condition of the roads,

---

1 Bodl., Wood MS F33, fos 69–70, list of the king's servants appointed to attend his majesty into Scotland, 11 May 1633; K. Sharpe, 'The image of virtue' in Sharkey (ed.), *The English court*, p. 251; H.C.G. Matthew and B. Harrison (eds), *Oxford dictionary of national biography* (60 vols, Oxford, 2004), xxiv, pp 842–3.

and towns along the route were decorated and cleared of beggars. The Scottish border was eventually reached on 12 June. In the state entry into Edinburgh three days later, the Scots nobility rode immediately ahead of Charles, with the English contingent just behind their sovereign. There was pomp and pageantry in the streets. Scotsmen, who had waited eight years for this occasion, received their king with great enthusiasm.[2]

The coronation itself, which took place in the abbey church of Holyroodhouse Palace on 15 June, was a splendid affair. There was, however, much disquiet at the form of the ceremony. This was conducted according to the liturgy of the Church of England, which was unfamiliar in Scotland. Bishops attired in robes and clergy in white surplices genuflected to the crucifix on the altar. This was in stark contrast to the black gowns worn by the Scottish Calvinistic clergy, and the lack of the use of ornaments in the Scottish Church ritual. The Scots disliked the religious reforms that were then being introduced into the Anglican Church with the backing of the king. In their eyes, these changes resembled too closely the liturgy of the Roman Catholic Church. Despite their grievances, the coronation was a dignified and impressive occasion, after which the archbishop of St Andrews and the lord high constable of Scotland presented the monarch to his people.[3]

Charles I spent the rest of June in Edinburgh attending to official and ceremonial duties. On 20 June, he opened the Scottish parliament and attended its sessions for several days to ensure that some bills relating to church matters were passed. The king's visit cost the city of Edinburgh some £40,000 to stage. One of the functions that the city council hosted in his honour was a banquet on 23 June. An invited guest on this glittering occasion was Sir Frederick Hamilton, who had, some days previously, been created a burgess and guild-brother of Edinburgh by the council. This honour was no doubt bestowed on Sir Frederick on account of his nationality and his position in the king's entourage. Once again, the titles may have been conferred at the promptings of his cousin, the marquis.[4]

On 1 July, the king set out on a tour of central Scotland to confer honours and receive tributes. Over the next fortnight, he created twelve new knights, a viscount, two earls and a marquis. Charles and his retinue stayed in royal residences such as Linlithgow, Stirling and Falkland, all of which had been recently repaired. The Scots still cheered him as he processed through the country. His visit ended on 14 July, when he set out again for London to be with the queen, who was expecting their fourth child. The king was pleased with the

---

2 J.S. Wheeler, *The Irish and British wars, 1637–1654* (London, 2002), p. 13.   **3** Donaldson, *Scotland: James V to James VII*, pp 305–7.   **4** C.B. Watson (ed.), *Roll of Edinburgh burgesses and guild-brethren, 1406–1700* (Edinburgh, 1929). A burgess was a member of the city council.

reaction to his sojourn in Scotland, feeling that it had brought him closer to his Scottish subjects. Sir Frederick Hamilton must also have been delighted, not only to have been part of Charles I's entourage in his native country, but also with the honorary titles conferred on him in the Scottish capital.[5]

CURTAILED, HUMILIATED AND PENALIZED BY WENTWORTH

When Lord Deputy Falkland was recalled from Ireland in October 1629, he was temporarily replaced by Richard Boyle, earl of Cork, and Lord Chancellor Adam Loftus, viscount of Ely, who were commissioned lords justices. During their tenure of office, Charles I gave particular consideration as to how that kingdom might be governed with greater authority and efficiency. The necessity for decisive action became more apparent as the annual subsidies, paid by the Old and New English since 1628 in the hope of being granted the 'Graces', were due to expire in 1632. Ireland was then running an annual deficit of £20,000, as well as carrying an outstanding debt of £100,000. The king was anxious that this drain on the English exchequer should not be allowed to continue, as he himself was responsible for state funding, since he had dissolved the English parliament in 1629.[6]

The man chosen by Charles to make Ireland financially self-sufficient and more subservient to the king was the new lord deputy, Sir Thomas Wentworth (pl. 5). Born in London in 1593, Wentworth studied law at the Inner Temple. He became MP for Yorkshire in 1614 and opposed King James' denial of the rights and privileges of parliament. He later spoke out against King Charles' war with Spain, and the taxes imposed to maintain it. He was a strong supporter of the English parliament's Petition of Right, which attempted to restrict the power of the king in 1628. But when Charles reluctantly accepted the Petition, Wentworth switched sides and backed the king against parliament. From then on he became totally committed to upholding absolute royal authority. He became an English privy councillor in 1629 and was a key advisor to the king during his eleven-year personal rule without parliament. Wentworth was appointed lord deputy of Ireland in January 1632, but only took up his post in Dublin after Charles had returned from his Scottish coronation at the end of July 1633. Wentworth was a man of high intelligence and great determination. He set out to use the full powers inherent in his new office to rule in an autocratic, ruthless and thorough manner. He would be unwilling, like his royal master, to compromise on anything.[7]

5 Donaldson, *Scotland: James V to James VII*, p. 302.   6 W. Knowler (ed.), *Letters and despatches*, i, p. 287.
7 See A. Clarke, 'The government of Wentworth, 1632–1640' in Moody et al. (eds), *A new history of Ireland, iii*, pp 243–4.

The new lord deputy identified three, sometimes interrelated, areas that needed reform. The first of these involved a radical restructuring of the Irish finances. In 1634 he manipulated the Irish parliament into voting six subsidies, amounting to £250,000 in total, which would be paid over the course of four years. In the same year, he reactivated the Commission for Defective Titles, whereby land titles of powerful landowners, regardless of whether they were native Irish, Old English or New English and Scottish settlers, were re-examined. If found to be defective in any way, the commission could rectify the title, but would then increase the rents due to the crown, often by as much as 50 per cent. He also penalized planters who had not adhered to the original conditions of their grants. A spectacular example was that of the London Companies who were fined £70,000 by the Court of Star Chamber in London, in collusion with Wentworth, for failing to fulfil some of the regulations of the Ulster Plantation in Derry. The lord deputy also set about preparing for a plantation of Old English lands in Connacht, Clare and Tipperary, whereby a quarter of the land would be confiscated for the king, and the original owners given valid title to the rest, in return for a specified rent. Further revenue-generating procedures included the promotion of trade and industry, the introduction of a monopoly on tobacco imports and sales, and the reforming of the customs. The cumulative effect of all of these measures resulted in the Irish debt being wiped out and a significant surplus created for the crown within five years.[8]

The second area that Wentworth set out to reform was the Irish adminis-tration. Soon after taking up office, he came to the conclusion that many of the New English settlers, who held important positions of power, were more interested in promoting their own advancement than in serving the crown. Within two years, he had succeeded in removing from office, often following corruption charges, such government officials as Lord Chancellor Loftus, Vice-treasurer Mountnorris, Lord Wilmot and the earl of Cork. In the Irish House of Commons, he set about creating his own party of government supporters, which held the balance of power between the Old and New English groups, thus controlling whatever legislation was enacted. Moreover, rather than relying totally on parliament, or the law courts (which were open to influence), to uphold his policies, he reinvigorated the Court of Castle Chamber to deal with those who disputed his decisions. This effective institution had the power to fine, imprison and even inflict corporal punishment, and was fully under the control of the lord deputy. Those found guilty by this court, such as the earl of Cork and Lord

8 See Gillespie, *Seventeenth-century Ireland*, pp 97–103; D. Scott, *Politics and war in the three Stuart kingdoms, 1637–49* (Basingstoke, 2004), p. 14.

Mountnorris, were also refused the traditional permission to travel to London to appeal its judgments to the king.[9]

Wentworth's third priority was to see that a strong and united Church of Ireland supported royal authority in Ireland. He took steps to ensure that the church adopted the same doctrinal and liturgical reforms that William Laud, archbishop of Canterbury, was then introducing into the Anglican Church in England. These reforms were aimed at curbing the perceived radical Puritan influences that had become prevalent in both countries during the reign of James I. Bishop Bramhall of Derry, who led Wentworth's church reforms from 1635, made sure that nearly all newly appointed bishops and deans were pro-reform, and that non-conforming ministers, especially Presbyterians in north-east Ulster, were pressurized to comply or leave the country. The lord deputy also realized that considerable finance was needed to strengthen the physical structures of the church. In previous decades, powerful Protestant and Catholic landowners had acquired ownership of over 50 per cent of Church of Ireland parishes by legal or other means. As a result, the only source of income for many clergy was what the landowner paid them. Such ministers were often obliged to hold two or more parishes to support themselves. Many church buildings were consequently in a state of disrepair. Wentworth substantially rectified the situation by introducing legislation to control the leasing of church property, by requiring landowners to surrender any unlawful acquisitions and by imposing fines on those found guilty.[10]

Sir Frederick Hamilton came to Wentworth's attention on many occasions during his lord deputyship. Wentworth seems to have taken quite a dislike to Hamilton from the very beginning, describing him to the secretary of state, Sir John Coke, in 1634 as 'a gentleman of a strange extravagant humour and judgement as any other indeed I know'. He would therefore 'keep him on this side [that is, in Ireland] and free His Majesty from his trouble'. But he would do so, while giving Hamilton no cause to complain, which 'is a great work to accomplish, the condition of the gentleman considered'. Wentworth's opinion of Sir Frederick did not change over the years. In a letter to the assistant secretary of state, Sir Francis Windebank, in 1639, he states that 'the violence and assurance of Sir Frederick in his own particular appetites are … understood for such as show their earnestness and metal equally, let the cause be good or bad'. With such a powerful and uncompromising lord deputy holding so poor an opinion of him, times were going to be difficult for Hamilton during Wentworth's tenure of office.[11]

Sir Frederick, who had returned to Ireland in the autumn of 1633, first clashed with Wentworth the following spring over the issue of arrears of army pay. These

9 Rushworth, *The tryal of Thomas, earl of Strafford*, p. 26.   **10** See Gillespie, *Seventeenth-century Ireland*, pp 66–8, 108–17.   **11** Knowler (ed.), *Letters and despatches*, i, pp 281, 406, 407; ii, p. 285.

arrears probably related to the time of his absence in Germany, when he still
retained and paid his company in the army in Ireland. He now wished to recoup
that money from the lord deputy. Because of the large crown debt that existed
when he took up office, Wentworth's policy was not to pay any such arrears until
the Irish parliament had voted the subsidies in July 1634. He therefore refused
Sir Frederick's request. When Hamilton pleaded poverty, Wentworth offered to
lend him the money privately, provided that Sir Frederick gave him security and
arranged for repayment. This, Hamilton refused to do, and instead told
Wentworth to recoup the money out of the arrears. The lord deputy declined, as
this would mean breaking his own rule on the matter of payment of arrears.
Instead, he got a warrant from the king to repay himself out of Sir Frederick's
current payments.[12]

Sir Frederick was furious and appealed directly to the king. Charles sided with
the lord deputy and wrote to Wentworth, through Sir John Coke, on 30 June
1634, telling him that Hamilton was not to be allowed to leave his army
company in Ireland, but that the situation should be handled diplomatically.
In his reply to Coke some weeks later, the lord deputy stated that he was
implementing the king's wishes, and was careful to ensure that no other army
officer would be permitted to cross over to England, so that Sir Frederick would
not feel that he was being unfairly singled out.[13]

Sir Frederick, however, would not take 'no' for an answer. He realized that he
would have to gain personal access to the king in order to have the lord deputy's
ruling overturned. He therefore requested some of his 'noble friends' at court,
probably again including the marquis of Hamilton, to persuade the king to order
his attendance at court for his quarterly service as privy chamberman. The plan
seemed to be working when Coke wrote to Wentworth in February 1635,
instructing him to give Sir Frederick licence to travel over, unless he 'know just
cause to keep him [in Ireland)]'. Wentworth, not wishing to be outmanoeuvred,
reminded Coke of the king's letter of the previous June. He added that he would
only give Hamilton permission to travel if the king clarified the situation with
another directive. Moreover he went so far as to point out to Coke the inconven-
ience of allowing such a disagreeable character as Sir Frederick near the court.[14]

When he learned about Coke's letter to Wentworth, Sir Frederick went
immediately to the lord deputy to enquire if he might now travel to England.
After keeping him waiting for nine days, Wentworth reiterated that he was

---

12 H. O'Grady, *Strafford and Ireland* (2 vols, Dublin, 1923), ii, pp 918–20.   **13** Knowler (ed.), *Letters and
despatches*, i, pp 281, 406; see also Rushworth, *The tryal of Thomas, earl of Strafford*, p. 460.   **14** Knowler
(ed.), *Letters and despatches*, i, p. 406. The marquis himself was shortly to become a bitter enemy of
Wentworth because the lord deputy would oppose several of his attempts to acquire plantation land in
Ireland; see BL, Add. MSS 64,911, Sir Frederick to Sir John Coke, 3 Dec. 1635.

unable to give him permission because of the king's initial overriding order that all captains in the army in Ireland must reside with their companies. He did add that he had replied to Coke and would respect whatever further directions he would receive from him.[15]

On hearing this, Sir Frederick himself wrote to Coke on 14 April, requesting him to tell the king that, 'if I shall not be suffered at this time to come over, it may turn to my great ruin and prejudice, which I do hope His Majesty would not willingly wish'. This letter provoked no response from the secretary of state. Hamilton then let the matter rest for a further eight months, before writing again to Coke on 3 December. This time, after repeating his request to have the king's authorization for him to travel, Sir Frederick enclosed a draft for £10, which seems to have been meant as an inducement. There is no evidence to show whether or not Coke procured the desired royal permission. Wentworth, at his subsequent trial in 1641, claimed that it was he who requested the king to allow Hamilton over, after Sir Frederick had threatened to complain him to Charles. The lord deputy, however, may have been disingenuous in this statement, as he seems to be referring to a later occasion when Hamilton again appealed to the king over Wentworth. One way or the other, there is no record of Sir Frederick in England until September 1637, when he was preparing to undertake his voyage to Sweden.[16]

While still embroiled with Wentworth over issues of pay and travel restrictions, Sir Frederick clashed again with the lord deputy over the question of seniority among captains in the army. Early in 1635, Wentworth, in his capacity as general of the army in Ireland, commanded that Sir Arthur Terringham, a junior captain to Sir Frederick, should take precedence over Hamilton at musters and parades. Sir Frederick was quick to complain in writing to the lord deputy. Wentworth consulted with some officers, and on their 'most partial report', he reaffirmed Terringham's position. Sir Frederick again protested, presenting certified copies of army muster rolls to prove his own seniority. He also requested that the Irish Council of War – of which both he and Terringham were members at the time – be convened to decide on the issue, but Wentworth refused to listen. To add insult to injury, the lord deputy commanded Hamilton in public to change his company's colours. Wentworth seems to have enjoyed bringing Sir Frederick to heel, if one is to judge by his comments to an army officer shortly after the first of these incidents took place: 'Sir Frederick Hamilton is going mad, I believe, because his colours may not fly before Arthur Ternagan's'.[17]

15 BL, Add. MSS 64,911.   **16** BL, Add. MSS 64,909, Sir Frederick to Sir John Coke, 14 Apr. 1635; Rushworth, *The tryal of Thomas, earl of Strafford*, pp 26–7; TNA, SP 16/366–8, the council to the officers of the navy re: Sir Frederick's ship, 29 Sept. 1637.   **17** *To the right honourable the lords now assembled in the upper house of parliament, the humble petition of Sir Frederick Hamilton, knight and collonel*, 14 Jan. 1641;

In December 1636, Hamilton again suffered as a result of one of Wentworth's measures. His title to his north Leitrim estate came under investigation by the Commission for Defective Titles. This may have resulted from the fact that he had not fulfilled all the conditions of his original grant, or that he had breached plantation regulations by acquiring without permission the lands of other planters. There is also evidence to suggest that he had acquired, perhaps illegally, some Church of Ireland land. The Commission's investigations would probably therefore have resulted in a fine and a significant increase in his rent.[18]

Sir Frederick came into conflict once more with Wentworth in 1637, when his father-in-law, Sir John Vaughan, governor of Derry, appointed him to represent him in a dispute over the ownership of the Lifford estate in Co. Donegal. Sir Richard Hansard had received, during the Ulster Plantation, a grant of the manor of Lifford, incorporating the borough and the emerging county town of Donegal. Sir Richard, who died in 1619, left the estate to his brother, William, in Lincoln. William sold the lands, and Sir John Vaughan acquired a third share in them. In 1622, a Robert Hansard from London claimed the property, but the Court of Chancery in Ireland found in favour of the original beneficiary, William of Lincoln, in 1627. However, when Wentworth came to Ireland in 1633, Sarah Hansard, widow of Robert, petitioned the king for the lands on behalf of her son, who was also called William. The king referred the matter to Wentworth, who made an out-of-court ruling in favour of young William the following year. Sir John Vaughan continuously challenged the ruling up to 1637, but to no avail. He therefore handed the matter over to Sir Frederick in June of that year.[19]

In the spring of 1638, on his return from Sweden, Sir Frederick appealed to the king to review the lord deputy's decree, on the grounds that the judges whom Wentworth consulted in 1634 had represented Robert and Sarah Hansard in the 1627 case. The king then wrote to the lord deputy, asking him to respond to Hamilton's allegation. Wentworth agreed to allow the case to be retried in England, though only after Sir Frederick had entered on a bond that he would abide by the 1634 decision if his appeal failed. Wentworth was actually so annoyed by Hamilton's conduct in the whole affair that he spoke of charging him with attempting to pervert and oppose the course of justice. King Charles submitted the case to three judges, Lord Keeper Finch, whom Sir Frederick later called a pawn of Wentworth's, and the chief justices of the King's Bench and Common Pleas. 'Upon mature reflection', they upheld the 1634 decree. Although

CSPI, Charles I, 1633–47, pp 100, 117: lord deputy to Lord Conway and Killultagh, 12 Mar. 1635 and Lord Cromwell to same, 17 Dec. 1635. Sir Arthur Terringham later became governor of Newry. **18** Balfour Paul, *The Scots peerage*, i, p. 44.   **19** *The several petitions of William Hansard and Sir Frederick Hammiltoun*, pp 7, 9–20; PRONI, D580/1, power of attorney given by Sir John Vaughan to Sir Frederick, 9 Apr. 1641; PRO, SO 1/3, 92, king to the lord deputy for Sir Frederick Hamilton, Kt, 25 Jul. 1638.

the king approved of their judgment, Sir Frederick did not let the matter rest and in March 1640 was still complaining to the king over Wentworth's decree.[20]

Wentworth penalized Hamilton on at least two further occasions – both while he was in England in the king's service during the First Bishops' War in the summer of 1639. The first incident was an out-of-court ruling that the lord deputy made in favour of a tenant of Hamilton's. Richard Lynch had leased land in Cos Leitrim and Mayo from Sir Frederick for a number of years up until his death in 1627. Hamilton then renewed the lease in favour of Lynch's widow, Evelyn, but sometime later terminated it when she failed to pay the rent. Lynch complained to Lord Deputy Falkland, who submitted the case to the vice president of Connacht, Sir Roger Jones. At the conclusion of the trial that followed in the provincial court, a decree was granted against Sir Frederick. Hamilton then appealed the judgment to the Court of Castle Chamber and the High Court of Chancery in Dublin, both of which decided in his favour. In 1633, the widow Lynch petitioned Wentworth, who had just been appointed lord deputy, for a retrial. He referred the case once more to Jones, who by then had become Lord Ranelagh and joint president of Connacht, but the decision of the high court was upheld. However, in May 1639, Lynch secured an extrajudicial decree from Wentworth directing Hamilton to pay her £323 10s. because he found that her lease had been unfairly discontinued, thus depriving her of the benefit of the lands between 1627 and 1639. Sir Frederick's tenants were forced by the sheriff to vacate the property, their houses were demolished and their goods seized. Moreover, £400 of his Leitrim rents were confiscated, and he later claimed that he had been unjustly penalized overall to the value of £3,000.[21]

Wentworth inflicted more hardship on Hamilton two months later at Dublin, where the whole standing army in Ireland was assembled for manoeuvres. At the final inspection of the sixty or so companies of horse and foot, only two – Sir Frederick's and Sir William Stewart's – were found to 'have been neglected by their officers'. For their punishment, and as an example to others, Wentworth detained them an extra fortnight until he 'saw them perfect as the rest in the use of their arms, and all the duties belonging common soldiers'. Wentworth wrote that he would 'be sure to have Sir Frederick bawling after him' as a result of his action, and he was right. Hamilton later complained to the English House of

---

20 TNA, SO 1/3, p. 92; *The several petitions of William Hansard and Sir Frederick Hammiltoun*, p. 7; Knowler (ed.), *Letters and despatches*, ii, p. 285: lord deputy to Assistant Secretary of State Windebank, 15 Feb. 1639; *CSPI, Charles I, 1633–47*, p. 238: king to lord lieutenant, 21 Mar. 1640; Mac an Ghallóglaigh, 'Sir Frederick Hamilton', 67.   **21** The Mayo property involved the former Dominican friary and lands of Rathfran, four miles north of Killala. M. Jansson (ed.), *Proceedings in the opening session of the Long Parliament: House of Commons, vol. 1: 3 November–19 December 1640* (New Haven, CT, 2000), p. 637; Jansson (ed.), *Proceedings in the opening session, vol. 6: 19 July–9 September 1641* (Rochester, NY, 2005), pp

Lords that his men were kept, not two but four weeks, in Dublin, which personally cost him £30 to £40. He also claimed that the lord deputy openly admitted to Sir Frederick's lieutenant, Laskleg (Lesley), that he had a score to settle with Hamilton and that he was taking this opportunity of doing so.[22]

As a result of all of these confrontations with the lord deputy, Sir Frederick became convinced that Wentworth was his 'mortall enemy'. He later complained of the 'hard measure I met withall in Ireland, by the power and greatness of the late earl of Strafford, whose whole design was apparent, the ruine of my honour and fortune'. In a petition to the English House of Commons in 1646, he stated that his 'losses and sufferings have not been few [because he had opposed Wentworth's] tyrannical courses'. He also alleged that his appeal to the king in the Hansard case, and

> his several other oppositions to the late earl of Strafford … for divers unsufferable injuries and extrajudicial proceedings against him and his late deceased Father-in-law Sir John Vaughan [left him, as Vaughan's heir] with a great burden of debt, by means of the crosses put upon him by the said Earl of Strafford.

Sir Frederick was obviously very bitter about the way he had been treated by Wentworth. It is not surprising, therefore, that he, like several other prominent settlers with similar grievances against the lord deputy, would play a part in Wentworth's eventual downfall.[23]

MANORHAMILTON CASTLE AND TOWN

As one of the principal undertakers in the plantation of Co. Leitrim, Sir Frederick Hamilton was responsible for the military security of his estate. He was required, therefore, according to the terms of his grant, to build a castle thirty feet long by twenty feet wide by twenty-five feet high within three years. It was to be surrounded by a bawn wall, three hundred feet in circumference and fourteen feet in height. Both castle and bawn wall were to be built 'of stone or bricke'. The fine for not adhering to this directive was £780. Hamilton, like many other settlers, was slow to comply with several of the plantation regulations, and even by 1630 he had made no move to build a castle. In December of that year, when he was regranted his enlarged estate, the king directed that he should not be fined

639–41.   **22** Knowler (ed.), *Letters and despatches*, ii, p. 427: lord deputy to Sir Henry Vane, 24 Jul. 1639; *The humble petition*.   **23** *The information of Sir Frederick Hammilton*, p. 59; *The humble remonstrance*, p. 2; *The several petitions of William Hansard and Sir Frederick Hammiltoun*, pp 7, 26, 27.

for any breaches of the original plantation regulations, provided he build 'in convenient time' a castle and bawn. The recruitment of a regiment for Swedish service, his participation in the Thirty Years War in Germany and his accompaniment of the king to Scotland, all prevented him from undertaking this project for several years. The reactivation of the Commission for Defective Titles by Wentworth in the summer of 1634 finally provided him with the stimulus to regularize his situation by building a castle. Moreover, the lord deputy, by confining him to Ireland in the years 1634 to 1636, unwittingly allowed him the time to devote his whole energy to this project.[24]

Sir Frederick decided to make an impression with his new castle (pl. 2). He modelled it directly on Rathfarnham Castle, the residence of a former lord chancellor and archbishop of Dublin, Adam Loftus, who built it in 1583. This castle was, in the 1630s, the abode of another Adam Loftus, knight, privy counsellor and treasurer-at-war in Ireland. Sir Frederick would have been familiar with the building, as he was friendly with Adam's brother, Nicholas, who was paymaster of the army in Ireland.[25]

Rathfarnham was really an imposing fortified house. Its design marked a critically important stage in the transition from military castle to country home in Ireland. It sought to combine a Renaissance-style harmonious balance between retaining the defensive features of a medieval castle and creating an elegant country mansion, which afforded more ample and comfortable living conditions. To further ensure its safety, it was probably enclosed by a protective bawn wall.[26]

Sir Frederick's original grant of land in Leitrim in 1622 was located entirely in the barony of Dromahair. However, a substantial amount of the new lands that he had purchased since then were situated in the neighbouring barony of Rosclogher. It was on the boundary of these two baronies, seven miles to the west of his original settlement of Cloonmullen, that he chose to establish his castle in late 1634. The green-field site was a slightly elevated one, which commanded extensive and picturesque views of the surrounding countryside, to the west, south and east. Bordered on the east by the Owenbeg River, it lay at the meeting place of the four main valleys that crisscross the north Leitrim uplands. Consequently, it also marked the intersection point of the east–west Sligo to Enniskillen, and the north–south Ballyshannon to Carrick-on-Shannon and Jamestown routes.

24 'Royal instructions for the plantation of Leitrim', 1620, no. 16, in B. MacCuarta (ed.), 'Leitrim plantation papers', pp 120–1; *CPRI, 19 James I*, p. 539; Marsh, MS Z4.2.6, king to lords justices, 12 Jan. 1630. **25** B. McGrath, 'A biographical dictionary of the membership of the Irish House of Commons, 1640–1641' (PhD, TCD, 1997), pp 195–200; Parliamentary Archives, HL/PO/JO/10/1/192, request of Nicholas Loftus for protection in relation to Sir Frederick Hamilton's debts, 10 Sept. 1645. **26** E. McParland, 'Rathfarnham Castle, Co. Dublin', *Country Life* (9 Sept. 1982), 734–5.

Like Rathfarnham, Sir Frederick's castle was a massive, semi-fortified, but very habitable house of three storeys over a basement. It reflected both the relatively peaceful times that pertained in Ireland since the beginning of the seventeenth century, and Sir Frederick's concern, as a recent veteran of the Thirty Years War in Germany, for providing a secure haven in the event of any future unrest in Ireland. The building consisted of a rectangular central block, with spear-shaped towers at its four corners. Some of the corner towers extended to four storeys in height. The castle, which was almost four times larger than what was required by his plantation regulations, measured 105 feet in width, ninety in length and over forty-five in height. Its walls were four feet thick. Unlike Rathfarnham, it had a large recess in the centre of its rear wall. In the literature of the time, it was referred to as both a 'stronge and commodious place' and as 'a spacious, beautiful and well-built' castle. A modern authority on Irish medieval architecture believes it must have been 'one of the most imposing seventeenth-century houses in Ireland'.[27]

The principal entrance to the south-facing building was in the centre of the front façade on the storey above the basement. It was accessed by a flight of steps and flanked on either side by Ionic stone columns. Large multi-light windows, set in cut sandstone frames, adorned the building at second- and third-floor levels. These windows were particularly prominent to the front and rear of the castle. Cut-stone string courses marked the different floor levels, while reddish quoin stones showed off the excellent workmanship of the masons. Twenty tall diamond-shaped chimney stacks were clustered in groups on the high gables and corner towers. The interior of the building probably featured some large rooms and open spaces, such as an entrance hall on the first floor, a banqueting hall on the second and a long gallery on the third. It is difficult, however, to be certain of the internal layout of the building, since all internal walls, floors and stairways were made of wood.[28]

Although elegant and very habitable, Castle Hamilton was essentially a fortified building. Its four corner towers were provided with numerous musket

---

27 J.T. Gilbert (ed.), *A contemporary history of affairs in Ireland from AD1641 to 1652* (3 vols, Dublin, 1880), ii, p. 119; R. Stalley (ed.), *Daniel Grose (c.1766–1838): the antiquities of Ireland* (Dublin, 1991), p. 74; see also M. Salter, *Castles and stronghouses of Ireland* (Worcester, 1993), p. 38; D.M. Waterman, 'Some Irish seventeenth-century houses and their architectural ancestry' in E.M. Jope (ed.), *Studies in building history* (London, 1961), pp 258, 264; M. Craig, *The architecture of Ireland from earliest times to 1800* (London, 1982), p. 117; P. Kerrigan, *Castles and fortifications in Ireland, 1485–1945* (Cork, 1995), p. 65; A. Day and P. McWilliams (eds), *Ordnance Survey memoirs of Ireland: counties of south Ulster, 1834–8, Cavan, Leitrim, Louth, Monaghan and Sligo* (Belfast, 1998), p. 51; D. Faughnan, *Topographical and general survey of Co. Leitrim* (Clonrush, 1943), p. 3; J. Logan, 'Tadhg Ó Roddy and two surveys of Co. Leitrim', *Breifne*, 4:14 (1971), 329, 332. **28** NLI, MS 10,442, A.S. Green papers: notes and text by A.S. Green and F.J. Biggar towards a history of Co. Leitrim; see also D. Sweetman, *Medieval castles of Ireland* (Cork, 1999), p. 175; strategy report for the Heritage Council on Manorhamilton Castle by Dedalus Architecture

and pistol loops, which permitted flanking fire, protecting especially the approach to the main entrances. At higher level, defence was provided from wall-walks behind the battlements. However, the principal security structure that protected the castle was the bawn wall that encircled it. This wall reached a height of some fourteen feet, and had two-storey towers at each of its four corners. These towers were also spear-shaped and equipped with gun loops. In addition, a gate house was probably located at the main entrance to the bawn.[29]

One can only speculate as to the identity of the person responsible for overseeing the construction of the castle. It may have been Revd John Johnson, Church of Ireland rector of nearby Dromlease parish, who is reputed to have built Lord Deputy Wentworth's much larger mansion at Jigginstown, near Naas in Co. Kildare.[30] Sir Frederick engaged masons, carpenters and other craftsmen, probably from England or Scotland, to do the actual construction work, although these were probably assisted by Irish labourers. The likely cost of the project, which took about eighteen months to complete, would have been in the region of £5,000. This was the equivalent of two and a half years' rents from Hamilton's north Leitrim estates. There is no record of Charles I having provided any funds towards the cost of the building, as his father, James I, had done for such undertakers as Sir William Cole or Captain Basil Brooke during the Ulster Plantation. Sir Frederick did borrow £800 on the Dublin staple on 4 December 1635, and it seems likely that this money went towards his construction costs. He may well have also sourced credit on the nearby Sligo staple, but we have no records of any such transaction.[31]

In the early decades of the seventeenth century, orchards, gardens and private parks were fashionable among the cultured classes of society in England. The settled conditions of the 1620s and 1630s in Ireland encouraged prominent British settlers there to commission such amenities in the vicinity of their castles. Such a move was a real vote of confidence in the future political stability and security of the country. Sir Frederick had a fairly large orchard planted on the sloping ground to the south-west, between the bawn wall of the castle and the

---

(unpublished, Nov. 2005). **29** NLI, 16M10 and 16F11, Leitrim county estates maps: J. Leonard, 'A plan of Manorhamilton, 1749' and W. Larkin, 'The town of Manorhamilton, 1807'; see also H. Leask, *Irish castles and castellated houses* (Dundalk, 1944), p. 125. **30** Jane Fenlon, '"They say I build up to the sky": Thomas Wentworth, Jigginstown House and Dublin Castle' in Michael Potterton and Thomas Herron (eds), *Dublin and the Pale in the Renaissance, c.1540–1660* (Dublin, 2011), pp 207–23 at p. 220. **31** *The several petitions of William Hansard and Sir Frederick Hammiltoun*, pp 27–8; kildare.ie/heritage//history/ historic castles/jigginstown castle.htm, accessed on 18 June 2007; Ohlmeyer and Ciardha (eds), *The Irish statue staple books*, p. 234; M.J. Moore (comp.), *Archaeological inventory of Co. Leitrim* (Dublin, 2003), pp 212–13; Bishop John Leslie's castle in Raphoe, Co. Donegal, which is a smaller model of Rathfarnham and Manorhamilton, was begun in 1636 and built in fifteen months. Sir Frederick's castle, though now in ruins, is still a very imposing edifice. The present owners, Anthony and Maura Daly, have carried out much conservation and consolidation work on the castle and on the bawn walls in recent years.

Owenbeg river. The area was then enclosed by a ditch. To the south-east of the bawn wall, he established his gardens, and to the north-east the castle park. He also laid down a terraced lawn, inside the bawn wall, in front of the castle. The supreme status symbol for leading settlers at the time was a deer park. Hamilton had been granted permission by the king in 1630 'to convert any part of the said manor not exceeding 1,000 acres into a park for deer'. He certainly created such a park some distance to the north-east of the castle, but it is possible that he used it to corral his 'highly esteemed and valued breed of four hundred horse and mares', rather than a herd of deer.[32]

Even as Hamilton's castle was being built in the mid-1630s, the town of Manorhamilton was already beginning to develop along the Sligo to Enniskillen route, on the other side of the Owenbeg from the castle. Many of the houses would have been built of stone walls and a slated roof, with a chimney 'according to the English manner'. The pre-1641 settlement may have amounted to between thirty and forty houses, with a population of perhaps 140, not including the army company – although some of the soldiers were also servants of Sir Frederick. It was therefore somewhat smaller than Ballyshannon, Donegal town and Enniskillen, all of which numbered about fifty houses. Sligo, on the other hand, was much larger, with sixty British households alone by 1641. It also had a substantial native Irish population, since Sir Frederick claimed to have killed up to three hundred of these when he burned that town on 1 July 1642.[33]

The early buildings in Manorhamilton included a Church of Ireland parish church, which was constructed about the year 1638, following a visit to the town by Bishop William Bedell of Kilmore, to discuss local church matters. The town had then at least one inn, where Bedell, his retinue and several of his ministers lodged during this visit. It is very likely that there was also a small sessions house and market house, since Hamilton had been authorized, in accordance with his plantation grant, to conduct a manorial 'court of record to hold pleas of £3 or under', as well as a weekly Tuesday market. When Sir Frederick built his castle in Manorhamilton, he also moved his company of fifty soldiers there. He may have constructed the star fort, with its spear-shaped bastions, quite similar to those of the castle bawn, as a garrison for his men, some two hundred yards from the

---

32 *Another extract of severall letters*, pp 19, 24; Leitrim county estates maps: J. Leonard, 'A plan of Manorhamilton and Manorhamilton gardens, 1749'; Marsh, MS Z4.2.6, king to lords justices, 12 Jan. 1630; *The several petitions of William Hansard and Sir Frederick Hammiltoun*, p. 28; see also M. McCarthy Morrogh, 'The English presence in early seventeenth-century Munster' in Brady and Gillespie (eds), *Natives and newcomers*, pp 185–7; J. Logan, 'Tadhg Ó Roddy and two surveys of Co. Leitrim', 329. 33 Parliamentary Archives, HL/PO/JO/10/1/198, the humble petition, c.June 1645; R.J. Hunter, 'Plantation in Donegal' in W. Nolan, L. Ronayne and M. Dunlevy (eds), *Donegal, history and society* (Dublin, 1995), p. 314; R.J. Hunter, 'Sir William Cole, the town of Enniskillen and plantation County Fermanagh' in Murphy and Roulston (eds), *Fermanagh, history and society*, p. 124.

castle. He also had two corn mills and probably a tuck mill erected in the town before 1641.[34]

Some of the earliest residents of the town were certainly the British craftsmen – 'masons, carpenters and other workemen' – who built the castle, and who remained in Sir Frederick's employment at least up to 1643. It is quite likely that any Irish labourers who assisted these craftsmen also resided there or in the near vicinity. Then there were the Hamiltons' servants who worked in the castle. Sir Frederick mentions that twelve men servants accompanied him on a visit to Derry in 1641. Hamilton's seneschal, or most senior manor official, who presided over the local court, lived there. So too did Revd John Cunningham, the Church of Ireland clergyman, who was appointed rector of Cloonclare parish on 2 August 1637. The inhabitants included one or more innkeepers, as well as several millers who operated the local corn and tuck mills. The new town would also have needed merchants, such as a clothier and a tavern keeper, and tradesmen like shoemakers, weavers and blacksmiths, to supply provisions and services for all of these men, their families and the soldiers.[35]

While on the subject of attempting to estimate the number of people in the town of Manorhamilton in the late 1630s, it is tempting to speculate also on the likely population of Co. Leitrim as a whole, just prior to the 1641 rebellion. The Sligo historian, Mary O'Dowd, surmises with the help of the Strafford Survey of 1635 that the population of Co. Sligo was then in the region of eighteen thousand persons. Now, the principal landowners and church authorities of that county were charged in 1627 with the task of raising a subsidy of £600 for the maintenance of the army in Ireland. Co. Leitrim's contribution was fixed at £400. Assuming that the levy was calculated on a per capita basis, one could perhaps argue that the population of Co. Leitrim at the time might be somewhere in the region of twelve thousand, or two thirds of that of Co. Sligo.[36]

SIR FREDERICK: THE ENTREPRENEUR

In the early decades of the seventeenth century, the Irish economy performed very well, resulting in a substantial growth in such Irish exports as live cattle,

---

34 *The several petitions of William Hansard and Sir Frederick Hammiltoun*, pp 26, 28; *CPRI, James I*, p. 539; Marsh, MS Z4.2.6; E.S. Shuckburgh (ed.), *Two biographies of William Bedell, bishop of Kilmore* (Cambridge, 1902), pp 34–5. The ruins of the church, which measured 18.6 by 6.45m, are still present. The structure, built of randomly coursed masonry, has a large window opening in the east gable and a round-headed doorway and a single bellcote in the west gable. The weathercock above the bellcote, as shown in Leonard's 'Plan of Manorhamilton, 1749', has long since disappeared. The star fort, with coursed limestone masonry walls that rise to 6m in places, is happily well preserved. **35** *Another extract of severall letters*, pp 18, 34, 46; Revd W.A. Reynell, 'Lists of parochial clergy of the late Established Church in the diocese of Kilmore', *Breifny Antiquarian Society's Journal* (1926), 394. **36** *CSPI, Charles I, 1625–32*, pp

hides, yarn, wool, tallow, timber and iron. A rise in the Irish population during the same period led to a significantly expanded labour force. Many of the progressive British planters in Ireland sought to capitalize on these favourable circumstances, and set about exploiting the resources of their estates and the surrounding areas. These men, who had adequate funds to establish various enterprises and a ready supply of tenants to staff them, were in an ideal position to assume the role of entrepreneur. They erected corn and tuck mills, established tanneries and ironworks, and organized a trade in cattle, sheep, flax, timber and other commodities.[37]

Sir Frederick Hamilton was a typical example of such enterprising planters. He soon became involved in both the cattle and horse trade. After importing improved strains of cattle from England and Scotland, he began breeding them on his estate. By 1641, he had between four and five hundred cows. He also bred mares, and valued his herd of four hundred, which were driven off by the rebels in 1642, at £5,000. Sligo town had a reputation for having a good cattle and horse market, and it is possible that Hamilton brought his animals there for sale before the rebellion.[38]

Sir Frederick grew a large quantity of corn (probably wheat and oats) on his estate and encouraged his tenants to do likewise. He had two 'sufficient corn mills', of the English or vertical type, erected near his castle. It must have been quite a profitable operation, since his tenants were obliged to bring their corn to his mills and charged for the use of them. It is possible that the tuck mill, referred to in Leonard's map of Manorhamilton Gardens in 1749, was also set up by Hamilton. Such mills, which thickened and toughened woven cloth, were introduced by many British settlers to Ireland in the early seventeenth century.[39]

There was a plentiful supply of woodland in north Leitrim, particularly in the Glenfarne, Rossinver, Glenade, Cornastauk, Dromahair and Drumkeeran areas, in the 1620s. At that time, woods all over the country were being exploited on a large scale for the manufacture of staves for export and in the smelting of iron. Although there is no evidence to show that Sir Frederick got involved in the timber trade as such, he did set up at least one ironworks. By the 1630s, there were six such works operating in Leitrim or just outside the county borders. Sir John Dunbar, the Fermanagh planter, set up one at Garrison and another at Dromcro, near Belcoo. Sir Charles Coote of Castlecoote, Co. Roscommon, was responsible for those at Creevelea, Arigna and Doobally. Sir Frederick erected his

250–3; O'Dowd, *Power, politics and land*, pp 63–6.   **37** Gillespie, *Seventeenth-century Ireland*, pp 79–80. **38** *Another extract of severall letters*, pp 21, 27; *The several petitions of William Hansard and Sir Frederick Hammiltoun*, p. 28.   **39** *The several petitions of William Hansard and Sir Frederick Hammiltoun*, p. 28; *Another extract of severall letters*, p. 22; *Leitrim county estate maps*, J. Leonard, 'Manorhamilton gardens, 1749'.

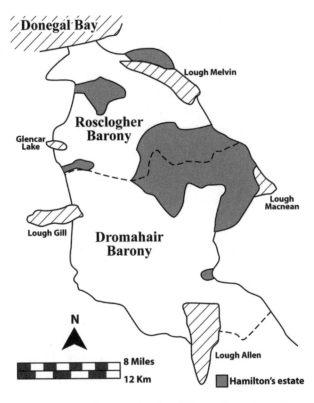

16 Sir Frederick Hamilton's estate in Leitrim in 1641 (sources: Books of survey and distribution; Petty's maps and index of forfeited lands; Chancery inquisitions for Co. Leitrim).

ironworks at Furnace Hill, just west of Drumshanbo. The work in the mines, furnaces and forges of ironworks in Ireland was done by Englishmen, since it required specialized skills, but also, reportedly, to conceal the methods of manufacture from the native Irish. The iron was frequently used to manufacture weapons and cast cannon. Ironworking was labour intensive, and Coote was said to have employed about 2,500 men at his works in Leitrim, Sligo, Roscommon and Leix. It was an expensive industry, both to set up and to maintain. A minimum of £3,000 was given for starting and stocking one ironworks in 1610, and nearly half that for maintaining another in 1626. We have no details, however, of Sir Frederick's expenditure at Drumshanbo, or about the number of workers he employed there.[40]

Sir Frederick's involvement in the above-mentioned enterprises, his construction of an impressive castle, the expansion of his estate (fig. 16), his recruitment of a regiment in the Thirty Years War, his hire of a ship to Sweden in 1637, not to mention his costly confrontations with Wentworth, all drew attention to his

40 *Another extract of severall letters*, pp 19, 21, 26, 32, 41; E. McCracken, 'Charcoal-burning ironworks in seventeenth- and eighteenth-century Ireland', *Ulster Journal of Archaeology*, 20 (1957), 123–33; P. Flanagan, 'Some notes on Leitrim industry', *Breifne*, 4:15 (1972), 415–20.

undoubted wealth. The lord deputy, in fact, referred to Hamilton's 'private fortune' in a letter to Sir John Coke, secretary of state, in 1635. Sir Frederick himself alluded to his wealth when he stated that Wentworth's 'design was ... the ruine of my honour and fortune'. It seems certain that he inherited most of this affluence, but he supplemented his resources with the rents, market tolls and court fees he collected from his Leitrim tenants, his army pay and the profits from his various enterprises. As long as these funds continued to materialize, he would be able to maintain his comfortable lifestyle. The future, in fact, seemed very promising for Sir Frederick in the 1630s, as he looked forward to inheriting the estates of his ageing father-in-law, Sir John Vaughan, in Derry, Donegal and Tyrone in due course.[41]

RELATIONS WITH HIS IRISH AND BRITISH NEIGHBOURS

The 'civill men' among the native Irish gentry who were awarded grants of land in the Ulster, Leitrim and midland plantations, were beginning to integrate with the new British settlers by the 1630s. They were now part of the new order and were benefiting from it. The native gentry of Co. Offaly actually petitioned Lord Deputy Wentworth at this time to 'take away all manner of distinction between the natives of Irish blood and birth and other [of] His Majesty's subjects of this kingdom'.[42]

Prominent native Irish landowners were not only beginning to use the common law, but were also participating in its administration, as well as playing a role in local government. A significant number of the Irish gentry filled the offices of justice of the peace and sheriff in many counties. Mulmurry MacTernan, chief of his clan, was one of the justices of the peace in Leitrim in 1641, whose function was to conduct the quarter-sessions, where all cases except treason and murder were tried. These justices also presided over the petty sessions, which dealt with minor offences. Some years earlier, MacTernan was also the county sheriff. As such, he was the most important official in the county, with responsibility for carrying out the directions of the central administration in Dublin. His duties involved receiving and implementing royal writs, collecting and accounting for crown revenue at the exchequer, and presiding over the assizes. Mulmurry MacTernan was quite a substantial landowner who had received over five hundred acres in the plantation of Leitrim. Con O'Rourke, one of the leading members of the O'Rourke clan, held the office of county sheriff in

---

41 *The humble remonstrance* (undated, prob. May 1645), p. 2.　　**42** 'Royal instructions for the plantation of Leitrim', 1620, no. 11 in Mac Cuarta (ed.), 'Leitrim plantation papers', 120; Gillespie, *Seventeenth-century Ireland*, p. 69.

1641. He was a son of Tiernan Bán, a former tánaiste to Sir Brian of the Ramparts O'Rourke, lord of Breifne from 1566 to 1591. Con got a grant of three hundred acres during the plantation of Leitrim, but must later have greatly increased his holding, as he had mortgaged almost one thousand acres to Robert Parke of Newtown, near Dromahair, by 1641. Sometime during the 1630s, he acquired Castle Car, seat of the O'Rourkes of Car (or Carre), chiefs of Leitrim during the fifteenth century, whose territory had formed one of the six original baronies in the county. The willingness of such members of the Irish gentry in Leitrim and elsewhere to take part in county and legal administration, certainly facilitated their integration with the settler community.[43]

Integration was also helped along by the enthusiasm with which many Irish landowners embraced English ways and customs. They adopted English speech, dressed in the English fashion and imitated English farming techniques. The English language became more prevalent as a steady supply of books, including grammars and children's books, were imported from England. In the fashion line, shoes began to replace brogues, and English hats, caps, breeches, stockings and even spectacles became popular. The native Irish were beginning to look like English men and women. The integration process was not, however, entirely one-sided. A number of the British settlers could understand Irish. Some planters also developed an appreciation of Irish music and culture. Robert Parke of Newtown near Dromahair, for example, employed Dermond O'Ferry as his Irish harper. Another north Leitrim settler, Lieutenant Walter Harrison, fostered out his son, also called Walter, with Cormick MacRobert MacTernan. And there was one instance of even closer integration when a neighbour of Sir Frederick's, James Witherspin, married 'a meer Irish woman'.[44]

Given the assimilation that was taking place between the native Irish gentry and the British planters during the 1630s, it is not surprising that good personal relationships and even bonds of friendship had developed between members of both communities. Sir Frederick Hamilton formed a close friendship with Tadhg O'Connor Sligo, chief of the O'Connors of that county, and one of the leading native Irish landlords in north-east Connacht. He was also MP for Sligo in the 1634 Irish parliament. Since his estate was situated in the barony of Carbury, which incorporates the town of Sligo, O'Connor lived only fifteen miles from

43 *Another extract of severall letters*, pp 17, 23; Mac Cuarta (ed.), 'Leitrim plantation papers', 132; *Down Survey, County Leitrim* (RIA); J. Meehan (ed.), 'Catalogue of the high sheriffs of the county of Leitrim from 1605 to 1800', *JRSAI*, 5:18 (1908), 386; J. Byrne, *Byrne's dictionary of Irish local history* (Cork, 2004), pp 165, 166, 284. The ruins of Castle Car still stand in the townland of Castletown, some three miles from Manorhamilton. **44** *The information of Sir Frederick Hammilton*, pp 36, 77, 78, 83; see also N. Davies, *The isles: a history* (London, 1999), p. 569; McCarthy Morrogh, 'The English presence in early seventeenth-century Munster', p. 189.

Manorhamilton. The friendship lasted up until O'Connor's death in November 1640. Tadhg's son, also called Tadhg, later acknowledged Sir Frederick's affinity with his late father when he wrote to Hamilton several months into the 1641 rebellion: 'I cannot forget in times past there was a mutual correspondency of love and affectionate friendship between my father and yourself'.[45]

There is no evidence to suggest that Sir Frederick was on as friendly terms with native gentry in Leitrim, such as O'Rourke or MacTernan. But neither are there records of any disputes between them before the rebellion. We may conclude that they at least coexisted peacefully in their respective military, judicial or administrative roles, despite their different ethnic and religious backgrounds.

Hamilton was, however, involved in a prolonged legal dispute with at least one native Irish gentleman. Tirlagh O'Michan was a Dublin merchant who had acquired land in Leitrim. On 15 November 1633, he brought a lawsuit against Sir Frederick in the Court of Chancery over disputed rights to lands in Drumlease, near Dromahair. O'Michan was awarded a decree granting him the lands. Three months later, O'Michan was again in the Court of Chancery to secure assurances from Hamilton's two tenants, Revd William Browne and Captain Andrew Adair, that they would abide by the earlier judgment and henceforth pay the rents to O'Michan, if they wished to remain on the property. Brown, an Englishman, and registrar of the dioceses of Achonry and Killala, was an enterprising Sligo landlord who had land rented in Leitrim. Adair also had associations with Killala and was probably a relative of Archibald Adair, the Scottish-born Church of Ireland bishop of Killala. In late February 1634, Hamilton succeeded in getting the original decision overturned in the Court of Chancery. But, in June of that year, O'Michan got a second injunction and a letter from Lord Deputy Wentworth to the sheriff in Leitrim to give him possession. Hamilton again secured another chancery order on 19 December allowing him to continue in place. Sometime later, O'Michan went to the Court of Chancery once more, but this time was ordered to give Sir Frederick joint ownership of the property. Incidentally, Revd Browne was still renting ninety acres in Drumlease from Sir Frederick at the outbreak of the 1641 rebellion.[46]

With the increasing adoption of the English way of life and culture by the native Irish in the early decades of the seventeenth century, there was a realization among some Irish scholars that vital primary sources for researching Gaelic civilization and tradition were in danger of being lost forever. This perception was

---

45 *Another extract of severall letters*, pp 52–3; see also O'Dowd, *Power, politics and land*, pp 15–18.   46 BL, Add. MSS 19,842, fo. 135r: land dispute between O'Michan and Hamilton, Febr. 1634; *Another extract of severall letters*, p. 18; deposition of William Browne, 8 Jan. 1644, and of Revd John Layng, 24 June 1653, printed in W.G. Wood-Martin, *History of Sligo, county and town* (3 vols, Dublin, 1889), ii, pp 198–202, 224; Jansson, *Proceedings in the opening session of the Long Parliament*, i, pp 473–4.

particularly strong among Irish Franciscan communities who had established colleges on the Continent. Friars from the Irish college at Louvain in the Spanish Netherlands set out initially to compile the lives of illustrious Irish saints as well as an ecclesiastical history of Ireland, with the dual purpose of edifying their fellow Irishmen and impressing other Europeans. A lay Franciscan brother, Mícheál Ó Cléirigh, was sent back to Ireland in 1626 to collect material for such a compilation. On completion of this work, which involved transcribing the contents of old vellum books and manuscripts, it was decided to greatly broaden the scope of his research to include data for a full history of Ireland from the earliest times up to the year 1616, when Hugh O'Neill, earl of Tyrone, died. After having secured the financial backing of Fergal O'Gara, a Sligo landowner and member of the Irish parliament, Ó Cléirigh gathered a team of educated lay chroniclers around him to assist with this work. These included Cúcoigcríche Ó Cléirigh, a distant cousin, Fearfeasa Ó Maolchonaire, a poet and historian from Co. Roscommon, and Cúcoigcríche Ó Duigenan from Co. Leitrim, who together with Brother Michael became known as the Four Masters. 'The Annals of the Kingdom of Ireland', as the historical work was originally entitled, were begun in 1632 and took over four years to complete.[47]

The annals were written mainly in the convent of the Franciscan friars of Donegal, which was on the banks of the River Drowes. This short river, four miles in length, flows from Lough Melvin to the sea. The first quarter of its course lies entirely in Co. Leitrim, while its last three miles form the boundary between Donegal and Leitrim. The friars had abandoned their residence in Donegal town after the Flight of the Earls in 1607 and lived by the Drowes during the 1620s and 1630s. The river is mentioned nearly forty times by the annalists when signing off on various sections of their work. It was from this convent that Brother Mícheál would set off every summer to many parts of the country in search of old historical manuscripts. And it was to here that he would return again in wintertime to transcribe, compile and edit, along with his collaborators, their important work.

Sir Frederick Hamilton owned the land that bordered the Drowes to the north-east. As a firm advocate and promoter of Britishness in Ireland, Hamilton would have strongly disapproved and surely reported to the authorities an activity such as the writing in Irish of a history of Gaelic Ireland, had he been aware of its existence. It is not surprising, however, that the convent of the friars escaped his attention, as the lands he owned by the Drowes were situated some ten miles

47 B. Cunningham, 'Native culture and political change in Ireland, 1580–1640' in Brady and Gillespie (eds), *Natives and newcomers*, pp 164–9; Gillespie, *Seventeenth-century Ireland*, p. 22; see also B. Cunningham, 'Writing the Annals of the Four Masters' in E. Bhreathnach and B. Cunningham (eds), *Writing Irish history: the Four Masters and their world* (Dublin, 2007), pp 27–30.

from his base at Manorhamilton. Moreover, the friars once described their abode as being 'in the wilderness of our residence' and thus difficult of access. The fact that Sir Frederick was absent from Ireland for several years in the early 1630s, due to his involvement in the Thirty Years War, may also account for his failure to be aware of the friars and their scholarly guests. In the end, the annalists managed to avoid unwelcome interference from any hostile source, and successfully completed their project on 10 August 1636.[48]

Sir Frederick's relations with the Church of Ireland bishop of Kilmore, local clergymen and his fellow British settlers could at times be described as intimidating, rude or even hostile. The recently ordained Matthew Moore, for example, was appointed vicar of the parishes of Cloonclare (in which Manorhamilton was situated) and neighbouring Cloonlogher on 24 September 1635. Hamilton had already acquired the extensive church lands in both of these parishes, which gave him the right to collect tithes therein. This situation was quite common in the mid-1630s, when laymen owned over 60 per cent of Church of Ireland rectories in Connacht, Leinster and Munster, with the result that clergymen in such parishes were dependent on whatever the owner of the lands paid them. This amount was often small, and consequently clergy were often appointed to two or more parishes in order to be guaranteed a respectable income. Revd Moore complained to the bishop of Kilmore, William Bedell, that 'he had made a disadvantageous bargain out of servile fear with a great person that held two livings of his, for less than either of them was worth'. Bedell wrote to Sir Frederick, requesting him to increase Moore's income, but Hamilton would have none of it. The bishop reacted very astutely by transferring Moore to a parish that was more profitable than the other two put together. He then appointed more capable ministers to Cloonclare and Cloonlogher on 2 August 1637. This new arrangement actually seems to have worked to the advantage of all concerned, as John Cunningham, the new vicar of Cloonclare, got on well with Sir Frederick and fought under his command during the 1641 rebellion.[49]

Hamilton and Bishop Bedell met personally in Manorhamilton about a year after the above event, when the bishop called a meeting of local Church of

---

48 Down Survey, barony and parish maps of Co. Leitrim (RIA); P. Ó Gallachair, *Where Erne and Drowes meet the sea* (Ballyshannon, 1961), pp 45–51; S. Fox, 'The Annals of the Four Masters: a reappraisal' (unpublished paper, 1976). There has been much speculation over the years as to the exact location of the convent of the friars where the annals were compiled. Scholars have suggested various sites in Cos Donegal and Leitrim on one or other bank of the River Drowes. A 'compromise' was arrived at in 1975 when representatives from both sides of the debate were present at the unveiling by President Cearbhall Ó Dalaigh of a memorial to the Four Masters, erected on Mullinaleck Bridge, which spans the river. **49** Reynell, 'Lists of parochial clergy of the late Established Church in the diocese of Kilmore', 394; Books of survey and distribution for Co. Leitrim (in Leitrim County Library, Ballinamore); *The information of Sir Frederick Hammilton*, p. 88; *Another extract of severall letters*, p. 46; Shuckburgh (ed.), *Two biographies of William*

Ireland ministers to 'consult of matters of weight properly concerning their spiritual function'. He had already booked an inn for the gathering when he received an invitation from Sir Frederick to stay at his castle. Bedell declined due to the fact that arrangements had been made with the innkeeper, but assured Hamilton that he and his party would pay him a courtesy call when their discussions had concluded. Sir Frederick was unhappy with the reply and now invited 'not only the bishop and all his company, but all the ministers; assuring them that they should have freedom and privacy, the best his house could afford, for their consultations'. He added that he felt embarrassed that the distinguished visitors should stay anywhere else than at his residence. He also sent 'a threatening messenger to the host of the house for making provision for them without his advice'. Bedell, perhaps recalling his previous dealings with Hamilton, stood by his decision to remain at the inn, but again promised to call on Sir Frederick before leaving the town.[50]

The following morning, the bishop and his entourage arrived at the castle, only to find the doors shut and nobody there to receive them. They knocked and shouted many times but got no response. Then they spotted some people 'peeping out at windows and laughing'. Bedell's followers were furious and urged the bishop to leave immediately. Bedell, however, retained his composure and decided to stay a while longer, assuring them that Hamilton was only in a sulk, which would not last too long. Finally, after half an hour, Sir Frederick 'caused the doors to be opened and himself met and embrac'd the bishop'. He was impressed with Bedell's wisdom, patience and humility, and tried to make amends for his discourtesy by hosting a fine meal for the bishop and his company.[51]

Hamilton's relations with two of his fellow British settlers were much more hostile and involved several court cases. The first of these concerned John Waldron, who had been granted one thousand acres in the Leitrim plantation at Mullies and Rassaun, some four miles from Manorhamilton. Waldron brought a lawsuit against Sir Frederick over a title to land, and won the case in about 1640. Around the same time, there were court cases pending in both Ireland and England involving Hamilton and James Witherspin, another Scottish settler who had married the 'meer Irish woman'. Witherspin was a former tenant of Waldron's and a witness for him in his lawsuit against Sir Frederick. Hamilton later wrote that Witherspin was 'known to be of a most wicket base disposition from his childhood, and one who had been accused of fellony, and found guilty before the rebellion'. The speaker of the English House of Commons summoned Witherspin to London to answer charges made against him by Sir Frederick. Witherspin duly arrived there in April 1641 and spent the next few months

Bedell, pp 106–7. **50** Shuckburgh (ed.), *Two biographies of William Bedell*, pp 34–5. **51** Ibid., p. 35.

waiting for his case to be heard. Not being able to remain any longer, he returned to Ireland in September of that year. Although some witnesses were examined before he left, the eventual outcome of the case is not recorded. Relations between Hamilton and Witherspin would deteriorate further during the rebellion that followed, with disastrous consequences for Witherspin.[52]

IN THE SERVICE OF THE KING DURING THE BISHOPS' WARS

The Church of Scotland, or Kirk as it was popularly called, reformed its doctrines, government and liturgy in 1560, based on Calvinistic teachings to which John Knox had been exposed while living in Geneva. An important element of the reformed doctrine taught that man, due to original sin, is incapable on his own of doing any good. He is totally dependent on God's grace if he is to live a moral and spiritual life. God would therefore be just in condemning all people for their sins, but he has chosen to be merciful to some – those who follow the Calvinistic way of life – and bring them to salvation. The remainder will suffer eternal damnation.

The government of the reformed church was based on the presumed structures intended by the New Testament and the earliest churches. Councils of ministers and elders, collectively called presbyters, governed together as a group. The supreme council was the general assembly. Regional administrations were called presbyteries and local ruling bodies were known as kirk sessions. This Presbyterian form of government rejected domination by archbishops and bishops. In the first two decades of the seventeenth century, King James I reintroduced bishops into the Church of Scotland, thus curbing the powers of the general assembly. These changes were, however, resented and opposed by Scottish Presbyterians.

Worship in the Kirk was strictly regulated by what is commanded in the Bible. Preaching the word of God therefore became the central focus of church services. There was also an emphasis on simplicity, and an absence of ornaments and ritual in the Church's liturgy. Clergy wore black gowns instead of vestments, and used improvised prayers. Statues, crucifixes, church organs, incense and candles were all excluded, and genuflection was considered idolatrous.

The authorities of the Church of Scotland were offended by the highly ritualistic coronation service of Charles I in Edinburgh in 1633. The grandeur of the Church of England ceremony, with its use of ornaments and vestments,

---

52 *Books of survey and distribution for Co. Leitrim*; *The information of Sir Frederick Hammilton*, pp 7, 8, 36; MacCuarta (ed.), 'Leitrim plantation papers', 131; *CSPD, 1641–3*, p. 122.

resembled too closely in their eyes the liturgy of the Roman Catholic Church. Anything to do with popery they could not tolerate. They were further disquieted when the king, before leaving Edinburgh, pushed through an act in the Scottish parliament giving him power to introduce similar changes in the Scottish ritual. The fact that he also held deep discussions with the Church of Scotland bishops was also resented by Presbyterian leaders within the Kirk.[53]

In the years that followed, Charles began to exert more and more control over the Church of Scotland. This process often involved elevating the status of the bishops, while reducing that of the Presbyterian authorities. In 1634 Archbishop Spottiswoode of St Andrews was installed as chancellor of Scotland, the highest office in the state. Other bishops were appointed to the privy council. Two years later, Charles issued a new set of canons for the Kirk without having first consulted with the general assembly. These regulations forbade improvised prayer and gave directions about the furnishings of churches, but made no mention of general assemblies, presbyteries or kirk sessions. The king's most provocative action, however, was his imposition on the Kirk of a new prayer book and liturgy in 1637. These were designed to bring Scottish worship into line with that of the Church of England. Moreover, the fact that the prayer book permitted such 'popish' practices as kneeling to receive communion, and the repositioning of the communion table from the centre to the east of the church, like the altar in the Roman Catholic Church, inclined Scottish Presbyterians to believe that Charles was moving the Kirk back to Rome.[54]

When the first service according to the new prayer book was held in St Giles' Church in Edinburgh on 23 July 1637, in the presence of the Scottish bishops and privy council, a riot erupted and the congregation walked out. Demonstrations broke up similar services across the country. Scottish nobles and gentry now joined Presbyterian Church leaders in their opposition to the king. They had already resented Charles' Act of Revocation in 1625, whereby he quashed many of the titles to church land that they had acquired over the years. He had also withdrawn their hereditary rights to crown offices such as sheriffships. Moreover, they felt isolated from the corridors of power, since they were no longer consulted on matters of Scottish importance. In November 1637, delegates of nobles, gentry and clergy set up a body known as the Tables, which became a rival administration to the Scottish privy council.[55]

Three months later, nobles and clergy signed and issued a manifesto called the National Covenant at Greyfriars Church in Edinburgh. The document reaffirmed

53 J. Kenyon with J. Ohlmeyer, 'The background to the civil wars in the Stuart kingdoms' in Kenyon and Ohlmeyer (eds), *The civil wars*, p. 16. **54** Wheeler, *The Irish and British wars*, pp 12–14. **55** Scott, *Politics and war*, pp 13, 15, 16.

the covenant drafted by Scottish Presbyterians in 1581 to protect the Kirk from innovation, superstition and Roman Catholicism. The signatories pledged themselves to resist the changes recently made by Charles I, and to defend their own religion, their national rights and one another. Within months, the covenant had got the backing of forty thousand signatories from all over Scotland.[56]

The general assembly of the Church of Scotland met in Glasgow in November 1638. The covenanters had manipulated the elections to the assembly, and many nobles and gentry were selected as elders. Despite the efforts of Charles I's personal representative, the marquis of Hamilton, the assembly not only annulled the king's new canons and prayer book, but also deposed the Scottish bishops. Charles and his Scottish subjects were now on a collision course, and war was inevitable. The covenanters began recruiting men and building up supplies at home. They also summoned professional Scottish soldiers, serving in the Swedish armies in the Thirty Years War to return home to defend their country and the covenant. Hundreds responded to the call, and played a key role in training and leading the Scottish army. These included such officers as Field Marshal Alexander Leslie and colonels Alexander Master of Forbes, Alexander Hamilton and Robert Monro. Leslie was made commander-in-chief of the new force.[57]

Not all Scottish veterans of the Swedish armies joined the covenanters' cause. Some, including Sir Frederick Hamilton, remained loyal to the king. It is not at all surprising that Sir Frederick took this stand. He had, after all, been granted his estates in Leitrim by Charles' father, James I. He was also a British courtier in regular attendance on a king who had bestowed on him quite a number of favours since the beginning of his reign. In addition, it was to be expected that he would side with that other Scottish veteran of the Thirty Years War, his patron, the marquis of Hamilton, who was a key player in the king's confrontation with the covenanters.

King Charles planned a four-fold attack on Scotland in what became known as the First Bishops' War in 1639. His main army would assemble in the north of England near Newcastle, from where they would cross the Scottish border and advance on Edinburgh. The marquis of Hamilton intended to land a fleet carrying five thousand men in the Firth of Forth. These would then link up with local anti-covenanter forces in the north-east led by the earl of Huntley. The navy was to transport an army led by Randal MacDonnell, earl of Antrim, from Ulster to western Scotland. Finally, Lord Deputy Wentworth would send a force of five hundred men to garrison Carlisle, the chief English border fortress on the west coast.[58]

56 Donaldson, *Scotland: James V to James VII*, pp 313–16. 57 R. Greenwood, 'Colonel William "Blowface" Forbes: a Scot who fought for parliament in Yorkshire during the first English Civil War' (unpublished paper, 2005), pp 96–8. 58 Kenyon with Ohlmeyer, 'The background to the civil wars in the Stuart kingdoms', p. 17.

Sir Frederick Hamilton demonstrated his loyalty to the king by participating in two of these ventures. He himself was a member of the special group of mounted privy chambermen appointed to guard the king's person during the hostilities. They set about their task on 27 March 1639 when they escorted the king on his journey northwards from London. Hamilton also provided a number of soldiers from his company in the standing army in Ireland for the five hundred-strong detachment that Wentworth sent to reinforce Carlisle.[59]

In the event, much of Charles' grand strategy to defeat the covenanters failed to materialize. The earl of Antrim had neither money nor men to raise an Ulster army for an attack on western Scotland. The marquis of Hamilton was unable to land his force on the north-east coast because the covenanters had already subdued most of the local royal sympathizers. Although Wentworth did send men to garrison Carlisle, he was unable to provide any more troops for an invasion of western Scotland. In May he had stationed half of the army in Ireland in Ulster to ensure that all Scots there took the 'black oath', disassociating themselves from the rebellious activities of the covenanters. He could not afford to relax his grip on that province.[60]

Charles was now totally dependent on his main army of twenty thousand men for an invasion of Scotland. This force was, however, quite undisciplined and lacked training. Moreover, its officers had inadequate military experience. When confronted by Leslie's covenanter army just inside the Scottish border on 3 June 1639, a section of the royal army retreated. Leslie then advanced to within five miles of the royal camp. Fearing defeat, Charles' nobles advised him against engaging in battle. The king had little alternative but to negotiate with the covenanters. In the Pacification of Berwick that followed, the Scots consented to disband their army provided the king did likewise, and that he agreed to attend meetings of the Scottish parliament and the general assembly. When many of the covenanter leaders refused to meet with the king in Berwick in July, Charles decided that it would be pointless to attend either parliament or assembly. So, accompanied by his privy chamber guard, he returned to London.[61]

The general assembly of the Church of Scotland met in August 1639. After once again rejecting the king's canons and prayer book, it now abolished the office of bishop in the Kirk. When the covenanter-dominated Scottish parliament ratified the decrees of the assembly the following month, it became obvious that a Second Bishops' War was inevitable. Charles recalled Lord Deputy Wentworth from Ireland to be his chief advisor in London. He devised a strategy consisting

---

59 *CSPD, 1638–39*, pp 377–8; Parliamentary Archives, HL/PO/JO/10/1/47, petition of Sir Frederick Hamilton to the House of Lords, 14 Jan. 1641; *Another extract of severall letters*, p. 17. **60** D. Stevenson, *Scottish covenanters and Irish Confederates* (Belfast, 1981), p. 18. **61** See Wheeler, *The Irish and British*

of a multi-pronged attack on Scotland, broadly similar to that planned in the first war. A main royalist army of twenty-three thousand men would invade Scotland from Berwick. A naval force would attack the Firth of Forth on the east coast, and troops from Ireland would invade western Scotland. This time, however, the military force from Ireland would be much more dependable, as it would consist of a new army of ten thousand men raised by Wentworth himself.[62]

It quickly became obvious to Wentworth that the substantial amounts of money required to finance the armies in England and Ireland could not be raised by the king from existing taxes. He therefore convinced Charles to convene parliaments that could then be persuaded to vote subsidies to fund the military ventures in both countries. The Irish parliament met in March 1640. Wentworth, who had recently been created earl of Strafford and lord lieutenant of Ireland, soon prevailed upon it to grant four subsidies totalling £180,000 to fund a new Irish army for the king against the Scots. He then set out for England to manage the parliament in London, which was due to convene one month later. He hoped it would provide twelve subsidies, amounting to £720,000 to finance the king's war preparations in England. In his opening address to parliament, Charles made a dramatic appeal for immediate support on the grounds that the covenanters had already sought assistance from Louis XIII of France. The House of Commons, however, resolved not to provide any money until it had first discussed its grievances with the king over his imposition of unlawful taxes and religious reforms in England. Some MPs were also in sympathy with the defiant stand that the covenanters were making against the king. Charles was forced to dissolve this Short Parliament after only three weeks, in order to prevent the Commons from petitioning him to come to terms with the Scots. He would now have to raise an English army at his own expense.[63]

Meanwhile in Ireland, preparations were already being made for the mobilization of Wentworth's new army. It would consist of ten regiments of foot and three of horse. Eleven of the regiments would be raised in Ireland, with the remaining two recruited in England. James Butler, earl of Ormond, a protégé of Wentworth, was appointed commander-in-chief. The Irish privy council decided that normal religious tests for the army should not apply. Officers were generally Protestant, but sometimes included members of landowning Catholic families of Old English and native Irish backgrounds. Most of the common soldiers, though, were Catholic. Recruitment was voluntary, but captains probably formed their companies from tenants and men on neighbouring estates. One thousand soldiers were drawn from the standing army to form a nucleus of experienced officers and

---

wars, pp 22–5. **62** See ibid., pp 26–7. **63** Gillespie, *Seventeenth-century Ireland*, pp 124–7; A. Clarke, 'The breakdown of authority, 1640–41' in Moody et al. (eds), *A new history of Ireland, iii*, pp 270–5.

men in every regiment. Despite his differences with Wentworth, Sir Frederick Hamilton was one of the captains from the standing army who offered his services for the new royal force being 'raised for the intended invasion of Scotland'. Sir Frederick's company was placed in Colonel John Butler's regiment, which was raised mainly in Leinster and Munster. Another captain in the same regiment happened to be Rory Maguire of Fermanagh. Sir Frederick's brother, George, was in charge of a company assigned to Sir Henry Bruce's regiment, which was raised in Connacht. John Waldron, Hamilton's neighbour in Leitrim and court adversary, became a lieutenant in a second Connacht regiment under Sir Charles Coote. It was originally intended that the army should be ready by May 1640, but the necessary finance was delayed. As a result, the entire force only began to assemble in Carrickfergus in Co. Antrim in July. It still needed some further training, though, before it was ready for battle.[64]

Charles I did manage to mobilize a royal army in England. The fact that he used conscription to levy his force resulted in many of his soldiers being untrained and undisciplined misfits. They marched slowly northwards, assembling at Selby in Yorkshire in July. From there, a substantial detachment under Viscount Conway proceeded towards Berwick, just south of the Scottish border.

The covenanters, who were far more united and committed than the English, had also moved with much greater speed. In June and July 1640, they sent Robert Monro and the earl of Argyll to crush royalist opposition in the Highlands, before it could be properly organized. This greatly reduced the possibility of a rising by Scottish supporters of the king, in the event of an English invasion. Argyll was also commissioned to defend the west coast of Scotland against a possible attack from Ireland. Alexander Leslie was once again given command of the main army of about twenty thousand men. Rather than wait for the English to attack, he decided on this occasion to invade England. The Scots crossed the border at Coldstream on 20 August. Skirting Berwick, they headed south to Newburn. Here, they were confronted by Conway's troops, who, after suffering several hundred casualties, fled in panic. Within a week of the Battle of Newburn, Leslie's army had also taken Newcastle and Durham. The covenanters now controlled London's coal supply and held a secure base in northern England. On the advice of a council of his nobles, Charles agreed to call a truce. The Scots insisted on remaining in occupation of England's northern counties until a proper peace treaty was concluded. Moreover, they demanded that the king pay £850 a day for the maintenance of their army there. Charles was forced to accept the covenanters' terms at an armistice signed at Ripon in October 1640.[65]

64 Bodl. MS Carte 1, fos 181–187v: a list of the officers of the army for my lord of Ormond, Aprill the 23rd 1640.   **65** Kenyon with Ohlmeyer, 'The background to the civil wars in the Stuart kingdoms', pp 23–6.

The covenanters' clever campaign in both Scotland and England during the summer of 1640 prevented Wentworth's new Irish army from taking any part in the Second Bishops' War. By cutting out any potential royalist opposition in the Highlands, by policing the west coast of Scotland and especially by capturing Dumbarton Castle near Glasgow on 27 August, they made certain there could be no successful invasion of Scotland by troops from Ireland. In addition, by decisively invading England and defeating the royal army so quickly, they ensured that the war was over before the Irish troops were ready to come to the king's assistance. But it is doubtful, even if the Irish army had been ready to engage in battle, whether there were adequate funds to provide for its transportation across the North Channel. In the end, Wentworth's army remained on in Carrickfergus until its disbandment in May 1641, following the Treaty of London between Charles and the covenanters. Sir Frederick Hamilton had left the Antrim seaport six months earlier. After entrusting his company to his lieutenant, he set out for London where he had more important business to attend to.[66]

ACTIVE INVOLVEMENT IN WENTWORTH'S DOWNFALL

Having failed to get loans from abroad, Charles was forced at the end of September 1640 to call another English parliament. He hoped it would provide him with the money required to pay the covenanters until a peace treaty could be negotiated. He also needed funds to maintain his own army in Yorkshire.

The Long Parliament, which was to last for almost twenty years, met amid much disquiet and civil unrest. The king's supporters had lost heavily at the polls and a strong opposition emerged in the Commons, led by the Puritan, John Pym. Puritans were followers of the Calvinistic doctrines, but who remained members of the Church of England. They were opposed to the ever-increasing interference of the king in religious matters, and took issue with the power of the bishops. They disagreed fundamentally with many of Archbishop Laud's doctrines and reforms, such as the importance he attributed to free will, as against their own belief in predestination, in the matter of salvation. They were sympathetic towards the Scots covenanters, with whom they shared many similar doctrines, and whom they regarded as defenders of their own rights and liberties against the king. Right from the early days of the Long Parliament, Pym and the Puritans were in collusion with the covenanters, whose army in northern England helped strengthen their hand against the king.[67]

---

66 T.L. Coonan, *The Irish Catholic Confederacy and the Puritan revolution* (Dublin, 1954), p. 57.   67 D. Scott, *Politics and war*, p. 25.

Rather than deal with parliamentary grievances or fiscal matters in the early sessions of parliament, Pym and his followers concentrated on warning their fellow members of a popish plot to destroy Protestantism in England. The king, Laud and the Anglican bishops were all conspirators in that plot because their reforms had brought the Church of England much closer to Catholicism. Only the 'godly', as the Puritans described themselves, remained to oppose such a move. Rather than attack the king directly, the Puritans decided that the best way to achieve their aims was to remove Laud, one of the king's evil counsellors. Within a short time he was accused of treason, and some months later committed to the Tower of London.[68]

Pym was even more trenchant in his criticism of the other evil counsellor, Sir Thomas Wentworth, earl of Strafford, who had led the king astray. He denounced him as the 'greatest promoter of tyranny that any age hath produced'. Wentworth, he alleged, had deprived Englishmen of both their property and their freedom. Moreover, he had recruited an army of Irish Catholics to subdue the king's opponents, and root out Protestantism, in England and Scotland. Pym called for Wentworth's impeachment on a charge of high treason. The lord deputy was arrested and imprisoned in the Tower, while a case against him was being prepared in parliament.[69]

Pym knew that it would be difficult to convict Wentworth of a single act of treason, even if he could prove that the lord deputy had actually intended to land his Irish army in England. So he decided instead to use a combination of several of Wentworth's policies and actions to demonstrate his intention to 'subvert the fundamental laws and government of the realms of England and Ireland', and to usurp royal power. As Wentworth had exercised power in England for only one year, his service in Ireland would have to form the main basis of charges against him. Therefore Pym had to depend largely on the lord deputy's opponents in Ireland to testify against him. The first such person to denounce Wentworth was Sir John Clotworthy, a Puritan planter in Co. Antrim. Clotworthy had been a member of the 1634 Irish parliament, but now sat in the English House of Commons. He strongly condemned the high-handed nature of Wentworth's government, and also referred to the lord deputy's pro-Catholic rule in Ireland, as evidenced by the Catholicism of the new Irish army.[70]

A committee, representative of both Catholics and Protestants in the Irish parliament, provided more compelling evidence when it presented a list of grievances against Wentworth's administration in the English House of Commons in

---

68 See Coonan, *The Irish Catholic Confederacy and the Puritan revolution*, p. 65.   **69** Wheeler, *The Irish and British wars*, pp 39–40.   **70** Rushworth, *The tryal of Thomas, earl of Strafford*, p. 8; see also Clarke, 'The breakdown of authority, 1640–41', pp 279–82; H. Kearney, *Strafford in Ireland, 1633–41: a study in*

late November 1640. These included the lord deputy's denial of the Graces, his extrajudicial rulings, his cruel treatment of the British inhabitants of Derry and his prohibition on travel without licence from Ireland to England. Sensing that the occasion was timely, Sir Frederick Hamilton now brought before the Commons four charges against Wentworth 'showing the unjust proceedings of the Lord lieutenant' against him. He accused Wentworth of making unlawful extrajudicial rulings in favour of some of his fellow settlers and tenants – the Hansards, Tirlagh O'Michan, Evelyn Lynch, John Waldron and James Witherspin – with whom he was in dispute over land. He also cited the lord deputy's ban on his freedom of passage from Ireland to England. The Commons found in favour of Hamilton on several counts and by the end of December had not only lifted his travel restriction, but also put a stay on the lord deputy's ruling that obliged him to pay a substantial amount of money to the widow Lynch for the non-renewal of her lease, and ordered that the Lifford estate be taken from the Hansards and held in trust by three independent gentlemen.[71]

During the months of January and February 1641, the Irish parliament provided further material for the articles of impeachment against Wentworth. At the lord deputy's trial, which began on 22 March, seventeen of the twenty-eight charges against him related to his government of Ireland. The witnesses who testified against him were former government officials and New English settlers such as the earl of Cork, Lord Mountnorris, Lord Wilmot, Viscount Loftus and other Protestant 'men of quality' whom Wentworth had alienated during the course of his lord deputyship in Ireland. Sir Frederick Hamilton was one of those 'men of quality' who testified at the trial. He repeated his evidence that the lord deputy had prevented him from travelling to England to appeal to the king. Wentworth, in his defence, admitted that he had done so, but claimed that he was acting on the king's orders. As soon as Sir Frederick had threatened to complain to the king, he successfully appealed to Charles to let Hamilton make the journey. Sir Frederick was not content to confine his involvement in the trial to his own testimony. He procured – for the second time in four years – a bill of attorney from his father-in-law, Sir John Vaughan, authorizing him on this occasion to present evidence for Vaughan against Wentworth in the 'high and honourable Court of Parliament'. There is, however, no record to show that he was ever given the opportunity to speak for Vaughan at the trial.[72]

Despite the numerous charges made against him, Wentworth was able to successfully refute most of them. He pointed out that even if they were true, his

---

absolutism (Cambridge, 1959), p. 200.   **71** Rushworth, *The tryal of Thomas, earl of Strafford*, pp 11–13; *The several petitions of William Hansard and Sir Frederick Hammiltoun*, p. 3; Jansson, *Proceedings in the opening session of the Long Parliament*, i, pp 654, 657.   **72** Rushworth, *The tryal of Thomas, earl of Strafford*, pp 26–7; PRONI, D580/1, Sir John Vaughan's power of attorney to Sir Frederick Hamilton, 9 Apr. 1641.

alleged offences were actions carried out lawfully in the service of the king. Even the most serious accusation of his having plotted to use the Irish army in England, could not be substantiated by a second witness. In desperation, the English parliament was forced to abandon the impeachment procedure and attaint the lord deputy instead. This meant that parliament could vote to condemn him as a traitor, with no evidence beyond the belief that he was guilty. On 19 April, the Commons voted by 204 to 59 for Wentworth's attainder. Within three weeks, the House of Lords had done likewise, though by a very slim majority. The bill received reluctant royal assent on 10 May and Wentworth was executed on Tower Hill two days later.[73]

The king never forgave the parliamentarians and others who were involved in Wentworth's trial. Sir Frederick Hamilton later admitted that he was 'in some disfavour with His Majesty for prosecuting the earl of Strafford'. Nevertheless, it seems certain that he would have agreed with Richard Boyle, the earl of Cork, that Wentworth's execution was 'well deserved'. The lord deputy had been a thorn in his side ever since Wentworth first landed in Ireland. He had, in Hamilton's opinion, made harsh judgments against him, imposed unlawful restrictions upon him, denied his legitimate pay claims and publicly humiliated him. Sir Frederick now hoped to consolidate his position and estates in Leitrim, Donegal and Mayo, which had been adversely affected by the activities of the late lord deputy. He could not have known that there would be a much more deadly assault of a very different nature directed against himself and the other British settlers in Ireland within a matter of months.[74]

73 Gillespie, *Seventeenth-century Ireland*, p. 130.   74 *The information of Sir Frederick Hammilton*, p. 31;
The several petitions of William Hansard and Sir Frederick Hammiltoun, p. 4.

CHAPTER SIX

Rebellion, reprisals and early Confederate War, October 1641–September 1643

EVENTS LEADING UP TO THE 1641 REBELLION

In 1641 the native Irish gentry in Ulster were descendants of those who had supported the English during the Nine Years War. Their grandfathers and fathers had been rewarded with lands and pensions in the Ulster Plantation, and had passed on their property and wealth to their offspring. The present generation was still Catholic, but had otherwise integrated quite successfully with the British settlers, sometimes even through intermarriage. They also participated widely in local government and the administration of justice at county level. Despite their integration and achievements, many of the native Ulster gentry were unhappy with the way they had been treated by Lord Deputy Wentworth and the British authorities in Ireland.[1]

They held Wentworth responsible for the difficult economic circumstances in which they found themselves in the early 1640s. It is true that, like other landlords throughout the country, they had to endure an examination by the lord deputy into the validity of their land titles, and to submit to the payment of fines, dues and increased rents arising from his Commission for Defective Titles and Court of Wards. However, their difficulties were compounded by the fact that they themselves were often improvident and spendthrift, and unable to adjust to the British economic system, which was based on the exchange of money and centred on markets. To make matters worse, they were unable to recover rents from their tenants because of a series of bad harvests in the late 1630s and early 1640s, which affected all parts of the country, but Ulster in particular. As a result, many of them now found themselves heavily in debt and were forced to sell or mortgage substantial parts of their property to British settlers or Dublin speculators.[2]

The native Ulster gentry were also aggrieved by rumours of the imposition of anti-Catholic measures and by threats of physical force to be used against Irish

---

1 See P.J. Corish, 'The rising of 1641 and the Catholic confederacy, 1641–5' in Moody et al. (eds), *A new history of Ireland, iii*, p. 289; R. Gillespie, 'The end of an era: Ulster and the outbreak of the 1641 rising' in Brady and Gillespie (eds), *Natives and newcomers*, pp 193–4.   2 Kenyon with Ohlmeyer, 'The background to the civil wars in the Stuart kingdoms', p. 30; see also Gillespie, *Seventeenth-century Ireland*, pp 139–40; B. MacCuarta, 'Introduction' in B. MacCuarta (ed.), *Ulster 1641: aspects of the rising* (Belfast, 1993), pp 2–3.

Catholics. During Wentworth's term of office in Ireland, Catholics had been allowed to practise their religion fairly freely, although anti-recusancy legislation still remained on the statute book. However, when the Puritan lords justices, Parsons and Borlase, replaced him in February 1641, there were reports of a likely anti-Catholic clampdown. There were also fears of what religious constraints the Puritan-dominated Long Parliament in London might introduce in both England and Ireland. In addition, there was some alarm at the prospect of a covenanter army arriving from Scotland to forcefully impose Presbyterianism on Irish Catholics, following its success against King Charles in the Bishops' Wars. This was all happening at a time when increasing numbers of Continentally trained Franciscans and diocesan clergy were spearheading a reorganization and revival of the Catholic religion in Ireland. These priests were unhappy with the level of religious tolerance permitted in Ireland, and would certainly have strongly expressed their views to influential members of their flock.[3]

Although several of the Ulster native gentry were active members of the Irish parliament of 1640–1, they felt politically ineffective and sometimes marginalized. While two of them were involved in unsuccessful attempts to impeach Lord Chancellor Bolton, a supporter of Wentworth, early in 1641, none of their group had been selected on the committee sent to England the previous November to present the Irish parliament's grievances to Charles I. They also shared the frustration felt by many MPs in Ireland at the little progress made to win greater autonomy for the Irish parliament in the spring of 1641. Their disillusionment was complete when the lords justices prorogued parliament the following August, before it could ratify some of the Graces that had finally been sanctioned by the king.[4]

Inspired by the success of the Scots covenanters' armed resistance to royal authority in Britain, a small group of these discontented Ulster Catholic gentry decided to capture Dublin Castle, the seat of Irish government, as well as the principal fortified places, first in Ulster and then throughout the rest of the country, with a view to negotiating a resolution of their grievances from a position of strength. Just as the covenanters had used Scottish officers with military experience in Swedish armies during the Thirty Years War to lead their campaign, so too did the Ulster rebel leaders conspire with some Irish colonels in Spanish Habsburg service, who had returned temporarily to Ireland in May 1641 to recruit soldiers from Wentworth's disbanded army. Several of these officers had become disenchanted with their Continental experience and were now willing to

3 Coonan, *The Irish Catholic Confederacy and the Puritan revolution*, pp 13–16; M. Perceval-Maxwell, 'Ulster 1641 in the context of political developments in the three kingdoms' in MacCuarta (ed.), *Ulster 1641*, p. 103. 4 Clarke, 'The breakdown of authority, 1640–41', p. 280.

fight for freedom of religion and other entitlements for their fellow countrymen at home.[5]

The tightly-knit group of Ulster gentry who plotted the 1641 rebellion comprised prominent landowners and members of parliament. Several of them were related to one another. Notable among the conspirators were the young Maguire brothers. Conor, Lord Enniskillen, then aged twenty-four, had an estate of thirty thousand acres, but was heavily in debt. His brother, Rory, two years his junior, was MP for Fermanagh and had been a captain in the same regiment as Sir Frederick Hamilton in Wentworth's Irish army. He had recently married Deborah Blennerhassett, the daughter and widow of wealthy local planters. The Maguires were nephews of Owen Roe O'Neill, who would return to Ulster from the Spanish Netherlands in July 1642 to take overall command of the Irish insurgents. Sir Phelim O'Neill of Kinard, or Caledon, Co. Tyrone, was MP for Dungannon and a justice of the peace. A kinsman of Owen Roe, he owned substantial estates in Tyrone and Armagh, but was now in financial difficulty, having mortgaged lands for £13,000 to individuals in Dublin and London and locally. Philip MacHugh O'Reilly was MP for Cavan and had been sheriff of that county some years earlier. He was a brother-in-law of Owen Roe O'Neill and thus an uncle by marriage of the Maguires. Rory O'More, a descendant of the former lords of Laois, was an army officer who owned lands in Armagh and Kildare. Colla MacBrian MacMahon had been an MP for Monaghan in the 1634 parliament, while his kinsman, Hugh, was a justice of the peace. Mulmore O'Reilly was sheriff of Cavan and Turlough Oge O'Neill, a brother of Sir Phelim, held a similar position in Tyrone.[6]

The first proposal to stage a rising was made by Rory O'More to Lord Maguire in February 1641, with the aim of trying to prevent further intrusion on Catholic lands and rights. No further action was taken at that stage, although the pair remained in contact. A second plot was instigated by recruiter colonels such as Bryan O'Neill, Hugh MacPhelim O'Byrne and Richard Plunkett in the summer. When the English parliament halted the levying of men from Wentworth's disbanded army for the service of Catholic Spain in July, these officers, plus thousands of former ordinary soldiers, were at a loose end in the country. The colonels contemplated taking Dublin Castle with its arsenal of arms and ammunition, but once again the plan came to nothing. In August, however, a third plot emerged when some of the colonels approached O'More and Maguire. These were soon joined by Sir Phelim O'Neill and the other native Ulster MPs when the Irish parliament was prorogued. For a time, the plot seemed to merge

5 N. Canny, *Making Ireland British, 1580–1650* (Oxford, 2001), pp 469–71.   6 McGrath, 'A biographical dictionary', pp 205–6, 230–2.

with secret manoeuvres by the earls of Ormond and Antrim to reassemble Wentworth's army and use it to secure Dublin for the king. In the end, the Ulster leaders and the colonels decided to go their own way, and on 5 October in Glaslough, Co. Monaghan, final plans were agreed to fix the rising for the 23rd of that month.[7]

THE OUTBREAK IN ULSTER

The northern leaders and colonels realized that, due to a lack of arms and ammunition, the element of surprise was essential if their plans to take Dublin Castle and the principal Ulster strongholds were to succeed. In the event, the attempt to seize Dublin Castle failed because the plot was revealed to the lords justices by Owen O'Connolly, a foster-brother of Hugh MacMahon, one of the insurgent leaders, on the eve of the rebellion. O'Connolly was opposed to the rising as he was a tenant of the English settler, Sir John Clotworthy, and a convert to Protestantism. Lord Maguire, MacMahon and other leaders in Dublin were apprehended and the castle's garrison was reinforced. Meanwhile, the rebellion in Ulster had been put in jeopardy by Bryan Maguire of Tempo, a cousin of Lord and Rory Maguire, who informed Sir William Cole, governor of Enniskillen, of the plot on the 10th and 21st of October. Cole seems to have taken little action, however, beyond strengthening his own position in Enniskillen. As a result, the rising came as a total surprise to the British authorities and settlers in the province. Even Audley Mervyn, MP for Tyrone, whose sister, Deborah, was married to Rory Maguire, later wrote that 'the suddennesse of our surprisall, and the nature of it, was so unexpected that the inhabitants could scarcely believe themselves prisoners, though in their chains'. William Skelton, a tenant of Sir Phelim O'Neill, was also amazed, since, before the rebellion, natives and settlers 'differed not in anything … save only that the Irish went to mass and the English to the Protestant church'. The Ulster settlers were thus caught unawares by the speedy capture of many of their castles and garrisons in the first few days of the rising.[8]

The seizure, by stealth, of Charlemont Fort in Co. Armagh and Dungannon Castle in Co. Tyrone by Sir Phelim O'Neill and his kinsmen on the evening of 22 October signalled the outbreak of the rebellion in Ulster. Senior figures of the O'Reillys, MacMahons, Maguires, O'Hagans, Quinns and O'Hanlons led the revolt in their own areas, and within days the main strongholds and towns in the

---

7 Wheeler, *The Irish and British wars*, p. 45; Stevenson, *Scottish covenanters and Irish Confederates*, pp 40–1. **8** *The information of Sir Frederick Hammilton*, pp 1, 3, 4, 22–5; Lord E. Hamilton, *The Irish rebellion of 1641* (London, 1920), pp 143–5, 185–6; P. Ó Gallachair, 'The 1641 war in Clogher', *Clogher Record*, 4:3 (1962), 138–9; R. Gillespie, 'Destabilizing Ulster, 1641–2' in Mac Cuarta (ed.), *Ulster 1641*, p. 110.

centre of the province had been taken. By the end of November, most of Tyrone, South Derry, Armagh, West Down, Monaghan, Cavan and Fermanagh were in the hands of the rebels. Significantly, however, important seaports such as Derry, Coleraine, Carrickfergus, Donegal and Ballyshannon, as well as inland towns like Enniskillen, Newtownstewart, Raphoe and Lisburn, all remained in settler control. After the first month or so, the insurgents made few further gains in Ulster. Nevertheless, the Catholic Old English gentry of the Pale joined the rebellion in early December, and, by the summer of 1642, most parts of the country were in open revolt.[9]

At the outbreak of the rebellion, the Ulster leaders had ordered,

> upon pain of death, that no Scotch man should be stirred in body, goods or lands, and that they should to this purpose write over the lintels of their doores that they were Scotch men, and so destruction might passe over their families.

By exempting the Scots from attack and, in some instances, by appealing to their common Celtic ancestry, the insurgents aimed at seeking their support for the rising, or at least reducing their opposition to it. In the first few weeks, this strategy seems to have been partially successful. Although some Scottish settlers played an active role in combating the rebels, there were numerous reports of Scots in several counties who refused to assist English refugees, allowing them to be robbed, stripped or killed by the Irish. It was also alleged that they handed over English settlers to the rebels, and even joined with the latter in attacking the English. Within a month or so, as the rebellion turned more violent, and as the Scots realized that the revolt was more or less confined to Ulster and that Dublin Castle was still in government hands, they took a more united stand with their English neighbours. In fact, the decision by the insurgents to initially exempt the Scots from attack backfired, as it allowed many of them a sufficient reprieve to prepare themselves for an Irish assault when it eventually did come.[10]

Sir Phelim O'Neill and the other Ulster leaders found it hard to maintain control of their own followers almost from the beginning. Few of them had any military training and their overall command structure was weak. Once they were seen to be challenging the political and social order in the province, their example was quickly followed by many of the lower Irish who had motives and grievances of their own. These ranged from a sense of envy at the apparent wealth of their Protestant neighbours in these difficult economic times to an opportunity to

9 Wheeler, *The Irish and British wars*, p. 46.   10 D.M. Schlegel, 'A Clogher chronology: October 1641 to July 1642', *Clogher Record*, 16:1 (1997), 85.

settle local scores. At first, the violence consisted of robberies, beatings, lootings and expulsions, but as the settlers resisted, it degenerated into torture and murder. A number of gruesome atrocities took place at Portadown, Clones, Belturbet, and Lisgoole and Tully in Co. Fermanagh, where sometimes as many as one hundred defenceless civilians, including women and children, were drowned, burned alive, hanged or put to the sword. In all, as many as twelve thousand settlers perished in the first few months of the rising. One third of them were murdered, while the rest died from cold and exposure during the very harsh winter. Many of them fled to various centres of refuge, including Dublin, where depositions of their terrifying experiences were recorded. Allied to the strong anti-British sentiments that inspired these expulsions and killings was an antipathy towards all things Protestant. Bibles and prayer books were torn up and desecrated. Protestants were refused burial in consecrated ground and ministers were often singled out for particularly violent treatment.[11]

The initial British response to the rebellion in Ulster was mixed. King Charles, who was then in Scotland trying to win support from the covenanters in his difficulties with the English parliament, immediately requested the Scottish parliament to send troops to quell the rising. He himself dispatched 1,500 fighting men as well as arms and ammunition to the beleaguered settlers. Before returning to London in mid-November, he also appointed James Butler, earl of Ormond, lieutenant general of the British army in Ireland, and signed commissions authorizing a number of prominent Ulster landlords to raise regiments as a charge on the state. The Scottish parliament, which was suspicious of the king's motives, was much slower in reacting to news of the rebellion. It did offer to send troops to Ulster, but only if the English parliament requested them. Otherwise, it felt it could not intervene as Ireland was an English dependency. When the Long Parliament in London eventually agreed to finance such an expedition, the Scots sent ten thousand men to Ulster between April and August 1642. The Long Parliament, then involved in a growing power struggle with the king, was also rather tardy in sending English reinforcements to deal with the crisis. Initially, it dispatched arms and powder from Carlisle to Ireland. However, after having secured reluctant royal approval, it succeeded in shipping twelve thousand men mainly to Dublin, between 30 December 1641 and June 1642. Meanwhile, the lords justices in Dublin had organized that city's defences and sent Ormond and Sir Charles Coote on indiscriminate punitive expeditions in the Pale. They were unable to provide any practical help to the embattled Ulster settlers, however, beyond sending commissions to some landlords to raise troops at local level.[12]

11 See M. Elliott, *The Catholics of Ulster* (London, 2000), pp 100–1.   **12** I. Ryder, *An English army for Ireland* (Leigh-on-Sea, 1987), pp 5–19.

In the early months of the rebellion, then, it was left up to individual settler landlords to organize themselves as best they could. In western Ulster, Sir William and Sir Robert Stewart – both Scottish veterans of the Thirty Years War – set up the Laggan force from among their tenants, neighbouring settlers and refugees. They also got strong backing from Sir William Cole of Enniskillen and Sir Ralph Gore of Ballyshannon. In the east of the province, Lords Montgomery and Chichester took the initiative in assembling similar corps. Once they had recovered from the initial shock of the insurrection, such military groups prevented rebel attempts from capturing vital seaport towns and inland strongholds. From many of their besieged garrisons, they sallied forth to rout the attackers, carry out cattle raids and conduct scorched-earth campaigns. They often engaged in brutal treatment of Irish prisoners and civilians, as well as in retaliatory massacres such as those at Templepatrick and Islandmagee in Co. Antrim and in the Mourne mountains in Co. Down. By the spring of 1642, such gratuitous violence had become a commonplace occurrence on both the Irish and the British sides.[13]

THE REBELLION QUICKLY SPREADS TO LEITRIM

The principal native Irish gentry in Leitrim in 1641 belonged to the former ruling Dromahair branch of the O'Rourkes. Their fathers or grandfathers had been 'civil men' who had sided with the English authorities during the rebellion of Sir Brian of the Ramparts O'Rourke in 1590. They and their families had been rewarded with substantial grants of land during the plantation of Leitrim, in recognition of their services to the state. Like the native Ulster gentry, the O'Rourkes had integrated well with the British settlers and were participating in local government. Some of them were also heavily in debt by 1641. In the north of the county, the three sons of Tiernan Bán O'Rourke, the former loyal tánaiste, were the most prominent family representatives. The eldest son, Owen Mór lived in Kilcoosy, near Corrigeencor Lake, but also owned lands in southwest Sligo, where his wife, Mary O'Connor, widow of Rory MacSweeney, came from. The second son, Con, owned seven hundred profitable acres in Glencar, and had a thousand acres more in the same area mortgaged to the English planter, Robert Parke of Newtown. Con had acquired Castle Car, the former residence of another branch of the O'Rourkes, and in the early months of 1641 was appointed sheriff of the county. The youngest son, Brian Ballagh, lived in Newtownmanor, but also

---

13 The Laggan force got its name from the Laggan Valley, which lies between Lough Swilly and Lough Foyle, in the barony of Raphoe in Co. Donegal: K. McKenny, *The Laggan army in Ireland, 1640–1685* (Dublin, 2005), p. 40.

owned land around Belhavel Lake, south of Killargy village. Tadhg O'Rourke was another member of the family who had not supported Brian of the Ramparts' rebellion. By 1641, his grandson, Con MacDonnell O'Rourke, owned eight hundred acres of profitable land in Cloone parish in south Leitrim. Other significant Leitrim gentry were members of different branches of the O'Rourkes, as well as the Mac Clancys, Reynolds, MacMorrows, MacTernans, MacConsnamhas, Mac Loughlins, Mac Shanleys, O'Morans and O'Mulveys.[14]

Conor Lord Maguire and his brother Rory were responsible for drawing the O'Rourkes and the other Leitrim gentry into the rebellion. Before his arrest in Dublin on 22 October, Lord Maguire had written to Owen Mór and Con MacDonnell O'Rourke 'to go on with the plot in those parts'. Rory Maguire was more specific in his directions. He sent word to both O'Rourkes to attack and burn Sir Charles Coote's ironworks at Arigna, on the Roscommon–Leitrim border, and Creevelea, east of Killargy. It is likely that he also prompted the MacMorrows and the MacLoughlins to assist the O'Flannagans of Fermanagh in destroying the ironworks at Garrison on the Fermanagh–Leitrim border, even though these were owned by the Scotsman, Sir John Dunbar. Ironworks became a particular target of the rebels in various parts of the country, since iron was frequently used to make weapons, and those employed in the ironworks were generally Englishmen. On Sunday 24 October, Owen Mór and Con MacDonnell O'Rourke who, as the senior native leaders in the north and south of the county respectively, became colonels of the local insurgents, assembled their followers and destroyed Coote's ironworks. They then proceeded to rob the eighty English workers who were forced to flee for safety to the garrison towns of Jamestown and Carrick-on-Shannon. The same day, the O'Flannagans, MacMorrows and MacLoughlins set fire to the works at Garrison and attacked and robbed the tradesmen. These, together with their families, numbering 150 persons in all, quickly made their way to Manorhamilton, seven miles distant. All were given refuge in the castle by Sir Frederick Hamilton's wife, Sidney.[15]

Hamilton kept his own personal record of the events that followed over the next two years in Manorhamilton and the surrounding area. He later directed one of his clerks to transcribe it. On comparison with independent sources, the diary's datings are substantially accurate. Given the lack of corroborated accounts of

14 *CSPI, 1588–92*, p. 464; *Books of survey and distribution for Co. Leitrim* (NAI); Down Survey maps of Co. Leitrim (RIA); Meehan (ed.), 'Catalogue of the high sheriffs of the county Leitrim from 1605 to 1800', 386; Mac Cuarta (ed.), 'Leitrim plantation papers', 134; see also Mac Dermot, *O Ruairc of Breifne*, p. 143. **15** W. Prynn and M. Nudigate, *The whole triall of Connor Lord MacGuire* (London, 1645), p. 18; deposition of Captain Andrew Adair (TCD, MS 831, fos 174–178); McCracken, 'Charcoal-burning ironworks in seventeenth- and eighteenth-century Ireland', 123–33; W.C. Trimble, *The history of Enniskillen* (3 vols, Enniskillen, 1921), i, p. 101.

some of his engagements with Irish rebels, however, as well as Hamilton's tendency to brag, it is important for the reader to keep an open mind regarding the truth of some of his seemingly exaggerated claims.[16]

Sir Frederick himself and his two teenage sons, Frederick and James, were in Derry visiting his father-in-law when the rebellion broke out in Ulster. On Wednesday 27 October, a messenger arrived from Sidney informing him of the events at Garrison and the refugees in Manorhamilton. He decided to return home at once, but before setting out, he wrote a letter to his cousin James, marquis of Hamilton, in Edinburgh, requesting him to use his influence with the king to secure for him a royal commission to raise local troops to suppress any disturbances in Leitrim. Then, accompanied by twelve of his servants, he embarked on the hazardous seventy-five-mile journey back to Manorhamilton. Every man carried a musket and a smouldering cord ready to fire it. Sir Frederick frequently sounded his trumpet, while his servants created as much of a din as possible, trying to give the impression that there were far more than a dozen of them in the party. After riding through the night, they arrived in Donegal town the following morning. There they found Sir Ralph Gore and the local British settlers, who had already been robbed of their cattle, now expecting a rebel attack at any moment.[17]

Against all advice, Hamilton and his servants continued on their journey that same evening, this time with a convoy of twenty Scottish horsemen. They reached Ballyshannon and found the town burned down, with the castle under siege. After dispersing the attackers, Sir Frederick spent some hours helping Captain Folliott, the castle's commander, pursue the rebels. They killed some and took twenty-two prisoners. Hamilton then sent a messenger to his wife requesting an escort for the final stage of his journey home through Belleek, Garrison and Rossinver – 'the most dangerous way in Ireland'. The following day, Friday 29 October, a detachment of his own soldiers and servants arrived from Manorhamilton and accompanied him safely home.[18]

That very evening, Sir Frederick wrote to the most important settler in the general region, the Englishman, Sir William Cole, MP for Fermanagh, provost of Enniskillen town and commander of the strongly fortified castle there. He described the state of affairs in Donegal, outlining his own involvement at Ballyshannon, and assured Cole of any support he could give him in Enniskillen. Cole replied, expressing appreciation of Hamilton's offer of assistance, and bemoaning the fact that some of Sir Frederick's fellow countrymen in Fermanagh were not siding with the English in their hour of need, due to the insurgents'

<hr />

16 *Another extract of severall letters*, p. 16.   **17** Ibid., pp 16–17; NRS, GD 406/1/885.   **18** *Another extract of severall letters*, p. 17.

policy of sparing the Scots. There were obviously tensions between Cole and many Scottish settlers, especially during the first weeks of the rebellion. Hamilton became aware of these when, within days of his return to Manorhamilton, he was contacted by four Scottish neighbours of Cole – Sheriff Adam Cathcart and captains William Acheson, Hugh Rosse and George Greir – all of whom offered their services and those of their companies to Sir Frederick, rather than to the English commander of Enniskillen. Hamilton, however, persuaded all four to return home and assist Cole, so that Co. Fermanagh might not be lost to the rebels.[19]

Following the burning of the ironworks on Sunday 24 October, the rebellion quickly spread to various areas in south Leitrim. In this part of the county, several hundred English settlers were robbed, stripped and issued with an ultimatum to leave their homes or be killed. According to the settlers' subsequent depositions, the instigators of these acts were Colonel Con MacDonnell O'Rourke, other local native gentry and some Catholic clergy. In sharp contrast to such activity, the situation around Manorhamilton and north Leitrim in general remained quiet. Colonel Owen O'Rourke did take possession of his ancestral castle in Dromahair on Thursday 28 October, but only with the full consent of its then English owner, William Parke, brother of Robert who lived in nearby Newtown Castle. Parke and O'Rourke had reportedly agreed that if the rebellion was not successful, Parke should have the castle returned to him, but if the insurgents were victorious, O'Rourke would treat Parke more favourably than any other English settler. On 31 October, Sheriff Con O'Rourke called on Sir Frederick Hamilton to congratulate him on his safe return from Derry, and to assure him of his loyalty. Hamilton received similar expressions of support in letters from Brian Ballagh O'Rourke and Tadhg O'Connor Sligo in the days that followed. The absence of any immediate escalation of the violence that accompanied the burning of the ironworks can, no doubt, be largely explained by the rebel directive not to interfere with the Scots, who made up the majority of the settlers in the northern half of the county. But it may also have been partially due to the willingness of some English settlers such as William Parke and his brother Robert – an important landowner with many business interests – to collaborate to some degree with the rebels, in an attempt to minimize their potential losses.[20]

In the continuing uneasy calm, Sir Frederick Hamilton was delighted when six of his soldiers – 'good musketeers bred with himself' – who had been stationed in Carlisle since the First Bishops' War in 1639, arrived back in Manorhamilton on

---

19 *The information of Sir Frederick Hammilton*, pp 24–6. 20 Ibid., pp 67–70; depositions for Cos Leitrim, Sligo and Mayo (TCD, MSS 830–831); see also D. Mac an Ghallóglaigh, '1641 rebellion in Leitrim', *Breifne*, 2:8 (1966), 441–8.

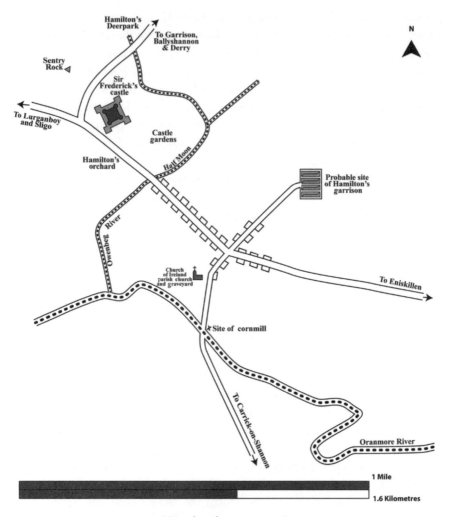

17 Manorhamilton town, *c.*1641.

Saturday 6 November. The following day, he formed a troop of fifty horsemen from among his servants and tenants. From now on, these would patrol the area around his castle and garrison both day and night. He also took the opportunity to write to his immediate superior, Viscount Ranelagh, president of Connacht and commander of the standing army in the province, outlining the weakness of both Manorhamilton (fig. 17) and Sligo town in the event of a rebel attack, and requesting immediate assistance.[21]

21 *Another extract of severall letters*, pp 17–19.

The first indicators of an extension of the violence in the north of the county occurred in mid-November, when two English Protestant clergymen – Mr Bushe and William Browne – were robbed of their possessions. Revd Browne was a tenant of Sir Frederick in Drumlease, near Dromahair. The alleged perpetrators of the crimes were Sheriff Con O'Rourke and his brother, Brian Ballagh. Despite their recent expressions of loyalty, Hamilton had both men arrested and questioned. It would seem, however, that the accusations could not be substantiated, and that both O'Rourkes were released shortly afterwards.[22]

Probably on learning that Sir William Cole had received a commission from the lords justices, as well as one from the king, to raise several new companies of soldiers from among the British settlers of Co. Fermanagh, Sir Frederick Hamilton wrote to Parsons and Borlase on 19 November. He outlined the volatile situation in Leitrim at the time, and requested arms, ammunition and a commission to raise local troops. Not being content, though, to wait for an ideal situation to develop before taking action, he sent a party of his existing company of men the following night to an ale-house in the Garrison area, which was frequented by insurgents from Fermanagh and Donegal. The ale-house keeper and six rebels were arrested and brought back to Manorhamilton, along with sixty head of cattle.[23]

If Hamilton had hoped to prevent the rebellion from spreading to his own estates by launching an attack on the Fermanagh and Donegal insurgents, he was soon to be disappointed. On Wednesday 24 November, none of his Irish tenants appeared at the manor court, which was being presided over by his seneschal. Sir Frederick interpreted their absence as treacherous and as a sign that he had lost their allegiance. His analysis proved to be correct. Hugh MacCahill MacMorrow, his chief Irish tenant, joined up with 'a great body' of Cavan rebels, who marched to within two miles of Hamilton's castle on the last day of November. They captured one English settler, whom they later hanged, and drove away cattle belonging to many of Sir Frederick's British tenants.[24]

Sir Frederick Hamilton wrote once more to the lords justices on 2 December, stressing the serious deterioration of the situation in Leitrim, and again requesting authorization to levy extra troops. He also sent a second letter to James, marquis of Hamilton, who had returned with the king to London in November, expressing his disappointment that the marquis – 'so neare a kinsman' – had not procured a commission for him from the king, like the one that was sent to Sir William Cole the previous month. Two days later, however, realizing that he could no longer trust the native Irish, and despairing of receiving any help from Viscount Ranelagh or the lords justices, he decided to take drastic action

---

22 Ibid., pp 18–20.   **23** Ibid., p. 18; *The information of Sir Frederick Hammilton*, pp 5, 89.   **24** *Another extract of severall letters*, p. 18.

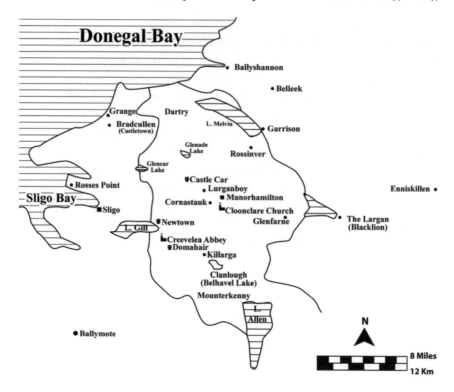

18 Sir Frederick's field of operations, 1641–3.

himself. Having erected a gallows on the little hill beside the castle, he hanged eight of the twenty-four prisoners he had brought to Manorhamilton from Ballyshannon and Garrison. Two of 'the rogues centries', whom his own mounted patrol had discovered in the fields around the castle, soon suffered the same fate. Acting on intelligence, he then sent a party of horsemen to Glenfarne Wood to search for Hugh MacCahill MacMorrow, the ringleader of his 'traiterous' tenants. Three of the rebels were killed, although MacMorrow himself made a narrow escape in the fading light.[25]

The escalating hostilities and the increasing likelihood of all-out warfare, as well as the overcrowded living conditions were also causing tensions within Castle Hamilton itself. Possibly up to two hundred displaced men, women and children were being given refuge there by the end of November. The majority of these belonged to Sir John Dunbar's party from Garrison ironworks. In the first week of December, the Dunbars, allegedly feeling threatened by Sir Frederick, decided to leave Manorhamilton with their workers and families and go to Cole's castle in

25 Ibid., pp 18–19; *The information of Sir Frederick Hammilton*, p. 89; NRS, GD 406/1/885.

Enniskillen. Cole later stated that the group was sent away from Manorhamilton, without either an accompanying convoy of troops to protect them or sufficient food for the journey, and that several of them were killed en route by the Irish. Hamilton insisted that the Dunbars left because there were no longer enough provisions to feed all the refugees in his castle. Moreover, he utterly denied that any Protestants ever left his castle without sufficient supplies and the protection of whatever armed escort he could spare.[26]

In the meantime, events were unfolding in the neighbouring county of Sligo (fig. 18), which were to have a direct impact on the escalation of the rebellion in north Leitrim, and which in turn would result in one of the most notorious massacres of the rebellion taking place in Sligo town itself. Centrally involved were the Catholic gentry of the county, who were drawn from native Irish families such as the O'Connors Sligo, the MacDonaghs and the Creans, but also included the descendants of Old English families of the Pale, like the Taaffes, the Plunketts and the French family, who had acquired land in Sligo. Both groups resented state restrictions limiting the full expression of their religion, as well as the collection of tithes from them by Protestant clergymen. They had also taken exception to the forced acquisition of the heavily mortgaged O'Connor Sligo estate by Wentworth, at a bargain price in 1634, and to the more recent threatened plantation of the county. However, they initially made no move to get involved in rebellion or take out their frustration on the significant number of British settlers that resided in Co. Sligo, even when the disturbances had spread from Ulster to neighbouring Leitrim. On the contrary, at a meeting in Ballysadare in early November, these Catholic gentry resolved to prevent Leitrim rebels from entering Co. Sligo, while at the same time deal with the problem of considerable numbers of disbanded soldiers from Wentworth's Irish army who were attacking and robbing British settlers within the county.[27]

It was only when Sheriff Andrew Crean of Grange called a second meeting of the Sligo Catholic gentry about the 8 December that a decision was taken to join the rebellion. It would seem as if the resolution was largely influenced by the Old English members present, whose associates in the Pale had thrown in their lot with the Ulster insurgents some days previously. After gathering their forces, the Sligo gentry, under the temporary command of Bryan MacDonagh, who was married to a daughter of Viscount Taaffe and had been an officer in Wentworth's Irish army, besieged the two centres of defence in Sligo town – Lady Jones' and O'Crean's castles. The Sligo men were later joined by some Leitrim insurgents

26 *The information of Sir Frederick Hammilton*, pp 6, 12, 40.   **27** *Another extract of severall letters*, pp 52–3; deposition of Edward Braxton (printed in Wood-Martin, *History of Sligo*, ii, pp 197–8); O'Dowd, *Power, politics and land*, pp 53, 89, 103, 112–17.

under the command of Colonel Owen O'Rourke and the MacClancys. Both castles held out for over a week. Sir Frederick Hamilton later alleged that many of the British settlers, who had taken refuge there, lost their lives during the capture of the strongholds, although he may have been referring to an event that took place one month later in Sligo Gaol. Ensign Cotton, who commanded a company of Viscount Ranelagh's regiment in O'Crean's castle, finally agreed to surrender on condition that the besieged in both castles, who wished to leave Sligo, be given safe passage to Boyle. Those who expressed a preference to remain in the town were to be allowed to do so, although they would forfeit half their property. Despite these guarantees, many of the British settlers were robbed of their possessions. The majority were eventually escorted to Boyle, although three or four fled to Manorhamilton for refuge. Those who chose to remain in Sligo were destined to suffer a terrible fate within a matter of weeks.[28]

While the siege of Sligo was in progress, some of the rebel captains there wrote to Sir Frederick Hamilton threatening to destroy him and his castle if he would not submit peacefully. Patrick Plunkett of Markree Castle followed up these messages on 13 December with a personal letter to Sir Frederick's wife, Sidney, to whom he claimed to be related. In it, he attempted to frighten her by mentioning the thirty-five companies of soldiers that the Irish had, or were about to have, in Sligo. These would all march on Manorhamilton, once the castles in Sligo were taken. Judging by Sir Frederick's response to a similar letter from Tadhg O'Connor Sligo some weeks later, it is likely that on this occasion also the Hamiltons completely disregarded the threats.[29]

Shortly after the arrival of Plunkett's letter, Sir Frederick had to deal with a more immediate problem almost on his doorstep. Thomas Abercromy, one of his nearest planter neighbours and fellow Scotsman, sent word to him on 15 December that he had heard that Manorhamilton Castle was soon to be attacked by the insurgents from Leitrim and surrounding counties. Consequently, he and his wife and family were going to take refuge with Sheriff Con O'Rourke in nearby Castle Car, where he was assured that they would be looked after, until provided with safe passage out of the area. Abercromy, a former sheriff of the county himself, who lived in a 'pretty stone house' in Lurganboy, a mile and a half north-west of Manorhamilton, had already been invited by Sir Frederick on

28 *Another extract of severall letters*, p. 19; depositions of Edward Braxton, William Walsh, Richard Jones, Revd John Layng and Hugh Gasgein in Wood-Martin, *History of Sligo*, ii, pp 197–8, 205–9, 224, 253–6; deposition of Owen O'Rourke, 17 May 1653 (printed in Mac Dermot, *O Ruairc of Breifne*, pp 145–6); NRS, GD 3/5/309, Sidney Hamilton to her sons in Glasgow, 4 July 1643; Parliamentary Archives, HL/PO/JO/10/1/198, petition of Sir Frederick Hammilton to the House of Lords, c.June 1645; *The information of Sir Frederick Hammilton*, p. 88; see also Wood-Martin, *History of Sligo*, ii, pp 38–41. **29** *Another extract of severall letters*, pp 50–1.

several occasions to join his garrison, but had always declined. Now, after moving to Castle Car, he allowed the local rebels, including a Catholic cousin of his who had married an Irishwoman, to take over his house in Lurganboy. The following day, Sheriff Con O'Rourke's men again robbed some of Hamilton's tenants and servants, and this time even stole produce from his own private gardens. The raiders, however, were followed and captured. While they were being led back to Manorhamilton, Abercromy's cousin tried to intercede on their behalf, but Sir Frederick had him arrested also, and his newly acquired house demolished. Hamilton then sent a reconnoitring party towards Sligo on 20 December to try and establish the level of rebel activity in that town. His soldiers encountered a number of rebels, and after killing three, they brought home their heads. One insurgent was also taken prisoner, and was hanged the following day in Manorhamilton.[30]

Beheading had been a feature of warfare practised by both English and Irish soldiers during the sixteenth-century Tudor conquest of Ireland. Some English authorities admitted that the killing and mass beheading of civilians were at times unavoidable in their attempts to subdue the native population. The custom of decapitation was obviously now being readopted by at least some British commanders in their attempts to crush the 1641 rebellion. The gruesome practice was intended to demonstrate the defeat of an enemy. Moreover, the severed heads of important foes were often taken as trophies and affixed to spikes over the main gate of a castle for the purpose of striking terror into any opposition that remained. Perhaps the heads of Sir Frederick's three victims on this occasion were later impaled above the main entrance to Castle Hamilton as a reminder to the rebels of his dominance in the north Leitrim-Sligo area.[31]

As the year 1641 drew to a close, two letters were sent to Sir Frederick. One of them contained disappointing news, while the other was more positive. The first was written by his cousin, James, marquis of Hamilton. After acknowledging receipt of Sir Frederick's letter to him earlier in December, the marquis said that he did not believe that he received his cousin's original one from Derry, since he had not been at court at that time. He regretted therefore not having been able to secure a commission for him from the king, like the one sent to Sir William Cole in November. Moreover, while assuring Sir Frederick that he 'was never wanting upon all occasions to do you the best offices that lay in my power', the marquis feared that he could not be of any assistance at present, as he had not attended court, due to illness, since his return to London. Incidentally, the marquis was not very forthcoming in his letter about the reasons for his absence from court in

30 Ibid., pp 19–20. **31** D. Edwards, 'Some days two heads and some days four', *History Ireland* (Jan./Feb. 2009), 18–21.

October. He had actually fled the court at Edinburgh on 12 October, following a plot – known as 'the incident' – to assassinate him and the covenanter leader, Argyll, with whom he had developed a close political alliance. Charles I was believed to have approved of the plot. However, the marquis seems to have been reconciled with the king within a matter of weeks, as they returned together to London in November.[32]

The second letter, dated 30 December, was from the lords justices Borlase and Parsons. They thanked Sir Frederick Hamilton for his efforts in combating the rebels, and hoped to be in a position to send him supplies of arms and ammunition before long. They also enclosed a commission authorizing him to suppress the rebellion in the counties of Leitrim and Sligo with 'the power of martiall law'. They commanded

> the sheriffs of the said counties … and all other officers, ministers and loving subjects … to be … always ayding, helping and assisting, whenso-ever they shall be required by you, as they shall answer the contrary at their uttermost perils.

The commission conferred on him the military governorship of both counties, with freedom to act 'as your conscience and discretion shall guide you therein'. It also authorized him to 'raise such numbers of men of those counties, for your assistance, as you shall think fit' for the purpose of restoring law and order. In the event, he increased the number of soldiers in his foot company from fifty to two hundred, while retaining also his recently formed troop of fifty horse. In virtue of his commission, the newly raised soldiers would, at least in theory, be paid for by the state and also form part of the regiment of locally recruited British forces, which was then being created in Connacht, under the command of Colonel Francis Willoughby.[33]

In the months that followed the outbreak of the rebellion, several other local commanders and gentlemen in various parts of the country were appointed governors of their respective counties. They were all granted authority to kill, by martial law, 'traitors and their adherents'. One such gentleman, John Bellew from Co. Louth, received his commission at the end of October allowing him to dispense summary execution upon any in rebellion or found 'robbing or spoiling'. Hanging was then the accepted method of killing in accordance with martial law. Thus, Sir Frederick Hamilton was authorized to 'proceed with … all traitors and traiterous persons … and their adherents … in the course of martiall

---

32 NRS, GD 406/1/885; H.C.G. Matthew and B. Harrison (eds), *ODNB*, xxiv, p. 844. **33** *The information of Sir Frederick Hammilton*, pp 89–91; *The humble remonstrance*, pp 6–7; *The several petitions of William Hansard and Sir Frederick Hammiltoun*, p. 26; Ryder, *An English army for Ireland*, pp 11, 38.

law, by hanging them, till they be dead, as hath been accustomed in time of open rebellion'.[34]

The rebellion in north Leitrim had gained little real momentum by the end of 1641. With the advent of a new year, however, the situation would change dramatically. Sir Frederick would then need all his recently acquired recruits, power and status to withstand the repeated attacks about to be made on him, his men and his castle. He would have to draw on all the military training he had received as a captain in the old standing army in Ireland, and especially on his experience as a senior officer during the Thirty Years War in Germany to outmanoeuvre and overcome the rebels from Leitrim and neighbouring counties who were far superior in number, though less well armed and disciplined. He had already hanged at least twelve insurgents from the gallows at Manorhamilton by 31 December. Now that he had the express authorization of the lords justices to carry out such executions, this figure would rise substantially in the months ahead.

BURNINGS, BLOCKADES AND DEADLY REPRISALS

The north Leitrim insurgents made their first attempt on Castle Hamilton in the very early days of 1642. On Thursday 6 January, Colonel Owen and Bryan Ballagh O'Rourke, at the head of over one thousand men, advanced on the castle, firing their muskets. When one of their number was shot dead by the castle's garrison, however, they withdrew to a safer distance. That night, the general army of the rebels set up camp at Lurganboy, while their leaders were accommodated in Castle Car by Sheriff Con O'Rourke, who up till then had not publicly joined the rebellion. Over the course of the next few days, Castle Hamilton was encircled by the insurgents, who tried to intimidate the garrison with an ever-increasing show of strength. Led by Sheriff Con, all of the rebels marched to within half a mile of the castle on 11 January, seemingly with the intention of making an assault. Sir Frederick Hamilton then drew up his horse and foot soldiers in battle formation in front of the castle and challenged the Irish to fight. At the same time, he instructed some horsemen to set fire to several good houses and barns belonging to his own tenants behind the castle, in case the rebels would use these for cover or for quartering their men. Seeing the fire, the insurgents believed that other British forces were arriving to relieve the garrison. So, when Sir Frederick's soldiers advanced towards them, the Irish retreated in disorder and abandoned their camp. Two rebels were caught and hanged on the gallows that evening.[35]

---

34 *The information of Sir Frederick Hammilton*, pp 90–1; R. Armstrong, *Protestant war* (Manchester, 2005), pp 20–2. **35** *Another extract of severall letters*, pp 20–1.

Hamilton was quick to exact revenge for this 'kind visit' of the O'Rourkes and their followers. The next day, he sent a contingent of men to Castle Car, but they found that Sheriff Con and his family had already fled, leaving the building in the possession of Thomas Abercromy, with his wife and children. The soldiers ordered these to leave, and after seizing as much meat, butter and meal as they were able to carry back to Manorhamilton, they set fire to the castle, as well as to the many thatched houses in the vicinity. On 13 January, another group of soldiers was sent in the direction of Dromahair, where they burned many good houses and barns of corn within a five-mile radius of Colonel Owen O'Rourke's castle. The following day, they torched the house and barns of Bryan Ballagh, his brother, in Newtownmanor. A further raid was carried out in Glenade, where a strong stone house with a bawn wall, built by Sir Roger Jones of Sligo, as well as many Irish houses and barns, were destroyed. On the way home from there, Hamilton's men captured and beheaded Tiernan Oge MacArt O'Rourke, one of the leading men of the Car branch of that family. The final foray of the week was to Rossinver, where sixty soldiers set fire to all the houses and barns belonging to the O'Meehans, MacGloins and O'Friels. On the return journey, they were ambushed by three hundred insurgents. Five soldiers and eight rebels were killed in the engagement. The scorched-earth campaign carried out by the Manorhamilton garrison in those few days was so thorough that, according to one of the soldiers, the rebels had 'not so much left as a cabbin to campe in' within six miles of Manorhamilton.[36]

While Sir Frederick's soldiers were taking their revenge on the Irish for the first blockade of Castle Hamilton, terrible events were taking place in Sligo town that would practically wipe out the settler population there. The forty-five or so British settlers who had chosen to remain in the town, after the siege one month earlier, were at first allowed to go about their business uninhibited. Some even joined the regiment of Sligo insurgents, which Colonel Tadhg O'Connor now commanded. However, a meeting of rebel leaders from Sligo, Leitrim and south Donegal was held in the town on Thursday 13 January, most likely to discuss plans for a co-ordinated attack on Manorhamilton, the strongest planter castle in the region. Sometime during the day, two Donegal rebels attacked and killed four Protestants in the street. Shortly afterwards, Hugh and Charles O'Connor, younger brothers of Colonel Teige, persuaded the rest of the settlers to take refuge in Sligo Gaol, where they would be accorded protection. Later that night, almost all of them were 'most inhumanely and barbourously muthered [with] swords and skiens', allegedly by the two O'Connor brothers, with about twelve of their followers who apparently had all been drinking heavily during the previous few

36 Ibid., p. 21.

hours. Only four settlers, including a former provost of the town, managed to survive the frenzied attack. The next morning, the pregnant wife of one of the victims was stabbed to death by the rebels as she attempted to leave the town. The murders caused widespread revulsion, even in insurgent circles, and the suspects were later arrested and imprisoned. The native Irish civilian population would also pay a deadly price in the months ahead for the atrocity that happened in Sligo that day.[37]

On 25 January 1642, almost two weeks after the Sligo Gaol massacre, Colonel Owen O'Rourke set up camp once again at Lurganboy. This time he was joined by some Sligo companies under captains Luke Taaffe and Bryan MacDonagh, as well as by the MacGaurans of Co. Cavan. The rebel forces, which now numbered almost 1,400 men, succeeded in driving off some five hundred of Sir Frederick's cows at dawn the following morning. Later that day, they advanced to within half a mile of the castle, where they set fire to two houses and barns of corn belonging to Sir Frederick's lieutenant, William Lesley. This action so annoyed Hamilton that he sallied forth from the castle with horse and foot soldiers, and, after killing eight rebels, he forced the rest to abandon their camp once again.[38]

The Irish did not retreat very far, however, and two days later set up a new camp in the grounds of Cloonclare Church, one mile south of the castle. This time their numbers were significantly augmented with the arrival of Colonel Con Mac Donnell O'Rourke from south Leitrim and Colonel Tadhg O'Connor Sligo. On Sunday 30 January, their combined forces burned the town of Manorhamilton, including Sir Frederick's garrison quarters and his two corn mills. Hamilton was unable either to prevent this destruction or to engage with the insurgents, since he had to ensure the safety of the townsfolk, who were all given shelter within the bawn walls of the castle. He took his revenge the following day, though, by hanging, in full view of the rebels, the recently captured Sheriff Con O'Rourke and Connor MacLoughlin, chief of his clan – 'two of the ablest and most dangerous men in this county', and the most valuable of the twenty-four prisoners then held in the castle.[39]

In retaliation, the insurgents hanged two Protestant ministers, William Liston and Thomas Fullerton, as well as a third man, Patrick Dromond, at their camp in Cloonclare. These had belonged to a party of 120 Scottish and English settlers, led by Sir Robert Hannay, who had earlier surrendered Belleek Castle near Ballina in Co. Mayo to the rebels, on condition of being given safe passage to Ballyshannon, Co. Donegal, where they could board a ship for Scotland. All had

---

37 Depositions of William Welshe, Hugh Gasgein, Edward Braxton, Peter O'Crean, James Butts, Colonel Francis Taaffe and others, printed in Wood-Martin, *History of Sligo*, ii, pp 194–260; O'Rorke, *The history of Sligo: town and county*, i, pp 150–3; *Another extract of severall letters*, pp 24, 51, 53. 38 *Another extract of severall letters*, pp 21–2. 39 Ibid., p. 22; *The information of Sir Frederick Hammilton*, pp 55, 56, 77, 78.

gone well until they reached Enniscrone, where the settlers were attacked, and many of them killed, by local insurgents. The survivors – Hannay himself, Captain Andrew Adair, a former tenant of Sir Frederick Hamilton, and the Protestant ministers, together with their respective families and servants – were eventually handed over to Colonel Owen O'Rourke in Dromahair, who hoped to exchange them for his brother, Sheriff Con, and other prisoners held in Manorhamilton. In a letter to Sir Frederick, Hannay, Adair and the ministers had pleaded with him to spare the life of Sheriff Con and the other prisoners, otherwise they would suffer the same fate. Hamilton replied on 19 January, regretting their misfortune, but while encouraging them to hope for a satisfactory outcome, firmly asserted that he would never do a deal with 'those disloyall traytours' who held them captive. When Sir Frederick hanged his prize prisoners eleven days later, the two ministers and Adair's servant, Dromond, were chosen by the rebels to pay the penalty. Sir Robert Hannay and the rest of his party remained in captivity in Dromahair Castle.[40]

After the executions, Colonel Owen and Bryan Ballagh O'Rourke, together with six hundred MacClancys from Dartry (Kinlough and Glenade areas), returned again to the houses and haggards of Sir Frederick's lieutenant, where they continued to burn and carry off whatever stocks of corn remained. However, Hamilton sallied forth from the castle with a party of horse and foot on 5 February and killed several of the rebels, bringing home 'three of their ablest men's heads'. Owen himself had a narrow escape, with one bullet passing through his hat and another striking the pike in his hand. The wives and sons of the soldiers from the castle came and gathered up whatever corn was left. Sir Frederick then ordered that the houses and haggards be burned, so that they could never again be used by the Irish.[41]

On hearing that Robert Parke was blockaded in his castle at Newtown (pl. 6), Sir Frederick sent a party of eighty horse and foot, under the command of Lieutenant Lesley and Ensign Vaughan on 24 February, to assess the strength of the insurgents, and if possible to raise the siege and speak with Parke. On arriving at their destination, they encountered no rebels there at all. Parke advised them to return to Manorhamilton immediately, saying that they had been lured to Newtown under false pretences and would shortly be attacked. Lesley was surprised that Parke knew this, but asked him for twenty or thirty of his men to strengthen his cohort for the journey home. Parke refused, saying that he did not

40 Depositions of Revd John Layng, Captain Andrew Adair, Pat Dowda and Oliver Albanagh in Wood-Martin, *History of Sligo*, ii, pp 220–32; *Another extract of severall letters*, pp 56–7; *The information of Sir Frederick Hammilton*, pp 20, 21, 56, 57.   41 *Another extract of severall letters*, p. 22; *The information of Sir Frederick Hammilton*, pp 77–8.

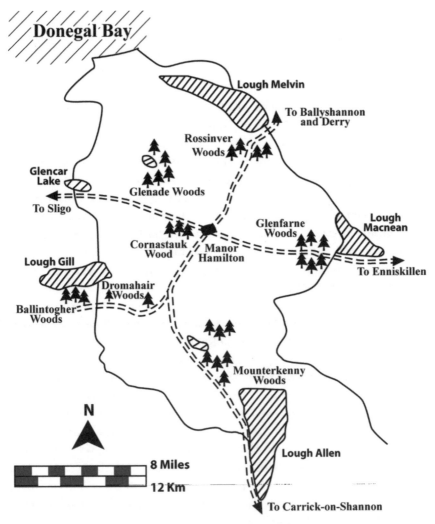

19 North Leitrim: routes and woods, *c.*1641.

wish to draw the wrath of the Irish upon himself. The lieutenant's men were later surrounded by almost one thousand rebels 'in a most dangerous rocky place, where our horses could make no play', less than three miles from Manor-hamilton. After an initial discharge of musket shot by the soldiers, the fighting consisted of hand-to-hand combat. The British used their pikes, swords and musket butts, while the Irish engaged with pikes and skeans, as well as stones, which they hurled with great dexterity. After a fierce struggle, Lesley's men routed their attackers, killing sixty of them, including Mulmurry MacTernan, a justice of the peace and former sheriff of Leitrim, together with many other 'prime gentlemen of these two counties'. The soldiers claimed that they lost only one musketeer and one pike man, though many of the others suffered from pike cuts and were 'sore bruised with stones'. They then returned home with a large amount of rebels' weapons and clothes, after having stripped up to thirty of the dead ambushers.[42]

The most prolonged blockade of Manorhamilton began on 1 March 1642. Colonel Tadhg O'Connor Sligo set up camp in Cornastauk Wood, beside Benbo Mountain, about one mile west of the castle (fig. 19). Colonel Owen O'Rourke and his men joined O'Connor three days later. Both regiments marched around the castle in impressive manner on 8 March, but kept out of the garrison's musket range. That evening marked the arrival once again of Colonel Con MacDonnell O'Rourke, which brought the insurgent numbers up to almost two thousand. The following day, some of them advanced as far as Sir Frederick's orchard, which lay almost directly in front of the castle, and took shelter behind its perimeter ditch. Hamilton, however, managed to shoot two of them, who were then carried back to the camp by their comrades.[43]

Tadhg O'Connor Sligo tried a different strategy to gain the upper hand a few days later. In a letter to Sir Frederick, he stated that he had come to Manorhamilton to support his cousins, the O'Rourkes, who were sorely aggrieved by Hamilton's killing and hanging of several of their family and friends. He added that the combined insurgent forces were numerous, with even more reinforcements expected shortly from Co. Mayo. Nevertheless, on account of Hamilton's friendship with his late father, O'Connor now wished to give Sir Frederick a chance to conclude a treaty and surrender before the Mayo rebels arrived. Once that happened, it would be too late to save Manorhamilton Castle. O'Connor therefore sought an immediate response to his letter, which he had delivered by a seven-year-old boy. Sir Frederick's reply was brief and to the point. He would never trust the Sligo colonel who had turned his back on his king and his former friends. Moreover, he was contemptuous of O'Connor's dishonourable boasting. So, instead of surrendering, he would look for every opportunity to take his revenge on the Irishman.[44]

Having learned that the insurgents had resolved to destroy his castle and kill the garrison on St Patrick's Day 1642, Sir Frederick himself took the initiative that morning and led out his full cohort of soldiers, complete with trumpeters, drummers and flag-bearers, towards the Irish. These were drawn up in battle formation on the opposite bank of the River Bonet, with a bog also separating them from the British. Hamilton challenged them to come forward and defeat

42 *Another extract of severall letters*, pp 22–4, *The information of Sir Frederick Hammilton*, p. 72.
43 *Another extract of severall letters*, p. 24. 44 Ibid., pp 24, 52, 53.

his men, in accordance with their earlier boasts. Seeing that they were unwilling to do so, he ordered that one of his prisoners be hung 'in honour of St Patrick'. The hangman on the gallows shouted to the rebels that if they had any humanity, they should send a priest to administer the last rites to the condemned man. The Irish fell to their knees at the sight of the execution, not realizing that the victim was only 'an old sack of straw, long stockings being sowed to it'. They no longer had the stomach for a fight and withdrew to their camp after the incident.[45]

No further action was taken by the insurgents in the weeks that followed, allowing Sir Frederick's servants the opportunity to plough the fields in the vicinity of the castle. On the night of 2 April, their sixteen plough-horses were driven off by the Irish, due to a lapse in security by the castle sentries. The next morning, however, Hamilton ordered that ploughing should continue, using his soldiers' troop horses, which for security reasons had been kept inside the bawn walls. The initiative proved a success, with the British managing to sow nearly eighty barrels of corn.[46]

By now, the Irish were becoming so confident that Colonel Owen O'Rourke had brought his cattle to graze within two miles of Castle Hamilton. On being informed of this fact, Sir Frederick sent out a party of men at dawn on Good Friday, 8 April, to round them up and drive them back to the castle. While doing so, they were attacked by the rebels, who almost got the upper hand in the encounter. Finally, though, the soldiers prevailed, killing six of the insurgents' principal officers, including James Murragh MacClancy, chief of his clan. The British then raided the rebel camp, where they seized a store of weapons including muskets with bandoliers, halberds, pikes and skeans, many of which had originally been captured by the Irish at the siege of Sligo the previous December. They also retrieved many crowbars and similar instruments, with which – as one of Hamilton's men scornfully remarked – the 'poore churls believe ... they were to pull downe ... our colonels castle and bawne'. The soldiers later destroyed the camp, after their wives and sons had taken possession of the large amount of food which the attackers had left behind.[47]

It is interesting to note how the insurgents managed to recruit, feed and pay such large numbers of men during the various blockades of Manorhamilton. Among papers taken from the pockets of Mulmurry MacTernan, the former Leitrim sheriff, who was killed in February 1642 by Hamilton's soldiers, was a letter dated 31 January 1642, from Colonel Owen O'Rourke, ordering that a levy of two hundred men be imposed on the barony of Dromahair. The MacLoughlins and the Murrays were to provide eighty of these, with the balance coming from Killargy, Dromlease, Mounterkenny and Ballymakenna. Other

45 Ibid., pp 24–5.   **46** Ibid., p. 25; *The information of Sir Frederick Hammilton*, p. 87.   **47** *Another*

letters found on the corpses of some Sligo rebels revealed that Colonel Tadhg O'Connor Sligo authorized the captains of his regiment to collect meal and money in the barony of Carbury for the maintenance of his men during the March blockade of Manorhamilton. Each rebel fighter was to get fourteen quarters of meal and twelve pence a week for as long as the siege lasted. This pay-scale seems small when compared with the eight pence a day that a foot soldier in the British army received at the time, although his payment had to cover the cost of food and lodgings.[48]

A week or so after Easter, Sir Frederick, with a party of horse and foot, burned some villages and killed a number of rebels two miles from Sligo town. He returned home via Newtown Castle and village, which he noticed had not been attacked at all by the insurgents. He was then informed that the rebels' cows had been allowed to graze right up to the bawn walls of the castle, without any interference from Robert Parke and his sixty-strong garrison, even while Manorhamilton was blockaded. Moreover, the Irish apparently passed freely by Parke's castle, with provisions from Sligo town, on their way to their camp at Cornastauk. So Hamilton decided there and then to burn Newtown village, which 'so long had relieved and sheltered the rogues', and to put some of its inhabitants to the sword. As for Parke himself, he would be made to answer for his collusion with the rebels on another occasion.[49]

During the course of the last week of April and the first fortnight of May, Sir Frederick carried out devastating raids on various locations to the north, south and west of Manorhamilton. The forays were certainly in retaliation for the recent blockade of his castle, but it seems clear that civilians in many of the targeted districts often bore the brunt of these attacks. In the first raid, forty people were killed and many good houses burned in the Dromahair area on 23 April. The soldiers brought home 150 cows, as well as a sizeable number of horses, sheep and goats. They later learned that they had unwittingly disrupted plans for another blockade of Manorhamilton, which had been arranged for the following day. Sir Frederick's foot soldiers struck in the Mounterkenny area, near the present town of Drumkeeran, at dawn on 1 May. There they killed up to sixty inhabitants in houses belonging to the local chieftain, Garret MacConsnamha (Forde). Garret's wife was one of the casualties, as she had not been recognized by the soldiers. The chieftain himself and his two daughters were taken prisoner and brought back to Manorhamilton, along with 170 cows and two hundred sheep and goats. One week later, a party of horse and foot killed a dozen rebels and burned houses belonging to the O'Connors in the barony of Carbury in Co.

---

extract of severall letters, p. 25.   **48** Ibid., pp 51, 53, 54; Gentles, 'The civil wars in England', p. 106.
49 *Another extract of severall letters*, pp 25–6.

Sligo. Most of the local population had already fled the barony and were taking refuge in Sligo town. Moreover, the countryside was almost devoid of farm animals, and the soldiers managed to take only a small prey of sheep. Another dawn raid took place on 13 May in Co. Fermanagh, where the wife of Donnacha MacFlaherta Maguire, together with forty other rebels and civilians, were killed in their homes. Five prisoners were brought back to Manorhamilton Castle and hanged. The soldiers also took possession of 180 cows, two hundred sheep and goats, 47 horses and 30 pigs. Some days later, Hamilton's men marched once more to Dromahair, this time to attack the Franciscan friary of Creevelea (pl. 7). The guardian of the friars, Fr Bernard MacKeegan, had been named as one of the instigators of the rebellion in November 1641. By the time the soldiers arrived, the friars had fled and the thatch had been removed from the building. While in Dromahair, the soldiers killed twenty rebels and seized many pikes, as well as a halberd that had once belonged to Lord Ranelagh's sergeant in Sligo. They also drove one hundred English and Scottish cows (which had obviously been stolen earlier by the rebels), 150 sheep and some horses back to Manorhamilton.[50]

Five hundred insurgents from Dartry or Rossinver were preparing to attack Castle Hamilton on 20 May. When they were spotted by the sentries, who raised the alarm, they retired to the hills. True to form, Sir Frederick led a party of soldiers to Glenade the following night to search for the would-be attackers. He found none, but burned 'many faire Irish-houses' in the area. On the way home in the morning, they spotted a large number of Sligo rebels at Lurganboy, who were about to make an assault on the castle. Hamilton taunted them by enquiring whether they had come to take the castle, to rescue MacConsnamha and his daughters or to steal his cows. He then had a prisoner brought out from the castle and hanged on the gallows. The Irish dropped to their knees, thinking it was Garret MacConsnamha. Sir Frederick then ordered that the two hundred cows, which his men had taken when they broke up the insurgent camp at Cornastauk, should now be driven towards the rebels in an attempt to entice them to advance and fight. But even though they were five times more numerous than the British, they would not cross the bog and the River Bonet, which lay between the two armies. Hamilton then engaged in a ruse. He directed his men to withdraw towards the castle. The rebels, who thought the soldiers were retreating, crossed the river and pursued them with great speed. When the insurgents were within musket range, the British were ordered to wheel around and confront the advancing throng. The musketeers shot many of the rebels as

50 Ibid., pp 26, 27, 56; deposition of Revd William Browne, former tenant of Sir Frederick's in Dromlease, in Wood-Martin, *History of Sligo*, ii, pp 201–2; C. Mooney OFM, 'The Franciscan friary of Jamestown', *Ardagh and Clonmacnoise Antiquarian Society Journal* (1946), 6–7; B. Millett OFM, *The Irish Franciscans, 1651–1665* (Rome, 1964), pp 49–50.

they fled back across the river, and chased others for three miles in the direction of Sligo. The insurgent leader was killed and Sir Frederick's men recovered many weapons, two drums, a good store of meal, as well as 'one hundred of their mantles, coates and cloakes', which they had discarded when crossing the river. Two prisoners later confessed that insurgents from Leitrim, Sligo, Donegal, Fermanagh and Cavan had all been planning to blockade the castle once again that very night, and not to give up until it had been captured or the garrison starved into submission.[51]

Over the course of the next three weeks, Hamilton's men carried out deadly raids on rebels and civilians alike in various parts of Sligo and Leitrim. Once again, they took preys of significant numbers of farm animals, which would provide a useful supply of food for Sir Frederick's household, the castle garrison and the townspeople who were still being afforded refuge within the bawn walls. During the first raid on 22 May, which took place in Co. Sligo, the soldiers killed thirty people in their cabins at daybreak and brought home a prisoner as well as two hundred cows and sheep. They then hanged their guide, 'a most desperate, obdurate villaine', who had confessed, presumably under torture, to having planned to betray them. Five days later, they invaded Mounterkenny again, killing a dozen people in their cabins and driving off a greater number of animals than they had taken from Co. Sligo. On the return journey, they were attacked by Colonel Owen O'Rourke and the sons of Garret MacConsnamha, with three hundred men. The British succeeded in killing and stripping a number of the attackers, while still holding on to their prey. The following week, they killed fifteen rebels on lands belonging to Colonel Owen O'Rourke and seized some of his horses, cows, sheep and goats. Finally, in the middle of June, they put to death the same number of insurgents in Glenfarne Wood, as well as taking some prisoners and prey.[52]

Around this time Sir Frederick had prevailed upon Robert Parke to let him have the loan of twenty men, in accordance with the commission he had received from the lords justices the previous December. In return, Hamilton sent a party of soldiers, which included Parke's men, with twenty cows to supply the rest of the Newtown garrison. Parke accepted the animals, but would not allow his twenty men to go back to Manorhamilton, even though Sir Frederick had explicitly ordered them to do so. The next day, Hamilton sent Lieutenant Lesley with a detachment of horse and foot to estimate the number of men needed to defend Newtown, and to request Parke to let him have the remainder for 'some speciall speedy piece of service intended'. Lesley believed that Newtown could be secured with half of Parke's sixty strong garrison, and therefore wished to take

---

51 *Another extract of severall letters*, pp 27–8.   **52** Ibid., pp 28–9.

thirty men away with him. Parke, however, refused once again to let any man go.[53]

Fearing that Parke might now surrender his castle to the insurgents, since he seemed to be in touch with them on a daily basis, Sir Frederick himself led a strong party of 120 horse and foot to Newtown on the night of 1 July. Parke eventually admitted Hamilton to the castle, but was shortly afterwards arrested on suspicion of treason and for having disobeyed Sir Frederick's previous orders. He was replaced as commander of Newtown by an officer from Manorhamilton. Hamilton then selected twenty of Parke's best men to join his own party, which now set off for Sligo town, less than six miles away.[54]

On arriving at the outskirts of Sligo as dawn was breaking, Sir Frederick exhorted his soldiers to help him burn down the town, which harboured so many rebels who had reduced Manorhamilton town and garrison quarters to ashes, who had blockaded his castle on many occasions and sought its destruction, and who had 'murthered and massacred many poor British' in Sligo itself. He also called upon them to liberate whatever British prisoners were being held there by the rebels. No houses were to be entered for plunder, but 'with fire and sword to destroy all that [they] could come at'. Lieutenant Lesley and Ensign Vaughan were both absent that day due to illness, so Hamilton himself led the troop of horse, while Sergeant Leviston took command of the foot soldiers. Many good houses, as well as humble cabins, were set on fire and their inhabitants burned alive. The Dominican church and friary, with all 'their superstitious trumperies belonging to their masse' were also torched. Some friars were believed to have perished inside the buildings, while two of those who escaped were killed outside. The friars may have been specifically targeted because of the alleged involvement of some of their members in the rebellion. Edmond MacBryan MacSweeney, the prior, had supposedly taken part in the siege of Sligo, whereas Friar Charles O'Connor, brother of Colonel Tadhg O'Connor Sligo, was said to be one of those responsible for the Sligo Gaol massacre. Sir Frederick later claimed that three hundred people in all had been put to death in their homes, in the streets or by drowning. Even if his assertions are somewhat exaggerated, the slaughter and destruction carried out in Sligo that morning must surely rank as one of the deadliest and most brutal retaliations carried out by either side during the course of the 1641 rebellion.[55]

Hamilton's soldiers would have been quite familiar with the 'fire and sword' command that he issued to his men that morning in Sligo, as well as on other

53 Ibid., pp 29–30. **54** Ibid., p. 30; *The information of Sir Frederick Hammilton*, pp 2, 9, 35. **55** *Another extract of severall letters*, pp 30–1; *The information of Sir Frederick Hammilton*, p. 37; Parliamentary Archives, HL/PO/JO/10/1/198, petition of Sir Frederick Hammilton to the House of Lords, *c.*June 1645; depositions in Wood-Martin, *History of Sligo*, ii, pp 197, 206–7, 242, 243, 256–9.

occasions in Leitrim. In Scottish tradition, the king would invoke such an order when wishing to force insubordinate clans into submission. The strategy involved the killing of any supporters of the enemy – often without regard to sex or age – and the burning of their houses, food-stocks and crops. The tactic was used by both Scottish and English commanders in 1642 in an attempt to strike terror into the Irish population and to destroy the rebels' subsistence and their will to resist. In June 1642, for example, the English authorities in Dublin described how their army acted 'against the rebels, their adherents, relievers and abettors ... with fire and sword, the soldiers not sparing the women and sometimes not the children, many women being manifestly very deep in the guilt of this rebellion'. On these occasions, the common rules of humanity were ignored, atrocities were committed and the civilian population paid a huge price for the conflict that was being waged in their name. While the existence of a 'fire and sword' tradition or strategy neither excuses nor mitigates the brutality of Sir Frederick Hamilton's actions in Sligo, it does put some of his harsher attempts to defeat the rebels into perspective.[56]

As the Manorhamilton raiding party concluded its business in Sligo, the soldiers were informed by some prisoners that Colonel Tadhg O'Connor Sligo had that very night linked up with Colonel Owen O'Rourke and some Cavan rebels for the purpose of blockading Castle Hamilton once more and driving off Sir Frederick's cattle. On hearing this news, Hamilton decided to return home immediately. When his men were less than three miles from the castle, they were ambushed by one thousand insurgents at a narrow pass, between a rocky wood and an extensive bog. Many of the soldiers' horses began to get stuck in the soft ground. Hand-to-hand fighting ensued, and Sir Frederick was knocked from his horse on three different occasions. His men eventually forced their way through the pass, but were still closely pursued by the Irish until they came to within sight of the castle. In the end, quite a number of the insurgents were shot and killed, whereas the soldiers claimed that they had lost only three of their comrades. This failed attack resulted in the cancellation of the planned rebel blockade of Manorhamilton. Another sequel to the Sligo raid was the hanging for treachery in Manorhamilton of James Witherspin, a Scottish neighbour of Sir Frederick's, who had joined the Sligo rebels, but was captured during the incursion.[57]

During the first seven months of 1642, while Hamilton and the insurgents of Leitrim, Sligo and Cavan were engaged in a desperate struggle for supremacy, the fortunes of the insurgents in other parts of the country varied significantly. In

---

56 E.M. Furgol, *A regimental history of the Covenanting armies, 1639–1651* (Edinburgh, 1990), p. 12; R. Bagwell, *Ireland under the Stuarts* (3 vols, London, 1909), ii, pp 14–16; Armstrong, *Protestant war*, pp 34–5.
57 *Another extract of severall letters*, p. 31; *The information of Sir Frederick Hammilton*, pp 7–9, 36–7.

south Leitrim, the Irish were the dominant party and had the British pinned down in the garrison towns of Jamestown and Carrick-on-Shannon. The situation in the rest of Connacht was somewhat similar. Despite the efforts of the earl of Clanricard, lieutenant of Galway, to keep that county peaceful, much of the province had fallen to the insurgents, leaving only a few castles and strongholds in Protestant control.[58]

By the summer of 1642, the rebellion had achieved considerable success in large areas of the provinces of Leinster and Munster. There had, however, been some serious setbacks, due in part to the arrival from England of nine or ten British regiments, including a naval squadron led by Alexander Master of Forbes, with whom Sir Frederick had collaborated some ten years previously in raising regiments for Sweden. In Ulster, on the contrary, the rebellion was on the wane, having been gradually suppressed by the Laggan army, under the Stewart brothers in the north-west of the province, and by Major General Robert Monro in the eastern counties. Monro, another veteran of the Thirty Years War, had landed at Carrickfergus with a well-equipped advance party of 2,500 Scottish troops on 15 April. Despite the uneasy relationship between the British settlers in Ulster and Monro's Scots, both groups had achieved significant victories over the rebels, even before the arrival of 7,500 further Scotsmen under General Alexander Leslie in early August.[59]

In an attempt to better manage the war and control the disorder that followed the rebellion, a nationwide provisional government was set up in Kilkenny by the Catholic hierarchy and gentry of both Old English and native Irish extraction in June 1642. Four months later, a general assembly of 'Confederate Catholics of Ireland' would meet in the same city and appoint a supreme council to organize its armies and administer the Catholic controlled parts of the country, pending a final settlement of the war. However, even though a Connacht confederate council met in Ballinrobe, Co. Mayo, in the summer of 1642 to restore law and order in the province and to nominate representatives to attend the assembly in Kilkenny, it seems to have had little immediate impact on the deadly conflict that continued unabated between Sir Frederick Hamilton and the insurgents in north Leitrim.[60]

---

58 See Mac an Ghallóglaigh, '1641 rebellion in Leitrim', pp 448–51; Canny, *Making Ireland British*, pp 499–500; M. Ó Siochrú, *God's executioner: Oliver Cromwell and the conquest of Ireland* (London, 2008), p. 13. **59** Ryder, *An English army for Ireland*, pp 7–12; R. Greenwood, 'Col. William "Blowface" Forbes', p. 98; K. McKenny, 'British settler society in Donegal, *c.*1625–1685' in Nolan et al. (eds), *Donegal, history and society*, pp 331–3; R. Gillespie, 'An army sent from God: Scots at war in Ireland, 1642–9' in N. MacDougall (ed.), *Scotland and war, AD79–1918* (Edinburgh, 1991), pp 116–17. **60** P.J. Corish, 'The rising of 1641 and the Catholic confederacy, 1641–5', pp 297–9; S.J. Connolly (ed.), *Oxford companion to Irish history* (Oxford, 1998), p. 115.

CONTINUING CONFLICT DESPITE CHANGES IN THE INSURGENT
LEADERSHIP

When the rebellion had broken out in October 1641, Hamilton wrote to Sir
William Cole in Enniskillen, offering him any help that he could give. He also
encouraged four Scottish captains in Fermanagh to join Cole's garrison, even after
they had volunteered their services to Manorhamilton. Cole commanded a
regiment of some six hundred horse and foot, which was more than twice the
number of men that Sir Frederick could muster. Despite repeated requests for
assistance during the first nine months of the rebellion, Hamilton had received
no support at all from his powerful planter neighbour. However, when a
messenger from Manorhamilton informed Cole towards the end of July 1642
that a 'store of cowes were to be had in our county of Leytrim', the Enniskillen
colonel, who was then experiencing a severe shortage of food, immediately sent a
party of four hundred soldiers to Manorhamilton. Sir Frederick offered the
visiting officers the hospitality of his castle for the night, and arranged that the
rest of the men would be quartered in his own soldiers' cabins. Cole's officers
declined the invitation, suggesting instead that Hamilton 'should imploy them
upon some peece of service'. Sir Frederick eventually decided to use the opportunity, with such a substantial body of soldiers now at his disposal, to try and take
Owen O'Rourke's castle in Dromahair, and to secure the release of Sir Robert
Hannay and his fellow prisoners, who had been held there since the previous
February. On arriving at Dromahair, Hamilton sent his own 'masons, carpenters
and other workemen with their instruments' to make a breach in the castle wall.
Once this was achieved, he placed some of his musketeers in the opening. These
were soon forced to abandon their position, however, due to the sustained gunfire
of the defenders, which killed two of the musketeers. Meanwhile, Cole's soldiers
had made no attempt whatsoever to take part in the assault. Instead, 'their horsemen were rambling the countrey, driving in horses and cowes, their foot-men
running after muttons, catching, killing and waiting under every bush'. One
member of the Enniskillen party was particularly responsible for the non-
cooperation with Hamilton's men. This was the Revd Robert Barkley, dean of
Clogher and son-in-law of Sir William Cole. Despite the fact that he was not a
military man, the dean behaved as if he had been given supreme authority over
Cole's soldiers. After publicly discouraging them from joining in the attack, he
refused to allow them to undertake a short siege of Dromahair, which Hamilton
felt would result in the capture of the castle within a day or so.[61]

61 Cole had a regiment of almost 1,000 men garrisoned at Enniskillen during the first eight months of the
rebellion. 400 of these had to be disbanded on 1 Jul. 1642, when the English parliament sent money and
supplies to sustain only 600. *The information of Sir Frederick Hammilton*, pp 1–2, 4–6, 31–2, 48–9;

When the visiting party was returning to Enniskillen the following day, the officers allowed thirty of their men to remain in Manorhamilton to reinforce the local garrison. However, Dean Barkley created such a fuss that half of the delegated men were so frightened that they rejoined their own detachment. Sir Frederick was disgusted with the cleric's antics and claimed that Barkley 'carried himselfe more like a devill then a deane'. When Sir William Cole was notified of the incident, he justified his son-in-law's actions, and even insisted that the fifteen soldiers who had remained in Manorhamilton, should be immediately sent back to him. To make matters worse, some of Hamilton's own men began absconding to Enniskillen in the weeks that followed, after having observed the freedom and lack of discipline that prevailed in that garrison.[62]

In the weeks before and after the visit of the Enniskillen party, Sir Frederick Hamilton embarked on a series of devastating raids in Leitrim and the surrounding counties. The first of these took place at dawn on 10 July, when his men attacked a strong camp of insurgents at Killargy, five miles south of Manorhamilton, killing and stripping about thirty of them, and seizing many weapons as well as 160 cows. Two weeks later, he sent a party of men into Co. Fermanagh to look for a group of '100 Irish rogues' led by Bryan Maguire of Tempo. Sir William Cole had afforded protective status to this man because of his non-involvement in the rebellion and his services to the British authorities. Hamilton, on the contrary, believed that Bryan could not be trusted, as he was a close relative of Lord Conor and Rory Maguire, the leaders of the rebellion in Fermanagh. Moreover, he and his followers posed a threat to Sir Frederick, since Cole had allowed them to set up camp along the Enniskillen to Manorhamilton road. Although Hamilton's men failed, on this occasion, to find Maguire, they burned 'many goodly Irish houses' and brought home some prisoners and cows. Another party of foot soldiers was dispatched on 8 August to Co. Cavan, where they killed more than twenty of the local inhabitants, and brought home two prisoners and a large prey of cows, sheep and goats. A further raid took place a fortnight later near Ballyshannon in Co. Donegal, where the Manorhamilton soldiers killed seventeen people and burned many houses. Finally, after hearing that corn was being cut at Doonally and Calry in Co. Sligo, Sir Frederick sent a detachment of horse and foot to the area on 25 August. Unable to find the corn, they burned four villages and drove off seventy cows and a hundred sheep. As they were doing so, they were attacked by a force of local insurgents, led by the O'Connors and the O'Hartes. After killing forty of them and repulsing the rest, some of the soldiers drove the cows and sheep to Newtown Castle, three miles

---

Another extract of severall letters, pp 32–5; see also Hamilton, *The Irish rebellion of 1641*, p. 139.   **62** *The information of Sir Frederick Hammilton*, p. 50; *Another extract of severall letters*, pp 35–6.

away. The rest of the party marched to Rosses Point on the Sligo coast, where they took a much larger prey of animals. On their return journey, they were set upon by a very large contingent of insurgents near Sligo town, who had, at the time, been planning another blockade of Castle Hamilton. However, Sir Frederick's soldiers killed 'neare sixty of their ablest men', including two priests, Conor O'Harte and Donal O'Lynch. They also brought home seven prisoners, five of whom were hanged the next day at Manorhamilton.[63]

Around the time that Hamilton was carrying out raids in Doonally, Calry and Rosses Point at the end of August 1642, changes were being made in the leadership of the insurgent forces in Co. Sligo. The recently formed Connacht council of the confederates appointed Luke Taaffe, younger brother of Viscount Theobald Taaffe of Ballymote, to be its new colonel and commander in Sligo. Lieutenant Bryan MacDonnagh was designated as his assistant. Tadgh O'Connor Sligo was demoted, possibly on account of his alleged association with the Sligo Gaol massacre of British civilians the previous December. Further action would be taken against the former Sligo colonel in March 1643, when Colonel Luke Taaffe would order his arrest, that of his two brothers, captains Charles and Hugh, as well as other former insurgent officers, for 'severall incursions, massacres, robberies, outrages and many other enormities and pillages within the county of Sligo'. It is not clear if O'Connor Sligo was ever apprehended, although Charles and Hugh were imprisoned for some time in Ballinafad Castle.[64]

Towards the end of 1642 or early 1643, Colonel Owen O'Rourke found himself relegated from his position as leader of the Leitrim insurgents. The confederates appointed Richard Farrell of Longford, a veteran of Habsburg service in the Thirty Years War in Germany, to be the new commander in Leitrim. O'Rourke's demotion may also have been due to allegations about his possible involvement in the Sligo Gaol massacre, or in the killings of three Church of Ireland ministers at Dromahair and Manorhamilton in December 1641 and January 1642. O'Rourke does not figure in accounts of the war in Leitrim after April 1643, so he may have left the county at that time and gone to live in Kilmacteige parish in south-west Sligo, where his wife Mary O'Connor owned lands. Owen's younger brother, Bryan Ballagh, had earlier gone to reside in the neighbouring parish of Killasser in east Mayo. The changes in leadership in Sligo and Leitrim, brought about by the confederate authorities, caused division and faction fighting among Irish insurgent forces in both counties, and did little

63 *The information of Sir Frederick Hammilton*, pp 2, 14–16, 43–4; *Another extract of severall letters*, pp 31–2, 36–7; deposition of Bryan of Tempo in Trimble, *The history of Enniskillen*, i, pp 100–2, 274–5; see also P. Livingstone, *The Fermanagh story* (Enniskillen, 1969), pp 88–9. **64** *Another extract of severall letters*, pp 44, 48–9, 54–5; depositions of William Walsh, Hugh Gasgein and Francis Taaffe in Wood-Martin, *History of Sligo*, ii, pp 48–9, 205–59; O'Rorke, *History of Sligo: town and county*, i, pp 150–3; see also O'Dowd,

1 Paisley Abbey or the 'Place of Paisley' in Scotland, where Frederick Hamilton was born (photograph by William Roulston).

2 An impression of Castle Hamilton in the 1630s by Marie McDonald.

4 King Charles I, by Sir Anthony Van Dyck (© National Portrait Gallery, London).

3 (*previous page*) King James I of England and VI of Scotland, by Daniel Mytens
(© National Portrait Gallery, London).

5 Thomas Wentworth, first earl of Strafford, by Sir Anthony Van Dyck
(© National Portrait Gallery, London).

6 Parke's Castle, Newtown, Co. Leitrim (courtesy of the National Monuments Service, Department of Arts, Heritage and the Gaeltacht).

7 Creevelea Abbey, Dromahair, Co. Leitrim (courtesy of the National Monuments Service, Department of Arts, Heritage and the Gaeltacht).

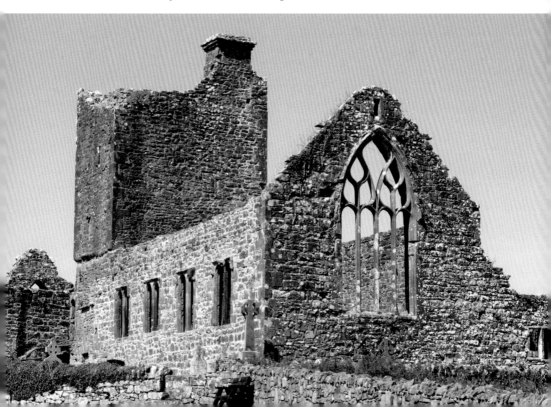

8 Enniskillen Castle (photograph by Bryan Rooney).

9 Title page of a folio of maps of Manorhamilton estate belonging to Nathaniel Clements, second earl of Leitrim, by William Larkin, 1807 (NLI MS 16F11, courtesy of the National Library of Ireland).

10 Portrait of Sir Frederick Hamilton (*c.*1590–1647) in a slashed doublet and hose. Oil on canvas. Circle of Daniel Mytens (*c.*1590–1647) (private collection).

11 Castle Hamilton in 2012 (photograph by James Molloy).

12 Ruins of the seventeenth-century Church of Ireland parish church in Manorhamilton (photograph by the author).

to improve their chances of victory against Sir Frederick Hamilton or other British garrisons in the general region.[65]

Sir Frederick heard canon fire coming from the Sligo direction on 10 September 1642, leading him to hope that a British force had arrived in the area, and was perhaps coming to bring aid to Manorhamilton. The following day, he sent a party of horse and foot towards the Sligo coast to try and establish where the shooting had come from. On reaching Sligo Harbour, they came across four hundred confederates trying to prevent the landing of men from two ships that were anchored there. The Irish fled to an old castle on the coast when Hamilton's men appeared. The soldiers, however, succeeded in taking a prisoner, from whom they learned that some O'Donnells and O'Gallaghers from Donegal had joined with Sligo insurgents to prevent the landing, since they believed that the ships were bringing money, food and ammunition for the relief of Castle Hamilton. The men on the ship later managed to put ashore on Oyster Island, off Rosses Point, where they burned some houses and took on board cattle and corn, before sailing away. Sir Frederick never established their identity or the purpose of their visit.[66]

By early October, the Manorhamilton garrison was in an almost desperate situation, having received neither supplies nor help from any quarter since the beginning of the rebellion, some twelve months previously. So, on 2 October, Hamilton decided to send most of his men to Enniskillen to collect arms and ammunition that had recently been brought there for them from Derry by Sir Robert Stewart. While in Enniskillen, Stewart had written to Sir Frederick to tell him the amount of supplies that he was leaving for him with Sir William Cole, who had promised to deliver these to Manorhamilton as soon as possible. When Hamilton's men arrived at Enniskillen Castle (pl. 8), they found the gate shut and the drawbridge raised, as if they had come to attack the fortress. Moreover, they were not offered 'so much as one bit of bread, or cup of small beere', despite the fact that four hundred of Cole's men had been entertained at Castle Hamilton two months previously. On demanding the arms and ammunition, the officer in charge was informed that he could have them, but would be offered no convoy of Enniskillen soldiers to ensure their safe transportation back to Manorhamilton. He was forced, therefore, to abandon his plans, since he had earlier heard reports that some Leitrim confederates intended to attack his men in the woods and mountains on the way home. The officer also failed in his attempt to get Cole's men to return the fourteen or fifteen deserters who had run away from

Power, politics and land, pp 126–7. **65** J.T. Gilbert (ed.), *A contemporary history of affairs in Ireland*, i, p. 50; depositions of Edward Braxton, William Walsh, John Layng, Andrew Adair in Wood-Martin, *History of Sligo*, ii, pp 197–232; deposition of Bryan Ballagh O'Rourke in MacDermot, *O Ruairc of Breifne*, pp 146–50. **66** *Another extract of severall letters*, p. 37.

Manorhamilton to Enniskillen in previous months. To add insult to injury, Sir William Cole himself did not put in an appearance during this visit of Sir Frederick's party.[67]

The Manorhamilton garrison was also running short of food at this time. So the soldiers, accompanied by their wives and sons, spent the rest of that first week of October raiding Irish corn stocks in Leitrim, Sligo and Fermanagh. They succeeded in bringing home a good supply, although one soldier pointedly remarked that, had they got help from Enniskillen, they could have seized so much more wheat, rye and barley, to the benefit of both strongholds. In the middle of the month, the soldiers, whom Hamilton had placed in Newtown Castle, attacked corn reapers near Sligo town, killing four of them and chasing away the rest. They then commandeered the twenty or so carts that the workers had been using to transport the corn. They also brought back to Manorhamilton a prisoner who confessed under torture that two companies of Donegal confederates had recently joined up with Captain Teige MacPhelomy O'Connor of Castletown in north Sligo, for the purpose of launching an attack on Castle Hamilton. During the night of 21 October, Sir Frederick sent a party of men to Castletown, in a pre-emptive strike against the Irish. They killed sixty of them, including the two Donegal captains and Teige O'Connor and his wife. After burning Castletown and some neighbouring villages, the soldiers returned home with O'Connor's brother as a prisoner and a prey of two hundred cows. The captive was hanged shortly afterwards.[68]

Hamilton was expecting that Sir William Cole would convey his allocation of arms and ammunition, as well as his fifteen deserters to Manorhamilton by the middle of October, as he had more or less promised to do. As the month drew to a close, however, there had been no communication whatsoever from Enniskillen. Sir Frederick's stores of ammunition, as well as his supply of salt – an essential preservative for meat – were almost exhausted. So, hearing that Cole had received a recent delivery of salt from Ballyshannon, Hamilton sent most of his men to Enniskillen once more on 29 October. Lieutenant Lesley was given a letter for Cole explaining their plight, and money to buy whatever quantity of salt he could get. Once again, Cole was no more accommodating to the Manorhamilton party than on their last visit. They were handed their supply of arms and ammunition, but afforded no convoy to escort them home. Nor were they successful in obtaining any salt or in having their runaways returned. Nevertheless, they did succeed in making it safely back to Manorhamilton.[69]

Sir Frederick claimed that up to one thousand confederates from Fermanagh and Cavan, under the command of Sergeant Major Hugh MacBryan Maguire,

67 Ibid., pp 37–8.　68 Ibid., pp 38–9.　69 Ibid., p. 39.

lay in ambush in the fields around Castle Hamilton throughout the night of 11 November, with the intention of driving off his herd of cattle the following morning. However, they were discovered at dawn by two of the castle sentries, who managed to raise the alarm before being attacked and killed. The garrison succeeded in rescuing the cattle and then set about confronting the attackers. Despite making the best stand of any confederates up to then, the Irish were eventually forced to make a hasty and disorderly retreat, after the soldiers 'did pepper them both with horse and foot'. One of the captured officers was Captain Charles Maguire, who had bravely led eighty of his musketeers by example. As one of his legs was broken, Maguire was wheeled in a barrow to the gallows, despite his plea for a soldier's death by shooting. The condemned man lamented that he had spent many years in both French and Spanish service, and even that very morning was in command of three hundred confederates, never realizing that he would 'dye like a dogge on Mannour Hamilton's gallowes' before the end of the day. The Irish casualties also included Shane Roe Maguire and Conaught MacFlaherta MacHugh, a son-in-law of Garret MacConsnamha of Mounterkenny. In revenge for the confederate attack, Sir Frederick hanged MacConsnamha, who had been a prisoner in the castle for the previous six months.[70]

As the Manorhamilton garrison was still in great need of salt, Hamilton sent a detachment of men to Ballyshannon to seek a supply on 30 November. Although they travelled throughout the night, their journey was monitored by confederate sentries. Nevertheless, they arrived safely at their destination before dawn. When Captain Folliott, the British commander there, heard Lieutenant Lesley's trumpet, he dispatched a boat to bring the officer to the castle. Folliott first informed the lieutenant that four barrels of powder, together with match and lead, had recently been sent from Derry to Donegal town for transmission to both Enniskillen and Manorhamilton. Upon hearing about this, Sir William Cole had asked Folliott to bring his portion as far as Ballyshannon, where it was then collected by members of the Enniskillen garrison. Lesley felt that Cole might easily have requested Folliott to transport all of the ammunition from Donegal, and then the Enniskillen men could have delivered Sir Frederick's share, since they passed within six miles of Manorhamilton on their way from Ballyshannon to their own garrison. As regards a supply of salt, Folliott had only four barrels in his castle, but gave Lesley two of them, although Hamilton had been hoping for twenty. The Ballyshannon commander also sent a midwife, Una Hale, for Sidney Hamilton, who was then pregnant with her fourth child. On their return journey, the soldiers noticed that 'the fields [were] fowle on all quarters' with confederates. Just as they arrived at the boundary of Hamilton's

70 Ibid., pp 39–40.

estate, they were suddenly ambushed by 'a pickt party of the best and ablest men' of the MacClancys, MacLoughlins, O'Friels and O'Meehans of Dartry and Rossinver, and the O'Flannagans, Maguires and MacCaffreys of Fermanagh, who all appeared out of nowhere. It took half an hour for the British pike men and musketeers to overcome the Irish, who fought 'most desperately'. Sixty insurgents, including Bryan Darragh O'Treacy, who had served in the Spanish army, were killed and stripped. Amazingly, the soldiers suffered no loss of life – if one can believe Sir Frederick's account of the incident – although 'many [of them were] hurt with push of pike and darts'. They later seized the weapons and cloaks of the defeated confederates. The British chronicler of the event stated that 'this glorious victory broke the hearts of the most daring dangerous men' of Leitrim and Fermanagh, before adding wryly that 'the service was performed upon Saint Andrewes day, for the credit of our Scottish-patron'.[71]

Sir Frederick Hamilton had good reason to resent the involvement of the Old English Catholic gentry family, the Taaffes of Ballymote, in the rebellion. Colonel Luke Taaffe, now commander-in-chief of the Sligo confederates, and his younger brother, Captain Francis, had joined the insurrection at the siege of Sligo, and subsequently took part in several attacks on Manorhamilton. Even though their eldest brother, Viscount Theobald Taaffe, was still a loyal supporter of the crown, many of his tenants were among the confederates. In Hamilton's eyes, the viscount himself was an 'arch-rebell and wicked incendiary' because these tenants had participated in the burning of Manorhamilton town in January 1642. So, eleven months later, on Christmas night, he sent a party of men to burn Taaffe's town of Ballymote, some thirty miles from Manorhamilton. After they had marched only a short distance, however, many of the soldiers began complaining of tiredness and feeling faint – something that had never before happened. Lieutenant Lesley was forced to turn his men around and head for home. Sir Frederick, who was amazed to see the soldiers return within a matter of hours, quickly discovered that many of them had planned to use the occasion to run away to Enniskillen. They had been influenced by reports of the lax discipline that prevailed among Sir William Cole's men, who allegedly would obey neither their captains not superior officers. Hamilton blamed Cole for the incident, because he had never returned the fifteen men who had run away during the summer. In addition, Cole had recently sent word covertly, through a messenger, that any deserters from Manorhamilton would be made very welcome in Enniskillen.[72]

---

71 Ibid., pp 40–1. The references to Captain Charles Maguire and Bryan Darragh O'Treacy in insurgent attacks on Manorhamilton, during the month of November 1642, would seem to be indicative of the increasing number of Irishmen with service in Continental armies, who were returning to fight in Ireland, as the rebellion developed into the Confederate War. **72** *Another extract of severall letters*, p. 42; *The*

The new year (1643) began with further acts of terrorism carried out by Hamilton's men against the local population in north Leitrim and Cavan. On 9 January, they attacked a group of confederates, burned many houses and stole corn and two hundred cows near Belhavel. The following week, the soldiers killed some insurgents and took a prey of 160 cows at Blacklion, then known as Largane. The next day, they marched further into Co. Cavan and drove off an even greater number of animals, 'most of them as fat as if it had been at Michaelmas'. On the way home through Glenfarne, they killed five local inhabitants and captured 'a most arch-rogue named Cormack O'Quillan, who had all that yeere stolne a many of our colonels horses'. The next incursion took place on 4 February at Drumkeeran, where once again several insurgents were killed, and the wife of Owen Oge MacMurray, chief of his clan, was taken prisoner. MacMurray himself narrowly escaped being captured. Finally, on hearing, a fortnight later, that over a thousand confederates from Leitrim and Sligo, under the command of Luke Taaffe and Bryan MacDonnagh, had assembled at Creevelea Abbey in Dromahair to plan a new blockade of Castle Hamilton, Sir Frederick sent a party of men to reconnoitre the scene early one morning. While in Dromahair, they managed to kill a few confederates, take two prisoners and drive off seventy cows from the nearby woods.[73]

One of the prisoners – a young girl, aged about ten or eleven – was sent back to the confederate encampment later the same day with a curious letter, allegedly written by six Irish soldiers in Sir Frederick's garrison. These 'loyall' Irishmen addressed the confederates as 'dishonourable and unworthy countrymen'. In derisive tones, they declared themselves to be ashamed at the confederates' cowardice in not coming sooner to raid Sir Frederick's cows. They advised that there would be very few animals left to prey on if the confederates delayed much longer, and that instead it would be the Manorhamilton garrison who would be carrying out the raids, as they had done that morning in Dromahair 'looking for our breake-fast'. The letter-writers went on to say that the local Irish insurgents were threatening to complain to Owen Roe O'Neill, the Ulster general, that their leaders were wasting their ammunition by shooting at Castle Hamilton from the top of Benbo Mountain, more than a mile away. They added that the confederates' boasting about their prowess counted for little as far as the castle garrison was concerned. The writers' message to Teige and Turlough MacConsnamha, sons of the already executed Garret, was that if they ever came near Manorhamilton, their two sisters who were still prisoners there, would also be hanged. Colonel

---

information of Sir Frederick Hammilton, pp 2, 46–8, 57–8, 65, 68; see also McGrath, 'A biographical dictionary', pp 280–2. Sir Frederick Hamilton would later make a reference to Cole being 'chast', on one occasion, by his own officers and men.   **73** *Another extract of severall letters*, pp 42–4.

Luke Taaffe and Lieutenant Colonel Bryan MacDonnagh were also warned that if they persisted in their attacks on the castle, they would likely end up on its gallows themselves. They should be mindful that they had already lost many men in their attempts to steal Hamilton's cows over the last twelve months. The six signatories, who concluded by wishing their fellow countrymen failure and misfortune in 'this abhominable, barbarous and detestable rebellion' and advising them to forsake their 'lying and seducing leaders', were Shane Roe MacRoy, Cormac O'Clery, Edmond O'Kelly, Connor O'Feeney and Hugh and Bryan O'Phelan. There are no corroborated sources to confirm the existence of these 'loyall' Irishmen, although, around the same time, a Connor O'Feeney made a deposition against his former master, Robert Parke of Newtown, which is recorded in *The information of Sir Frederick Hammilton*. It should also be remembered that Sir William Cole took Bryan Maguire of Tempo and fifty of his followers into his service after they had refused to join the rebellion. Cole claimed that these men were of great use to him as spies and guides. So we should not dismiss out of hand the possibility that some Irishmen also served in Sir Frederick's garrison and that the letter was in fact genuine.[74]

The letter provoked no response from the confederates at Dromahair. They did, however, continue to build up their large camp beside Creevelea Abbey. Upon hearing that there were now as many as eight thousand cows in the vicinity of the camp, and that the confederates had a good supply of corn, Hamilton sent word to Enniskillen that there would be plenty of animals and grain for both garrisons if Cole's men would join with Sir Frederick's soldiers in a raid on Creevelea. The authorities in Enniskillen, although acknowledging their shortage of food, were non-committal in their response, because they were 'in such confusion and disorder amongst themselves'. For several weeks, Hamilton was reluctant to venture an attack on his own against such a huge band of confederates. As Easter approached, though, his own stock of provisions was dwindling fast. Realizing that Cole was, at this stage, unlikely to show up, Sir Frederick himself led a party of men to Dromahair on Spy Wednesday, 29 March 1643. They fought their way 'through a great body of the rogues, where we kild divers, hurt above 40 [and] chast the rest into woods and boggs'. They brought home three prisoners, 'neere 400 cowes, with pretty store of sheepe, goates and mares, with some small supply of butter and meale'. The soldiers themselves lost nobody in the raid, although one of their musketeers sustained an injury. They afterwards concluded that if the Enniskillen garrison had listened to Hamilton's advice, their combined forces could have 'had a faire pull of at least 7 or 8,000 cowes, with abundance of wheate and other corne besides'.[75]

---

74 Ibid., pp 43–4; *The information of Sir Frederick Hammilton*, pp 14–16, 86.   75 *Another extract of*

Colonel Luke Taaffe was furious at Sir Frederick's lightning raid on his camp at Creevelea, and resolved immediately on a retaliatory attack on Castle Hamilton. On Holy Saturday morning, 1 April, his regiment, consisting of three divisions, including 130 musketeers, marched to within a mile of the castle. From there, they spotted Hamilton's cattle and horses grazing in the fields nearby, guarded by a few dozen soldiers. The castle sentries sounded the alarm when they saw the confederates approaching the herd. There were only about fifty foot soldiers left in the castle at the time, as the rest of the garrison were out collecting firewood and other necessities. Sir Frederick nevertheless ordered the fifty to rescue those guarding the herd, who were now in imminent danger of being cut off by Taaffe's men. On seeing the small band of soldiers marching out from the castle, the Irish turned swiftly in their direction, firing their muskets. Hamilton's men withdrew behind a ditch for cover, while the confederates, imagining that the soldiers were retreating, began cheering as if they were already victorious. However, Sir Frederick's musketeers 'did from that ditch so pepper [the Irish] that it is not to be beleeved what a sudden alteration our handful made amongst their multitude, our pike-men flying in upon them'. Bryan MacDonnagh, who fought 'most desperately as ever man did [even] upon his knees', was killed. Even the British acknowledged that it was a 'pitty so great courage should have beene in so arch a traitour, who was thought to have beene one of the greatest fire-brands of Connaght in this rebellion'. Once the insurgents realized that their lieutenant colonel had been slain, they fled in disorder across the River Bonet. Many of them were killed in the confusion of the retreat. The British, meanwhile, lost only one man in the encounter. Revd John Cunningham, Protestant minister of Cloonclare parish and a member of the castle garrison, was struck by a musket ball and died two days later. On Easter Sunday morning, Sir Frederick sent some soldiers out of the castle to see if the insurgents had come back during the night to carry away their dead. As this had not happened, twenty soldiers spent the next two days burying the sixty corpses that were found. It was also believed that the Bonet, which was then in flood, had already swept away many others. The soldiers' wives and sons recovered enough muskets, pikes, swords and skeans to arm 150 men. Hamilton regarded the event as a 'great and miraculous victory', which had been achieved by so few defenders, and 'without the help of Enniskillen'. As for the confederates, this engagement marked the end of their attempts to take Manorhamilton Castle. Incidentally, Owen O'Rourke, although still resident in Dromahair Castle at the time, did not take part in this attack, and probably left the area soon afterwards.[76]

severall letters, pp 44–5. **76** Ibid., pp 45–8; deposition of William Walsh in Wood-Martin, *History of Sligo*, i, p. 207.

Six weeks later, the Manorhamilton garrison was again running low in provisions. So on 15 May, Sir Frederick himself led a strong party of men to the Grange area of north Sligo, upon learning that a huge herd of cows had been brought there by confederates from Co. Donegal. After having killed many insurgents in the vicinity of Grange Castle, which was then occupied by a Donegal man, Hugh MacDowell O'Gallagher, and burned several villages and houses in the area, the soldiers took a large prey of animals. On the way home, they were ambushed by as many as five hundred Donegal confederates, according to Hamilton. He claimed that his men succeeded in killing and stripping sixty of these, including Marcus O'Clery, who had served in the Spanish army. They also seized many new muskets and a large bag of gunpowder from the Irish.[77]

On his return to Manorhamilton, Sir Frederick, temporarily setting aside his previous differences with Sir William Cole, wrote a letter to the Enniskillen commander, requesting his help to defeat the remainder of the Donegal confederates. In return, he promised that Cole could have as many of their cows as he could get his hands on. On this occasion, Cole reacted quickly and positively, no doubt motivated by the size of the prey on offer, and arrived on 20 May, with four or five hundred men, near Castle Hamilton. He would not approach any closer, however, as he had heard a report that Sir Frederick had threatened to imprison him if he ever entered his castle. Hamilton, who was ill in bed that day, sent his minister, Revd John Long, to dispel any doubts that Cole might have regarding his safety. Cole soon relented, and he and his officers entered the castle, where they were courteously received by Sir Frederick and his wife, Sidney. Hamilton then gave the Enniskillen officers directions on how to get to Grange, and also sent fifty of his own soldiers to accompany the Enniskillen party. He could not spare any more, as many of his men were still recovering from their recent engagement with the Donegal confederates. The raiders were successful in Grange, returning to Manorhamilton two days later with almost two thousand cows, as many sheep and a large amount of booty. To Sir Frederick's annoyance, however, they had killed very few confederates, which was the principal reason he had notified Cole of their existence in the first place. The Enniskillen commander and his officers had no qualms about spending that night in Castle Hamilton. The following morning, at the division of the prey, Cole took nearly 1,700 of the cows, leaving Hamilton and his officers with only 155 between them, which were not fit to be driven back to Enniskillen. He also commandeered many horses to carry home the booty. Cole later claimed to have given half of the sheep as a gift to Sidney Hamilton, but Sir Frederick scornfully described these as 'a number of poor sheep, which his party had left uneaten and

77 *The information of Sir Frederick Hammilton*, pp 50–1.

could not drive with them'. Before the Enniskillen party departed, Hamilton nevertheless invited Sir William Cole to attend the christening of his youngest son, Gustavus, who had been born a few weeks earlier. Despite this gesture, Cole left Manorhamilton when the ceremony was over, complaining that he and his officers had been shown much disrespect during the course of their visit.[78]

There was no confederate activity of any significance in the north Leitrim area during the month of June 1643. This did not mean that Sir Frederick Hamilton could afford to be in any way complacent about his security. In fact, a new menace developed when Owen Roe O'Neill retired, with his remaining Ulster forces, to south Leitrim after his defeat at the Battle of Clones on the 13th of that month. When writing some weeks later to the lords justices in Dublin, Hamilton stated that 'your lordships may judge of my condition, who am daily threatned by Owen Roerke O'Neale, and most of the rest of the Ulster rebels who are driven into this county'. It was probably at this time, therefore, that Hamilton constructed a half-moon fortification outside the bawn wall of his castle. It consisted of a rampart and a ditch laid, in a convex shape, along the bank of the Owenbeg nearest the castle. This south-eastern outer defence would have controlled access to the bridge that spanned that river, thus giving further protection to the main entrance of his stronghold. Perhaps he felt that an attack by O'Neill would most likely come from that direction. Despite the threat of such an assault, there is no evidence that the Ulster general ever set foot in Manorhamilton.[79]

On 4 July, Sir Frederick's wife, Sidney, wrote to their two eldest sons, Frederick and James, in Glasgow, where they had just completed their first year at university. While attending the college, the young men also had their own personal tutor, a Mr Allan Cunningham. In a letter to Cunningham in May, Hamilton had expressed satisfaction with the tutor on his success 'in breeding' the youths. Sir Frederick's first cousin, Alexander Seton, sixth earl of Eglinton, also kept a watchful eye over his two young relatives from Manorhamilton, and saw to it that they were kept free from distractions and provided with all the college books they required. Sidney Hamilton, in her letter, announced the death of a close relative or friend called Mary. His wife must have been quite upset, as Sir Frederick wrote to Eglinton the following day, asking that his sons be sent home with his servant who had delivered the letter, so that they could be a

---

78 Ibid., pp 18, 50–5.   **79** Ibid., p. 66; *Another extract of severall letters*, pp 9–12; Mac an Ghallóglaigh, 'Sir Frederick Hamilton', 99; see also R. Hutton and W. Reeves, 'Sieges and fortifications' in Kenyon and Ohlmeyer (eds), *The civil wars*, pp 203–25 for further information on half-moons and other earthwork defences that were created around some cities and towns in England, Scotland and Ireland during the wars of the 1640s. There are no remains of the half-moon fortification in Manorhamilton, but the small field where the defence was located is still called the half-moon.

comfort to their grieving mother. There were many references in both letters to the continual presence of some confederates in the Manorhamilton area. Sidney wrote that she would have sent a better token to Frederick and James 'if the feeldes were cleare', while Sir Frederick promised to 'keape the passage ... cleere' for his sons' return.[80]

Hamilton had taken Robert Parke, commander of Newtown Castle, into custody on 1 July 1642, for disobeying his orders and allegedly collaborating with the Irish. Parke was still a closely guarded prisoner, held in solitary confinement, in Castle Hamilton, twelve months later. This was despite the fact that some of Parke's relatives and friends had, on two separate occasions, lodged petitions for his release with the lords justices. The most influential of these relatives was Parke's father-in-law, Sir Edward Povey, a prominent settler and military officer in Roscommon. It was due to his patronage that Parke, although resident in Newtown, had been elected MP for Roscommon in the Irish parliament of 1640–1. Other significant allies were relatives of his uncle, Sir Roger Jones, who had been a large landowner and wealthy businessman in Sligo. Parke had actually been a business partner of his uncle's in the years leading up to the rebellion. In response to the first of these petitions, the lords justices had, on 24 January 1643, ordered Sir Frederick to send Parke, under escort by Viscount Ranelagh, president of Connacht, for trial to Dublin. Hamilton later claimed that he had never received that order. Povey and others again petitioned the lords justices for Parke's release about the beginning of May, and this time agreed to put up a surety of £10,000 that he would present himself to answer the charges against him. The lords justices reacted some weeks later by ordering Sir Frederick to bring Parke to Ballyshannon, from where he would be sent to Derry and then on to Dublin for trial. Hamilton wrote in reply on 6 July that Povey's petition was both scandalous and seditious, and portrayed him in a very bad light for having imprisoned Parke. He added that the former Newtown commander, through his collaboration with the Irish, almost caused the defeat and ruination of all who sheltered in Castle Hamilton. Sir Frederick maintained that he was finally forced to seize Parke and imprison him, following information received from Parke's own servants and soldiers, who also made subsequent depositions regarding his guilt. Hamilton then greatly exaggerated both the dangerous circumstances in which he found himself and the distance between Manorhamilton and Ballyshannon in order to justify his refusal to comply with the lords justices' order. He said that he was 'living in the bozom of the rebels', and could not therefore afford to reduce the

---

80 *Records of the University of Glasgow from its foundation till 1727* (3 vols, Glasgow, 1854), iii; NRS, GD 3/5/298, Alexander, sixth earl of Eglinton, to Mr Allan Cunningham, tutor to Sir Frederick Hamilton's children at Glasgow, 26 Dec. 1642; NRS, GD 3/5/308, Sir Frederick Hamilton to Cunningham, 4 May 1643; NRS, GD 3/5/309, Sidney Hamilton to her sons in Glasgow, 4 July 1643; NRS, GD 3/5/310, Sir

size of his small garrison by sending a convoy of men with such a dangerous prisoner as Parke, on the long and hazardous road to Ballyshannon, which lay in another province altogether. Moreover, he expressed his grievances with their lordships for appearing more concerned about someone like Parke, who had colluded with the Irish, than with himself, who had unsuccessfully requested help and supplies from them three months previously. Finally, he enclosed, with his own reply to the lords justices, a letter from the prisoner to Sir Edward Povey. In that letter, Parke was put under pressure to back up Sir Frederick's account of the reasons he was arrested. He was also forced to mention what great work Hamilton was doing with so small a garrison against the insurgents.[81]

One week after Sir Frederick had replied to the lords justices, a messenger arrived at Castle Hamilton with a letter from Viscount Taaffe of Ballymote, who offered, in the absence of Viscount Ranelagh, to take Parke to Dublin to stand trial. Hamilton was incensed that someone, whom he believed to be associating with the insurgents, should now have the audacity to meddle in a private matter between him and their lordships. He immediately arrested the messenger and reportedly had him hanged. Some weeks later, he sent a detachment of soldiers to Ballymote. On this occasion, they reached their destination and burned Taaffe's town to the ground. It is not known if there were any civilian casualties during the course of this arson attack or if the townspeople managed to take refuge in Ballymote Castle before the assault began. One way or the other, this was to be the last major violent offensive carried out by Sir Frederick Hamilton on either confederates or civilians in Leitrim or its neighbouring counties.[82]

By the end of August 1643, hostilities had almost ceased in Leitrim and the surrounding area. The twenty-one months of almost continuous attacks, raids and plundering had, however, taken a terrible toll on local insurgents and civilians. Hamilton's men claimed to have killed almost 1,200 persons during this time, including three hundred at the burning of Sligo and 58 on Manorhamilton gallows. Among those who died by hanging were Con O'Rourke, sheriff of Leitrim, Turmultagh MacGarraghy, deputy sub-sheriff of Donegal, Connor MacLoughlin and Garret MacConsnamha, chiefs of their respective clans, and one woman – the wife of Cormac O'Hoey. The total number of victims killed by the soldiers from Castle Hamilton was, nevertheless, no greater than that slain by neighbouring British garrisons, and – if we allow for Sir Frederick's tendency to brag – it may have even been significantly less. Troops from Ballyshannon and Donegal town, for example, were said to have put to death two thousand Irishmen

Frederick to Eglinton, 5 July 1643.   **81** *The information of Sir Frederick Hammilton*, pp 9, 64–7; McGrath, 'A biographical dictionary', pp 234–5; see also O'Dowd, *Power, politics and land*, pp 99–101, 104, 121. **82** *The information of Sir Frederick Hammilton*, pp 65, 68; J. Lowe (ed.), *Letter-book of the earl of Clanricarde, 1643–47* (Dublin, 1983), pp 10–11.

between them. Sir William Cole's men in Enniskillen were even credited with having killed as many as 2,417. Hamilton also claimed that he lost only about twenty to twenty-five of his own soldiers in the fighting. Their military training, superior weaponry and a skilled though ruthless commander, experienced in Continental warfare, all combined to ensure that they suffered such a low level of casualties, despite being greatly outnumbered in many encounters with the Irish.[83]

A YEAR'S TRUCE IN IRELAND

Tensions between Charles I and the Long Parliament in Westminster had continued to increase after the execution of Lord Deputy Wentworth for treason in May 1641. Towards the end of that year, parliament brought forward measures to reduce the king's authority over the armed forces. Pym, leader of the parliament, and his majority of Puritan MPs also presented Charles with their Grand Remonstrance – a list of grievances that denounced Jesuits, Church of England bishops and many of the king's counsellors and courtiers. As a result of the power struggle between the two parties, neither side was able to send sufficient military forces to crush the insurgents during the early months of the Irish rebellion. In January 1642, the king had treason charges drawn up against Pym and five other parliamentary leaders, and tried to have them arrested. He was unable to do so, because parliament, believing that he was trying to use force to crush legitimate opposition, refused to comply with the royal command and became more united in its hostility towards him. Soon afterwards, Charles left London and set up his headquarters at Hampton Court Palace, twelve miles away. From then on, parliament was master of the capital, and Pym controlled a united parliament. The king began to raise a royal army during the first six months of 1642. He also sent Queen Henrietta Maria to the Continent to seek military support from Holland and Denmark, and to pawn the crown jewels for money and arms. Parliament in turn began raising its own forces from April onwards. Charles declared war on 22 August, and the first engagement between both sides occurred near Worcester one month later. The balance of military power had tilted in favour of the royalists by the summer of 1643, due in part to the arms and money that the queen had brought back to England. By early August of that year, it looked as if the parliamentarian cause would collapse. Although the parliamentarians rallied in the weeks that followed, it had been clear for some time that neither side could win the English Civil War without help from Ireland or Scotland.[84]

83 *Another extract of severall letters*, pp 55–6; McGrath, 'A biographical dictionary', p. 107; P. Ó Gallachair, 'Tirconnell in 1641' in Revd T. O'Donnell OFM (ed.), *Fr John Colgan OFM* (Dublin, 1959), p. 87.   84 See

While, on the one hand, he employed the marquis of Hamilton to try and ensure that the Scottish covenanters did not enter into an alliance with the English parliament, the king, at the same time, felt that his best chance of getting military support in England lay with Ireland. The commander of the army there, James Butler, whom Charles had created marquis of Ormond in August 1642, was unable to defeat the Irish because of a lack of men, money and supplies. If, however, a peace treaty could be concluded with the confederates, many of Ormond's troops could then be withdrawn for royal service in England. The king might even manage to persuade Irish confederates, by offering them significant concessions, to contribute troops and money to his cause as well.[85]

There were many reasons why, by 1643, a truce might also suit the confederate Catholics in Ireland. Although they then controlled large areas of three provinces – Leinster, Munster and Connacht – the maintenance of a bureaucracy in Kilkenny and four provincial armies in the field was a costly business, and money and arms were in short supply. Customs could not be accessed because government forces controlled most of the Irish ports. Loans from wealthy merchants were not easily acquired, and levies on the territories held by the confederates proved difficult to collect. There was little likelihood either of foreign military assistance. Moreover, an alliance with Ormond might help prevent a victory by the anti-Catholic Westminster parliament in the English Civil War, which could have disastrous consequences in Ireland.[86]

As early as 11 January 1643, the king had secretly authorized the marquis of Ormond to meet with some confederate Catholics and hear their grievances. By the end of February, the confederates had agreed to engage in exploratory talks with the king's commissioners at Trim, Co. Meath. At the meeting, which took place on St Patrick's Day, it soon became obvious that both sides were very far apart in their demands. The confederates would agree to end the war if the penal laws were repealed, if Poyning's Law was suspended during a meeting of a free Irish parliament, and if Catholic lands, confiscated since 1607, were returned. The king, however, would not contemplate rescinding Poyning's Law. Nor would he tolerate free worship for Irish Catholics, as this would seem in England that he was backing an Irish cause. Moreover, any wholesale restoration of land to Catholics might cost the king the allegiance of his New English subjects in Ireland who had been granted substantial estates from this appropriated land over the previous thirty-five years. Although little had been achieved at the meeting, Charles ordered Ormond, at the end of April, to seek a year's truce with the confederates, during which they could have further negotiations with the king

Wheeler, *The Irish and British wars*, pp 49–60, 77–87. **85** Stevenson, *Scottish covenanters and Irish Confederates*, p. 145. **86** See Gillespie, *Seventeenth-century Ireland*, p. 161; Hamilton, *The Irish rebellion of*

himself at his headquarters in Oxford. Tense discussions about such a temporary ceasefire eventually took place at Castlemarten, near Kilcullen in Co. Kildare, the residence of Sir Maurice Eustace, speaker of the Irish House of Commons and one of the royalist commissioners, during the last week of June 1643. These were adjourned one week later and hostilities on the battlefield were even renewed between Ormond and the confederates. Talks were reconvened at Jigginstown House, near Naas, the residence of the former Lord Deputy Wentworth, at the end of August, and a cessation of arms was finally signed by both parties on 15 September.[87]

It was agreed that the ceasefire would last for one year. According to its terms, the confederates would contribute £30,000 and supplies to the royalist military campaign in England. In return, they would be allowed to retain control of the territories they had captured in the previous two years. Charles would also consider repealing some penal laws and granting the confederates significant political independence. The cessation brought hostilities in Ireland to a temporary end. It was generally honoured by most commanders on both sides throughout the country. Even the Scots forces in Ulster, who had not been represented at the negotiations, reluctantly agreed in early October to observe it – at least until they would receive instructions from Scotland and the English parliament on how to proceed. Otherwise, they feared they would be attacked by the Irish for being cessation breakers. Almost at once, Charles ordered the marquis of Ormond to ship as many of his regiments as possible to Welsh seaports. Over the course of the next five months or so, almost five thousand English troops who had originally been sent over to Ireland in the early months of 1642 to suppress the rebellion were now repatriated to fight for the king. At least a similar number of troops, raised in Ireland by New English commanders, were also dispatched across the Irish Sea to serve the king in England. Meanwhile, the ceasefire provided the confederates with the opportunity to select delegates who would attempt to negotiate a permanent treaty with the king at Oxford, in the spring of the following year.[88]

The earl of Clanricard, the leading royalist in Connacht and one of Ormond's principal associates in the negotiations for a cessation, had written to Sir Frederick Hamilton on 23 August 1643 to inform him of the possibility of a temporary ceasefire in Connacht being agreed to, pending final talks on a countrywide truce. Although Hamilton's reply has been lost, it is obvious from Clanricard's next letter to him that Sir Frederick strongly opposed the provincial settlement as it would have exposed him to attack from nearby Ulster confederates who would not have been bound by such an agreement. His antagonism to any truce with the Irish, be it at provincial or national level, was, however, much more fundamental. He felt that he could never trust the 'cruell and bloody rebell[s]' who had instigated the insurrection, and had caused him so much grief over the previous two years. He believed, moreover, that the confederates were already beaten in Leitrim and the surrounding counties, and therefore saw no reason to compromise with them. In common with a number of other British commanders in Ireland, he opposed from the beginning any idea of a cessation. He gave effect to his disapproval by allowing the contents of a detailed diary of his achievements against the insurgents, which had been compiled by one of his clerks or clergymen in Manorhamilton, to be published in an anti-cessation pamphlet in London, probably about the middle of August 1643. Furthermore, as soon as he heard that the countrywide ceasefire had been agreed on 15 September, he went immediately with his wife and youngest children to Derry in an attempt to try and persuade the authorities there not to adhere to the new settlement.[89]

Sir Frederick made several powerful enemies, at least in part as a result of his position and actions against the cessation. Among these was the marquis of Ormond, who was severely critical of Hamilton's disparagement of those British officers in Ulster who even partially observed the truce. But there was also Sir William Cole of Enniskillen, who was extremely annoyed at the 'scandalous calumnies and aspersions digested in fifteen places of that pamphlet, printed at London in Anno Dom. 1643'. He resented the fact that he had been in this very public way, 'most injuriously taxed, with often reiterations of unworthy and mean carriage towards him [Sir Frederick]'. In consequence, he would take every opportunity he could from then on, not only to strongly justify, to the English parliament, his own behaviour during the rebellion and cessation, and make many counter-allegations against Hamilton, but also to try and block any chances of promotion of his hostile and ambitious neighbour.[90]

---

89 The diary outlining Sir Frederick's accomplishments against the rebels is entitled: *A true relation of the manner of our collonell Sir Frederick Hamiltons returne from London-derry in Ireland, being 60 miles from his castle and garrison, where he was at the beginning and breaking out of this rebellion, with the particular services performed by the horse and foote companies which he commandes garrison'd at Manor Hamilton in the county of Leitrim in the province of Connaught*. The word *cleric* was also spelt *clerk* in documents of the time, so it is not possible to say with certainty whether the author was a secretary of Sir Frederick or a clergyman in his castle. Hamilton had sent the diary to a friend named Thornton of Derry, who brought it to London and showed it to various people, before the parliamentary authorities directed that it be published. The diary fills forty-two of the sixty-two pages of the pamphlet called *Another extract of severall letters from Ireland, intimating their present state*. See also *The information of Sir Frederick Hammilton*, introduction and pp 2, 44–5, 63; Lowe (ed.), *Letter-book of the earl of Clanricarde*, pp 10–11. **90** *The information of Sir Frederick Hammilton*, p. 17; Carte, *The life of James, duke of Ormond*, iii, pp 164–5.

CHAPTER SEVEN

The committed covenanter, November 1643–February 1647

THE SOLEMN LEAGUE AND COVENANT

While Charles I was negotiating a truce with the Irish confederates in 1643, the English parliament was, at the same time, seeking an alliance with the Scots. In fact, the Westminster parliamentarians had made an initial request for military aid to the Scottish privy council as early as November of the previous year. Despite the efforts of the marquis of Hamilton, whom the king elevated to the dukedom in April 1643, and those of his younger brother, William, earl of Lanark, the covenanter-dominated council ensured that the English parliament's plea was given widespread publicity throughout Scotland. The covenanters, who had defeated Charles in the Bishops' Wars some years previously, now called upon the king to allow a meeting of the Scottish parliament to discuss the issue. Although Charles naturally refused to sanction such a request, the privy council voted on 12 May 1643 to convene, without royal warrant, an alternative assembly, called the convention of estates.[1]

As arrangements were being made to hold the Scottish convention, an event happened in Ulster that alarmed the covenanters. Randal MacDonnell, the earl of Antrim, whom Charles I had commissioned to raise an Irish army to invade Scotland during the First Bishops' War in 1639, was captured by Robert Monro's Scots forces in Co. Down. A search of his papers revealed plans for a new royalist uprising in Scotland, supported by an Irish Catholic army. This news strengthened the covenanter case for an alliance with the English parliament, when the convention of estates met on 22 June. The leading covenanter, Archibald Campbell, marquis of Argyll, had copies of Antrim's documents conveyed to Westminster, and also requested the English parliament to send representatives to Edinburgh to discuss ways of combating the common danger posed by the king and his Catholic allies.[2]

Four English House of Commons commissioners arrived in Edinburgh on 7 August 1643 to negotiate an alliance with the Scots. Within ten days, members of

---

1 Donaldson, *Scotland: James V to James VII*, pp 330–1; M. Lynch (ed.), *The Oxford companion to Scottish history* (Oxford, 2001), p. 111. 2 Wheeler, *The Irish and British wars*, pp 89–90. Archibald Campbell, earl of Argyll, had been created a marquis in 1641.

the Scottish convention, the general assembly of the kirk and the English commissioners had drafted a treaty known as the Solemn League and Covenant. The pact was reminiscent of the Scottish Presbyterian covenants of 1581 and 1638, and in fact was drawn up with the assistance of the authors of the 1638 covenant. The Solemn League and Covenant was a religious-political-military agreement that would bind together the fortunes of Scotland and the English parliament for the next four years. Religiously, the signatories promised to preserve Presbyterianism in Scotland, to extend the Presbyterian doctrine, worship and form of government to England and Ireland, and to 'extirpate all forms of popery and prelacy' in all three kingdoms. Politically, the sides agreed to preserve the rights and privileges of both parliaments, as well as the 'firm peace and union' of Scotland and England. Militarily, the two countries pledged to mutually defend each other. When the treaty had been signed in Edinburgh, the convention of estates sent it to Westminster for ratification by the English parliament. The convention itself then adjourned until January 1644, leaving an executive called the 'committee of estates' to govern Scotland in the interim.[3]

The new treaty was discussed at Westminster during the month of September 1643. While the parliamentarians there favoured a political and military alliance with Scotland, as well as the abolition of the office of bishop in the English church, many had serious reservations about replacing the existing Church of England form of worship and structures of government with those of Scottish Presbyterianism. The English parliament did finally ratify the Solemn League and Covenant on 25 September, but only after accepting to reform the English church 'according to the Word of God' – a phrase that afforded them plenty of latitude regarding the type of changes that they themselves would be willing to introduce. For the English then, the treaty was primarily a military one, entered into for the purpose of securing an ally in their conflict with the king. For the Scots, however, one of the primary commitments of the pact was its religious component. Consequently, although the treaty did help to turn the tide in favour of parliament in the English Civil War, it also bore the seeds of future discord between the covenanters and the parliamentarians, on account of the differences of interpretation of some clauses by both sets of signatories.[4]

Even while the English parliament was still discussing the pact at Westminster, Argyll and the English commissioners in Edinburgh were already working out details of the proposed military alliance between the two sides. The covenanters began to raise troops for a new Scots army and commanders were selected.

---

3 E. Furgol, 'The civil wars in Scotland' in J. Kenyon and J. Ohlmeyer (eds), *The civil wars*, p. 49; Hamilton, *The Irish rebellion of 1641*, p. 297; Lynch (ed.), *The Oxford companion to Scottish history*, p. 436. The committee of estates would continue to govern in the years ahead, whenever the convention was not in session. 4 Lynch (ed.), *The Oxford companion to Scottish history*, pp 436–7; Scott, *Politics and war*, pp 65–6.

Alexander Leslie, now earl of Leven, was once again chosen as general. A final military settlement between Westminster and the covenanters, which committed the Scots to sending an army into England to support the parliamentarians, and bound the English to pay for the Scottish armies in England and Ulster, was reached on 29 November. Within weeks, the Army of the Solemn League and Covenant had assembled in the south-eastern Scottish Lowlands. On 19 January 1644, a confident Leven entered England at the head of twenty-one thousand men and quickly secured the north-east of the country.[5]

SIR FREDERICK TAKES THE COVENANT OATH

The English parliament condemned the marquis of Ormond, Charles I's lieutenant general of the army in Ireland, for having concluded a cessation with the Irish confederates in mid-September 1643. Westminster was also critical of the lords justices and the Dublin parliament for having accepted the deal. It realized that the English troops, which had been sent over to Ireland in the early months of 1642 to suppress the rebellion, would now be repatriated to fight for the king against the parliamentarians in the English Civil War. But it also had no wish to see the Irish insurgents being treated with apparent leniency, accorded legitimate status and given a chance to regroup and re-supply. It set out, therefore, to try and win the loyalty of both the Scots army in Ulster and the British settler forces in Ireland. On 25 September, the very day it signed the Solemn League and Covenant, it mandated the Revd James Traile to go to Ulster to persuade both sets of troops there to oppose the cessation. Some days later, Westminster sent a petition against the agreement to British units in Dublin, Munster and Ulster. Again, in a letter dated 3 November, it promised substantial supplies to British commanders in Ulster if they would renew the war against the confederates.[6]

While the cessation came as a welcome relief to the British commanders in Leinster, Munster and much of Connacht, because they lacked the necessary military supplies to continue the war against the confederates, it was quite a different situation for the Ulster and north-east Connacht Protestant leaders. They had achieved a position of relative strength over the insurgents and were much more secure in their territories. On 13 June 1643, the Laggan army had defeated Owen Roe O'Neill's confederate forces at Clones, Co. Monaghan, and had destroyed his army. As a result, Charlemont was the only fort still held by the

---

Ulster Irish. Meanwhile, Sir Frederick Hamilton had decisively beaten the Sligo insurgents at Manorhamilton as far back as the previous April. The local O'Rourkes had already been forced to leave the area some months earlier. As we saw in chapter six, Sir Frederick went from Manorhamilton to Derry with his family in September to voice his opposition to the cessation. There, he found that the officers of the Laggan army, despite their loyalty to Ormond and the king, also had serious reservations regarding the advisability of the agreement.[7]

Nevertheless, the British commanders in Ulster adhered in general to the terms of the cessation in the months that followed its signing, although they did continue to harass the confederates by stealing or destroying their corn. It may have been their lack of adequate ammunition and food stocks, however, as much as their regard for Ormond, that prevented them from fully re-engaging with the enemy. In a reply to Loudoun, the Scottish lord chancellor and president of the convention of estates, who had expressed surprise that they had ceased to wage war against the insurgents, a group of Derry commanders, headed by Sir William Stewart, Sir Robert Stewart and Mayor Robert Thornton, as well as Sir Frederick Hamilton, who was then resident in the city, declared on 8 November that they had lost too much in terms of friends and estates during the rebellion for them now to allow the Irish to prevail. They had only ceased to fight, they said, because of a shortage of supplies and the difficulty of conducting a winter campaign. They justified their recent inaction by alleging that even Monro's soldiers were more or less abiding by the cessation, since they had now withdrawn to their base in Carrickfergus. The signatories to the letter assured Loudoun, however, that if he would refrain from recalling Monro's forces to Scotland to serve in the Army of the Solemn League and Covenant, provide the Derry leaders with ammunition and food, and petition the English parliament to send its long-promised money and supplies to Ulster, then they would willingly renew the war against the confederates.[8]

Within weeks of ratifying the Solemn League and Covenant, the English parliament decided that the covenant oath should be imposed on Protestants in England, Scotland and Ireland. Such an imposition in Ireland would, if success-ful, drive a further wedge between Monro's army and the British forces on the one hand, and the marquis of Ormond, who would shortly be appointed lord lieutenant of Ireland by the king, on the other. In early October, Charles had declared that the covenant was 'a traitorous and seditious combination' against himself, the Protestant religion and the kingdom of England. He therefore ordered all his subjects to refrain from taking it. Shortly afterwards, Ormond

---

7 Armstrong, *Protestant war*, p. 101.   **8** HMC Portland MSS, i, pp 149–150; Carte, *The life of James, duke of Ormond*, iii, p. 69.

reiterated the king's command to the officers of the British forces in Ireland. By the middle of the month, however, the English parliament requested the Scottish government to ensure that the covenant was taken by all Scots, both military and civilian, in Ireland, while it pledged that it would administer the oath to English Protestants there. Then, on 4 November, Westminster sent Captain Owen O'Connolly (who, in 1641, had informed the lords justices in Dublin about the rebellion) to Ulster to urge the British commanders there both to subscribe to the covenant and to renew the war against the confederates. In spite of these measures, the covenant had still not been enforced in Ireland by the end of 1643, although it was reported that many of the British forces in Ulster, especially those of Scottish nationality, were disposed towards accepting it, and that many among the civilian Protestant population were even requesting it.[9]

The commanders of the British regiments in Ulster were now in a particularly difficult situation. They had received no pay since the beginning of the rebellion and had expended most of their wealth on maintaining their regiments. Although their allegiance was still directed towards the king, they now believed that their only hope of receiving supplies lay with the English parliament. They decided, therefore, to call a meeting in Belfast on 2 January 1644 to consider their attitude to the covenant. Most of the British leaders, including Sir Robert Stewart, Sir Audley Mervyn, Sir William Cole and Robert Thornton from the north-west of the province, and Lord Montgomery, Sir James Montgomery and Colonel Chichester from Cos Antrim and Down, were in attendance. They decided in the end not to denounce the covenant in front of their regiments as Ormond had ordered, since so many of their own men were in favour of taking it. Nevertheless, they privately resolved not to subscribe to the covenant themselves, or to accept the English parliament's proposal that Monro be appointed commander-in-chief of the British as well as the Scottish forces in Ulster. They omitted, though, to mention these details when informing Westminster shortly afterwards that they were willing to renew the war against the insurgents, but urgently needed supplies in order to do so.[10]

One might have expected that Sir Frederick Hamilton would have followed the example of the Ulster British commanders and rejected the covenant. He had, after all, served with Sir Robert Stewart in Germany under Gustavus Adolphus some ten years previously, and had also been sent supplies by Stewart from Derry on several occasions in 1642. It is likely, moreover, that Thornton – Hamilton's friend from Derry who had circulated his *Exact relation of the good service of Sir Frederick Hammilton* in London in the summer of 1643 – was related to Robert

---

9 *The information of Sir Frederick Hammilton*, p. 41; Carte, *The life of James, duke of Ormond*, iii, pp 70–2.
10 Carte, *The life of James, duke of Ormond*, iii, pp 71–3; Armstrong, *Protestant war*, pp 104, 113.

Thornton, mayor of Derry. However, circumstances had changed in the intervening months and relationships between Hamilton and many of the other
settlers in the north-west were now far from cordial. When Sir Frederick arrived
in Derry with his family in September 1643, he found to his annoyance and
disgust that the British regiments in the Derry and Lifford areas had taken
possession of the property and lands that he had recently inherited from his late
father-in-law, Sir John Vaughan, who had been governor of the city. The
regiments' commanders and officers had also appropriated his tenants' rents to
the value of £3,000 to £4,000. Hamilton singled out Sir Robert Stewart's
regiment as the guiltiest party, but may also have been referring to his brother, Sir
William, whose forces were stationed at various times in Raphoe and Letterkenny. Sir Frederick was deeply resentful of these confiscations, since he felt that
he had campaigned as much as either of these colonels during the rebellion, and
had in fact prevented rebels from Connacht from invading Ulster. The colonels
were unwilling to return any of the inheritance to him, even though, according to
Hamilton, they had been supplied several times by both the English parliament
and the Scottish state. They had also seized other estates and had taken large
preys of cows from the rebels. Sir Frederick found himself with little sympathy
from these men, despite the fact that he had few means of support or likely
prospects since his arrival in Derry.[11]

Some weeks after writing to Chancellor Loudoun on 8 November, indicating
their willingness to renew the war against the confederates if they were properly
supplied, the Derry commanders decided to send Sir Frederick to Scotland to
describe in person their poor circumstances. Hamilton used this occasion to
highlight his own particularly difficult situation. He was fortunate in that his first
cousin, Alexander Seton Montgomerie, sixth earl of Eglinton, was a prominent
member of the convention of estates. Sir Frederick had always been on friendly
terms with the earl, and it was he who had seen to it that Hamilton's eldest sons,
Frederick and James, were properly housed, looked after and provided with the
books they required while attending the University of Glasgow in 1642 and
1643. Not surprisingly, therefore, Eglinton and some other of Sir Frederick's
'noble friends … were pleased to take my hard condition and great charge into
their honourable and charitable care and consideration'. He was promised that if
he took the covenant, he would be given command of a regiment in the Army of
the Solemn League and Covenant. He was also given to understand that representations would be made on his behalf with the English parliament for a similar

11 *The information of Sir Frederick Hammilton*, p. 44; *The humble remonstrance*, p. 3; *The several petitions of
William Hansard and Sir Frederick Hammiltoun*, p. 29; The register of deaths of Derry Cathedral lists Sir
John Vaughan's death on 20 Feb. 1643.

position with the British forces in Ireland. It seems pretty obvious therefore that it was on this occasion in Edinburgh that Hamilton took the covenanting oath because of the assurances given him. There is no significant evidence to show that he acted from any great Presbyterian conviction, although several of his writings do contain a number of biblical quotations and references. For their part, the covenanting leaders probably felt that their promises were more than justified, since Sir Frederick was 'a gentleman of considerable influence' in both Ulster and Scotland, who would hopefully be very useful in winning over other British leaders in Ireland to the covenant.[12]

On his return to Ulster, Sir Frederick would have been pleased to observe that the covenant was being received with great enthusiasm there by significant numbers of both the Scottish and British forces and settlers. It probably had not gone unnoticed by these groups that there had been calls somewhat previously in both Westminster and Edinburgh for adequate supplies to be sent to both Monro's army and the British units in Ulster. Moreover, the convention of estates and the English commissioners who had been working out the final details of the Solemn League and Covenant in Edinburgh, had agreed in November 1643 that the English parliament would send £10,000, clothes, food and ammunition to Monro's forces as soon as possible, and that a further £50,000 of arrears would follow by 1 February 1644. There was naturally much unease in both Ulster and Edinburgh when none of the money or supplies had been dispatched by early January. On 11 January, therefore, the convention of estates wrote to Monro telling him that they were making plans to bring his army back to Scotland if the money had not arrived by 2 February. Some of his troops would then be used to reinforce the Army of the Solemn League and Covenant in England, while the rest would become part of a reserve army to defend Scotland against a possible royalist uprising. When they heard of these proposals, some Scots Presbyterians in Ulster, fearing that they would be overrun by the Irish if the army were withdrawn, sent Sir Frederick Hamilton, the newly converted covenanter, to Scotland once again to plead with the convention of estates to change its mind. Sir Frederick was also requested to petition the Scottish administration to send some authorized persons to administer the covenant in Ulster. It was during this visit to Scotland in January and February 1644 that the convention of estates recommended that Hamilton be given special consideration by the committee of

---

12 *The humble remonstrance*, p. 3; J.S. Reid, *History of the Presbyterian Church in Ireland* (3 vols, Belfast, 1867), i, p. 433; E.M. Furgol, *A regimental history of the covenanting armies*, pp 85,134–5, 147; Stevenson, *Scottish covenanters and Irish Confederates*, p. 151; NRS, GD3/6/9, item 10. Eglinton was colonel of a regiment of foot in Monro's army in Ulster, but in the autumn of 1643, he was also commissioned to raise a horse regiment for the new Army of the Solemn League and Covenant. It is quite possible that Sir Frederick also counted Loudoun among his friends, since the lord chancellor was related to the wife of

estates, in view of his 'valorous caradge … against the rebells in Ireland thir tuo yeeres bygane, with the losse he hes susteened and extreemities he hes beene put to, throw his constant and religious opposeing of the saidis rebells'. On 27 February, the committee responded to the proposal by commissioning Sir Frederick colonel of a regiment of horse in the Army of the Solemn League and Covenant.[13]

Despite the ties of kinship and loyalty that had bound the Hamiltons to the Stuart monarchy over several generations, Sir Frederick's decision to withdraw his allegiance from Charles I and join the covenanters may not have been that difficult to make. Tensions had been building for some time between Hamilton on the one hand and the king and his representatives in Ireland on the other. Sir Frederick's numerous differences with Wentworth, and his testimony against him at the lord deputy's trial in the spring of 1641, apparently led to Hamilton being overlooked when the king dispatched commissions to several commanders in the north-west of Ireland following the outbreak of the rebellion later that same year. Sir Frederick also disagreed fundamentally with the marquis of Ormond who, at the king's command, had concluded the cessation of arms with the Irish confederates. Around the same time, moreover, Ormond had ordered Hamilton to hand over his prisoner, Robert Parke of Newtown, whom Sir Frederick believed had colluded with the rebels, to Sir William Cole, so that he could be brought to Dublin for trial. To make matters worse, in Hamilton's eyes, Ormond later restored Parke to his castle at Newtown after Sir Frederick had gone to live in Derry. In the end, though, it was probably the fact that neither the king nor Ormond was capable of offering him any support in his difficult situation in Derry, whereas the covenanters quickly extended the hand of friendship to him, with firm promises of advancement in his career, that prompted him to change sides.[14]

Sir Frederick was not the only member of the Hamilton clan to switch his allegiance from the king to the covenanters at this time. His cousin, William, earl of Lanark, the younger brother of James, duke of Hamilton, escaped from custody after he and his brother had been arrested by the king, following their failure to prevent the signing of the Solemn League and Covenant in Scotland. William then returned to Edinburgh, where he took the covenant in April 1644. He was immediately admitted to the convention of estates as secretary of state, and was also commissioned colonel of horse and foot regiments in the Army of the Solemn League and Covenant. It is interesting to note, however, that Sir Frederick's older brother, the Catholic Sir George of Greenlaw and Roscrea,

James, first earl of Abercorn, Hamilton's brother. **13** *The acts of the parliaments of Scotland* (12 vols, Edinburgh, 1872), vi, pp 75, 698; Carte, *The life of James, duke of Ormond*, iii, p. 72, 74, 75; Reid, *History of the Presbyterian Church in Ireland*, i, p. 433. **14** *The information of Sir Frederick Hammilton*, pp 2, 3.

remained a staunch royalist, and became an important intermediary between Ormond, to whom he was related through marriage, and the confederates.[15]

FROM SUBSCRIBER TO PROMOTER OF THE COVENANT

Before Sir Frederick Hamilton had an opportunity to take up his commission in the Army of the Solemn League and Covenant, the committee of estates decided to send him back to Ulster on an entirely different multifaceted mission. The Scottish forces there were in a 'dangerous discontented condition', because the money and supplies promised to them by the English parliament had still not arrived. On 13 February 1644, the officers of the army met at Carrickfergus and resolved of their own accord to leave Ireland immediately and return to Scotland. Moreover, they took an oath not to lay down their arms or disband in their native land until all arrears due to them were paid. As the whole army was anxious to go as soon as possible, and the number of ships available to transport them was limited, the officers drew lots to determine the order in which the various regiments should depart.[16]

Attempts were meanwhile being made in Edinburgh by Lord Chancellor Loudoun and others to try and get the convention of estates' earlier decision to withdraw the army reversed. At a joint meeting of the Scottish privy council and the committee of estates on 22 February, it was decided to retain Monro's forces in Ulster in order to defeat the confederates, to preserve the Protestant religion and to ensure that the British population there remained in situ. The meeting agreed to send them, within a short space of time, £10,000 sterling, as well as food, suits of clothes, arms and ammunition. If, however, the promised supplies from England had not reached Ulster by the end of March, then the Scots army would after all be allowed to leave.[17]

The new decision of the Scottish authorities came almost too late. Three regiments of Monro's soldiers – Sinclair's, Lothian's and Lawers' – had already procured some ships, and were finalizing arrangements for the crossing. By 26 February, Sinclair's regiment had already reached Scotland and would be followed shortly by the other two. There was now a danger, if the remaining seven regiments of Monro's army left Ulster, that the British forces there would also disband and flee, and that the province would be taken over by the insurgents.[18]

15 *The acts of the parliaments of Scotland*, vi, p. 89; Balfour Paul, *The Scots peerage*, i, 43; R.J. Hunter, 'Style and form in gravestone and monumental sculpture in Co. Tyrone in the 17th and 18th centuries' in C. Dillon and H.A. Jefferies (eds), *Tyrone, history and society* (Dublin, 2000), p. 295; H.C.G. Matthew and B. Harrison (eds), *ODNB*, xxiv, p. 844. 16 *The humble remonstrance*; Carte, *The life of James Duke of Ormond*, iii, p. 74; Reid, *History of the Presbyterian Church in Ireland*, i, p. 432. 17 Stevenson, *Scottish covenanters and Irish Confederates*, pp 152–5. 18 Carte, *The life of James Duke of Ormond*, iii, p. 74;

The committee of estates reacted immediately. Sir Frederick Hamilton and Sir Mungo Campbell of Lawers (whose own regiment was about to set sail from Carrickfergus) were dispatched to Ulster on 27 February – the very day Sir Frederick had received his commission in the Army of the Solemn League and Covenant – to try and dissuade any further Scottish troops from returning to Scotland. To this end, they were to brief the army directly on the money and supplies that the Scottish state had recently agreed to send it. While Hamilton and Campbell were unable to prevent the latter's regiment from following Sinclair's and Lothian's, Sir Frederick was later to write that

> it pleased God, beyond expectation, so to blesse our indeavours and instructions, as we prevailed with them [the remaining seven regiments], and our words were taken for a time, to stay, until the State of Scotland were advertised with what we had undertaken for, in their names, should be speedily sent them from Scotland.

On 14 March, the officers of the seven regiments agreed to delay their departure for another fortnight to give the Scottish authorities time to fulfil their promises. When the pledged money and supplies did finally arrive at the beginning of April, the officers voted to remain in Ireland, pending the arrival of arrears and supplies from the English parliament and the granting of concessions by the convention of estates.[19]

The committee of estates also mandated Hamilton and Campbell to try and persuade the British commanders in Ulster to cooperate with Monro in renewing the war against the Irish. In return, the estates would encourage the English parliament to send them money. Moreover, the Scottish authorities were also making arrangements to supply them with various provisions, including 'a thousand bolles of meal from this kingdome for Sr Wm and Sr Robt Stewart and another thousand for Londonderrie'. Once again, the two envoys were successful in their mission, if one is to judge by a letter from some British leaders in north-west Ulster to Loudoun on 26 March, which rejected the cessation and pledged collaboration with Monro, but stressed the need for supplies before any operation could be undertaken.[20]

Sir Frederick was also given a third directive by the committee of estates when setting out for Ulster in February 1644. He had gone to Scotland the previous month at the behest of Ulster Scottish Presbyterians to petition the Scottish authorities to send them some authorized persons who would administer the

---

Furgol, *A regimental history of the covenanting armies*, p. 89. **19** *The humble remonstrance*; Carte, *The life of James, duke of Ormond*, iii, pp 75, 78. **20** Armstrong, *Protestant war*, p. 113.

covenant in the province. Now he himself was requested to 'manage this affair'. By April, Hamilton was actively promoting the covenant in the Derry area. In a letter to Ormond on 17 April, Sir Robert Stewart blamed Hamilton for winning over the common people of Derry to the covenant in the absence of his brother, Sir William Stewart, and himself. Sir Frederick also succeeded in persuading all the officers of the regiments of both the Stewart brothers to take the oath while the commanders were away – Sir William in London and Sir Robert in Dublin.[21]

During the spring, the English parliament and the Scottish committee of estates had decided to make a concerted attempt to extend the covenant to Ulster. The general assembly of the Church of Scotland, which was given responsibility for the task, appointed four ministers, specially chosen because of their eloquence and enthusiasm for the covenant. The four Scotsmen – revds Hugh Henderson, James Hamilton, William Adair and John Weir – arrived in Ireland at the end of March. On 4 April, they tendered the oath to Major General Robert Monro and his officers at Carrickfergus. Some days later, they administered the pledge to the rest of the Scottish army. The ministers then continued their mission with much success among both Scottish and English settlers in various parts of Cos Antrim and Down.[22]

Revds William Adair and John Weir later set out for Derry (fig. 20), after having been invited there by Sir Frederick Hamilton and Captain Robert Lawson, one of the aldermen of the city. Despite receiving messages along the way from both the mayor, Robert Thornton, and the recently appointed governor, Audley Mervyn, 'prohibiting their coming there upon their peril … lest they bred division in the garrison and town', they continued on their journey and arrived at the city walls on about 22 April. Hamilton had the gates opened to allow them to enter, before bringing them to his own house and entertaining them to supper. The following morning they were visited by the mayor, who reminded them that they had disobeyed his orders by coming to the city. He now questioned them as to who had authorized their visit. They replied that the general assembly of the Church of Scotland had delegated them to bring the covenant to the Scots army and to all others who were willing to receive it in Ulster. The committee of estates had also received a petition from some British forces in the province to send them both supplies and the covenant. Moreover, the English parliament had recommended that the oath be taken by all the British forces there. In spite of these explanations, however, the mayor forbade them to proceed with their mission.[23]

---

21 *The information of Sir Frederick Hammilton*, p. 45; Carte, *The life of James, duke of Ormond*, iii, pp 81, 164; Reid, *History of the Presbyterian Church in Ireland*, i, p. 447. **22** Carte, *The life of James, duke of Ormond*, iii, p. 78. **23** Reid, *History of the Presbyterian Church in Ireland*, i, pp 433 and 445–7; P. Adair, *A true narrative of the rise and progress of the Presbyterian church in Ireland (1623–1670)*, ed. W.D. Killen

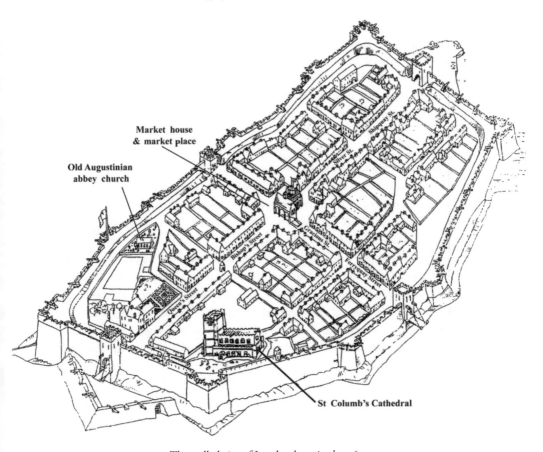

20 The walled city of Londonderry in the 1640s.

At that stage, Sir Frederick Hamilton came into the room and angrily confronted Thornton with the following words: 'Mr Mayor, take heed of what you do or speak to these gentlemen'! Thornton would still not lift his prohibition against them, although he did agree to take advice on the matter, saying that he would see them again in the afternoon. At this second meeting, which was held in the mayor's chamber, the ministers pointed out that Thornton would have to choose between the English parliament's endorsement of the covenant and Ormond's condemnation of it. They themselves were in no doubt about Westminster's good will towards, and support for, the British in Derry, as opposed to Ormond's 'corrupt disposition' and lack of assistance to them.[24]

(Belfast, 1866), p. 108; Carte, *The life of James, duke of Ormond*, iii, p. 82; B. Lacy, *Siege city: the story of Derry and Londonderry* (Belfast, 1990), pp 104–5. A petition for the covenant by captains Owen O'Connolly and Robert Magill, on behalf of the Laggan forces and some British regiments in Antrim and Down, was made to the committee of estates in February 1644. **24** Adair, *A true narrative*, pp 108–9.

The ministers then requested permission to preach in the cathedral on Sunday 25 April. The application was refused because the Church of Ireland communion service was due to be held there on that day. They were offered instead the old Augustinian Abbey church, but because of the large crowd that turned up they chose to preach outdoors in the market place. The theme of their sermon was the religious importance of the covenant. Sir Frederick followed the ministers' homily with an oration of his own, exhorting the attendance to take the oath. Ormond's biographer, Thomas Carte, alleged that Hamilton used coercive tactics on this occasion, by surrounding himself with Scottish officers and men of the Derry garrison who supported the covenant. Carte also believed that Sir Frederick had backed the ministers in Derry in an effort to upstage Thornton and Mervyn, since he was hoping to be appointed governor of the city by the English parliament in place of Mervyn. Be that as it may, the majority of those who listened to the oration then raised their hands and 'with many tears' entered into the covenant. The mayor and his retinue, who were coming out from the cathedral, were very surprised and impressed by the strange sight. The following day, the ministers requested the keys of the cathedral once again. This time, their application was successful. The bells were rung, and an even larger crowd than on Sunday assembled to hear the preachers. Once again, the enthusiastic audience, which included some important personages from the surrounding area, 'did embrace the covenant with much sign of affection'.[25]

After their success in Derry, the two ministers set out to administer the covenant to the various regiments of the Laggan army, even though many of the troops had already taken it at this stage. They first visited Raphoe, where Sir Robert Stewart's men – except the commander himself, who was still in Dublin – took or retook the oath. They then journeyed to Letterkenny, where Sir William Stewart's regiment followed suit. From there, they headed north to Ramelton. Sir Audley Mervyn's forces, who were based here, submitted to the covenant, despite their colonel's opposition. The ministers then received a request from some officers of the Enniskillen garrison for the covenant. There, the whole detachment – apart from Sir William Cole himself, who left the church before the end of the cere-mony – took the pledge. Several of the nearby garrisons, including Ballyshannon, did likewise. Although there is no record of the covenant being taken at Manorhamilton, it would seem rather surprising, in view of Sir Frederick Hamilton's support for it, if it were not administered there also at this time.[26]

The commanders of the British forces in Ulster were much more reluctant than their officers and men to swear the covenant. Some eventually took it purely

---

25 Carte, *The life of James, duke of Ormond*, iii, pp 82–3.   **26** *The information of Sir Frederick Hammilton*, pp 45–6.

out of expediency, just to retain control of their regiments and in the hope of receiving supplies from the English parliament and Scotland. Historians differ in their conclusions as to when exactly the various Laggan leaders took the oath. It seems likely that both Mervyn and Thornton took it in the weeks following the ministers' visit to Derry. Sir William Cole would certainly have sworn it before setting sail for London from Carrickfergus as a representative of the Ulster British forces to the English parliament at the end of June. Sir Robert Stewart, however, may not have acquiesced until even later. On the other hand, some of the east Ulster commanders, such as Colonel Chichester of Belfast, never took the covenant at all.[27]

Ormond's biographer, Carte, acknowledged that Sir Frederick Hamilton was 'the great instrument of propagating the covenant in those parts [Derry]'. Hamilton himself was not shy in taking credit for the significant part he played in winning over the military and civilians of that city to the covenant. Writing in early 1645, he claimed to have 'been the best means of taking it at the Derry'. Some months later, he maintained that he was

> the immediate instrument, and best help to the ministers, who were intrusted with the Solemn League and Covenant, to get it taken by the citizens of London-Derry, the regiments and countrey thereabouts, who will confesse, that without me, it had not so easily past, if at all, at that time.[28]

Through his vigorous promotion of the covenant, Hamilton had aligned himself closely with the parliamentarian side in the English Civil War against the king. He expected, therefore, that the English parliament, just like its allies, the Scottish authorities, would reward him for his achievements. But he also hoped for a substantial recompense from Westminster for his three-year campaign on behalf of the English state against the rebels in Ireland. He was already 'well known to both the honourable houses of parliament' on account of his status as a nobleman courtier, but also through his involvement with the trial of Lord Deputy Wentworth in 1641. He would therefore spend considerable time and energy over the next twelve months requesting parliament to grant him a fitting remuneration for his past services, as well as advancement in his career in the future.[29]

27 Reid, *History of the Presbyterian Church in Ireland*, i, pp 452–5. See also McKenny, *The Laggan army in Ireland*, pp 68–9 for speculation as to when the British commanders of north-west Ulster took the covenant.   **28** *The information of Sir Frederick Hammilton*, p. 45, *The humble remonstrance*; Carte, *The life of James, duke of Ormond*, iii, p. 164.   **29** *The several petitions of William Hansard and Sir Frederick Hammiltoun*, p. 31; *CSPD, 1641–3*, p. 122; M. Jansson (ed.), *Proceedings in the opening session of the Long Parliament*, i, pp 473, 474, 637, 654.

ASSIGNMENTS FROM THE ENGLISH PARLIAMENT WITH THE BRITISH
FORCES IN ULSTER

Sir Frederick had not long to wait before reaping the first of his rewards from the English parliament for having switched his allegiance from the king to the Solemn League alliance, and for his aggressive promotion of the covenant in Ulster. About the second week of April 1644, he was appointed commander of a force of two thousand British soldiers in the northwest of the province – most likely the pro-covenant regiments of Sir William and Sir Robert Stewart, in the absence of both colonels. The mandate may have come from Major General Robert Monro, who, one month earlier, had been confirmed by Westminster as commander-in-chief of the Scottish and British forces in Ulster. Monro now moved south-westwards, at the head of eight thousand men, from Carrickfergus into Co. Armagh. It was rumoured that he and Hamilton were going to join forces and march into Connacht, perhaps as far south as Galway. The apparent aim of their mission was to make a pre-emptive strike against the newly selected confederate general, the earl of Castlehaven, before the latter could assemble sufficient forces to attack the Scottish army in Ulster. Castlehaven was then in the western province capturing some small British garrisons that had not respected the cessation.[30]

The threatened offensive by Monro and Hamilton never materialized. Ormond's most loyal supporter and senior commander in Connacht, the earl of Clanricard, wrote to Castlehaven on 19 April: 'I am very glad to find that the rumours of the advancing of the Scotch army proves so uncertain … I am very confident there is no danger of a Scotch invasion upon this province'. He added that 'if those two thousand do follow Sir Frederick Hamilton, it is rather to secure his own [castle], upon the rumour of your lordship's army coming into this province'. It had also been reported to Clanricard that Sir Frederick intended returning to Manorhamilton purely to take away all his possessions to Scotland, and perhaps as well to inflict 'a parting blow where he can find or snatch a booty'. In the event, neither Monro nor Hamilton left Ulster on this occasion. Monro still had to procure the allegiance of many of the other Ulster British commanders. As for Sir Frederick, his plans were suddenly altered with the arrival in Derry of the two Scottish Presbyterian ministers a few days after Clanricard's letter to Castlehaven. It would appear as if both of the Stewart brothers' regiments then returned to their respective bases, and before long to their original commanders.[31]

The second of Hamilton's appointments came directly from the English parliament, or more precisely from the CBK. This body had been set up jointly

---

30 C.P. Meehan, *The Confederation of Kilkenny* (Dublin, 1882), pp 102–3; Stevenson, *Scottish covenanters and Irish Confederates*, p. 193.   31 J. Lowe (ed.) *Letter-book of the earl of Clanricarde*, pp 72–3.

by the English parliament and the Scottish convention of estates in February 1644 to centrally manage and direct the war against the king in England, Scotland and Ireland. It was answerable to Westminster, but had authority to act more or less independently in matters connected with the conduct of the war. The committee had a large majority of English parliamentarians – seven peers and fourteen MPs – among its members, with only four Scottish commissioners filling the remaining places. It was, nevertheless, well disposed towards Sir Frederick during much of 1644 for several reasons. Firstly, one of the Scottish members was Lord Chancellor Loudoun, who had earlier entrusted him with the successful mission to the Scots army and the British commanders in Ulster. Secondly, the sub-committee for Irish affairs, which the committee had established to specifically advise on the war in Ireland, was highly impressed by Sir Frederick's account of his exploits in suppressing the rebellion in Leitrim and the surrounding counties, as well as by his earlier service in Germany during the Thirty Years War. As a result, the sub-committee made at least two significant representations in his favour to its parent body during that year.[32]

Hamilton was also fortunate to have another influential organization in London promoting his advancement with the CBK. This was the Committee of Adventurers, which represented mainly English financiers who had subscribed over £300,000 to the English parliament for the conquest of Ireland in 1642 and 1643, in return for two and a half million acres of land to be confiscated from the rebels. This powerful body, which also comprised a number of MPs, was anxious that an effective campaign be waged against the Irish, so that it might be guaranteed a return on its investment. With this in mind, it called on the CBK in early March 1644 to appoint one commander-in-chief for all Scottish and British troops in Ireland, and to send a joint English and Scottish commission to Ulster to better regulate the war there. On this occasion, it also singled out Sir Frederick Hamilton 'for the good service he hath done against those rebels, his fidelitie to the parliament, and for his owne worth and merite', and recommended that he 'be made a collonel of a regiment of 1,000 foott, and of a troope of horsemen in the expedicion of warre against those rebels'.[33]

With such powerful bodies advocating on his behalf, it is not surprising that Sir Frederick was rewarded with the command of Colonel Chichester's regiment

32 'To the honourable Committee of Both Kingdoms: the humble remonstrance of the sub-committee at Grocers-Hall for Irish affairs, in the behalf of Sir Frederick Hammiltoun, Grocers Hall, 12 Aug. 1644' and 'To the honourable Committee of Both Kingdoms: the humble remonstrance of your subcommittee concerning Sir Frederick Hammiltoun, knight, Grocers Hall, 29 October 1644', *The several petitions of William Hansard and Sir Frederick Hammiltoun*, pp 21–4, 31–3; Armstrong, *Protestant war*, pp 106, 108, 109; Scott, *Politics and war*, p. 70.   **33** PRONI, T525/7/2, petition of the committee of adventurers to the Committee of Both Kingdoms, *c.*early March 1644; *The several petitions of William Hansard and Sir*

in east Ulster. Chichester, a nephew of Sir Arthur Chichester, a former lord deputy of Ireland, was the British governor of Belfast and a loyal supporter of Ormond. He had accepted the cessation and denounced the covenant. He had also received supplies from the lord lieutenant to enable him to hold Belfast against Monro, and thus deter the Scots general from marching on Dublin. On 13 May 1644, Chichester hosted a meeting of mainly east Ulster British colonels, but which was also attended by Sir Robert Stewart of the Laggan army, to decide on whether to accept or reject Monro's authority. The following morning, however, Monro surprised and captured the town. Chichester's garrison was expelled. The colonel himself fled first to Dublin and then to London to complain to the English parliament.[34]

Chichester received no satisfaction from Westminster and was in fact removed from his command. Sir Frederick was installed as colonel of the regiment in his place. It is not clear when this appointment occurred, but it may have happened sometime in June 1644, when Hamilton was listed by the Scottish authorities as being in command of a British regiment in Ulster. On 22 June, the committee of estates in Edinburgh took the decision to supply all the Ulster British colonels, including Sir Frederick, with money and food. These payments and provisions were conditional on the colonels accompanying Monro on a three-week expedition that he was about to undertake into north Leinster to try and disrupt Castlehaven's confederate army before it had fully assembled and trained. Monro, in his account of the mission, however, makes no mention of Sir Frederick. Nor did he leave Hamilton to garrison Belfast in his absence, since he had already appointed one of his own men, Colonel Hume, governor of the town and castle.[35]

It is more likely, therefore, that Hamilton's appointment as colonel in charge of Chichester's regiment did not take place until the autumn of 1644. On 12 August, the sub-committee for Irish affairs petitioned its parent body, the CBK, in favour of Sir Frederick – 'a gentleman ... being honourable both by birth and acquisition ... [who] hath had some command for a long time in Ireland (though not of such eminency as he deserveth).' The sub-committee suggested, therefore, that

Frederick Hammiltoun, pp 22–3.   **34** Carte, *The life of James, duke of Ormond*, iii, pp 83–6, 164. See also Stevenson, *Scottish covenanters and Irish Confederates*, pp 160–2; *ODNB*, xi, p. 401.   **35** Sir Frederick's name is included by the Scottish estates in a list of east Ulster colonels. Chichester's name does not feature on the list: *The acts of the parliaments of Scotland*, vi, p. 123; *A full relation of the late expedition of the right honourable the Lord Monroe, major general of all the Protestant forces in the province of Ulster, with their several marches and skirmishes with the bloody Irish rebels, and what towns and castles they have taken* (London, 1644); G. Benn, *The history of the town of Belfast* (Belfast, 1823), p. 26. Lord Conway was also removed from colonelcy of his regiment by the Committee of Both Kingdoms in favour of Lord Blaney.

he may be recommended to the honourable house of parliament to be made a colonel of a thousand foot, and to have the command of a troop of horse; either to be placed over such forces whereof the commanders shall now be displaced and removed there, or over such other forces as are now there in the province of Ulster, which are not yet regimented ... or over those forces not regimented in Connaught, where he hath a fair estate.

It may have been this strong endorsement of his suitability and merit for the post of colonelcy that finally led to his appointment.[36]

There are few indications as to how long Hamilton retained his new command. Ormond's biographer, Carte, seems to suggest that he held on to Chichester's regiment into the spring of 1645. A reference to 'Sir Frederick's regiment' in the calendar of state papers (domestic) on 19 February of that year would seem to substantiate this assumption. His name does not appear in a report on the strength of the British forces in Ulster, drawn up by the Ulster British commanders themselves about the second quarter of 1645, so we may assume that he no longer commanded the regiment at this stage. His position may have been difficult to maintain due to the strong royalist loyalties of some of Chichester's officers, and also because a substantial number of the regiment's soldiers were in fact Irish.[37]

EVENTUAL DISILLUSIONMENT WITH THE ENGLISH PARLIAMENT

Not satisfied with having been conferred with the command of Chichester's regiment, Sir Frederick Hamilton felt that he should also be remunerated by the English parliament for his military activities during the rebellion, and even compensated for the loss of his estates. He decided, therefore, to go to London himself in September 1644, 'in expectation of some course to be taken with me, for the recompence of my past services, and incouragements to go on'. He wished to be close to those advocating on his behalf – the Committee of Adventurers and the sub-committee for Irish affairs – so that he could provide them with any information they needed, and to encourage them to continue their efforts. He based himself in the English capital for the next eight months, confident, at least initially, that he would be amply rewarded by Westminster.[38]

His arrival in London was timely. The English parliament had just resolved to make a much greater investment in the war in Ireland, and on 18 October passed

---

36 *The several petitions of William Hansard*, pp 31–2.   **37** *CSPD, 1644–5*, p. 313; J. Hogan (ed.), *Letters and papers relating to the Irish rebellion between 1642–46* (Dublin, 1936) ix, pp 180–3; Carte, *The life of James, duke of Ormond*, iii, p. 164.   **38** *The humble remonstrance.*

an ordinance or decree to raise £80,000 in England and Wales for the relief of the British forces in Ulster, Munster and Connacht, 'who shall continue faithful in the service, and persist in the prosecution of the war against the rebels'. The monies collected were to be spent on paying the commanders, officers and soldiers, and supplying them with food, clothes, arms and ammunition. The CBK decided that just over half of the fund would be allocated to Ulster, with £10,000 going to Munster, £5,500 to Connacht and £2,500 to Duncannon fort in Co. Wexford, which was about to be besieged by the confederates. The rest of the money would be held in reserve. Nothing was earmarked for Leinster, as most British troops in that province adhered to the royalist marquis of Ormond. The contract for supplying the forces in Ireland was awarded to John Davies, an Ulster merchant. He was a close associate of Sir John Clotworthy, the son of an English planter from Co. Antrim, who had played a significant part in the trial and impeachment of the former Lord Deputy Wentworth, and who now commanded a British regiment in Ulster. In his other role as an MP at Westminster, Clotworthy had had a large input in the promotion and passage of the October ordinance through parliament.[39]

In anticipation of the passing of the ordinance, Sir Frederick presented a petition to the CBK on 14 October. The same body had already received a letter of recommendation of Hamilton's 'business' from the Scottish convention of estates. Although neither document survives, we may assume that both dealt with matters of advancement or compensation that were very much on Sir Frederick's mind at this time. In any case, the petition and letter were duly forwarded to the House of Commons for its consideration.[40]

The CBK also ordered its sub-committee for Irish affairs on 21 October to examine Hamilton's record of service in Ireland and to suggest 'what proportion of the money that is to come in upon the assessment for Ireland, shall be assigned unto him'. The sub-committee set about its task immediately and requested Sir Frederick to furnish it with a detailed account of his operations during the rebellion. Within a matter of days, Sir Frederick had presented an inventory of his services, achievements and losses. He mentioned how he had enlarged his garrison from fifty to 250 men in October 1641, and maintained these men at his own expense since then. He had suppressed the rebellion in Leitrim and Sligo, and kept Manorhamilton Castle intact, without any state aid or relief, despite attacks from Connacht and Ulster rebels. As a result of the rebellion, however, he

---

39 TNA, SP16/503, 'An ordinance of the lords and commons assembled in parliament for raising of fourscore thousand pounds by a weekly assessment through the kingdom of England and dominion of Wales for the present relief of the British army in Ireland' (London, 1645). Although passed by parliament in October 1644, the ordinance was not published until the following February; Armstrong, *Protestant war*, pp 129–30.   40 *CSPD, 1644–5*, p. 38; *Journals of the House of Commons* (Eng.), iii, p. 678.

had lost £2,000 per annum in rents from his estate in Connacht, the same again
from his late father-in-law, Sir John Vaughan's estate in Derry, £600 from
the lands in Lifford, as well as his rents from Valentia Island in Co. Kerry.
Manorhamilton town, with his army garrison quarters and two corn mills, had
been burned to the ground. His stock of cattle and corn were stolen and his herd
of four hundred stallions and breeding mares, worth £5,000 were driven off by
the rebels. Finally, for good measure, he mentioned £5,000 arrears of army pay,
which he and Sir John Vaughan had been due since before the rebellion, but
which had been withheld by Lord Deputy Wentworth.[41]

Hugely impressed with Sir Frederick's account of his services, the sub-
committee for Irish affairs wrote back to the CBK on 29 October saying that no
other commander of such a small force in Ireland deserved greater compensation
from the English state than Hamilton, since 'he hath behaved himself with such
valour and resolution, and hath gone thorow so many difficulties and dangers
with good successe'. It

> thinks him worthy of all encouragement, and a person fit to be employed
> in the service there, in whatsoever charge and command that shall be
> conferred upon him. And that men of his merit may be encouraged to the
> like undertakings, you may be pleased … to put some mark of honour and
> acknowledgement upon him accordingly.

The sub-committee therefore recommended that 'he may receive two thousand
pounds out of the moneys to come in upon the said ordinance … to satisfie and
discharge the engagements he hath contracted … [and] to supply himself, family
and souldiers withal, in this time of action'. It also proposed that Hamilton be
given the same payment and supplies as other British commanders in Ireland. Sir
Frederick must have been very happy with the sub-committee's strong support for
him. It now seemed that he would shortly be substantially recompensed for his
service throughout the rebellion. Other honours might follow. His decision to
switch loyalties from the king to the Solemn League alliance was surely about to
pay off.[42]

The first indication that things were not going according to plan occurred on
14 November. Following its meeting that day, the CBK sent Sir Frederick's
petition to the sub-committee for Irish affairs and ordered it to reconsider its

---

41 'The humble remonstrance of Sir Frederick Hammiltoun, knight and colonel, to the honourable sub-
committee sitting at Grocers Hall for Irish affairs', *The several petitions of William Hansard and Sir Frederick
Hammiltoun*, pp 4, 25–30. **42** 'The humble remonstrance of your subcommittee concerning Sir
Frederick Hammiltoun, knight, to the honourable Committee of Both Kingdoms, 29 October', *The several
petitions of William Hansard and Sir Frederick Hammiltoun*, pp 21–4.

recommendations on his behalf, after it had taken into consideration the opinions of some 'gentlemen of Ireland'. The sub-committee was then to report back its conclusions to its parent body. It would seem as if some of the Ulster British colonels were objecting to, or at least casting doubt on, the truth of the claims in Hamilton's petition. The committee was obviously trying to establish whether or not his assertions were genuine.[43]

It appears as if two Ulster colonels in particular were intent on undermining Sir Frederick's position. One of these was Sir William Cole, commander of the Enniskillen garrison, whom Hamilton had accused of failing to support him during the rebellion, in a pamphlet published in London in 1643. Cole was one of four representatives of the British forces in Ulster, chosen by their fellow officers at the end of June 1644 to go to London to request the English parliament to send them badly needed aid and supplies. Within a few months, Cole and the others, who remained at Westminster, had risen to positions of some prominence. By early December of that year, they were being styled 'commissioners of the British forces in Ulster' by the CBK, and some of the October ordinance money was already being directed their way.[44]

The other Ulster British colonel who objected to Sir Frederick's claims was Sir John Clotworthy, who had played a very significant part in promoting the October ordinance. Clotworthy was a Presbyterian and had initially been very supportive of the Solemn League and Covenant alliance with Scotland. He later developed an animosity towards the Scots after Monro had been given overall command of both the British and the Scottish forces in Ulster. Hamilton's Scottish identity and his collaboration with Monro in the spring of 1644 would not have endeared him to Clotworthy. The Antrim colonel had more personal reasons for opposing Hamilton, however. He was married to a daughter of Viscount Ranelagh, former president of Connacht, and one of Sir Frederick's 'mortall enemies'. He was also related through marriage to Colonel Arthur Chichester, whose regiment had been handed to Hamilton. Moreover, his sister Martha was married to Colonel Audley Mervyn, whom Hamilton had defied by introducing the two Scottish Presbyterian ministers to Derry in April 1644, and whose position as governor of that city Sir Frederick was said to be seeking. Like that of Sir William Cole, Clotworthy's and his associate John Davies' influence with the Committee of Both Kingdoms grew towards the end of 1644, while the leverage of the Committee of Adventurers, which had made several representations of behalf of Sir Frederick, began to wane.[45]

43 *CSPD, 1644–5*, p. 123.   44 *Another extract of severall letters*, pp 29, 32, 36, 39, 41 and 42; *CSPD, 1644–5*, p. 201; McKenny, *The Laggan army in Ireland*, pp 69–70.   45 *The information of Sir Frederick Hammilton*, pp 41, 59; Carte, *The life of James, duke of Ormond*, iii, pp 82–3; *ODNB*, xii, p. 198 and xxxvii, p. 933; M. Perceval Maxwell, 'Strafford, the Ulster-Scots and the covenanters', *IHS*, 18 (1973), 545;

There is no record of the outcome of the sub-committee for Irish affairs' interviews with the 'gentlemen of Ulster'. Nor does the sub-committee seem to have presented a revised report to the CBK during the month of December 1644. Meanwhile, Sir Frederick, who was becoming more and more frustrated, began making counter-allegations against his detractors. On 23 December, the CBK ordered 'that Sir Frederick Hamilton be desired to put in writing what he has to say concerning any person employed [by the English parliament] in Ireland'. Three days later, the same body directed that 'the paper given in by Sir Frederick Hamilton against Sir John Clotworthy be reported to the House of Commons and that, before it is done, Sir John Clotworthy shall hear it read'. The following day, Hamilton handed in his *Information* against Sir William Cole. The CBK demanded, on the last day of the year, that Cole be given a copy of Sir Frederick's accusations, and also that Clotworthy present himself before it the following afternoon to answer questions.[46]

There are no surviving documents to enlighten us on the nature of Sir Frederick's specific allegations against Clotworthy. We would probably not be too far off the mark, however, if we were to assume that they referred to Clotworthy's anti-Scottish bias. We may also speculate that Hamilton was critical of the Antrim MP's role in the allocation and administration of the October ordinance funds. Incidentally, Sir Frederick was not the only person to make accusations against Clotworthy at this time. As a result, both Clotworthy and Davies were investigated by the Committee of Accounts in connection with alleged abuses in their accounts. In contrast to his claims against Clotworthy, Sir Frederick's allegations against Sir William Cole, the latter's answers and Hamilton's 'replication' have all survived in a pamphlet entitled *The information of Sir Frederick Hammilton, knight and colonell*, which was published in 1645. The accusations, answers and replies will be examined in detail in the next section.[47]

The CBK continued to deal with issues arising from Hamilton's allegations against both men throughout the month of January 1645. It ordered that the information against Cole be reported to the Commons on 6 January. Five days later, it referred Cole's answers for consideration by the sub-committee of Irish affairs, which was to report 'if anything be therein not fit to be presented to the house'. The CBK directed on 13 January that Sir Frederick be given a copy of Cole's answer, and that both statement and answer be sent to the Commons. One week later, it also sent the allegations against Clotworthy and the latter's answer to the lower house. Much more alarmingly, though, from Hamilton's point of

Stevenson, *Scottish covenanters and Irish Confederates*, pp 148–9; McGrath, 'A biographical dictionary', p. 215. **46** *CSPD, 1644–5*, pp 195, 198, 200, 204; *The information of Sir Frederick Hammilton*. **47** See Armstrong, *Protestant war*, p. 129.

view, was the fact that the committee also decided during that same month to notify parliament that the remonstrance of the sub-committee for Irish affairs of 29 October in favour of Sir Frederick concerned arrears that could not be paid for out of the October ordinance. One can only speculate as to whether the notification resulted from the promptings of Sir John Clotworthy.[48]

While Hamilton, Cole and Clotworthy were levelling accusations and counter-allegations against one another, the CBK was taken up with much more important matters that temporarily sidelined the commanders' disputes. In its attempts to reinvigorate the war against the confederates in Munster and Connacht, it was planning to dispatch two thousand Ulster British troops to the southern province and 1,500 more to the west. In late December 1644, the sub-committee for Irish affairs had recommended that Sir William Cole and two other Ulster colonels should all be given £1,000 in order to bring their regiments up to full strength for such a venture. During the same month, Sir Frederick had given notification of his intention to raise one hundred foot and fifty horse, presumably with the same purpose in mind. As it is unlikely that he was planning to bring Chichester's regiment to the western province, he may have decided to levy these new troops in either Derry or Leitrim. On 7 February 1645, Hamilton and Sir Charles Coote junior, an army commander from Co. Roscommon, submitted a joint proposal to the CBK 'mentioning the way we intended to prosecute the war there [in Connacht]'. The committee later ordered Sir Frederick, Coote and Sir Robert King of Boyle to attend a meeting on 1 March to report on the number of men they had in pay, and to discuss how the money allocated for the war in Connacht should be divided up.[49]

The committee was at the same time still considering if there was any other way that Sir Frederick could be compensated from the October ordinance money for his past services and losses. On 5 March, it ordered that the remonstrance of the sub-committee for Irish affairs be reported once again to the House of Commons. Two weeks later, the Commons demanded that this remonstrance and another from the Committee of Adventurers be redirected to the CBK so that it could make a prompt recommendation on the matter. Playing for time, that body once again referred the whole question to its sub-committee for Irish affairs. However, on 24 March, it finally informed Westminster that it had 'considered the claim of Sir Fred. Hamilton for reward for his good service, but cannot pay it out of the October ordinance, by reason it is for service past; so desire the house to recompense him some other way'. In addition, it also directed that 'his troop of horse and newly levied foot, they not being yet on the

---

48 *CSPD, 1644–5*, pp 232, 244, 245, 249, 264.   **49** *The humble remonstrance*, p. 7; *CSPD, 1644–5*, pp 184, 200, 291, 313, 325; McGrath, 'A biographical dictionary', p. 113.

establishment, cannot receive allowance out of this money, unless the houses give order for it some other way'.[50]

Sir Frederick was incensed on hearing the news. As he saw it, he was being told that his loyalty in the past to the English state and parliament had not been appreciated, and that his present services were no longer required. Although the terms of the October ordinance did indeed specify that the £80,000 collected should only go towards the payment and supply of present forces, it would seem as if at least some exceptions had already been made to this rule. For example, the CBK itself recommended to the House of Commons less than a month earlier that it take Sir William Stewart's 'condition into consideration, as they have done others', since he had received no pay at a time when other British commanders in Ulster did. Moreover, the committee's decision to withhold payment from Hamilton for his current troop of horse and newly levied foot, until such time as they had been formally sanctioned, also appears rather harsh, in view of Sir Frederick's long record of unrecompensed service to the state, as well as his official involvement in plans for the reinvigoration of the war in Connacht. In disgust, Hamilton took the decision to cease any further involvement with the planned escalation of hostilities in the western province, proclaiming that he no longer had confidence in anything to do with it, except in his own castle at Manorhamilton. Apparently unconcerned, the CBK ordered on 7 April that Sir Charles Coote should decide on the allocation of parliamentary supplies to the various commanders in Connacht, although Sir Frederick should retain the right to say where those that had been set aside for his use should now be directed.[51]

A key element of the plan by the English parliament to step up the war against the confederates in Munster and Connacht was the appointment of lords president, with supreme authority in military, civil and criminal matters, in both provinces. The person chosen for the position in Munster in January 1645 was Murrough O'Brien, Baron Inchiquin, the principal Protestant commander in the province, who had defected from the Ormondite camp and declared his allegiance to parliament some six months earlier. The CBK was considering the appointment of Sir Charles Coote to the presidency of Connacht during the month of April 1645. Coote had parted from Ormond and espoused the parliamentarian cause at the beginning of that year. If selected, he would not be the first member of his family to hold such an office. His late father, Sir Charles Coote senior, had held the post of vice-president of the province in the 1620s.[52]

On hearing about the possibility of Coote's appointment, Sir Frederick wrote to the CBK, saying that the selection of Coote as lord president would have a

50 *Journals of the House of Commons (Eng.)*, iv, p. 81; *CSPD, 1644–5*, pp 334, 349, 365. **51** *CSPD, 1644–5*, pp 325, 384, 391. **52** McGrath, 'A biographical dictionary', pp 113–14; *ODNB*, xiii, pp 293–4.

detrimental effect on the efficient prosecution of the war in the province. He reminded the committee that Coote's place of residence, Castlecoote, was fifty miles from Leitrim and Sligo. As a result, Coote would find it very difficult to campaign in these counties, without neglecting the area in which he lived himself.[53]

Hamilton also stated that his own honour and personal interests would be compromised if Coote were chosen for the position. He believed that the Irish in Leitrim and Sligo would be absolutely delighted to hear that Coote had been given jurisdiction over both counties, which he himself had been placed in charge of by 'warrant and commission from the lords justices and councell of that kingdom [of Ireland]' at the outbreak of the rebellion. Without any assistance from Coote, he had successfully suppressed the insurrection in these counties at great expense to himself – £6,000 for the maintenance of his garrison at Manorhamilton, and the same amount again in loss of rent and stock. He believed that it would be most unjust that he should 'now be turned out of this trust, after all my long service, great losse and sufferings, unquestioned for any misdemeanours, or neglect in that charge'.[54]

Hamilton therefore pleaded that, just as he had earlier in the year submitted a joint proposal with Coote on how best to renew the war in Connacht, he might now be appointed joint president of the province with Coote. He suggested that, on account of his knowledge and experience of Leitrim and Sligo, he be given charge over these two counties, and that Coote be accorded responsibility for the rest of Connacht. Sir Frederick concluded by saying that if the English parliament would not listen to his opinion or advice on the matter, it should pay the arrears due to him, leave his castle and estate undisturbed and use his services somewhere else.[55]

Perhaps not surprisingly, the CBK was not inclined to let itself be swayed by Hamilton's emotional plea. The thirty-five-year-old Coote was formally commissioned lord president of Connacht, with special responsibility for the town of Sligo, on 12 May. In his frustration, Sir Frederick appealed this time to the House of Lords (fig. 21). In his petition, he stressed the fact that that the last president of the province, Viscount Ranelagh, had through his own carelessness allowed the rebels capture and slaughter 'many poore Brittishe soules' in Sligo town in December 1641. It fell to Hamilton, with 140 of his own men, to avenge that action by burning the town and killing almost three hundred rebels. He added that his successful campaign during the rebellion 'hath been a terrour to the powerfulest of those bloody rebels, and a comfort to a many distressed

---

53 *The humble remonstrance*, pp 5–7.   54 Ibid., p. 6; *The information of Sir Frederick Hammilton*, pp 90–1.
55 *The humble remonstrance*, p. 7.

21 Sir Frederick Hamilton's petition to the House of Lords, May 1645 (Parliamentary Archives, HL/PO/JO/10/1/198, courtesy of the Parliamentary Archives, London).

Protestants sheltered and relieved by that place [Manorhamilton]'. He finally begged their lordships not 'to subject himselfe and those parts (where God hath soe blessed him) unto the command of any privat governour untill it please your honnours to take furthere informacion of his great sufferings and services'. There is no record to indicate that the House of Lords made any attempt to intervene in the matter. Even if it had done so, it is difficult to see how it could have achieved any significant alterations to the terms of Coote's appointment, since the balance of power in the English parliament then lay with the lower house.[56]

Having been sorely disappointed by the reactions of the CBK and the House of Lords to his petitions, Hamilton made a third and final appeal – this time to the House of Commons. Although the document itself has been lost, it seems likely that it made similar requests to those contained in the other papers. After having listened to a reading of the application on 2 June, the Commons directed that the matter be referred for further consideration to the Committee for Examinations, which would report back in due course with its recommendations. In the meantime, however, Coote's appointment stood. Within days, the new president had set out for Ireland, armed with letters from the CBK to the British regiments in Ulster and Monro's Scots, requesting them to provide him with 1,500 men for an expedition into Connacht. The realization that his own jurisdiction over Cos Leitrim and Sligo had come to such a humiliating end was surely a bitter pill for Sir Frederick to swallow.[57]

By the middle of June 1645, Coote had assembled a force of 4,500 men, composed mainly of Laggan forces at Augher, in Co. Tyrone. With these, he marched to Sligo, which was then held by a regiment of confederate soldiers under Colonel Tadhg O'Connor Sligo. After a short siege, the poorly fortified town was captured with much loss of life on 8 July, and garrisoned with Ulster British troops. Coote's parliamentary army then took control of the rest of the British-held towns and castles in Leitrim and Sligo, including Robert Parke's Newtown, Carrick-on-Shannon and Jamestown. Although Sir Frederick's castle at Manorhamilton had been a parliamentarian stronghold for over a year, Coote may now have installed a new commander there to insure its allegiance to him personally. Many of the Irish-held castles and garrisons in the area, including Dromahair and Collooney, were abandoned and burned, as the confederates fled before the advancing troops. In an attempt to halt Coote's progress throughout the province, the marquis of Ormond commissioned the still loyal Viscount Taaffe of Ballymote to raise a cross-religious royalist army, composed of English

---

56 Parliamentary Archives, HL/PO/JO/10/1/198. 57 *Journals of the House of Commons (Eng.)*, iv, pp 158–9; Carte, *The life of James, duke of Ormond*, iii, p. 168; Stevenson, *Scottish covenanters and Irish Confederates*, p. 222.

troops and local confederates. During the months of August and September, Taaffe recaptured Castlecoote, Tulsk, Elphin and Jamestown. To avoid being attacked, other garrisons such as Roscommon, Boyle and Carrick-on-Shannon promised obedience to the king and observance of the cessation. Ormond withdrew Taaffe's commission at the end of September because he was suspected of associating too closely with the confederates. His English troops withdrew, thus making any attempt to recapture Sligo town impractical. Some two thousand Irish confederate troops under Archbishop Malachy O'Queely did, however, make an assault on Sligo one month later. While this was in progress, a British relief force, led by Sir Charles Coote, Sir William Cole and Sir Francis Hamilton, arrived quickly on the scene and routed the confederates. O'Queely and two hundred of his men were killed, leaving Coote once again master of north Connacht.[58]

Apart from the presidency of Connacht, Sir Frederick had set his sights on two other military commands. One of these was the governorship of Sligo town. It seems that the English parliament had intended to create such a position towards the end of 1644, and that Hamilton was being considered for the post. However, Sir William Cole and another unnamed 'gentleman of a deeper reach than his own' – possibly Clotworthy – objected to his candidature, on account of his Scottish nationality. As a result, Sir Frederick felt obliged to emphasize to the CBK the fact that he had been 'long incorporated with the English, both by marriage and otherwise'. In the end, the post was not filled until Sir Robert Stewart 'took possession of the government of Sligo' in July 1645, following Coote's successful capture of the town. By then, Sir Frederick had already cut his links with the western province.[59]

Hamilton had also targeted the much more prestigious position of governor of Derry, which had been held by his father-in-law, Sir John Vaughan, until his death in February 1643. The marquis of Ormond appointed the Laggan army colonel, Sir Audley Mervyn, to the post in April 1644 because of his opposition to the covenant and his criticism of the English parliament's lack of support for the British forces in Ulster. Thomas Carte alleged that Hamilton's principal reason for inviting the Scottish Presbyterian ministers to Derry shortly afterwards was to undermine Mervyn's position, with a view to his own advantage. Even though Mervyn did take the covenant within a month or so of the ministers' arrival, he still remained a royalist at heart, and it would appear as if the CBK was

58 Hogan (ed.), *Letters and papers relating to the Irish rebellion*, pp 189–92; Carte, *The life of James, duke of Ormond*, iii, pp 168–72. In some of the accounts of the defeat of O'Queely's forces at Sligo in October 1645, Sir Frederick Hamilton is mistakenly mentioned in place of Sir Francis Hamilton, Coote's brother-in-law.
59 *The information of Sir Frederick Hammilton*, p. 58; Carte, *The life of James Duke of Ormond*, iii, p. 169.

considering replacing him as early as August of that year. The sub-committee for Irish affairs then proposed Hamilton for the position, stating that

> no man is better able to discharge the trust, where his father-in-law, Sir John Vaughan, now deceased, had the government before, and with which the said Sir Frederick Hammiltoun is well acquainted, and no doubt but will be well accepted of the citizens.

In November 1644, some of Mervyn's letters and private papers were intercepted in Scotland and sent to London, where they were referred by the CBK to the sub-committee for Irish affairs for its consideration. Two months later, Sir William Cole accused Sir Frederick of passing on damaging information about Mervyn to the English parliament, and begged the committee not to make Hamilton governor of the city. The matter was still under consideration in March 1645, when the House of Commons requested the committee to once again examine Sir Frederick's suitability for the post.[60]

In the end, two not unrelated factors combined to ensure that Hamilton would not secure the Derry appointment. One was the growing tension between the English parliament and its allies, the Scottish covenanters who, throughout the winter of 1644–5, had been pressing Sir Frederick's claims for the position. Westminster was beginning to resent what it regarded as Scottish interference in English affairs, and also the lack of achievements on the part of the Scots in the English Civil War. With significant victories by its reorganized New Model Army under Fairfax and Cromwell at Naseby, east of Coventry, and Langport, in Somerset, during the summer of 1645, parliament was now, largely through its own efforts, gaining the upper hand in the war against the king. Many of its leaders were determined, therefore, to promote English interests, whenever possible, over and above those of the Scots. Hence, when Westminster sent over three commissioners to Ulster to strengthen the parliamentarian cause there at the end of October 1645, they were directed among other things to remove Audley Mervyn from the governorship of Derry, and replace him, not with Sir Frederick, but with Lord Folliott, the English commander of Ballyshannon.[61]

The other factor that militated against Hamilton's chances of success at Derry was the creation, by the English parliament, of the powerful Star Chamber Committee during the summer of 1645, for the purpose of directing the war in

60 'The humble remonstrance of the sub-committee at Grocers-Hall for Irish affairs in the behalf of Sir Frederick Hammiltoun, 12th August 1644', *The several petitions of William Hansard and Sir Frederick Hammiltoun*, pp 33–5; *Journals of House of Commons (Eng.)*, iv, p. 81; *The information of Sir Frederick Hammilton*, pp 21, 60; Carte, *The life of James, duke of Ormond*, iii, p. 82.   **61** H.W. Meikle (ed.), *Correspondence of the Scots commissioners in London, 1644–1646* (Edinburgh, 1917), pp 41–2, 51; Carte,

Ireland. One of the most influential members of this committee was Sir John Clotworthy. His personal differences with Sir Frederick, as well as his resentment at Hamilton's alleged part in the vilification of his brother-in-law, Mervyn, would certainly have led him to use all his power to ensure that Sir Frederick was not appointed to the post in Mervyn's place.[62]

Early in 1644, Hamilton had switched his allegiance from the king to the Solemn League alliance. He had not only taken the covenant himself at a very early stage, but had also vigorously promoted it in Ulster. In return, he expected that Westminster would show its appreciation for his wholehearted support, as well as for the successful campaign he had earlier waged on behalf of the English state at his own expense, against the Irish rebels. In his attempts at securing compensation and promotion from the English parliament, he was accused of maligning other Ulster British commanders such as Chichester and Mervyn. Writing from a royalist perspective, Thomas Carte remarked that by the summer of 1645, Sir Frederick 'was now grown universally odious to all the Protestant gentlemen and officers in the north'. He added that few of them had escaped 'his violence, rapines, cruelties and insupportable insolencies'. His undoing in Ireland, however, stemmed principally from his public criticism of Clotworthy and Cole, both of whom were firmly based within the parliamentarian fold and more closely connected than he to the centre of power in England. Their views were accorded more weight than his, for despite all his attempts at proclaiming his Britishness, he was still labelled a Scotsman by these rivals. Clotworthy and Cole also helped secure for their fellow Englishmen and close associates, Coote and Folliott, the promotion that Sir Frederick was denied.[63]

Hamilton was totally disillusioned with the English parliament's rejection of his numerous petitions. In disgust, he seems to have abandoned the Irish scene altogether sometime in the early summer of 1645, even before the issue of the governorship of Derry had been resolved. He returned via England to Scotland where he still had a horse regiment in the Army of the Solemn League and Covenant. Even though he would make one final unsuccessful plea for compensation to Westminster during 1646, he would never again set foot in Ireland, where he had spent the previous quarter of a century. His castle in Manorhamilton would remain under Coote's control, and it was listed by Sir Robert Hannay, Coote's lieutenant colonel, among five castles in Leitrim 'in the parliament's possession' in June 1646.[64]

The life of James, duke of Ormond, iii, pp 167–8. **62** R. Simson, *The annals of Derry* (Londonderry, 1847), p. 72; Armstrong, *Protestant war*, pp 149, 158, 159. **63** Carte, *The life of James, duke of Ormond*, iii, p. 164; see also *CSPD, 1644–5*, p. 337; W. Prynn and M. Nudigate, *The whole triall of Connor Lord MacGuire* (London, 1645); and Carte, *The life of James, duke of Ormond*, iii, p. 168; for references to associations between some of these English commanders. **64** *The several petitions of William Hansard and*

THE HAMILTON/COLE ALLEGATIONS AND COUNTER-CLAIMS

Sir Frederick submitted his hand-written *Information of Sir Frederick Hammilton, knight and colonell against Sir William Cole, knight* to the CBK at Derby House, London, on 26 December 1644. The document contained six potentially damaging allegations about Cole's conduct leading up to and during the 1641 rebellion and the Confederate War. These ranged from failing to inform the authorities in Dublin or his settler neighbours in Ulster of the impending rebellion, even though he himself had prior knowledge of its likely occurrence, to having inappropriate dealings with both the marquis of Ormond and the Irish confederates after the cessation had been concluded in September 1643.[65]

On 11 January 1645, Cole presented the CBK with his answer, in which he attempted to refute these allegations. Some two months later, he decided to defend himself more forcefully by publishing, for the same committee, an expanded version of his manuscript, which he now entitled *The answere and vindication of Sir William Cole, knight and collonel … unto a charge given in by Sir Frederick Hamilton*. He used the opportunity to clarify some of his original points and to rectify some earlier mistakes. In it, he also challenged 'the frivolous aspersions … cast upon the said Sir William and his regiment in a pamphlet set forth in Anno Dom. 1643, declaring the services of the said Sir Frederick'. This pamphlet was Sir Frederick's 'diary' of the rebellion in Leitrim, which had been published in *Another extract of severall letters from Ireland*.[66]

Hamilton was furious. He could not believe that

> there had been a man in the world having any drop of a gentlemans blood
> in him that could have invented so many grosse slovenly falshoods, much
> lesse to have presumed to publish such untruths to such an honourable
> committee and assembly.

He decided that he in turn would vindicate himself by way of a published reply, because Cole's scandalous answer is 'stuft with calumnies and aspersions cast upon this repliant [Sir Frederick] by way of recrimination'. His pamphlet, which he once again entitled *The information of Sir Frederick Hammilton, knight and colonell* and addressed to the CBK, appeared during the month of May 1645. It contained four sections: a two-page preface, his original accusations which took

Sir Frederick Hammiltoun; Hogan (ed.), *Letters and papers relating to the Irish rebellion*, pp 192–8. This was the same Sir Robert Hannay, who as a prisoner of the O'Rourkes in Dromahair in January 1642, had appealed in vain to Sir Frederick Hamilton to release his prime captive, Sheriff Con O'Rourke, in exchange for Hannay and two Protestant ministers. **65** *The information of Sir Frederick Hammilton*, pp 1–3. **66** *CSPD, 1644–5*, p. 245; *The answere and vindication of Sir William Cole knight and collonel* (London, 1645). A handwritten date on the first page of the document suggests that it was published on 31 Mar. 1645.

up the same amount of space, Cole's 'scandalous answer', which amounted to nineteen pages, and now his lengthy 'replication ... with divers letters and depositions for the clearing of the said Sir Frederick Hammilton' which ran to sixty-nine pages.[67]

In his preface, entitled 'To the impartiall reader', Hamilton claimed that he has acted honourably throughout this whole dispute with Cole. He had conducted himself with integrity, and his reputation remained intact despite having been forced to vindicate his good name against malicious allegations. He loved his country, was trustworthy in all his affairs, and was devoted both to the parliamentarian cause and to the Solemn League and Covenant. It was his zeal for these very principles that led him to accuse Cole. His rival, on the other hand, had totally breached the code of honour that Sir Frederick adhered to. He was dishonest, corrupt, small-minded, lacking in charity and abusive of his friends. He spoke ill of those who stood in his way to promotion, dreamed up wrong-doings that did not exist and betrayed his country. Such people as he were like wild animals who 'usually run under great trees in a storm for shelter and protection, where they leave nothing but dung and filth behinde them for their standing when the tempest is once over'. Hamilton pleaded, therefore, with the impartial readers – in the CBK and the Houses of Parliament – that just as 'justice layes the gold to the touchstone and findes out the counterfeit mettall, and esteems of both according to their value' to judge him by the inherent and obvious truth of his case, since his fate lay in their hands.[68]

In his *Answer* to Sir Frederick's first allegation that he had failed to notify the Dublin authorities or his neighbours of the imminent rebellion, Cole protested that he had indeed informed the lords justices twelve days beforehand, on 11 October 1641, after having been told by Bryan Maguire of Tempo 'of some evil intentions and practises of the Lord Magwire, Sir Phelem roe O'Neil ... and others of the Irish gentry of Ulster'. He believed that a copy of that letter was actually still preserved in the English House of Commons. On receiving more definite information two days prior to the rebellion, Cole said that he again wrote to Dublin, but this letter was intercepted by the Irish in Cavan. He also sent warnings to eighteen neighbouring settlements, including Manorhamilton and Derry, where Sir Frederick was then on a visit.[69]

Hamilton was still sceptical in the first section of his *Replication* about Cole's claim to have written to the lords justices on 11 October. But even if Cole had done so, Sir Frederick believed that he should also have alerted his neighbours

---

67 *The information of Sir Frederick Hammilton*, pp 30, 38. **68** *The information of Sir Frederick Hammilton*, introduction; see again Gillespie, *Seventeenth-century Ireland*, pp 89–90 on the importance which seventeenth-century society attached to the concept of honour. **69** *The information of Sir Frederick Hammilton*, pp 3–4.

and tenants on that occasion, so as to give them time to prepare their defences and arrest the conspirators. Indeed, he said, arms would have been much more useful than letters to those neighbours. Moreover, Cole, as a justice of the peace, should himself have apprehended Lord Maguire at that early stage. If he had needed assistance, the sheriff of Fermanagh lived only a few miles from Enniskillen. Sir Frederick strongly denied ever having received a letter of warning from Cole. Instead, it was he who, on his return to Manorhamilton, wrote to Cole first on 29 October to apprize him of the extent of the rebellion in neighbouring Co. Donegal, and to offer him any support he could give. This is evident from Cole's reply, a copy of which Hamilton included in his pamphlet. Sir Frederick also directed the Scottish captains of four companies in Co. Fermanagh to join the Enniskillen garrison (pl. 8), even though these men had already offered their services to him. Cole, on the other hand, was only concerned about his own safety and that of his castle, from which he rarely ventured during the early days of the rebellion. Sir Frederick therefore questioned whether Cole had 'performed the office of a faithfull magistrate, or the duty and courage of a judicious commander, or the care and providence of a good neighbour and faithfull subject'.[70]

In his second allegation, Sir Frederick accused Cole of raising nine companies of men to defend Enniskillen at the outbreak of the rebellion, even though a commission from the king had only authorized five. Then, some eight months later, when the English parliament sent provisions for his garrison, he dismissed four of these companies so that he and his son-in-law, Dean Barkley, might keep all the supplies for themselves. In his *Answer*, Cole said that he was entitled to raise nine companies by virtue of his other commission from the lords justices 'for raising, arming and banding all the Brittish within the county of Fermanaugh'. When the English parliament took five hundred (that is, five companies) of these men into its service and sent them suits of clothes and provisions on 1 July 1642, he was unable to divide that number of suits among nine hundred men, although he did offer to share the provisions with the other four hundred. Cole admitted that many of the latter were so annoyed that they left Enniskillen to seek their fortune elsewhere. He denied discharging them, however, in order to get all the provisions for himself and Barkley. He also maintained that he had to raise £1,300 on his own credit at that time to buy corn and other supplies to ensure the survival of his remaining five companies. Cole concluded the second part of his *Answer* by alleging that the root of Sir Frederick's problem lay in the fact that he was jealous of Cole and the other Ulster commanders who got royal commissions to raise troops, whereas he got none. As a result, he took every opportunity

70 Ibid., pp 22–30.

he could from then on to belittle the achievements of Cole and the others, while 'extolling his own unknown services'.[71]

Hamilton, in the second section of his *Replication*, stated, rather tongue in cheek, that he had never expected to get a royal commission, as he was in poor standing with the king ever since his involvement in Wentworth's trial. He denied that he was ever envious of Cole, since the Enniskillen commander 'never did any such actions … that deserved to be envied'. On the contrary, he had given Cole any help he could with his small number of men. Sir Frederick went on to insist that Cole did withhold provisions from four of his own companies, treated them badly and did in fact dismiss them. Otherwise they would certainly not have left their houses and properties where they had been born and bred, of their own accord. And even if Cole had wished to keep the five hundred suits for himself and the five companies that he retained, surely he could have shared the 1,200 old suits donated by the city of London, and the £500 contribution 'sent for the relief of the distressed Protestants in those parts', with the four disbanded companies. Hamilton then enquired if it were true, as was commonly reported, that Barkley sold the corn and other supplies that were bought with that £500, and used the proceeds to set up a tanning business in Enniskillen with Cole's blessing? In addition, Hamilton said that he had been reliably informed that the £1,300 that Cole claimed to have raised at his own expense had actually been put on the English parliament's account. As a result, Cole's creditors would have to wait for quite some time before being reimbursed.[72]

Sir Frederick alleged thirdly that Cole knowingly took two English Catholics, named Hetherington, who had been actively involved in the rebellion in Leitrim, and who had plundered the house of a tenant of Sir Frederick's, into his service in Enniskillen, and later allowed them to escape. In his *Answer*, Cole replied that the Hetheringtons were in fact good Protestants and servants of the Scotsman, James Dunbar, the son and heir of Sir John Dunbar who owned the ironworks at Garrison on the Fermanagh–Leitrim border. The Dunbars fled to Manorhamilton when their ironworks were burned by the rebels on 24 October 1641. Cole claimed that some five weeks later James and his party departed for Enniskillen because Hamilton 'thirsted after his life' since he would not sign over the ironworks to him. Sir William then entrusted James with the command of Lisgoole Castle, which was soon captured by Rory Maguire, who massacred all seventy-four inhabitants except James himself. After spending six months in prison, Dunbar escaped and returned to Enniskillen, this time with the two Hetheringtons. Cole had no proof that the two servants had been in league with the rebels or had attacked the house of Sir Frederick's tenant, Sergeant Abrel. He

71 Ibid., pp 1–6.   72 Ibid., pp 30–2.

was unwilling to imprison them on the evidence of Hamilton's word alone, since he knew of the animosity Hamilton bore towards the Dunbars. Instead, Cole took them into his service and found them to be good and brave soldiers who killed many insurgents. He did not allow them to escape, as Sir Frederick had claimed. Instead, they joined Major General Robert Monro's forces with their master, James Dunbar, who was related to Monro. Cole concluded this part of his defence by stating that Dunbar and the Hetheringtons were willing to answer any charges that Hamilton might bring against them.[73]

In the third section of his *Replication*, Sir Frederick said that Cole's third answer 'consisteth onely of invectives, fabulous inventions and scandalous calumnies'. He stated that he had far more pressing matters on his mind during the rebellion than trying to acquire Dunbar's lands. He denied that there had been any bad blood between him and the ironworks' owners or their servants. He added, however, that James Dunbar, whom Cole placed in charge of Lisgoole Castle, 'is credibly reported' to have concluded a cowardly deal with the rebels in order to save himself and his wife, at the expense of the other eighty British subjects who were burned to death when that castle was set on fire. As regards the Hetheringtons, Sir Frederick stressed that they must have been Catholics, since they lived among the Irish for many years prior to the rebellion, and nobody but Cole believed that they were of any use to the British. Regardless of their religion, Cole should not have employed them, since they were no better than Catholics or rebels. He should instead, according to the law, have brought them to trial once they were accused of treason by any of the king's subjects. As a justice of the peace, he should also have imprisoned them while they were awaiting trial. He plainly did not understand the obligations of his office, since he did not even examine the Hetheringtons after Sir Frederick had made his accusations, and instead allowed them to remain at large, just because he doubted Sir Frederick's word and motives. As a result, Cole was indeed guilty of the third charge levelled against him.[74]

Hamilton alleged fourthly that, after the cessation, Cole complied with an order from the marquis of Ormond to take Robert Parke of Newtown away from Manorhamilton, where he had been imprisoned for over a year for having collaborated with the insurgents. Cole waited until he knew that Hamilton was gone to Derry before effecting Parke's release from custody. He allowed Parke to return among the confederates, who later accompanied him to Dublin. There Parke procured a state order for the restoration of his castle, which he and the confederates now hold for the royalist Ormond. In his *Answer*, Cole maintained

---

73 Ibid., pp 2, 6, 7.   74 Ibid., pp 32–4; see D.M. Schlegel, 'A Clogher chronology: October 1641 to July 1642', *Clogher Record* (1997), 87, for references to some depositions about the Lisgoole massacre.

that, before the rising, Parke was a justice of the peace and was well-respected by his settler neighbours. He later opposed the rebellion as best he could, and had never colluded with the rebels. Hamilton arrested him, charged him with treason and kept him in solitary confinement in Manorhamilton for over a year. He also took possession of his castle and all his goods. He refused the lords justices' many orders to send Parke to Dublin to be tried. Towards the end of September 1643, Cole sent his lieutenant to secure the prisoner's release, although he claimed that he did not know at the time that Hamilton had already gone to Derry or that the cessation was in operation. He also denied returning Parke to the confederates, and believed that Parke was now loyal to the parliamentarian cause and that Hamilton's assertion to the contrary was 'merely surmized, invented and devised' so that he could acquire Parke's estate for himself. Cole also complained about Sir Frederick's harsh imprisonment of another neighbouring planter, Thomas Abercromy, a brother-in-law of James Dunbar and a former sheriff of Leitrim. On his release, Abercromy went to Enniskillen, from where Cole sent himself and his family to Scotland. Cole finally alleged that in July 1642 Hamilton executed two Scottish Protestants by the name of Witherspin, who were tenants of yet another north Leitrim planter, John Waldron of Mullies, because they had testified against Hamilton in a land dispute court case before the rebellion.[75]

Sir Frederick began the fourth section of his *Replication* by saying that Parke's planter neighbours did not share Cole's high opinion of the Newtown commander. Even if one accepted that he may have 'lived orderly and in good repute' before the rebellion, he had now become like many others who 'have basely betrayed their religion and their countrey, and joyned with the rebels against the parliament', in order to hold on to their estates. Parke's failure to follow Sir Frederick's lawful commands, and his complicity with the rebels are detailed in the sworn depositions of fourteen of Parke's own servants, soldiers and ministers, which implicate him in treasonable activities. Copies of these depositions, which were witnessed by Sir Frederick's lieutenants and ministers, are included in the pamphlet. Hamilton then denied having had designs on Parke's estate, since he scarcely thought that he himself would survive the rebellion. He added that Cole, who dismissed an old Scottish neighbour of his own, Captain Roger Atkinson, and took over that man's castle and lands, was now judging Sir Frederick by his own standards. Hamilton claimed that Cole was also putting the former Sheriff Abercromy up on a pedestal. Even if he had been a good servant of the state in times of peace, he did join the rebels in December 1641 and was captured by Sir Frederick while in their company. Hamilton, though, denied treating him with the harshness that Cole alleges, adding that if Abercromy had any complaints, he

75 *The information of Sir Frederick Hammilton*, pp 2, 7–12.

would surely have made them known in Scotland, where both he and Hamilton spent some time in 1644. With regard to the Witherspins, Sir Frederick insisted that they were executed simply because they were traitors. James, the son, had been convicted of serious crime even before the rebellion. In November 1641, he and his Irish wife joined the rebels. As a musketeer, he took part in an attack on Manorhamilton the following February. He was eventually captured and hanged when Sir Frederick burned Sligo in July 1642. Meanwhile, his elderly father, John, had taken refuge in Castle Hamilton at the start of the rebellion. One night during the February 1642 blockade of the castle, he stole out to give his son £12. When the blockade was lifted, he was caught among the rebels and hanged. Sir Frederick concluded this section by asking how he could possibly have shot this same man five months later, as Cole had claimed.[76]

Hamilton claimed fifthly that, in February 1644, several months after the signing of cessation, Cole requested assistance from the marquis of Ormond, the king's lord lieutenant of Ireland and therefore an enemy of the English parliament. He procured an order from Ormond for the return of cattle, which the Manorhamilton garrison had taken from some confederates who were then under his protection. Sir Frederick added that his own lieutenant in Manorhamilton naturally refused to comply with the order, a copy of which is reprinted in the pamphlet. In his *Answer*, Cole admitted that on the 29 January 1644 he had taken the MacGaurans from Co. Cavan into his protection and allowed them to settle on lands near Enniskillen in return for £70 or food for his own needy garrison. He insisted, though, that he was entitled to do so by virtue of his 1641 commission from the lords justices, Parsons and Borlace. He went on to describe how Hamilton's garrison seized three to four hundred cows from these MacGaurans on 2 February 1644. On hearing about the incident, Cole requested Hamilton's lieutenant to return the prey. The latter only partially complied with the demand. Cole then informed the Dublin authorities, which resulted in Ormond's warrant for the restoration of the remaining cows. Cole claimed that he did not know at the time that Ormond had been created lord lieutenant by the king, because Enniskillen was so isolated from Dublin. Moreover, he only realized that the marquis was an enemy of the parliament when he himself went to London in June of that year. Cole claimed as well that he had documents to prove that Sir Frederick's officers in Manorhamilton also gave protection to confederates, by the name of MacMurrays and MacCabes, in Glenfarne in January 1644.[77]

In the fifth section of his *Replication*, Sir Frederick said that Cole was seeking to excuse himself for having given protection to the MacGaurans five months

76 Ibid., pp 26–9, 34–41, 69–88; see also *Another extract of severall letters*, 19–21.   77 *The information of*

after the cessation was agreed, by maintaining that he was not aware of what was happening politically in Ireland or England at the time. This, according to Hamilton, was nonsense. Ormond had consulted with all the British colonels in Ulster, including Cole, before concluding the cessation, and had sought their approval for it. Then, after it was signed, he had ordered them to observe it. Cole would also have learned from letters, which Captain Owen O'Connolly and others had brought from the English parliament, that Westminster was opposed to the cessation, and that it had requested all British officers in Ireland to take the covenant. In addition, Cole had continuous intelligence from Derry and from other parts of Ulster, which left him in no doubt about Ormond's appointment as lord lieutenant. Cole's actions show that, by not informing parliament of his arrangement with the confederates, and by obeying Ormond's command, he had still not made up his mind in February 1644 whether he was going to back parliament or the king. He 'was resolved to keep both sides his friends, if possible he could' by observing a 'detestable neutrality'. In fact, he was even trying to keep up good relations with the Irish as well. Cole's preference for the royalist cause is evident from his allegations that Sir Frederick's officers were committing a crime by not complying with Ormond's directions to restore the cows to the MacGaurans. Sir William's agreement with the MacGaurans was, moreover, harmful to the parliamentarian cause because Sir Frederick's garrison, which backed parliament and opposed the cessation, was dismayed to see a party of confederates under Cole's protection settling on lands at Blacklion, midway between Manorhamilton and Enniskillen, and taking preys of cows that heretofore had been within its catchment area and had helped it to survive. Hamilton added that Cole continued to protect those same MacGaurans even after they had broken off their agreement to supply him with money or food. He concluded by saying that he knew nothing about any confederates having been given protection on his lands in Leitrim. But if his officers had done so, which he very much doubted, it was surely due to the bad example given by Cole, and the fault could not be attributed to Sir Frederick who was then in Derry.[78]

Hamilton alleged finally that one of the companies in Cole's regiment consisted entirely of Irishmen, whom he had taken on at the beginning of the rebellion. These men did great harm to the British cause in Ireland by passing on intelligence to the rebels about various British troops, especially the garrison at Manorhamilton. Not surprisingly, these Irishmen later deserted Cole and 'turned rebels again'. Sir Frederick concluded by saying that he could have mentioned many more of Cole's 'omissions and disservices', but had not done so because they affected only himself personally. He was therefore reporting the Enniskillen

Sir Frederick Hammilton, pp 2, 12, 13, 14.   **78** Ibid., pp 41–3, 61–2.

commander, not out of vindictiveness, but rather because his covenant oath was binding him to do so. Cole, in his *Answer*, justified the fact that he took Bryan Maguire of Tempo and fifty of his men into his regiment because they had refused to join the rebellion and were loyal to the British cause. They did not form their own company, however, but rather fought under British officers. They were of great use to him as spies and guides. When a few proved disloyal, Cole hanged their guarantor, whom he had been holding as hostage. Cole assumed that Hamilton's unmentioned criticisms of him referred to those contained in the pamphlet *Another extract of severall letters from Ireland*, published in 1643, wherein he accused Cole of refusing to come to his assistance on many occasions. Sir William said, however, that he had far more important work to do in Fermanagh and other neighbouring counties than to be acceding to Hamilton's every call for help. He did send reinforcements to Manorhamilton in response to an urgent message from Hamilton on 26 July 1642, but discovered that Sir Frederick only wanted help to capture Dromahair Castle. Cole and his men were later invited to the christening of Hamilton's son on 20 May 1643, but were then treated with great disrespect by their host. Cole concluded with a stinging attack on Hamilton himself, whom he described as quarrelsome, domineering, hot-headed and lacking in tact. He said that Sir Frederick was constantly bickering with his settler neighbours and ill-treating his own officers. Cole also blamed him for provoking the rebels into murdering ten or eleven Protestants, including two ministers, by hanging Sheriff Con O'Rourke while an exchange of prisoners was being sought in January 1642. He added that, with such a temperament, Hamilton was totally unsuitable for the position of governor of Derry. A former governor of that city, Sir George Paulet, suffered defeat at the hands of the Irish, with the loss of his own life and many of the citizens, because of his impetuosity. Cole therefore implored the CBK not to appoint Hamilton to the post, because the citizens of Derry hated him, would never tolerate him, and would 'quit their fortunes and stations there … rather than submit to his command'.[79]

In the final section of his *Replication*, Hamilton suggested that Bryan Maguire of Tempo, being a Catholic, was very unlikely to have been loyal to the British cause. But even if he had been this 'one black swan amongst the rest', Cole should still never have taken his followers into his regiment, because the lower class Irish

79 Ibid., pp 2, 3, 14–22; see the text of the Solemn League and Covenant oath, especially articles IV and VI, in *The Westminster Confession of Faith* (Glasgow, 1990), pp 355–60. It is rather surprising that Cole did not challenge Sir Frederick about the Irish soldiers in his Manorhamilton garrison in February 1643. These are mentioned in *Another extract of severall letters*, pp 43–4. In 1608 Sir Cahir O'Doherty of Innisowen burned Derry and put Paulet and his garrison to the sword. Paulet was said to have insulted O'Doherty and driven him into rebellion.

people could never be trusted. Sir Frederick then alleged that, rather than coming to help him when requested, Cole had actually tried to weaken his position by enticing a number of his soldiers to abscond to Enniskillen, as is evidenced by the depositions of four Manorhamilton soldiers, which are included in the pamphlet. Regarding Cole's attack on his character, Hamilton said that he 'utterly denieth that he hath willingly injured or done wrong to any man', although he admitted to having taken some of his neighbours to court because they had claimed part of his estate or damaged his reputation. He also denied having harassed any of his officers, and did not feel that he had anything to learn about man management from Cole, who, on one occasion ran away from his soldiers because he had not the courage to face them down. He acknowledged that he would not release Sheriff Con O'Rourke in return for Sir Robert Hannay and the two Protestant ministers, insisting that, had he done so, it would have spelled disaster for him and all the British under his care. He claimed that he hanged the sheriff only after the rebels had burned Manorhamilton town some weeks later. He went on to say that it was none of Cole's business whether or not he was appointed governor of Derry. He denied that he had applied for the position, but said that Cole was trying to ruin any chances he had of being awarded this or indeed any post just because he was a Scotsman. He would not even try and refute Cole's comparison of him to Sir George Paulet, since he believed that 'it is both uncharitable and unworthily done to knock at a dead mans grave'. In conclusion, Sir Frederick claimed that Cole had failed to clear himself of 'the crimes and misdemeanours' of which he had been accused. Instead, throughout his *Answer*, he had 'infinitely abused and traduced this repliant [Sir Frederick] with unsufferable scandals and reproaches', many of a personal nature, which in no way concern the common good. Hamilton therefore desired redress against Cole for all these transgressions.[80]

By the time Hamilton was finalizing his publication in late April 1645, he had already been refused an allocation from the October ordinance – in part, at least, due to the intervention of Sir William Cole. In this pamphlet, therefore, he was intent on refuting what he considered to be Cole's slurs on his character and on vindicating his honour and good name, so that he might still have some chance of securing either the joint presidency of Connacht or the governorship of Derry. He was convinced of the veracity of his own defence and begged the CBK to carefully examine the evidence provided in his *Replication*. He concluded by asking the committee to reflect on the case of the prophet Micaiah, who was made to suffer for prophesying the truth against hundreds of the false prophets of

80 *The information of Sir Frederick Hammilton*, pp 43–61; see pp 48–55 for Hamilton's account of what happened during the visits of Cole and men in July 1642 and May 1643.

Ahab, king of Israel. Unfortunately, Ahab was killed before he could make restitution to Micaiah. Sir Frederick was therefore appealing to the committee to believe him – and not Cole, 'this simple old man' – before it was too late in this situation.[81]

Unfortunately for Sir Frederick, however, the publication of *The information of Sir Frederick Hammilton* achieved little or nothing. As we have seen, he was not subsequently assigned to any military command in either Connacht or Ulster. The pamphlet itself, in conjunction with another petition of Hamilton's, was referred by the English House of Commons to the Committee for Examinations for its consideration on 2 June 1645. There is no record of that body having made any recommendations to the Commons on how the two adversaries should be dealt with. Sir Frederick left London for Scotland during the summer of that year. It also seems probable that Cole returned to Ireland during the month of June. In the absence of both men, the document may simply have been shelved and forgotten about.[82]

IN THE ARMY OF THE SOLEMN LEAGUE AND COVENANT

As we have seen earlier in this chapter, the committee of estates in Scotland commissioned Sir Frederick colonel of a regiment of horse on 27 February 1644. The unit would be known as Hamilton's Horse. Although it was assigned to the Army of the Solemn League and Covenant, which had invaded England some five weeks previously under Alexander Leslie, first earl of Leven, it was initially directed to assist in preventing 'forrane invasions [and] intestine plots of malignantis and there adherentis' within Scotland itself. The covenanters may have held a tight control over the Scottish government and armed forces, but they were aware at the time of the increasing possibilities of external attacks and internal revolts by royalist supporters from England, Ireland and Scotland. Even as the Scottish army was marching into England to assist the parliamentarians, Charles I was urging extreme royalist leaders in Scotland, such as James Graham, earl (and later marquis) of Montrose (fig. 24), and George Gordon, marquis of Huntly, to rise in revolt against the covenanters in an attempt to force its recall. At the same time, the king was also instructing Randall MacDonnell, marquis of Antrim, to negotiate with the Irish confederates to send two thousand Irishmen to Scotland to assist the expected royalist uprisings. The advantage for the

81 *The information of Sir Frederick Hammilton*, pp 54, 61; see also 1 Kings 22; Cole was then aged seventy – fifteen years Hamilton's senior.   **82** *Journals of the English House of Commons*, iv, p. 159; Parliamentary Archives, HL/PO/JO/10/1/192, request of Nicholas Loftus for protection in relation to a debt of Sir Frederick Hamilton on 10 Sept. 1645; *CSPD, 1644–5*, pp 471, 472, 620.

confederates would be the possible withdrawal of Robert Monro's Scots forces from Ulster to help defend and pacify their native country. The mission of Hamilton's Horse regiment, at least initially, would therefore be to help quell any internal royalist revolt and repel an invading army.[83]

Even though the committee of estates had stipulated that the new regiment should 'imediately be lifted', Sir Frederick was then in no position to personally undertake the project. On the very same day that he received his commission, he and Sir Mungo Campbell of Lawers were hastily sent back to Ulster to try and prevent Monro's disgruntled forces from returning to Scotland. He therefore chose Sir Patrick McKie (McKay) of Larg, near Kirkcudbright, in south-western Scotland, as his lieutenant colonel, and entrusted him with the task of raising the unit. As a veteran of the Thirty Years War in Germany and also commander of a regiment of Galloway Horse during the Second Bishops' War, McKie was well qualified for the position. He was, moreover, an ardent covenanter and an MP for the stewartry (county) of Kirkcudbright. A regiment of horse in the Army of the Covenant consisted of eight troops, each of which comprised sixty men. McKie had raised four troops – Drummond's, Lawers', Hamilton of Preston's and his own – by the late spring of 1644, while Sir Frederick was in Derry promoting the Solemn League and Covenant.[84]

Meanwhile, the first of the not unexpected royalist uprisings had broken out in the north-east of Scotland. In mid-March 1644, a kinsman of the marquis of Huntly raided Aberdeen and seized some of the leading covenanters there. Towards the end of the month, Huntly himself occupied the city, while his followers soon gained control of much of Aberdeenshire. Around the same time, Montrose had been assembling over one thousand English and Scottish royalists in the north-west of England, and in early April marched from Carlisle to the Scottish border. Once in Scotland, he advanced on Dumfries and captured the town without difficulty.[85]

On hearing of the revolts in the north-east and south-west, the committee of estates met to consider the situation. It decided on 16 April to appoint James Livingstone, earl of Callander, in charge, under Leven, of all government forces within Scotland and to send him at the head of an army to restore order in the south-west. At least three troops – Drummond's, Lawers' and Preston's – of the now partially raised Hamilton's Horse regiment were assigned to this army. Sir

---

83 *Acts of the Parliaments of Scotland, 1644–5*, p. 698; D. Stevenson, *Revolution and counter-revolution, 1644–51* (Edinburgh, 2003), pp 4–6; Stevenson, *Scottish covenanters and Irish Confederates*, pp 165–9; Furgol, *A regimental history of the covenanting armies*, p. 147.   **84** *Acts of the parliaments of Scotland, 1644–5*, p. 698; S. Reid, *Scots armies of the 17th century: 1. The Army of the Covenant, 1639–51* (Nottingham, 2001), pp 21, 74; C.S. Terry, *Papers relating to the Army of the Solemn League and Covenant, 1643–1647* (2 vols, Edinburgh, 1917), i, pp lxiv–lxv.   **85** See Furgol, 'The civil wars in Scotland', p. 51.

22 Archibald Campbell, first marquis of Argyll, by Guillaume Philippe Benoist (© National Portrait Gallery, London).

Frederick Hamilton, as colonel of the regiment, was appointed a member of the advisory committee to accompany Callander, even though he was at this time in Derry organizing two thousand British troops for a joint attack with Robert Monro's Scots' forces on the confederate earl of Castlehaven in Connacht. On 28 April, Callander assembled five thousand men at Douglas, some forty miles north of Dumfries, and advanced towards the rebels. Montrose, who was heavily outnumbered due to dissensions and lack of local royalist support, fled back to England. Rather than pursue him there, Callander quartered his forces north of the border to prevent any future royalist invasions into Scotland.[86]

Meanwhile, a second government army of four thousand men was sent to the north-east to subdue Huntly's rising. These forces were commanded by the leading covenanter, Archibald Campbell, marquis of Argyll (fig. 22). There is evidence to suggest that Sir Patrick McKie of Larg's own horse troop may have been assigned to Argyll on this expedition. When the army reached Aberdeen on 2 May, Huntly's men, like those of Montrose, deserted or surrendered. Huntly himself fled to Strathnaver. After having garrisoned Aberdeen, Argyll reduced the rest of the shire to submission over the course of the following four weeks. He

---

86 *Acts of the parliaments of Scotland, 1644–5*, p. 91; *ODNB*, xxxiv, pp 61–2; Sir Frederick would have known Callander personally from the 1630s when both men served as gentlemen of the privy chamber at

then led his army south on 1 July, when the royalist threat had finally been quelled.[87]

The royalist risings of Montrose and Huntly in the spring of 1644 might have had more success if, as planned, they had been joined by an Irish invasion force under the marquis of Antrim. The marquis had hoped to persuade the Irish confederates to provide men for such an expedition. However, the supreme council at Kilkenny would only agree to supply arms, ammunition and food for the project, leaving Antrim with the task of raising an army himself. The marquis eventually assembled some 1,600 native Irish troops from Cos Antrim and Derry, as well as some Scots-Irish MacDonalds from Antrim. To lead the expedition, he chose a Scottish-born kinsman of his own, Alasdair MacColla MacDonald, who had taken refuge in Ulster after Argyll had captured his father's estates in western Scotland some years previously. MacColla was finally forced to sail from Passage East and Ballyhack in the Waterford estuary at the end of June 1644, after the king's lord lieutenant in Ireland, the marquis of Ormond, had refused to allow him to leave from Carlingford Lough for British security reasons. When news of MacColla's landing in Morvern in the Sound of Mull on 8 July reached Edinburgh, the Scottish government appointed Argyll to command an expedition to his home territory of Argyllshire against the Irish invasion force. Two weeks later, Argyll, with 2,600 men, launched a campaign against MacColla.[88]

The government felt that Argyll would be able to defeat the Irish invaders with his own resources. If reinforcements were needed, Robert Monro, commander of the Scottish forces in Ulster, had been instructed to send men to help. In the event, none were dispatched by Monro at this time. However, Sir Frederick Hamilton brought two troops of horse from Ulster to Scotland, with the intention of bringing Hamilton's Horse regiment closer to full strength. He had no doubt been prompted to raise these troops by news of the various recent royalist uprisings in his native country. He himself took personal command of one of the troops, and withdrew his eldest son, Frederick, from the University of Glasgow to be routmaster (or captain) of the second. Young Frederick, who had completed almost two years study at the university, was then aged about twenty.[89]

Once in Scotland, Hamilton himself probably led both troops into north-east England to join Callander's army, which had gone there at the end of June to recapture strongholds taken by the royalists (fig. 23). By the 22 July, however, he was back again in Scotland settling an account for his sons' textbooks with a lecturer at the University of Glasgow. Five days later, he travelled to Edinburgh

the royal court. **87** Furgol, 'The civil wars in Scotland', p. 53. **88** Stevenson, *Scottish covenanters and Irish Confederates*, pp 166–74. **89** Furgol, *A regimental history*, 147; Terry, *Papers relating to the Army of the Solemn League and Covenant*, i, p. lxiv; *Records of the University of Glasgow*, iii, p. ix.

23 Places associated with Sir Frederick Hamilton's Horse regiment in Scotland and England, 1644–7.

where he delivered to the convention of estates a petition, the nature of which is not recorded. He may also have taken the opportunity while in the capital to discuss business pertaining to his regiment with his lieutenant colonel, Patrick McKie, whose own horse troop was then quartered in Haddington some twelve miles east of the city.[90]

On 27 July 1644 – the same day that he had presented his petition – the convention of estates appointed him one of fifteen Scottish commissioners to reside with the Scots army in Ulster. The nominations followed an agreement by both the English parliament and the covenanters some three months previously to establish a joint Anglo-Scottish commission to direct, in a coordinated way, the war efforts of the Scottish and British forces in Ireland against the Irish confederates. The English parliament failed to designate its promised commissioners in the months that followed, however, and so the Scottish committee could not function in Ireland.[91]

Hamilton crossed back to Ulster at the beginning of August, not only to take up his position as commissioner, but probably also in the hope of being awarded the colonelcy of Chichester's regiment of foot by the CBK in London. He did not return again to Scotland later that month when the committee with the Army of the Solemn League and Covenant authorized him to raise his Scottish regiment of horse. This permit can have been no more than a formality, since by then the entire unit had already been recruited. The last two troops to be levied – Omachie's and Auchterlonie's – were quartered with Sir Patrick McKie's troop during a rendezvous of northern covenanters at Inverness on 22 August. The other five – Drummond's, Lawers', Preston's and Sir Frederick's two troops of Ulster horse – were meanwhile at the siege of Newcastle in northern England with the combined forces of Leven's and Callander's armies.[92]

By the end of August 1644, Alasdair MacColla and his three Irish regiments had, after evading the marquis of Argyll's army, marched into the Central Highlands. At Blair Atholl, he was joined on the 29th of the month by Montrose, who had secretly re-entered Scotland some ten days previously. Montrose quickly assumed command of MacColla's men and some local Highlanders, and marched southwards towards Perth. On 1 September, his force of 2,500 men defeated an army of local covenanters twice its size at Tippermuir. Perth itself, some three miles away, then surrendered to Montrose.[93]

90 *Acts of the parliaments of Scotland, 1644–5*, p. 224; NRS, GD/3/6/9 item 10, receipted account by James Sanders, reader at Glasgow University, for books to Frederick and James Hamilton, 22 Jul. 1644. **91** *Acts of the parliaments of Scotland, 1644–5*, p. 222; *CSPD, 1644–5*, p. 201. It would be October 1645 before three English commissioners were eventually sent to Ulster, by which time Sir Frederick had already departed the Irish scene for good. **92** D. Warrand (ed.), *More Culloden papers* (5 vols, Inverness, 1923), i, p. 71. **93** Wheeler, *The Irish and British wars*, p. 123.

Over the next twelve months, Montrose achieved a series of spectacular victories over various covenanting armies throughout Scotland. Hamilton's Horse, under the command of the regiment's lieutenant colonel Sir Patrick McKie, were among the defeated forces at Fyvie, Inverlochy and Auldearn (Sir Frederick Hamilton had in the meantime gone from Ulster to London to seek further remuneration from the English parliament for his service in Ireland). Montrose's final victory at Kilsyth, south of Stirling, on 15 August 1645 left him for a short time master of Scotland. However, Lieutenant General David Leslie, with almost five thousand cavalry, was soon dispatched from the Army of the Solemn League and Covenant in northern England to deal with the crisis, and on 13 September he won a total victory over Montrose at Philiphaugh near Selkirk.[94]

Sir Frederick Hamilton arrived back in Scotland from London during the late summer of 1645. Perhaps it was news of the covenanters' defeat at Kilsyth that prompted his return. In any case, he had by then become disillusioned with the English parliament, which had both rejected all his compensation claims and refused to assign him any further military commands in Ireland. It is not known if Hamilton's Horse took any part in the Battle of Kilsyth. Nor do the records confirm that the regiment, under either Sir Patrick McKie or Sir Frederick himself, fought with Leslie at Philiphaugh. It is possible that it was engaged in garrison duty elsewhere in Scotland during this period. It is thought likely, however, that it was assigned to Major General John Middleton's army of horse and foot, which was dispatched to Aberdeen in late September to recapture that city from the royalists. From then on, Hamilton himself seems to have taken personal command of the regiment.[95]

Having left John Middleton to take care of the royalist threats in Aberdeen-shire, David Leslie returned to England to be reunited with Leven's forces. In mid-November, both Scots commanders joined the English parliamentary army that had just laid siege to Newark-on-Trent in Nottinghamshire. This extremely well-reinforced city was one of the most important fortified bases in England, and served as a centre of operations for most of the East Midlands. By the end of December, the majority of David Leslie's cavalry had returned from Scotland to support the siege. So too did other regiments – including Hamilton's Horse – that had formerly seen service in England before being ordered to Scotland at the outbreak of Montrose's and MacColla's rebellion. The Army of the Solemn League and Covenant mustered seven thousand men in nine

94 Greenwood, 'Col. William "Blowface" Forbes', pp 106–8, 113; J. Skene (ed.), *The history of the troubles and memorable transactions in Scotland from MDCXXIV to MDCXLV* by J. Spalding (Aberdeen, 1828–9), pp 458–61, 465–6; S. Reid, *Auldearn, 1645: the marquis of Montrose's Scottish campaign* (Oxford, 2003), pp 45, 87.   95 Parliamentary Archives, HL/PO/JO/10/1/192, request by Nicholas Loftus for protection in relation to a debt of Sir Frederick Hamilton, 15 Sept. 1645; *Acts of the parliaments of Scotland, 1644–5*, p. 436.

regiments of foot, ten of horse, two companies of dragoons and thirteen troops of horse outside Newark on 17 January 1646. Hamilton's Horse regiment comprised 316 men in eight troops with Sir Frederick personally in command. By now, Hamilton's second son, James, had joined the regiment, and, like his older brother Frederick, was routmaster of one of the troops.[96]

The Anglo-Scottish siege of Newark continued into the late spring of 1646, despite deteriorating relations between the English parliament and the covenanters. Parliament felt that it could defeat the king without the help of the Scots, who by now they regarded just a worthless burden on England. In addition, the parliamentarians resented the covenanters' attempts to impose the Scottish model of Presbyterianism – one strictly controlled by clerics – on England, where the church was subordinate to the state. The Scots, for their part, were angry that their army was being grossly under-funded, and at the same time criticized for underachievement, by their parliamentarian allies. They also doubted that the English church would ever be reformed according to their wishes. Moreover, they feared that when the king was defeated, the English parliament would conclude with Charles I its own deal, which might not be to the covenanters' liking. So they secretly entered into peace negotiations with the monarch, aimed at helping him recover his rights in England, in return for the imposition of a civil and religious settlement in that country that would be favourable to themselves. Following some verbal assurances to this effect by the Scots, the king, who was now in imminent danger of being trapped in Oxford by advancing parliamentarian armies, arrived at the covenanters' camp outside Newark on 5 May 1646, in the hope of concluding a deal.[97]

Not surprisingly, the English were outraged that the Scots had apparently made a secret pact with the king. So the covenanters, fearing that their forces might be surrounded by the New Model Army at Newark and cut off from Scotland, withdrew with the king 130 miles northwards to Newcastle. They soon realized, however, that Charles had no intention of signing the covenant and establishing Presbyterianism in England, although he did accept military defeat and ordered all his forces in England and Scotland to disband. They therefore quickly set about reassuring the English parliament of their continued loyalty to the Solemn League and Covenant alliance. The tactic worked, and on 13 July both governments sent a set of common demands – known as the Propositions of Newcastle – to the king, who was still unwilling to make concessions. The

---

96 Furgol, *A regimental history*, pp 6, 148, 168, 415–16; Terry, *Papers relating to the Army of the Solemn League and Covenant*, p. lxiv; Hutton and Reeves, 'Sieges and fortifications', 212–15. The Army of the Solemn League and Covenant was significantly larger than the number of men that mustered outside Newark on 17 January. The muster did not include, for example, the Scots garrisons in various towns in northern England or the regiments still in Scotland. **97** Wheeler, *The Irish and British wars*, pp 148–9, 154–6.

following month, the Scots also agreed in principle to withdraw entirely from England, without the king, as soon as they had been paid the substantial arrears owed to them by the English parliament under the covenant treaty. In September, Westminster agreed to pay the Scots £400,000 sterling, half of it before they withdrew. £200,000 was raised and paid over by 3 February 1647, and within a few days all of the Scottish army, including Hamilton's Horse regiment, had crossed the border into Scotland, after having abandoned the king to the English in Newcastle.[98]

Not all covenanters were happy with the convention of estates' decision to leave Charles I behind in England, particularly as they realized that he might quite likely be ill-treated or deposed by the parliamentarians. Chief among those who held this view was James, duke of Hamilton, despite his imprisonment for over two years by the king for failing to prevent the Scots from forming an alliance with the English parliament in September 1643. On his release by parliamentarian forces, he had taken the covenant, but was now once again on friendly terms with the king. The duke's younger brother, William, earl of Lanark, was also well disposed to the king. When the Army of the Covenant returned to Scotland, therefore, the Hamiltons wished to keep it intact in case it would ever be needed to help the king. The extreme covenanters, led by the marquis of Argyll on the other hand, feared that the growing sympathy for Charles I in his native Scotland could lead the country to become involved in a new war with England, if the covenanting army was not disbanded or at least radically downsized without delay. Argyll got his way, and on 5 February 1647 the convention of estates ordered that the army be reduced to just over seven thousand men, mainly infantry. The marquis also succeeded in controlling what officers and regiments were to be retained, thus excluding those suspected of royalist sympathies.[99]

Whether on account of his close relationship to James and William Hamilton, or because many of the horse regiments in the Army of the Solemn League and Covenant were deemed to be superfluous to this New Model Scots Army, Sir Frederick Hamilton's regiment was among those disbanded on 9 February. One week later, Hamilton was given an honourable discharge by the Scottish parliament, which gratefully acknowledged the 'faithfull and trew service' of himself and his sons to Scotland. It also released them from any further commitments to their country, leaving them 'frie to seik and accept of anie furder employment sutable to their worth'. Interestingly, this discharge reminds one of that which Sir Frederick procured from Chancellor Oxenstierna and the Swedish

---

98 See Stevenson, *Revolution and counter-revolution*, pp 55–66. **99** *ODNB*, ix, p. 711 and xxiv, p. 843; Scott, *Politics and war*, p. 122.

council of state some ten years earlier, when he went to Sweden to complain about the manner in which his regiment had been disbanded in Germany in December 1632. Both amounted to being good references, but were accompanied by little or no monetary compensation.[100]

Sir Frederick was unhappy with the level of arrears that were paid to him on his discharge. So he promptly drew up a statement of his own and his regiment's outstanding expenses for service in Scotland, and presented these to the convention of estates with a claim for much better remuneration. The convention reacted on 5 March by referring his petition to a committee that had already been set up to consider the case of another claimant – Sir Adam Hepburn of Humbie. This body was then to report back its findings to the convention. There is unfortunately neither any record of the outcome of its considerations, nor any account of the final decision of parliament. We may assume, however, that it is unlikely, in view of the Scottish state's shortage of cash at the time, that Hamilton ever received any further compensation for his services. It seems, therefore, that, for the third time in his military career, Sir Frederick believed that he had been inadequately remunerated – firstly by Sweden, then by the English parliament and now by the Scottish authorities. In view of his ardent commitment to the covenanting cause, and the fact that he was in reality a Scot at heart, despite his frequent protestations of Britishness, this last disappointment may well have been for him the most difficult pill to swallow.[101]

PERSONAL MATTERS AND FINAL PETITIONS

Of the many hardships that befell Sir Frederick during his covenanter years, perhaps the greatest was the premature loss of his wife, Sidney, which occurred sometime in late 1643 or during the first nine months of 1644. Sidney was still a relatively young woman at the time, since she had given birth to their youngest son, Gustavus, some twelve months previously. She had been the homemaker and estate administrator during her husband's frequent absences from Manorhamilton in the 1620s and 1630s, as well as his most loyal and devoted supporter during the 1641 rebellion and early Confederate War. Sidney and their two youngest children had left Manorhamilton in mid-September 1643 to accompany Sir Frederick to Derry, where he planned to speak out against the cessation. Hamilton mentions his children, but not his wife, in a petition written about 25 October 1644, so we may assume that she had passed away by then. It is likely

---

100 *Acts of the parliaments of Scotland, 1644–5*, p. 698; SRA Riksregistraturet, vol.192, fo. 96r–v: Swedish royal 'Dimissio' for Sir Frederick Hamilton, *c*.Dec. 1637. **101** *Acts of the parliaments of Scotland, 1644–5*, p. 722.

that she died and is buried in Derry, even though there is no record of her death in the city cathedral register.[102]

Despite his grief at the loss of Sidney, Hamilton married again sometime after his return to Scotland in the autumn of 1645. His second wife was Agnes, daughter of Sir Robert Hepburn of Alderstown in Haddingtonshire, or presently East Lothian. In 1605 Robert Hepburn had been lieutenant of the king's guard in Scotland and justice of the peace for Haddingtonshire. He had extensive estates in his native land, but also received a grant of 1,500 acres in Co. Tyrone during the plantation of Ulster. By 1629, however, he had sold all his Ulster lands to other settlers, before returning to Scotland. His daughter, Agnes, was a widow when she married Sir Frederick. She had originally wed Adam Whiteford of Milntown near Paisley in the early 1630s, but he passed away in 1637. Unfortunately, there are no records to indicate whether or not Hamilton's union with Lady Milntown – as she was known – was as happy as the years he had spent with Sidney.[103]

One of the reasons that Sir Frederick left England for Scotland during the summer of 1645 may well have been to escape the pressure he was coming under to repay a loan that he had taken out on the London staple some years previously. John Cornelius Linkebecke, a merchant of the staple, had advanced him a certain sum of money early in 1641. As part of the contract, Linkebecke gave him a bill of exchange, which was a written order requiring him to repay the loan by a fixed date. Apparently not being in a position to honour the agreement six months later, Sir Frederick persuaded his friend Nicholas Loftus of Rathfarnham, paymaster of the old standing army in Ireland, to accept responsibility for the bill of exchange, on the understanding that he could reimburse himself from Hamilton's future army pay. However, the rebellion broke out in October of that year, leaving both men bereft of their income and estates.[104]

---

102 *Another extract of severall letters*, pp 17, 28; *The information of Sir Frederick Hammilton*, p. 2; *The several petitions of William Hansard and Sir Frederick Hammiltoun*, pp 25–30. A letter dated 7 June 2002 from Aubrey Fielding, project manager, Derry Rural Deanery Genealogy Project, at St Columb's Cathedral, Londonderry, confirmed that there is no record of Sidney's death in the cathedral register. 103 Revd G. Hill, *A historical account of the plantation in Ulster* (Belfast, 1877), pp 287, 368, 547; M. Perceval-Maxwell, *The Scottish migration to Ulster in the reign of James I* (Belfast, 1999), p. 347; Sir W. Fraser (ed.), *Memoirs of the Maxwells of Pollok* (2 vols, Edinburgh, 1865), ii, p. 482; G. Hamilton, *The house of Hamilton* (Edinburgh, 1933), p. 922. G. Hamilton suggests that Agnes Hepburn was already the widow of Robert Ker of Ridpath when she married Adam Whiteford. 104 Parliamentary Archives, HL/POJO/10/1/192, petition of J.C. Lynkebecke to the House of Lords, 10 Sept. 1645 and the answer of Nicholas Loftus, 15 Sept. 1645; Ohlmeyer and Ó Ciardha (eds), *The Irish statute staple books*, p. xvii; McGrath, 'A biographical dictionary', pp 195–200. There is a wall monument to J.C. Linkebecke, who died in 1655 aged 63 years, in the Guild Church of St Ethelburga the Virgin in Bishopsgate in London. Nicholas Loftus of Rathfarnham was a cousin of Nicholas Loftus of the city of Dublin who had acted as surety for Hamilton in the loan which he took out on the Cork staple in 1637.

Linkebecke continued to pressurize the two men for the return of his loan in the years that followed, despite their difficult financial situations and their prolonged absences from London. By 1645, they had indicated that they were prepared to give the merchant any security they possibly could. However, during the summer of that year, Sir Frederick left for Scotland. Probably tiring of their vague reassurances, Linkebecke now demanded that Loftus sign a bond promising to repay the debt with 10 per cent interest within the year, or else be liable for double the amount of the loan. Moreover, he suggested that Nicholas' nephew, Sir Arthur Loftus, who was then in London, should join in the surety. Sir Arthur agreed, provided that Hamilton signed the bond first and also accepted entire responsibility for the actual repayment of the money. Increasingly frustrated by the length of time that all this was taking, Linkebecke petitioned the English House of Lords on 10 September to request permission to sue Nicholas Loftus for the long overdue debt. Five days later, Loftus sought the protection of the house from the courts, claiming that Hamilton would in fact sign the bond, once it had been delivered to him in Scotland. There are no further documents that reveal the outcome of the affair. It seems unlikely that Sir Frederick would ever have been able to raise the money to repay the loan, in view of the lack of compensation he received from the English parliament and the paucity of arrears from the Scottish authorities.[105]

While Hamilton was back in London sometime during the early months of 1646, a petition relating to a totally different matter was handed in to the English House of Commons, requesting it to order him to appear before the parliamentary court on a charge of contempt. The petitioner was William Hansard, who was still claiming ownership of the Lifford estate in Co. Donegal in a legal dispute between him and Sir John Vaughan, Sir Frederick's father-in-law, which had dragged on for over twenty years. Hansard said that, following an appeal by Sir Frederick in the closing months of 1640, the Commons had temporarily placed the estate in the hands of three trustees. Despite this, Hamilton had in recent years been violating the order by forcibly collecting rents from the estate's tenants. Hansard therefore appealed to the house to order Sir Frederick to cease doing so, and also to answer the charge against him. He also begged to be allowed to collect some of the rents himself, as he was then in dire financial straits.[106]

In a printed counter-petition, Hamilton alleged that Hansard was being encouraged to take this action by people who had become antagonistic towards him because of his 'former great zeal to the publike service, and antipathy to their

105 Parliamentary Archives, HL/PO/JO/10/1/192.   **106** *The several petitions of William Hansard and Sir Frederick Hammiltoun*, pp 3–4.

knavery'. He felt that Hansard had his petition printed and circulated widely to make more of an impression and to further discredit him. Moreover, it was issued on the very day that some MPs believed that Hamilton had just left for Newark, so that he would not be in a position to answer the charges in person. Sir Frederick was thus implying that some of his detractors were members of the Commons.[107]

Hamilton went on to claim in his petition that he only began collecting rents from the estate in 1643, after the death of his father-in-law, who had been doing so up until then. He hoped that the Commons was aware of all his hardships and losses since the outbreak of the rebellion, but also of his devotion to the parliamentarian cause, even though 'never as yet having received either preferment or other reward from the parliament, notwithstanding his constant service and great arrears due to him'. He alleged that Hansard's petition not only dishonoured parliament, but also disheartened all 'faithful generous spirits [like himself] who constantly adhere to the cause and covenant'. Sir Frederick therefore requested the house to make an example of Hansard to 'all scandalous and vilifying persons', so that parliament's honour and his own reputation might be vindicated.[108]

Hamilton then presented for the consideration of the Commons 'the true state of the case concerning the lands of Lifford', which appears to have been part of the defence prepared by his legal counsel back in 1638. He also included a copy of a 1644 petition of his own to the sub-committee for Irish affairs, in which he had outlined his many losses resulting from the rebellion, as well as copies of two letters from this sub-committee to the CBK that recommended that he be compensated and promoted. Although these endorsements had not as yet been acted upon, he concluded with the fervent wish that, even at this late stage, the Commons might still reward him properly. There is no record in the House of Commons documents to indicate that Sir Frederick was ever ordered to appear before the parliamentary court in the Hansard case. But neither is there any indication that he received his desired compensation from the English parliament.[109]

Sir Frederick Hamilton's involvement with the Scots covenanters and their allies, the English parliamentarians, lasted for just over three years. For the first twelve months or so, he enjoyed prominent attention from both governments, and was awarded significant military, diplomatic and advisory roles in Scotland and Ireland. However, despite considerable canvassing on his own part, and the support of powerful committees in London, he failed to obtain from the English parliament any permanent military position or compensation for the losses he had sustained during the 1641 rebellion. He was undermined by some English

107 Ibid., pp 5–6.   108 Ibid., pp 6–8.   109 Ibid., pp 9–37.

planters in Ireland, partially as a result of his own outspoken criticism of them. These men had achieved more influence than he at Westminster, where a strong anti-Scottish bias was beginning to manifest itself from early 1645 onwards. And, while he did retain command of his horse regiment in the Army of the Covenant until February 1647, he then seems to have been less than adequately remunerated for his services by the Scottish convention of estates. As a result of these setbacks, it would appear that he was in deep financial trouble, leading to his inability to repay at least two loans taken out some years earlier. So, for Hamilton, the covenanter period of his life, which had begun so brightly and promised so much at times, ended for him in disappointment, disillusionment and insolvency in the spring of 1647.[110]

24 James Graham, first marquis of Montrose, by Gerrit van Honthorst (© National Portrait Gallery, London).

110 One of these loans was from Linkebecke, the other from Thomas Skiddy of Cork. See PRONI, D430/142, bond of Sir Frederick Hamilton and others to pay Thomas Skiddy £600, 3 Aug. 1637 and W. Roulston, 'The Ulster plantation in the manor of Dunnalong, 1610–70' in Dillon and Jefferies (eds), *Tyrone, history and society*, pp 279–80.

CHAPTER EIGHT

Death, posterity and legacy

On his discharge from the Army of the Solemn League and Covenant, Hamilton and his two youngest children, Christina and Gustavus, seem to have retired to the home of his second wife, Agnes Hepburn, at Milntown near Paisley. She had inherited this property from her late first husband, Adam Whiteford. Although Sir Frederick had by then withdrawn totally from both military and public life, he must have still shared the concern and indignation felt by the majority of Scots covenanters when, on 4 June 1647, elements of the English New Model Army seized the king from his parliamentary keepers at Holmby House in Northamptonshire and brought him to the army headquarters at Newmarket. It is interesting to speculate whether this development would have prompted Sir Frederick to reconsider his former rejection of Charles I and now favour the approach being championed by his cousin, James duke of Hamilton, which advocated sending Scottish military aid to rescue the king and help him recover the throne of England in return for some concessions to Presbyterianism in that country. Whatever his sentiments, Sir Frederick would not live to see the signing of the treaty, known as the Engagement, on 26 December 1647 between Charles and the Scottish commissioners, or the actual invasion of England by the Scots and their humiliating defeat in the summer of 1648.[1]

During his retirement at Milntown, Hamilton received both bad and good news of a personal nature from Ireland. His two eldest sons, captains Frederick and James, on being discharged from the Army of the Solemn League and Covenant, had returned there to pursue their military careers. While not engaged in active military service, it seems likely that they both resided in Manorhamilton Castle, which was still owned by their father, even though Sir Charles Coote had probably placed his own lieutenant in charge of its garrison. Both Frederick and James joined Coote's parliamentarian forces in Connacht, which, despite a serious lack of resources, were still engaged in a struggle for supremacy with confederate troops in the province. Sir Frederick would no doubt have approved of his sons' involvement against the Irish confederates. However, a letter dated 10 May 1647 brought the sad news that Frederick had recently been killed in Connacht 'with

---

1 Fraser (ed.), *Memorials of the Maxwells of Pollok*, i, p. 482; Wheeler, *The Irish and British wars*, p. 179.

his to much fordwardnes in persueing of some feue rogs'. He died unmarried, aged twenty-three.[2]

Some few months later, the tidings from Ireland were much more positive. Captain James, now Sir Frederick's heir, had married Catherine Hamilton, the teenage daughter of his first cousin Claude, Lord Strabane and Master of Abercorn. Interestingly, Catherine was a Catholic. Her father, who had died in 1638, was, according to the Protestant bishop of Derry, 'poisoned with Popery' and had built up a sizeable nucleus of Scottish Catholic settlers on his Strabane estate. He had also allowed the Catholic vicar general of the diocese of Derry to reside on his estate during the 1630s, and had promised him protection when he was in danger of being arrested. It is unlikely that Sir Frederick would have had any serious reservations about giving his blessing to the marriage, since his own brother, Sir George, himself a staunch Catholic, had been guardian and close friend of Catherine's father during the latter's youth. Catherine almost certainly came to live in Manorhamilton Castle after her marriage to James, since she was later buried in Cloonclare cemetery on the outskirts of the town.[3]

Meanwhile, Sir Frederick and his wife, Agnes, were living in very straitened circumstances at Milntown. On receiving a bill on 31 May 1647 for 488 marks and ten pence, which amounted to £27 sterling, Hamilton was forced to plead inability to pay. The bill, which was for twenty-eight bolls of oats and six bolls of peas, probably dated from his days in the Army of the Solemn League and Covenant. He did, however, formally acknowledge the debt to Andrew Hepburn, the supplier of the provisions.[4]

Hamilton's financial situation worsened in the months that followed. On 17 November, he was forced to borrow £348 Scots currency, which was worth £29 sterling, from John Hamilton, a merchant and burgess of Glasgow. He signed a bond on that occasion, committing himself to repay the money before the following Whitsunday Eve, or else be obliged to pay extra interest on the sum. However, tragedy struck within a matter of days of his taking out the loan, and he died suddenly – or at least unexpectedly – on or about 20 November.[5]

2 Sir W. Fraser (ed.), *Memorials of the Montgomeries* (2 vols, Edinburgh, 1859), i, p. 283; Matthew and Harrison (eds), *ODNB*, xiii, p. 294. **3** *CSPI, Charles I, 1625–32*, pp 499, 512–13; Balfour Paul, *The Scots peerage*, i, pp 45, 50; Lt Col. G. Hamilton, *The house of Hamilton* (Edinburgh, 1933), p. 923; Roulston, 'The Ulster plantation in the Manor of Dunnalong, 1610–70', pp 294–5; RIA, OS memoirs, Box 28, 11, statistical memoir of the union of Manorhamilton, 1836. The author of the memoir, Lieutenant William Lancey, mistakenly believed Catherine to be a daughter of Sir Frederick Hamilton; J. Anderson, *Historical and genealogical memoirs of the house of Hamilton* (Edinburgh, 1825), p. 244. **4** NRS, CC8/8/63, fos 260r–262r: Sir Frederick Hamilton's testament dative and inventar, December 1647. A mark or merk was an old Scottish silver coin worth thirteen shillings and four pence Scots currency or thirteen pence sterling. A boll was an old Scottish measure used for grain etc. 28 bolls weighed about 3 tons, while 6 bolls of peas equalled 8.5 hundredweight. **5** NRS, CC8/8/63, fos 260r–262r. £1 Scots was worth twenty pence sterling. Whitsunday, which fell on 15 May, was a Scots quarter day on which contracts, leases and rents ended.

Probably anticipating that there would be other claims made against her late husband's estate, Dame Agnes Hepburn hastened to Edinburgh Commissary Court on 25 November on behalf of herself and Sir Frederick's two youngest children, Christina and Gustavus, to reclaim her 5,300 mark dowry in accordance with the terms of her marriage contract with Hamilton. Three weeks later, Robert Wallace, Sir Frederick's former quartermaster, brought a case to the same court against Hamilton's heirs for reimbursement of the money he had expended on settling some of the colonel's army debts which had amounted to £3,430 2s. 3d. Scots.[6]

During the month of December 1647, Edinburgh Commissary Court appointed four executors – all of whom were also creditors of Hamilton – to assess the value of the deceased's moveable estate (which did not include his castle or lands). The four were John Hamilton, the Glasgow merchant, who had loaned Sir Frederick money just before his death, Andrew Hepburn, who had supplied the oats and peas, John McQuisteme, servant to Sir Frederick's son, Captain James, and Andrew Paton, merchant and burgess of Edinburgh. These men set about their task immediately, and before the end of the month had furnished for the court an inventory of the 'goods, geir, sowmes of money and debts' of the late Sir Frederick Hamilton.[7]

According to the inventory, Hamilton's moveable estate consisted of:

5 stones, 13lbs, 6ozs of silver plate valued at	£4,333	6s.
10 stones of old pewter and tin	£96	
14 damask table cloths and cupboard cloths	£252	
9 damask towels	£54	
10 dozen damask napkins	£240	
6 coarse damask cloths and cupboard cloths	£108	
8 dornick linen table cloths and cupboard cloths	£96	
7 dornick linen table cloths	£21	
2 dozen dornick linen napkins	£24	
2 linen table cloths	£16	
1 dozen linen napkins	£6	
7 pairs of sheets	£98	
4 pairs of pillowcases	£16	
2 sets of curtains (one set red and the other green)	£133	6s. 8d.
6 pieces of hangings (2 small ones and 4 big ones)	£200	
2 pieces of black and white curtains, 2 old striped hangings and an old green tablecloth	£20	

6 Ibid. 5,300 marks amounted to £295 sterling, while £3,430 2s. 3d. Scots came to £286 sterling.   7 Ibid.

2 old feather beds	£20
12 old coffers, some of which are very old	£48
2 old wine skins	£10
4 old broken cabinets without locks or keys and a broken writing desk	£15
An old set of weapons	£24
Total value	£5,840 12s. 8d. Scots

If we exclude the silver plate, Hamilton's remaining possessions, consisting largely of household items, were worth only a very modest sum. The inventory illustrates clearly how seriously his financial circumstances had deteriorated in his final years.[8]

Once the four executors had compiled their inventory, the Commissary Court authorized them, on 25 December 1647, to claim back their debts and expenses from the estate. The court did, however, appoint five other gentlemen – John Nisbet, John Hamilton of Braidyards, Robert Hamilton, lawyer in Edinburgh, Thomas Nisbet, servant to Andrew Paton, and Francis Abercrombie, butcher and burgess of Edinburgh – to stand surety that the executors would carry out their duties correctly. As the value of Sir Frederick's moveable estate was less than the total value of the claims lodged, it seems safe to assume that none of the creditors was compensated in full.[9]

And so came to an end the colourful and chequered career of Sir Frederick Hamilton. It was one that had begun so brightly at the court of James I in 1615. Then, after having been granted a substantial estate in the plantation of Leitrim in 1622, Hamilton succeeded through his own efforts in enlarging it fourfold within a decade. His ten-month involvement in the Thirty Years War in Germany under Gustavus Adolphus in the early 1630s greatly expanded his military horizons and prepared him well for future conflicts. One of the most fruitful periods of his career occurred following his return to Ireland in 1633. Despite the curtailments of Lord Deputy Wentworth, he managed to build an imposing castle, found the town of Manorhamilton and establish many profitable enterprises on his estate. The successful defence of his castle and the suppression of the 1641 rebellion in Leitrim and neighbouring counties further added to his list of achievements. Even his switch of allegiance from the king to the Solemn League Alliance proved initially favourable. However, his status and fortunes began to

---

8 Ibid. Damask is a weaving style or technique that originated in the early Middle Ages in Damascus. This style typically produced very ornate and decorative pattern in fabric of silk, wool, linen or cotton. Consequently, damask was and still is closely associated with luxury. Dornick is a heavy damask cloth used for hangings and tablecloths that originated in Tournai, Belgium. £5,840 Scots amounted to £487 sterling. **9** Ibid.

decline when the English parliament would neither reward him with a significant military command in Ireland, nor compensate him for his losses during the rebellion. And his career lay in tatters when the Scottish parliament disbanded his regiment and discharged himself in February 1647 with little or no remuneration for his past service. Although Sir Frederick could have pointed to the political turmoil and civil unrest in Britain and Ireland throughout the 1640s as being the principal causes of his downfall, there can be little doubt but that his own aggressive personality contributed in no small measure to his eventual fall from grace. In any event, his bragging days were now well and truly over and he died a ruined man.

THE FORTUNES OF HIS IMMEDIATE FAMILY

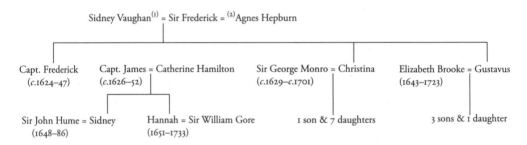

25 Sir Frederick's family.

On 9 July 1648, less than nine months after Sir Frederick's death, his widow Agnes married once again. Her third husband was John Maxwell of Pollok, a cousin and friend of the late Sir Frederick. This union turned out to be a very unhappy one, and on 25 July 1661 Agnes appealed to the lords of the privy council for protection against her abusive husband. She said that 'she was expecting nothing else [from Maxwell] bot to have lived a peaceable and quyet lyfe with him at bed and boord in all godlinesse, peace and honesty, conforme to the lawes of God and this kingdome'. However, her

> unnaturall husband, casting of all fear of God, and the affectione and deuty he owes to the said compleaner, hes without any just ground or offence on her pairt these sewerall yeirs bypast, caryed and behaved himself most harshlie, cruelie and baselie towards her, not only shunning to keip conjugall society with her, bot strykes and abuses her with staffs, hands and feett, to the perrill and hazard of her lyfe and frequent fear of death.[10]

10 Fraser (ed.), *Memorials of the Maxwells of Pollok*, i, p. 482, ii, pp 264–5.

She further alleged that on several occasions Maxwell turned her and their daughter Margaret out of the house, forcing them to spend the night in the stable with the animals. By refusing to allow her to use her own house at Milntown and by signing over her jointure to another, he had reduced her to 'extream miserie and necessitie, having little or nothing to maintaine her self, but by the charity of friends'. To make matters worse, Maxwell now planned to go into exile and leave her destitute. So she begged the council to oblige her husband to pay herself and her daughter a yearly maintenance. There is, unfortunately, no record of what penalties, if any, the council imposed on Maxwell. Nor do we have any knowledge of Agnes' subsequent fate.[11]

Sir Frederick's son and heir, Captain James, brought his young wife, Catherine, to live in Manorhamilton Castle after their wedding in 1647. Their first child, a daughter named Sidney, after her late grandmother, was born there the following year. The couple had a second girl in 1651 that they called Hannah.[12]

It is likely that James continued to serve under Sir Charles Coote during these years. By early 1648, the English parliament, through its military commanders – Coote in Connacht, Michael Jones in Leinster, George Monck in Ulster and Murrough O'Brien, Lord Inchiquin, in Munster – had seized the military initiative throughout Ireland. In the autumn of that year, therefore, the marquis of Ormond tried to form a royalist coalition, made up of his own forces, Irish confederates and the Scots army in Ulster, which he hoped would defeat the parliamentarians and even intervene on behalf of the king in Britain. Despite the beheading of Charles I by the English parliament in London in January 1649, the alliance in Ireland was proving to be quite successful until Colonel Michael Jones decisively defeated Ormond at Rathmines on 1 August of that year. This victory left the way free for Cromwell and his well-supplied army to land at Dublin later that month.[13]

The Cromwellian conquest of the country took another three years or so, with the native Irish leaders in particular offering stubborn resistance. Connacht was the last province to succumb. During the summer of 1651, Cromwell's son-in-law and successor, Henry Ireton, ably supported by Coote and commissary general Reynolds, invaded the western territory. They gradually captured the various towns and castles still under royalist and Irish control. In Leitrim, Jamestown and Carrick-on-Shannon surrendered in early April 1652. Galway submitted after a long siege one week later. Even then, various Irish leaders in the north-west of the province and in neighbouring Ulster were still holding out. So the earl of Clanricard, whom Ormond had appointed as his deputy when he fled

11 Ibid., i, p. 482; Hamilton, *The house of Hamilton*, p. 922.　**12** Balfour Paul, *The Scots peerage*, i, p. 45.
13 See Wheeler, *The Irish and British wars*, pp 209–11.

to France at the end of 1650, secured an alliance with these forces in a last desperate attempt to resist the aggressors.[14]

Just before Clanricard arrived in the north-west to take command of this new army in early May 1652, a strong party of native Irish from north Connacht and Ulster, under a Connachtman called Dowaltagh Caoch, decided to launch an attack on Manorhamilton Castle. Captain James Hamilton and his family were not in residence at the time. Neither was the parliamentarian castle garrison, which happened to be out on a foraging mission. The attackers surprised the garrison on its return and put every man to the sword. They then plundered the castle, which was 'riche and plentifull of both provision and amunition [and] covered with leade, a most necessarie ware for that armie'. Before leaving, they 'made havocke of all' and set fire to the castle, leaving it in a ruinous condition. While they were in the north Leitrim area, they also captured two or three other strongholds, including Parke's castle at Newtown. All this was accomplished 'with noe losse or labour and greate profitt' by the Irish.[15]

Shortly after these events, Clanricard arrived to take command of this sizeable army of north Connacht and Ulster troops. He captured Ballyshannon, but this was retaken by Coote on 26 May. One week later, the parliamentarians recaptured Parke's castle, and Sligo submitted to them on 18 June. Before the end of that month, Clanricard himself had surrendered to Coote, and, within a matter of weeks, most of the remaining outposts of Irish resistance in Connacht and Ulster had succumbed to the parliamentarians.[16]

After the destruction of Manorhamilton Castle by the Irish in May 1652, James and Catherine Hamilton went to live on Catherine's family estate at Strabane in Co. Tyrone. James died there on 27 December of that year, at the age of twenty-six. Seven years later, Catherine married the then high sheriff of Leitrim, Colonel Owen Wynne of Lurganboy Lodge near Manorhamilton, by whom she had four sons and three daughters. Some time after Wynne died in 1670, she remarried once again, this time to John Bingham of Foxford. He would later become MP for both Castlebar and Co. Mayo. He died in 1707, and, as there is no mention of Catherine in his will, we may assume that she predeceased him. She was buried in Cloonclare cemetery on the outskirts of Manorhamilton, where her effigy in stone, known as 'Lady Bingham', still lies today (fig. 26).[17]

14 R. Dunlop, *Ireland under the Commonwealth* (2 vols, Manchester, 1913), i, pp 163–73; M. MacMahon, *Portumna Castle and its lords* (Portumna, 1983), pp 16–17.   15 Gilbert (ed.), *A contemporary history of affairs in Ireland*, iii, pp 118–19. Dowaltagh Caoch may have been a MacSweeney from the barony of Tireragh in Co. Sligo: see Wood-Martin, *History of Sligo*, ii, p. 231.   16 Gilbert (ed.), *A contemporary history of affairs in Ireland*, iii, pp 119–22; Dunlop, *Ireland under the Commonwealth*, i, pp 212–35.   17 W.G. Jones, *The Wynnes of Sligo and Leitrim* (Manorhamilton, 1994), pp 9–12; R.E. McCalmont, *Memoirs of the Binghams* (London, 1915), p. 128; OS memoirs: statistical memoir of the union of Manorhamilton. Lieut. Lancey

26 Effigy of Catherine Hamilton, Lady Bingham,
in Cloonclare cemetery
(photograph by the author).

Sir Frederick Hamilton's only daughter, Christina, married, as his second wife, Sir George Monro of Newmore in northern Scotland. George was a son of Colonel John Monro of Obsdell, who had campaigned alongside Sir Frederick in Germany in 1631 and 1632. George himself had enlisted as an ensign in a Scottish regiment of the Swedish army in 1637. The following year, he married Anne, daughter of his uncle, Colonel Robert Monro, who also served in Germany. George left Swedish service in 1640, and two years later was appointed a lieutenant colonel in the Scottish covenanter army that was sent to Ireland under the command of his uncle, Robert. George's wife died in 1647. His allegiance transferred to the royalists around this time and in July 1648 he was commissioned as major general of two thousand Scots from the army in Ulster who were summoned to join the duke of Hamilton's engager army in the invasion of England. Following the defeat of the engagers, Monro fled to the court of the young Charles II in the Netherlands. He returned to Ireland early in 1649, however, to join Ormond's royalist coalition forces against the parliamentarians. After being knighted by Ormond at Kilkenny, he marched northwards and captured Carrickfergus and Coleraine from the parliamentarians during the summer of that year. It was while he was besieging the latter town in July 1649 that he married Christina Hamilton.[18]

The royalist resistance in Ireland began to crumble following Cromwell's arrival in the country during the month of August, and by the end of the year the Scots army in Ulster were a beaten force. So, George and Christina crossed over to Scotland to support the royalist uprising there on behalf of Charles II, who had landed in that country in June 1650. However, an English army – again led by Oliver Cromwell – invaded Scotland in July, and by the end of 1651 the Scots had been largely subdued.[19]

did a sketch of Catherine's effigy as it was in 1836. **18** *ODNB*, xxxviii, p. 649. **19** See Wheeler, *The*

27 Portrait of Gustavus Hamilton, first Viscount Boyne (1643–1723), in armour, with troops to the left in the distance. Oil on canvas. Attributed to Sir Godfrey Kneller (private collection).

When Charles II was restored to the British throne in 1660, Sir George Monro entered politics and represented his native Ross-shire in parliament for almost the next thirty years. In 1674 he was appointed major general of the army in Scotland and also admitted as a member of the Scottish privy council. He had strong Presbyterian sympathies, which were encouraged by his wife Christina, who herself was staunchly Presbyterian. The couple had one son and seven daughters. Sir George died in 1694 and Christina sometime after 1700. Both of them were buried in Newmore Chapel.[20]

Irish and British wars, pp 229–43.   **20** *ODNB*, xxxviii, pp 649–50.

Sir Frederick Hamilton's youngest son, Gustavus, was born in May 1643 (fig. 27). At the age of eighteen, he entered Trinity College Dublin, but, like his brothers Frederick and James two decades earlier in Glasgow, he left university without graduating. After joining the army in Ireland, he served as a captain in Sir George Hamilton's regiment in France from 1672 to 1676. While in attendance, as captain, on the duke of Ormond, chancellor of Oxford, he was conferred with a doctor of laws degree from that university on 5 August 1677. By 1685, he was serving as a major in Lord Mountjoy's regiment of foot.[21]

When the Catholic James II succeeded his brother Charles II as king of England, Scotland and Ireland in 1685, he wished to give Catholics the same status and liberties as Protestants throughout his three kingdoms. He appointed the Catholic Richard Talbot, earl of Tyrconnell, in charge of Irish affairs. Tyrconnell began by replacing many Protestant officers with Irish Catholics in the army. Despite being a Protestant, Gustavus survived the purge. However, after the Protestant William of Orange and his wife Mary (daughter of James II) landed in England and were received there as king and queen in November 1688, Gustavus resigned from the army and changed his allegiance to William. As governor of Coleraine, he successfully defended that town for a time against a Jacobite army in March 1689, before being forced to withdraw his small garrison to Derry. Soon afterwards, he crossed over to England, where he was given command of a new regiment, the first colonel of which had just died. When he had completed the formation of this regiment, he brought it over to Ireland in 1690, where it became known as the 20th Foot.[22]

Gustavus Hamilton took part in all the major engagements of the Williamite War in Ireland – the Battle of the Boyne (July 1690), the siege of Athlone (June 1691), the Battle of Aughrim (July 1691) and the siege of Limerick (August/ October 1691). He especially distinguished himself at Athlone, when he led an elite force of two thousand grenadiers across the Shannon in the perilous assault that gained the town for the Williamites. As a reward for his good service during the war, he was appointed vice-admiral of Ulster and governor of Athlone, as well as being granted 3,500 acres of confiscated land in Co. Meath. He was promoted to the rank of brigadier general in 1696 and to that of major general in 1704. He also became a member of the Irish privy council.[23]

After the Williamite War, Gustavus' principal residence was at Manor Vaughan, near Carrigart in Co. Donegal, which had been part of his late father's estate. He became MP for Donegal in 1692 and continued to represent that county in

21 *The information of Sir Frederick Hamilton*, pp 50–5; TCD, *Alumni of Trinity College Dublin*, p. 361; G.E. Cokayne, *The complete peerage*, ii, pp 266–7; *ODNB*, xxiv, pp 809–10.   **22** S. Duffy, *The concise history of Ireland* (Dublin, 2005), pp 118–19.   **23** *ODNB*, xxiv, p. 810.

parliament until 1713. Meanwhile, in 1704, he had purchased the Stackallan estate in Co. Meath for £5,350 and had gone to live there. He spent the next decade incorporating an existing castle and manor house on the property into an imposing and elegant new residence. In 1715 Gustavus was elevated to the peerage and given the title Baron Hamilton of Stackallan. Two years later, he was created Viscount Boyne. He married Elizabeth, daughter of Sir Henry Brooke of Brookeborough in Co. Fermanagh, and they had three sons – Frederick, Gustavus and Henry – and a daughter, Elizabeth. After his wife died in 1721, he married Anne, daughter of Sir George St George, baronet. Gustavus died at Stackallan on 16 September 1723 in his eightieth year, and was buried there.[24]

THE INHERITANCE OF SIR FREDERICK HAMILTON'S ESTATE

When Sir Frederick's son, Captain James, died in 1652, the inheritance of his estate passed to his two daughters, Sidney and Hannah. The elder daughter, Sidney, married Sir John Hume, baronet, of Castle Hume, Co. Fermanagh, sometime before 1666 and Hannah wed Sir William Gore of Manor Gore in Co. Donegal nine years later. The daughters divided up the estate between them, with Sidney opting for the Glenfarne section (fig. 28), which was closest to the Hume property in Co. Fermanagh, while Hannah acquired the smaller though more compact and populated western portion centred on Manorhamilton (fig. 29).[25]

The Glenfarne portion passed to the Loftus family of Loftus Hall in Co. Wexford when Sir John Hume's grand-daughter and heiress married Nicholas Loftus, first earl of Ely. Their son, Nicholas Hume Loftus, died unmarried, however, and the estate was eventually inherited by Charles Tottenham, MP for New Ross.[26]

The first member of the Tottenham family to take up residence in Glenfarne was Charles Henry, in the early years of the nineteenth century. He became sheriff of Leitrim in 1820 and built an imposing forty-eight-room mansion called Glenfarne Hall overlooking Lough MacNean. His son, Nicholas Loftus Tottenham, held the office of sheriff in 1841 and was elected chairman of the board of guardians of the Manorhamilton Poor Law Union the following year.[27]

24 Ibid.; C. Casey, 'Stackallan House' (unpublished booklet, 2005), pp 6–18.   25 Balfour Paul, *The Scots peerage*, i, pp 44–5; J. Anderson, *Historical and genealogical memoirs of the house of Hamilton*, p. 244. 26 www.proni.gov.uk/introduction_ely.pdf: Introduction Ely Papers (2007), 7–21, accessed on 10 Jan. 2009.   27 NLI, MS 9837, maps of the estate of Nicholas Loftus Tottenham, January 1797; www.tottenham.name/tree/sectionsB1, C1, C9 and C12–14, accessed on 10 Jan. 2009; A. Harrison, compiler, 'County of Leitrim: a roll of all gentlemen'; L. Ó Rúnaí, *From Rosclogher to Rooskey: the Leitrim story* (published privately, 1996), p. 208; P. Ó Duigneáin, *North Leitrim in Famine times, 1840–1850* (Manorhamilton, 1986), pp 28–9.

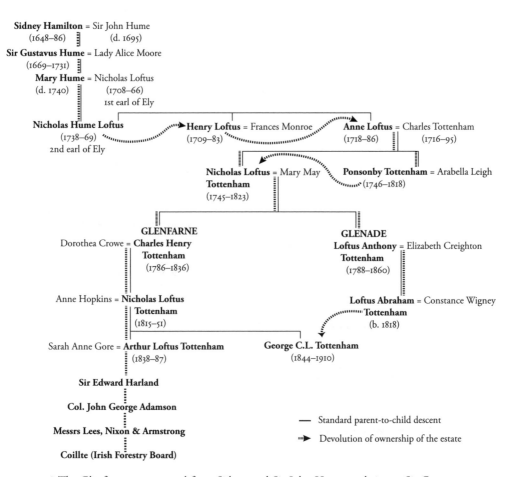

Sidney Hamilton = Sir John Hume
(1648–86)   (d. 1695)

Sir Gustavus Hume = Lady Alice Moore
(1669–1731)

Mary Hume = Nicholas Loftus
(d. 1740)   (1708–66)
              1st earl of Ely

Nicholas Hume Loftus   Henry Loftus = Frances Monroe   Anne Loftus = Charles Tottenham
(1738–69)   (1709–83)   (1718–86)   (1716–95)
2nd earl of Ely

Nicholas Loftus = Mary May   Ponsonby Tottenham = Arabella Leigh
Tottenham   (1746–1818)
(1745–1823)

GLENFARNE   GLENADE
Dorothea Crowe = Charles Henry   Loftus Anthony = Elizabeth Creighton
                 Tottenham   Tottenham
                 (1786–1836)   (1788–1860)

Anne Hopkins = Nicholas Loftus   Loftus Abraham = Constance Wigney
               Tottenham   Tottenham
               (1815–51)   (b. 1818)

Sarah Anne Gore = Arthur Loftus Tottenham   George C.L. Tottenham
                  (1838–87)   (1844–1910)

Sir Edward Harland

Col. John George Adamson

Messrs Lees, Nixon & Armstrong

Coillte (Irish Forestry Board)

—— Standard parent-to-child descent

⟶ Devolution of ownership of the estate

28 The Glenfarne estate passed from Sidney and Sir John Hume to their son Sir Gustavus, then to his daughter Mary and her husband Nicholas Loftus, and on to their son Nicholas Hume Loftus. When he died unmarried in 1769, the estate went to Henry Loftus, his uncle. When this man died childless, his sister, Anne Loftus, became the heir. She married Charles Tottenham. They had two sons, Nicholas and Ponsonby, who each inherited half of the Glenfarne estate, but Nicholas bought Ponsonby's share from him. The estate descended via Nicholas to his two sons, Charles (who inherited Glenfarne) and Loftus (who received Glenade). Glenfarne was held by Charles' son Nicholas and then Nicholas' son, Arthur Loftus Tottenham. The latter was forced to go surety for a loan from Sir Edward Harland of Harland & Wolff Shipbuilders of Belfast to complete the building of the Sligo, Leitrim and Northern Counties Railway. Being unable to repay the loan resulted in the bankruptcy of his Glenfarne estate. Tottenham emigrated to the UK and Harland acquired Glenfarne Hall (Tottenham's mansion) and demesne. Harland died in 1895 and in May 1902 the mansion and demesne were purchased by Col. John George Adamson. In July 1918, the property was bought by Lees, Nixon and Armstrong for £18,000. Glenfarne Hall was vandalized and burned to the ground during the War of Independence. The Land Commission acquired the whole estate some few years later and divided most of it up between former tenant farmers in the decade that followed. The Tottenham demesne was granted to the Forestry Commission and much planting of broadleaf trees took place there from the 1930s to the 1950s. Since 1988, this property has been administered by Coillte. Today it is a picnic resort known as Glenfarne Forest and Lake.

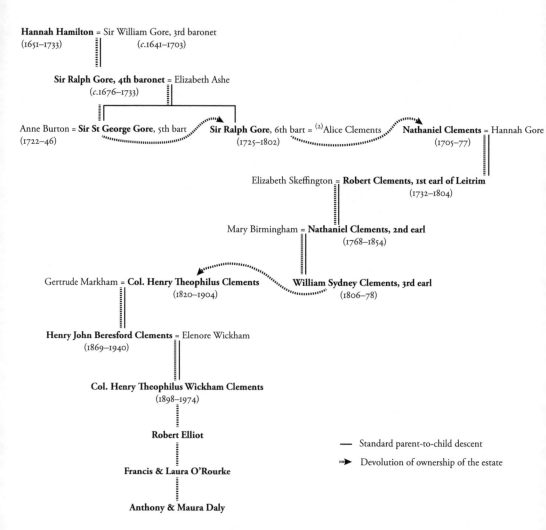

Hannah Hamilton = Sir William Gore, 3rd baronet
(1651–1733)   (c.1641–1703)

Sir Ralph Gore, 4th baronet = Elizabeth Ashe
(c.1676–1733)

Anne Burton = **Sir St George Gore**, 5th bart   **Sir Ralph Gore**, 6th bart = (2)Alice Clements   **Nathaniel Clements** = Hannah Gore
(1722–46)   (1725–1802)   (1705–77)

Elizabeth Skeffington = **Robert Clements, 1st earl of Leitrim**
(1732–1804)

Mary Birmingham = **Nathaniel Clements, 2nd earl**
(1768–1854)

Gertrude Markham = **Col. Henry Theophilus Clements**   **William Sydney Clements, 3rd earl**
(1820–1904)   (1806–78)

Henry John Beresford Clements = Elenore Wickham
(1869–1940)

Col. Henry Theophilus Wickham Clements
(1898–1974)

Robert Elliot

Francis & Laura O'Rourke

Anthony & Maura Daly

—— Standard parent-to-child descent

➠ Devolution of ownership of the estate

29 The Manorhamilton estate passed from Hannah Hamilton and her husband Sir William Gore, 3rd bart, to their son, Sir Ralph Gore, 4th bart, then to his son, Sir George Gore, 5th bart, and later to this man's brother, Sir Ralph, 6th bart. The estate was sold by Sir Ralph to Nathaniel Clements (a cousin of Gore's by marriage) for £21,822 in February 1759, and descended a further three generations in that family. William Sydney Clements, 3rd earl of Leitrim, bequeathed the estate to his relative, Col. Henry Theophilus Clements. His son, Henry John Beresford Clements, sold the major portion of the estate to the Land Commission during the early decades of the twentieth century, while his grandson, Henry Theophilus Wickham Clements, disposed of Castle Hamilton and the cottage – the last of the family's possessions in Manorhamilton – to Robert Elliot, a former tenant, in 1943. Both buildings were purchased in 1974 by Francis and Laura O'Rourke, who in turn sold them to Anthony and Maura Daly some twenty years later.

Arthur Loftus Tottenham, son of Nicholas Loftus, became sheriff in 1866 and was MP for Leitrim from 1880 to 1885. Though an obstinate landlord who refused to compromise with his tenants during the Land War, he was also the main driving force behind the construction from 1878 to 1882 of the Sligo, Leitrim and Northern Counties Railway, which gave much employment in the area.[28]

Arthur Loftus Tottenham was forced to go surety for a loan from Sir Edward Harland of Harland and Wolff Shipbuilders of Belfast in order to complete the railway project. Being unable to repay the money resulted in the bankruptcy of his estate. Harland then acquired Glenfarne Hall, using it as a holiday home and a hunting retreat. During the War of Independence, the mansion was vandalized and burned down. The Irish Land Commission divided up most of the estate between former tenant farmers in the 1920s and 1930s. The demesne itself was later afforested by the Irish Forestry Board. Today, it is known as Glenfarne Forest and Lake, and is a popular local amenity with a variety of walks, picnic areas and a boat quay.[29]

The marriage of Sir Frederick Hamilton's younger grand-daughter, Hannah, to Sir William Gore carried the Manorhamilton portion of the estate into the Gore family. The estate figured fairly prominently in the spring of 1689, when Brigadier Patrick Sarsfield set up his field headquarters in Hamilton's former walled deerpark after having been assigned the task of preventing supply ships from reaching Enniskillen through the port town of Ballyshannon.[30]

Sir Ralph Gore acquired the estate on the death of his father in 1703. He was appointed chancellor of the exchequer in 1729 and speaker of the house some four years later. He built a military barracks in Manorhamilton in 1716 to house an infantry company of forty men, but it was shut down in the more settled conditions of the 1750s.[31]

Sir Ralph's nephew, also called Sir Ralph, inherited the estate in 1746. He then commissioned the surveyor James Leonard to produce the earliest known maps of Manorhamilton and its town gardens. Ten years later, however, he sold the estate, comprising 5,393 acres, for £21,822 to Nathaniel Clements, his cousin by marriage. Clements had already acquired ten thousand acres of land at Lough Rynn near Mohill in the south of the county some years previously.[32]

28 P. Ó Duigneáin, *North Leitrim in Land League times* (Manorhamilton, 1987), pp 5, 21; P. Ó Duigneáin, *North Leitrim: the Land War and the fall of Parnell* (Manorhamilton, 1988), p. 62; N. Sprinks, *Sligo, Leitrim and Northern Counties Railway* (Leicester, 2001), p. 2; www.landedestates.ie: Connacht landed estates c.1700–1914 database, accessed on 20 Dec. 2010. **29** Ó Rúnaí, *From Rosclogher to Rooskey*, p. 208. **30** P. Wauchope, *Patrick Sarsfield and the Williamite War* (Dublin, 1992), pp 58–66. **31** P. Townend (ed.), *Burke's Peerage and baronetage* (London, 1970), p. 445; D. Rooney, 'Eighteenth-century military barracks in Manorhamilton and Lurganboy', *Leitrim Guardian 2003*, pp 90–3. **32** NLI, MS 16M10, maps and plans of the estates of Sir Ralph Gore and of the earl of Leitrim in the town of Manorhamilton and the county of Leitrim. Folio volume with 29 maps, 1749–1874; see also D. Rooney, '250 years of maps of

Clements was a powerful politician, property developer and financial figure in mid-eighteenth-century Dublin. In 1754 he was appointed chief ranger and master of the game in the Phoenix Park. He designed and built the impressive Ranger's Lodge, which later became the Vice-regal Lodge and eventually Áras an Uachtaráin.[33]

Nathaniel's eldest son, Robert, inherited his father's estates in Leitrim. As a reward for his loyal support for successive lords lieutenants, he was eventually ennobled in 1783 as Baron Leitrim of Manorhamilton, and was created earl of Leitrim twelve years later. Robert was succeeded by his son, Nathaniel, as second earl in 1804. Soon afterwards, he commissioned William Larkin to do a folio of maps of his Manorhamilton estate (pl. 9). He also erected a spacious and handsome new market house in the town in 1834.[34]

William Sydney Clements, on succeeding to the title as third earl in 1854, inherited a vast estate of over ninety-five thousand acres in Leitrim, Donegal, Galway and Kildare. His high-handed and domineering style of management, however, caused discontent and resentment among his tenants and he was assassinated on his north Donegal estate in April 1878.[35]

William Sydney left all his property to a second cousin, Colonel Henry Theophilus Clements, of Cootehill, Co. Cavan. The major portion of the Manorhamilton estate was sold to the Land Commission during the early decades of the twentieth century by the colonel's son. Sir Frederick Hamilton's castle itself was bought by a former tenant in 1956 and is presently owned by Anthony and Maura Daly, who have carried out significant consolidation and restoration work on the building (pl. 11).[36]

SIR FREDERICK HAMILTON'S LEGACY

Sir Frederick Hamilton claimed to have killed as many as 1,200 native Irish in Leitrim and the surrounding counties over a period of twenty-one months during the early 1640s. As far as their descendants were concerned, therefore, his

Manorhamilton', *Leitrim Guardian 1996*, pp 53–6; the text of the 'For Sale' notice that appeared in Faulkner's *Dublin Journal* is printed in the *Journal of the Breifny Antiquarian Society* (1926), p. 420. **33** F. Slevin, *By hereditary virtues: a history of Lough Rynn* (published privately, 2006), pp 14–17. **34** Ibid., pp 26–30, 32–40; NLI, MS 16F11, maps of Manorhamilton etc. in the county of Leitrim, the estate of the Rt Hon. the earl of Leitrim, surveyed by Wm Larkin 1807; O. Haslette, 'The Market House, Manorhamilton', *Leitrim Guardian 1983*, pp 95–7. **35** H. Coulter, *The west of Ireland* (Dublin, 1862), p. 333. **36** Manorhamilton Castle and the cottage house deeds. It is interesting to note that Colonel Henry Theophilus married Gertrude, a daughter of the English clergyman and amateur watercolour artist David Frederick Markham (1800–53), who had painted four scenes of Manorhamilton during a tour of Ireland in 1848. See D. Rooney, 'Mid-nineteenth-century watercolours of Manorhamilton by David Frederick Markham', *Leitrim Guardian 2005*, pp 92–4; www.manorhamiltoncastle.ie, accessed on 20 June 2010.

memory evoked sentiments of terror and hatred. The fact that fifty-eight of his prisoners were hanged on a gallows erected beside his castle, and also that the local civilian population was never spared during his fire and sword campaign, meant that he would also be recalled by successive generations as cruel and ruthless. It mattered little that Hamilton had justified his behaviour by claiming that he had received a commission from the lords justices to suppress the rebellion by military force. His assertion that he was only retaliating to a rebellion by Irish chieftains who killed his soldiers and tenants, burned his town and garrison, besieged his castle and made several attempts on his own life, also did not mitigate his guilt. And he was certainly not excused because of the low esteem in which he held the insurgents and their leaders. The former he described as 'wholly addicted to treacheries and perfidiousnesse ... naturally mercilesse and cruell upon avantages ... no savages have been so bloody and butcherly minded as they'. The latter, he believed, had proved disloyal to the king and could never again be trusted.[37]

It is not surprising, therefore, that several visitors to, and natives of, Manorhamilton over the course of the following centuries highlighted Sir Frederick's cruel and harsh nature. For example, John Wesley, the founder of Methodism, who preached in the town on 5 May 1769, wrote in his *Journal* that Manorhamilton was called after 'a poor wretch, famous in his day for nothing else but hanging up all the Irish who fell into his hands'. In his 1836 Ordnance Survey letters, John O'Donovan observed that the local population called Hamilton 'a bloody murderer', although he did add that the stories told about him were 'evidently the emanations of minds that detested him as their conqueror'. Later that century, Kate Cullen, who grew up in the town, of Anglo-Irish stock, described Sir Frederick in her memoir as a 'man of violent temper who had no scruples about shedding blood'.[38]

Hamilton's legacy of cruelty was further perpetuated by historians and other writers who used as their sources some of Sir Frederick's own publications, notably *A true relation*, in which he had given a detailed account of his 'services' against the rebels. The Liberator, Daniel O'Connell, for example, refers to Hamilton as an example of British inhumanity and cruelty towards the Irish during the 1641 rebellion. Quoting the historian and 'hostile witness' Edmund Borlase, a son of one of the lords justices in Ireland during the rebellion, O'Connell describes how Sir Frederick 'entering Sligo on first July 1642 burnt

37 *The information of Sir Frederick Hammilton*, pp 43–4; *Another extract of severall letters*, pp 55–6.   **38** R. Haire, *Wesley's one-and-twenty visits to Ireland* (London, 1947), p. 96; M. O'Flanagan (ed.), *Letters containing information relative to the antiquities of the counties of Cavan and Leitrim (Breifny) collected during the progress of the Ordnance Survey in 1836* (Bray, 1929), p. 131; Pyle, *The Sligo–Leitrim world of Kate Cullen*

the town and slew in the streets three hundred of the Irish'. Patrick G. Smith, author of *The Wild Rose of Lough Gill*, one of the most popular historical novels of late nineteenth-century Ireland, portrays Hamilton as a bitter scourge of the native Irish 'who outstripped all other "pillars of the state" in Ulster or Connaught in the extent of his tyranny and persecution'. For his part, Archdeacon Terence O'Rorke in his *History of Sligo* labels Sir Frederick the most ruthless monster in seventeenth-century Ireland who would have equalled or even eclipsed the savageries of certain human tigers of the East, like Genghis Khan or Tamerlane, if he had been given their opportunities. And in more modern times, Fr Daniel Gallogly in his article on Hamilton, makes mention of his 'unmitigated cruelty and sadism', depicting him as a precursor to Cromwell.[39]

Many of these damning assessments of Sir Frederick's violent nature were not, however, based on fact alone, but were also influenced by the many legends that grew up over time about the man. Chief among these were the stories describing Hamilton's supposed dinner or after-dinner murders and the brutal treatment of his victims. The first reference to such murders appears in a 1662 publication that set out to record the many atrocities committed by the British on innocent Irish Catholics during the 1641 rebellion. It recounts how 'the governour of Mannor Hamilton ... usually invited gentlemen to dine with him, and hanged them after dinner, and caused their thighes to be broke with hatchets before execution'. Almost two centuries later, Lieutenant William Lancey, in his Ordnance Survey memoir of the Manorhamilton area, wrote that, according to local tradition, Hamilton 'invited the Irish chieftains to dine with him, having prepared his servants at a special signal to dispatch them. The old Irish piper played the tune of "make your visits short and far between", but the hint had no effect and they were destroyed'. Some years afterwards, Kate Cullen recounted a story she had heard in Sligo about one of Sir Frederick's soldiers by the name of Rutherford who helped an Irish guest that was about to be murdered to escape, after he had taken pity on him. When Hamilton threatened to hang Rutherford in the Irishman's place, the rest of the garrison objected. 'So Rutherford went scatheless, and it is still said in Manorhamilton that if you call a little dog "Rutherford" it will cock its tail'.[40]

Another version of one of Hamilton's after-dinner murders is found in a poem penned by a local balladeer called Tommy Foley about the year 1865. The particular verse goes as follows:

(Dublin, 1997), pp ix, 1.   **39** D. O'Connell, *A memoir on Ireland, native and Saxon* (New York, 1843), p. 62; E. Borlase, *The history of the execrable Irish rebellion* (London, 1680), p. 88; P. G. Smith, *The Wild Rose of Lough Gill* (Dublin, 1883), p. 80; O'Rorke, *The history of Sligo, town and county*, i, p. 153; Mac an Ghallóglaigh, 'Sir Frederick Hamilton', p. 95.   **40** R.S., *A collection of some of the murthers and massacres committed on the Irish in Ireland since the 23rd of October 1641* (London, 1662), pp 7–8; RIA, OS memoirs,

He gives them gracious welcome and piles the banquet higher,
And freely flows the ruby wine, the weary guests retire.
O'Dowd is roused from slumber; in terror and dismay
He sees the headman axe in hand beside him where he lay.
Around the band of Frederick all crowding everyone,
And foremost stands the traitor, my lord of Hamilton.

Daniel Gallogly also referred to these murders and described how, according to tradition, Hamilton used to prolong the agony of his victims by beheading them with a blunt instrument like a reaping hook. He added that one man called Maguire from Co. Fermanagh was said to have been so terrified at the prospect of such suffering that he paid Sir Frederick a bag of sovereigns to have his head cut off quickly. It is interesting to note in passing, however, that there was also another legend in Co. Sligo that suggested that one such after-dinner murder was carried out by Catholics on their Protestant neighbours.[41]

Any account of Sir Frederick Hamilton's atrocities must be seen in the context of the times when massacres and pillaging were commonplace and carried out by all protagonists, Irish and British alike. Many of the crimes on the rebel side are recorded in the 1641 Depositions of Protestant settlers, who, after fleeing to Dublin in fear of their lives, made allegations of assault, stripping, imprisonment, robbery, arson and multiple killing against their Catholic neighbours. As against that, such publications as *A collection of some of the murthers and massacres committed on the Irish in Ireland* and Daniel O'Connell's *A memoir on Ireland* contain frightening examples of large-scale atrocities committed against the native civilian population by army garrisons throughout the country at this time. Even then, there is the added difficulty of trying to gauge the level of accuracy contained in all these accounts, and consequently the degree of credence that one can give to the numbers of casualties involved. Some accounts are purely hearsay. Moreover, both victims and perpetrators often had an interest in exaggerating their reports for propaganda purposes or in the hope of gaining compensation on the one hand or advancement on the other. Since Hamilton's ruthlessness, organization and energy as a military commander were obviously the key to his success, however, it is reasonable to assume that he spared neither insurgents nor innocent civilians in his grim determination to suppress the rebellion.[42]

Apart from the oral and written traditions of Hamilton's brutality, which have survived to this day in the north Leitrim area, local lore also abounds with stories

Box 28, 11; Pyle, *The Sligo–Leitrim world of Kate Cullen*, pp 1–2. **41** T. Foley, *Lines written on the destruction of Hamilton's Castle* (c.1865); Wood-Martin, *History of Sligo*, ii, p. 47. **42** TCD, MSS 809–841, depositions taken in the 1640s and 1650s; R.S., *A collection of some of the murthers and massacres*, pp 1–10; O'Connell, *A memoir on Ireland*, pp 54–62.

that relate to the capture of his castle and the supposed fate of the colonel himself. According to O'Donovan's Ordnance Survey letters, Sir Frederick's castle was said to 'have been set on fire by a family of the name of McLoughlin, who detested his name and power. After the burning of his castle, he [Hamilton] passed over to Scotland where he shortly after died of a lousy disease'. In Foley's poem, which was written some thirty years after O'Donovan's work, it was the Mayo man, O'Dowd, who, after having been spared a beheading and set free on condition that he return with a ransom, became the arsonist. Hamilton himself managed to escape the conflagration:

> The night being wild and windy, the revels lasted long,
> And Frederick's men were seated there with wassail, wine and song.
> Light flares upon the casement; loud shriek the startled dames.
> The Mayo men have gained the walls, the castle's wrapped in flames.
> The lead came down like molten mine and bubbling blue it run.
> That night saw Frederick fleeing far from Castle Hamilton.[43]

P.G. Smith in his 1883 novel credits Owen Roe O'Neill, Myles the Slasher O'Reilly and the fictitious Murty MacSharry, who was the childhood acquaintance of Kathleen Ny-Cuirnin, the Wild Rose of Lough Gill, with capturing the castle. Although they succeeded in setting fire to the building, they were unable to prevent Hamilton from seizing 'the most powerful horse in his stables, [riding] at full speed through the surrounding press of his enemies and escaping several shots that were fired after him'. Because Smith had framed his novel on historical data drawn mainly from authentic sources, several other writers in the decades that followed based their accounts of the destruction of Hamilton's castle on that narrative. T.C. Connolly in *Bundoran and its neighbourhood* and W.C. Trimble in his *History of Enniskillen*, for example, believed that O'Neill and some neighbouring chieftains, motivated by revenge, burned and sacked the castle. Connolly added that Sir Frederick and his two sons may have perished in the attack, or possibly escaped and watched the flames from four miles away at Saddle Hill.[44]

One other legendary incident relating to Hamilton still forms part of his legacy in the area. This is the well-known Scotsmen's leap or Lugnagall story, which tells how a detachment of Sir Frederick's men who were returning to

---

43 O'Flanagan (ed.), *Letters containing information relative to the antiquities of the counties of Cavan and Leitrim*, p. 131; Foley, *Lines written on the destruction of Hamilton's Castle*. The castle had a leaden roof as we are told in Gilbert (ed.), *A contemporary history of affairs in Ireland*, iii, p. 119. Foley imagines the lead liquefying in the intense heat and pouring on to the ground, as if it were gushing from a red hot mine or volcano. **44** Smith, *The Wild Rose of Lough Gill*, pp 156–65; T.C. Connolly, *Bundoran and its neighbourhood* (Dublin, 1896), p. 142; W.C. Trimble, *The history of Enniskillen*, i, p. 254–6.

Manorhamilton after the burning of Sligo town on 1 July 1642 were supposed to have been lured to their death over the cliffs of Glencar by a mad or mysterious guide. One version of the fable is recounted in Smith's *The Wild Rose of Lough Gill*. Here, the guide was the poor maniac Murty MacSharry, who managed to cling to a sapling that grew at the summit of the rock face as the mounted Scotsmen plunged to their deaths below. Another account is contained in one of William Butler Yeats' mythological tales *The curse of the fires and the shadows*, which was first published in 1897. In his story, the guide was a strange old man with a red cap and withered face, who was mounted on an old white horse. The soldiers he was escorting were powerless to prevent their horses from leaping over the precipice and falling, 'with a dull crash, upon the green slopes at the foot of the rocks'. The cliff face in question is to this day pointed out by locals.[45]

The physical aspect of Sir Frederick Hamilton's legacy is the town of Manorhamilton, which he founded in the early 1630s and which retains both his name and several reminders of his accomplishments. His ruined castle and a section of its bawn wall tower high above all other buildings. The original settlement has grown and developed over time, but its principal commercial artery remains the long Main Street, which emanates from the castle. The initial Church of Ireland parish church, built *c.*1638, is now in ruins (pl. 12). It was replaced as a centre of worship in 1783 by the present church, which is probably on the site of Hamilton's garrison's buildings. The fairs and markets established by the town's founder lasted for over 350 years before being eventually superseded by the present cattle mart. As for Sir Frederick's courts leet and baron, though, these have long since evolved into the present circuit and district courts in the town.

Hamilton's strategic siting of his settlement on a vein of fertile well-watered land at the intersection of four mountain valleys, where important north–south and east–west routes converge, has proved very advantageous over the centuries. Its situation mid-way between Sligo and Enniskillen resulted in the directors of the Sligo, Leitrim and Northern Counties Railway, which operated between these two towns, establishing the company's administrative headquarters and engineering works there in the 1880s. Because of its importance as the principal centre of population in the northern half of Co. Leitrim, the Industrial Development Authority and Enterprise Ireland have helped develop a number of international and indigenous industries in the town in more modern times. In the mid-1970s, when health administration was being regionalized throughout the country, Manorhamilton was chosen as the headquarters of the North Western Health Board because of its position between the neighbouring counties of Sligo and Donegal. In the recent restructuring of the service, the Health Service Executive

45 Smith, *The Wild Rose of Lough Gill*, pp 106–10; W.B. Yeats, *The Secret Rose* (London, 1897), pp 177–83.

has designated the former headquarters as a national project office under an assistant national director. The town has, therefore, due to its strategic location, acquired an importance far beyond what its size alone would merit.

Manorhamilton has moved on from its plantation origins. Today, it projects a progressive and self-reliant outlook, with citizens from several religious and ethnic backgrounds living and working in harmony for the common good. And while its ruined castle will always act as a reminder of the turbulent months of the 1641 rebellion, it can also be viewed as a means to a better understanding of the town's historical beginnings and the life and times of its colourful though controversial founder, Sir Frederick Hamilton.

THE EUROPEAN DIMENSION TO HAMILTON'S CAREER

Although primarily remembered in Ireland as the cruel suppressor of the 1641 rebellion in Leitrim and the surrounding counties, there were many other significant features of Sir Frederick Hamilton's varied career. He served as a part-time privy-chamberman at the courts of James I and Charles I for over a quarter of a century. He also participated on the fringes of the First and Second Bishops' Wars in 1639 and 1640. He subsequently commanded his own horse regiment in both the Scottish and the English Civil Wars. But it was his twelve-month campaign in the service of Gustavus Adolphus in Germany during the Thirty Years War that made the greatest impact on his later life.

The composite nations of Great Britain did not themselves play a major role in the Thirty Years War. Nevertheless, over one hundred thousand men from all parts of the British Isles fought in the armies of many European powers – most particularly those on the anti-Habsburg side – between 1618 and 1648. It has been estimated that half of these were Scots. In fact, as many as twenty-five thousand soldiers from Scotland served in Swedish armies alone between 1630, when Gustavus Adolphus intervened in Germany, and the end of the war. These included seventy or so officers such as Robert Monro, Robert Stewart, David Leslie and John Monro of Obsdell, who, like Sir Frederick Hamilton, held the rank of colonel. Many Scots enlisted because of their sympathy with the plight of their fellow Protestants in Germany. But they felt especially that they were fighting to uphold the honour of the Scottish House of Stuart following the Habsburg invasions of Bohemia and the Palatinate, and the expulsion from the empire of Frederick V and his Scottish-born wife, Princess Elizabeth.[46]

46 S. Murdoch (ed.), *Scotland and the Thirty Years War, 1618–1648* (Leiden, 2001), pp 14–15, 18–19; Grosjean, *An unofficial alliance*, 105–11.

Sir Frederick Hamilton had, no doubt, additional reasons for taking part in the war. As a distant relative of Charles I (and still very much a royalist in 1631–2), he would certainly have been eager to demonstrate his support for the British monarch. It would also have been natural for him to wish to campaign with his cousin, the marquis of Hamilton, general of the British army that arrived in Germany in the summer of 1631. And while mercenary motivation may well have been a factor, he probably also saw the war as an adventure where he, as colonel of a regiment, might serve with some distinction under Gustavus Adolphus, the illustrious leader of the Protestant cause at the time.[47]

It is likely that Sir Frederick owed his appointment to the Council of War in Ireland in the mid-1630s to his year-long experience at senior officer level on the battlefields of Germany. His involvement there also gave him a competitive advantage in his fight against the Irish during the 1641 rebellion and the later Confederate War. In the Swedish army, he had learned the most up-to-date tactics and strategy on how to deploy troops in action. Gustavus Adolphus ensured that his soldiers were trained regularly in exercises, forming and reforming ranks, drilling and using their weapons. Over a decade later, Hamilton recorded in some of his documents the use of several of these measures against the rebels. His military experience also stood him in good stead when he was confronted by Irish confederates who had formerly served in Spanish armies. While respecting their fighting qualities and admiring their bravery, he retained confidence in his own abilities and tactics.[48]

Extreme aggression, utter brutality and gratuitous slaughter were common-place features of the Thirty Years War. They resulted in huge loss of life, both within the ranks of the opposing armies and among the civilian population as a whole. While the carnage on many battlefields was appalling, fugitive soldiers and even entire units were also frequently killed in cold blood by the enemy or the local peasantry. In addition, war-related food shortages and epidemics drama-tically increased the mortality rate on occasion. The marquis of Hamilton's army, for example, lost two hundred men a week from plague, camp fever and other illnesses along the Oder in the autumn of 1631. At the same time, rival armies plundered the German countryside and destroyed entire towns, leaving the empire somewhat of a wasteland with a reduced population of some 20 per cent.[49]

It seems safe to assume that the violence and turbulence that Sir Frederick Hamilton experienced during the European campaign contributed in no small way to the cruel and pitiless streak in his nature that was so evident in his

---

47 SRA, AOSB E619, Hamilton's letter of grievances to the queen and senate of Sweden, *c.*end 1637.
48 *The information of Sir Frederick Hammilton,* p. 75; *Another extract of severall letters,* pp 28, 40–1, 45–6; *CSPI, Charles I, 1633–47,* p. 117.   **49** Parker et al. (eds), *The Thirty Years War,* pp 173, 180–2, 187–9.

treatment of insurgents, prisoners and the civilian population during the 1641 rebellion. He used ruthless and brutal tactics to suppress the Irish, whom he had come to mistrust and despise. Even civilians were considered a legitimate target because he suspected them of aiding and abetting those in arms. His memories of the European war would have allowed him to justify using 'the sword with the most keen and sharpest edge against a cruell and bloody rebell'.[50]

Hamilton's mission to Sweden in 1637 to seek redress for arrears of pay and the 'unlawful' disbandment of his regiment some five years earlier was not unusual. Other Scottish officers who had served in Swedish armies, such as Lieutenant General James King and Sir James Hamilton of Priestfield, did likewise around the same time. However, Sir Frederick's operation and the elaborate manner in which he carried it out are significant in that they highlight several of his most distinguishing personality traits – his acute sense of grievance at any attack on his honour, his readiness to appeal to the highest authority when seeking compensation or favours, and, finally, his desire to impress others by stressing his own importance and achievements. It was this last disposition in particular that earned him the sobriquet 'the Bragger'.[51]

50 *The information of Sir Frederick Hammilton*, Introduction.　51 SRA, AOSB E619, Hamilton correspondence: Sir James Hamilton of Priestfield to Oxenstierna, *c.*1636; SSNE Database, James King, ID: 2814.

Bibliography

Ireland

Marsh's Library (Marsh), Dublin

MS Z3.2.6 Miscellaneous papers, including letter from king to lord deputy authorizing Sir Frederick to nominate two baronets in Ireland.

MS Z4.2.6 Royal grants in Ireland, AD1604–31, including royal instructions for 1620 plantation of Leitrim.

National Archives (NAI), Dublin

Betham's genealogical abstracts.

MFS 42/6 & 42/7 Lodge's transcripts of the patent rolls.

RC 4/14 Calendar of chancery inquisitions for Co. Leitrim.

Repertories to chancery decrees.

National Library of Ireland (NLI), Dublin

MS 8014 (vi) Measurement of Co. Leitrim, probably taken in 1620.

MS 9837 Maps of the estate of Nicholas Loftus Tottenham, January 1797.

MS 10,162 A rental of the estate of Ponsonby Tottenham in Co. Leitrim, 1803.

MS 10,442 A.G. Green papers: notes and text by A.S. Green and F.J. Biggar towards a history of Co. Leitrim.

MS 16M10 Maps and plans of the estate of Sir Ralph Gore and of the earl of Leitrim in the town of Manorhamilton and the county of Leitrim, 1747–1874.

MS 16F11 Maps of Manorhamilton etc., in the county of Leitrim, the estate of the right hon. the earl of Leitrim, surveyed by William Larkin, 1807.

Royal Irish Academy (RIA), Dublin

MS 12W22 Description of Co. Leitrim by Mr Rody, 1683.

Ordnance Survey Memoirs, Box 28, 11. Statistical memoir of the union of Manorhamilton by Lieutenant William Lancey in 1836.

Trinity College Library, Dublin (TCD)

MS 672, 149r–162v Complaints of Leitrim natives for 1622 commission.

MSS 809–841 Depositions taken in the 1640s and 1650s.

MS 888/2 F16 Description of Co. Leitrim in1683.
Alumni of Trinity College Dublin.

Leitrim County Library, Ballinamore
Books of survey and distribution for Co. Leitrim (MS 2A2.14, fos 1–75 in
National Archives, Dublin).
Down Survey barony and parish maps of Co. Leitrim (originals in RIA, Dublin).

Northern Ireland
Public Record Office of Northern Ireland (PRONI), Belfast
D430/142 Bond of Sir Frederick Hamilton & others to pay Thomas Skiddy of
Cork £600, 3 Aug. 1637.
D580/1 Power of attorney given by Sir John Vaughan to Sir Frederick, 9 Apr. 1641.
T280/48 Tenison-Groves genealogical notes re. guardianship of Gustavus, Sidney
and Hannah Hamilton, 1661.
T525/7/2 Unsigned remonstrance, probably written by the Committee of
Adventurers for Ireland, *c.*early March 1644.

England
Bodleian Library (Bodl.), Oxford
MS Carte 1, fos 181–187v A list of the officers of the army for my lord of
Ormond, Aprill the 23rd 1640.
Wood MS F33, fos 69 & 70 A list of the king's servants appointed to attend his
majestie into Scotland, 11 May 1633.

British Library (BL), London
Add Mss 4,756 fo. 129v–130v Survey of plantation of Leitrim, 1620.
Add Mss 19,842 fo. 135r Land dispute between O'Michan & Sir Frederick,
Feb. 1634.
Add Mss 64,909 Letter from Sir Frederick to Sir John Coke, sec. of state, 14 Apr.
1635.
Add Mss 64,911 Letter from same to same, 3 Dec. 1635.

Parliamentary Archives, London
HL/PO/JO/10/1/47 Petition of Sir Frederick to the lords assembled in the upper
house of parliament, seeking redress against Strafford, 14 Jan. 1641.
HL/PO/JO/10/1/192 Request of Nicholas Loftus for protection in relation to a
debt of Sir Frederick Hamilton, 15 Sept. 1645.

HL/PO/JO/10/1/198 Petition of Sir Frederick Hamilton to the House of Lords that he not be made subject to the new governor of Connacht, *c.*May 1645.

The National Archives (TNA), London
SO1. Signet warrant book, Charles I.
SP16. State papers domestic, Charles I.
SP21/1–26 Records of the Committee of Both Kingdoms & the sub-committee on Irish affairs.
SP63. State papers Ireland, James I & Charles I.
T1/6535C Manuscript draft calendar of Irish patent rolls for part of the reign of Charles I.

Scotland
National Records of Scotland (NRS), Edinburgh
CC 8/8/63 fos 260r–262r Sir Frederick's Testament dative and inventar, Dec. 1647.
GD3 Papers of the Montgomerie Family, earls of Eglinton.
GD406 Hamilton collection.
PA. 2 Acts of the parliaments of Scotland.
PA 7/5/17 Petition of Robert Wallace, sometime quartermaster to umquhile Sir Frederick Hamilton's regiment, 23 Sept. 1647.
PC1 Register of the acts of the privy council.

Sweden
Swedish Riksarkivet (SRA), Stockholm
AOSB E601 Forbes correspondence:
(1) Alexander Master of Forbes to Chancellor Oxenstierna, 3 November 1633.
(2) Petition from captains A. and G. Forbes to Oxenstierna, *c.*1632/3.

AOSB E619 Hamilton correspondence:
(1) Sir Frederick Hamilton's petition to the Queen and Senate of Sweden, *c.*end 1637.
(2) Sir James Hamilton of Priestfield's appeal to Oxenstierna, *c.*1636.

Riksregistraturet, vol. 192, fo. 96r–v Royal 'Dimissio' for Sir Frederick, end of Dec. 1637.
Riksregistraturet, vol. 192, fo. 96v Reply from the Swedish chancellor, Oxenstierna, to James, marquis of Hamilton, regarding Sir Frederick, 30 Dec. 1637.

PRINTED PRIMARY SOURCES

The acts of the parliaments of Scotland, ed. T. Thompson and C. Innes (12 vols, Edinburgh, 1814–75; new ed. of vols v and vi, 1870–2), v–vi.

Acts of the privy council of England, vol. 46, June 1630–June 1631 (1964).

Another extract of severall letters from Ireland … as also, an exact relation of the good service of Sir Frederick Hammilton since the rebellion begun (London, 1643).

A repertory of the enrolments on the patent rolls of chancery in Ireland, commencing with the reign of James I (ed. J.C. Erck, i, pts 1, 2, Dublin, 1846–52).

Brev från Johan Adler Salvius, ed. Per-Gunnar Ottosson and Helmut Backhaus (Stockholm, 2012).

Calendar of Carew MSS, 1603–1624 (ed. J.S. Brewer and W. Bullen, London, 1873).

Calendar of state papers, domestic, Charles I, vols xii–xxii, 1637–49 (London, 1869–97).

Calendar of state papers, Ireland: 1603–1625 (eds C.W. Russell and J.P. Prendergast, 5 vols, London, 1872–80); *1625–1660* (ed. R.P. Mahaffy, 4 vols, London, 1900–4); *1660–70, addenda, 1625–70* (ed. R.P. Mahaffy, London, 1910).

Calendar of the patent and close rolls of chancery in Ireland, 1514–1633 (ed. J. Morrin, 3 vols, Dublin, 1861–3).

Harrison, A., comp., 'County of Leitrim: a roll of all gentlemen who filled the offices of high sheriff, sub-sheriff, foreman of grand jury, lieutenant of county, members of parliament for the county, with the date of office from the year 1600 to 1868' (Unpublished document, 1869).

Historical Manuscripts Commission 290: *Portland MSS, I* (1891): *Reply to Loudoun from British commanders in Derry, 8 Nov. 1643.*

Historical Manuscripts Commission: *Supplementary report on the manuscripts of His Grace, the duke of Hamilton* (1932).

Hogan, J. (ed.), *Letters and papers relating to the Irish Rebellion between 1642–46* (Dublin, 1936).

Jansson, Maija (ed.), *Proceedings in the opening session of the Long Parliament: House of Commons* (7 vols, New Haven, CT, 2000–7).

Journals of the House of Commons (Eng.) (12 vols, London, 1803), ii–vi.

Knowler, W. (ed.), *Letters and despatches of Thomas earl of Strafforde* (2 vols, London, 1740).

Kullberg, N.A., Severin Bergh et al. (eds), *Svenska Riksrådets Protokoll, 1621–1658* (18 vols, Stockholm, 1878–1959).

Lowe, J. (ed.), *Letter-book of the earl of Clanricarde, 1643–47* (Dublin, 1983).

Mac Cuarta, B. (ed.), 'Leitrim plantation papers, 1620–1622', *Breifne*, 9:35 (1999), 114–39.

Meehan, J. (ed.), 'Catalogue of the high sheriffs of the county of Leitrim from 1605 to 1800', *Journal of the Royal Society of Antiquaries of Ireland*, fifth ser., 18 (1908), 382–9.

Meikle, H.W. (ed.), *Correspondence of the Scots commissioners in London, 1644–1646* (Edinburgh, 1917).

Ohlmeyer, J., and Ó Ciardha, E. (eds), *The Irish statute staple books, 1596–1687* (Dublin, 1998).

Rikskansleven Axel Oxenstierna Skrifter och Brefrexling, first and second series (15 vols, Stockholm, 1888–1977).

Records of the University of Glasgow from its foundation till 1727 (3 vols, Glasgow, 1854), iii.

Register of the privy council of Scotland, second series (17 vols, Edinburgh, 1905–8), iv–viii.

Rushworth, J., *The tryal of Thomas earl of Strafford* (London, 1680).

The answere and vindication of Sir William Cole knight and colonell (presented to the right honourable the lords and others the committee of both kingdoms, and by them sent to be reported to the honourable the commons house of parliament of England at Westminster) unto a charge given in by Sir Frederick Hamilton knight, to the said committee, against the said Sir Will: Cole (London, 1645).

The humble remonstrance of Sir Frederick Hammilton, knight and colonell, to the right honourable the Committee of Both Kingdoms (London, 1645).

The information of Sir Frederick Hammilton, knight, and colonell, given to the Committee of Both Kingdoms, concerning Sir William Cole, knight, and colonell; with the scandalous answer of the said Sir William Cole, knight...(London, 1645).

The register of the privy council of Scotland, second ser., 4 (1630–2), ed. P. Hume Brown (Edinburgh, 1902).

The Swedish intelligencer: the fourth part (London, 1633).

To the honourable the knights, citizens and burgesses assembled in the Commons House of Parliament. The several petitions of William Hansard and Sir Frederick Hammiltoun knight and colonel ... As also, the several remonstrances of the committee at Grocers Hall for Irish affairs, in the behalf of Sir Frederick Hammiltoun ... (London, 1646).

Watson, C.B. (ed.), *Roll of Edinburgh burgesses and guild-brethren 1406–1700* (Edinburgh, 1929).

CONTEMPORARY WORKS

Adair, P., *A true narrative of the rise and progress of the Presbyterian Church in Ireland, 1623–70*, ed. W.D. Killen (Belfast, 1866).

Annals of the kingdom of Ireland by the Four Masters, from the earliest period to the year 1616, ed. and trans. John O'Donovan (7 vols, Dublin, 1851).

Boate, G., *Ireland's naturall history* (London, 1652).

Borlase, E., *The history of the execrable Irish rebellion* (London, 1680).

Brockington, W.S. (ed.), *Monro, his expedition with the worthy Scots regiment called Mac-Keys* (London, 1999).

Davies, Sir J., 'A discovery of the true causes why Ireland was never entirely subdued' in H. Morley (ed.), *Ireland under Elizabeth and James I* (London, 1890).

Dunlop, R., *Ireland under the Commonwealth: being a selection of documents relating to the government of Ireland from 1651 to 1659* (2 vols, Manchester, 1913).

Fraser, Sir W. (ed.), *Memorials of the Montgomeries, earls of Eglinton* (2 vols, Edinburgh, 1859).

Fraser, Sir W. (ed.), *Memoirs of the Maxwells of Pollok* (2 vols, Edinburgh, 1863).

Gilbert, J.T. (ed.), *A contemporary history of affairs in Ireland from AD1641 to 1652* (3 vols, Dublin, 1879–80).

Gilbert, J.T. (ed.), *History of the Irish Confederation and the war in Ireland* (7 vols, Dublin, 1882–91).

O'Sullivan, W. (ed.), *The Strafford inquisition of Co. Mayo* (Dublin, 1958).

Pender, S. (ed.), *A census of Ireland, circa 1659* (Dublin, 1939).

Prynn, W., and M. Nudigate, *The whole triall of Connor Lord MacGuire* (London, 1645).

Reynell, Revd W.A., 'Lists of parochial clergy of the late Established Church in the diocese of Kilmore', *Breifne Antiquarian Society's Journal* (1926), 389–99.

R.S., *A collection of some of the murthers and massacres committed on the Irish since the 23rd of October 1641* (London, 1662).

Shuckburgh, E.S. (ed.), *Two biographies of William Bedell, bishop of Kilmore* (Cambridge, 1902).

Spalding, J., *The history of the troubles and memorable transactions in Scotland from MDCXXIV to MDCKLV*, ed. J. Skene (Edinburgh, 1828–9).

Spenser, E., 'A view of the state of Ireland [1596]' in James Ware (ed.), *Ancient Irish histories: the works of Spenser, Campion, Hanmer and Marleburrough* (2 vols, Dublin, 1809).

Terry, C.S. (ed.), *Papers relating to the Army of the Solemn League and Covenant* (2 vols, Edinburgh, 1917).

The compossicion booke of Conought, transcribed by A. Martin Freeman (Dublin, 1936).

SECONDARY SOURCES

Allingham, H., *Captain's Cuellar's adventures in Connacht and Ulster, AD1588* (London, 1897). Reprinted under the title *The Spanish Armada* by Sligo County Council in 1988.

Anderson, J., *Historical and genealogical memoirs of the house of Hamilton* (Edinburgh, 1825).

Armstrong, R., *Protestant war: the 'British' of Ireland and the wars of the three kingdoms* (Manchester, 2005).

Bagwell, R., *Ireland under the Stuarts* (3 vols, London, 1909).

Balfour Paul, Sir J., *The Scots peerage* (9 vols, Edinburgh, 1904–14).

Benn, G., *The history of the town of Belfast* (Belfast, 1823).

Berg, J., and B. Lagercrantz, *Scots in Sweden* (Stockholm, 1962).

Besant, Sir W., *London in the time of the Stuarts* (London, 1903).

Bhreathnach, E., and B. Cunningham (eds), *Writing Irish history: the Four Masters and their world* (Dublin, 2007).

Birch, T., *The court and times of Charles I* (2 vols, London, 1848).

Brady, C., and R. Gillespie (eds), *Natives and newcomers: essays on the making of Irish colonial society, 1534–1641* (Dublin, 1986).

Burnet, G., *The memoirs of the lives and actions of James and William dukes of Hamilton and Castleherald* (1667, repr. 1852).

Byrne, J., *Byrne's dictionary of Irish local history* (Cork, 2004).

Canny, N., *Making Ireland British, 1580–1650* (Oxford, 2001).

Carlisle, N., *An enquiry into the place and quality of the gentlemen of His Majesty's most honourable privy chamber* (London, 1829).

Carte, T., *The life of James, duke of Ormond* (3 vols, London, 1851).

Casey, C., *Stackallan House* (Privately published booklet, 2000).

Casway, J., 'The last lords of Leitrim: the sons of Sir Teigue O'Rourke', *Breifne*, 7:26 (1988), 556–74.

Cheney, C.R., *A handbook of dates for students of British history* (rev. ed. Cambridge, 2000).

Cokayne, G.E., with V. Gibbs, H.A. Doubleday, G.H. White, D. Warrand, Lord H. de Walden (eds), *The complete peerage of England, Scotland, Ireland, Great Britain and the United Kingdom, extant, extinct or dormant*, new ed., 13 vols in 14 (1910–59, repr. in 6 vols, Gloucester, 2000).

Connolly, S.J. (ed.), *The Oxford companion to Irish history* (Oxford, 1998).

Connolly, T.C., *Bundoran and its neighbourhood* (Dublin, 1896).

Coonan, T., *The Irish Catholic Confederacy and the Puritan Revolution* (Dublin, 1954).

Čornej, P., and J. Pokarný, *A brief history of the Czech lands to 2004*, trans. A. Bryson (Prague, 2003).

Coulter, H., *The west of Ireland* (Dublin, 1862).

Craig, M., *The architecture of Ireland from earliest times to 1800* (London, 1982).

Cruickshanks, E. (ed.), *The Stuart courts* (Stroud, 2000).

Cunningham, B., 'The composition of Connacht in the lordships of Clanricard and Thomond, 1577–1641', *IHS*, 24:93 (1984), 1–14.

Curl, J.S., *The Londonderry plantation, 1609–1914* (Chichester, 1986).

Curtis, E., *A history of Ireland* (rev. ed. London, 2002).

Davies, N., *The Isles: a history* (London, 1999).

Day, A., and P. McWilliams (eds), *Ordnance Survey memoirs of Ireland: counties of south Ulster 1834–8: Cavan, Leitrim, Louth, Monaghan and Sligo* (Belfast, 1998).

Devine, T.M., *Scotland's empire, 1600–1815* (London, 2004).

Donaldson, G., *Scotland: James V to James VII* (Edinburgh, 1965).

Donaldson, G., *Scotland: the shaping of a nation* (third ed., Nairn, 1993).

Doodridge, P., *Some remarkable passages in the life of the hon. Col. James Gardiner, with an appendix relating to the ancient family of the Munros of Fowlis* (London, 1747).

Duffy, S. (ed.), *Atlas of Irish history* (Dublin, 1997).

Duffy, S., *The concise history of Ireland* (Dublin, 2005).

Dunlop, R., 'The plantation of Leix and Offaly, 1556–1622', *English Historical Review*, 6 (1891), 61–96.

Dunlop, R., *Ireland under the Commonwealth* (2 vols, Manchester, 1913), i.

Durand, S., *Drumcliffe: the Church of Ireland parish in its north Sligo setting* (Manorhamilton, 2000).

Elliott, M., *The Catholics of Ulster: a history* (London, 2000).

Faughnan, D.A., *Topographical and general survey of Co. Leitrim* (Clonrush, 1943).

Fenlon, Jane, '"They say I build up to the sky": Thomas Wentworth, Jigginstown House and Dublin Castle' in Michael Potterton and Thomas Herron (eds), *Dublin and the Pale in the Renaissance, c.1540–1660* (Dublin, 2011), pp 207–23.

Fischer, T.A., *The Scots in Germany* (Edinburgh, 1902).

Fitzgerald, P., 'Scottish migration to Ireland in the seventeenth century' in A. Grosjean and S. Murdoch (eds), *Scottish communities abroad in the early modern period*, (Leiden, 2005), pp 27–52.

Fox, S., 'The Annals of the Four Masters: a reappraisal' (unpublished paper, 1976).

Furgol, E.M., *A regimental history of the Covenanting armies, 1639–1651* (Edinburgh, 1990).

Gallogly, D., 'Brian of the Ramparts O'Rourke (1566–1591)', *Breifne*, 2:5 (1962), 50–79.

Gargan, P., 'St Clare's Roman Catholic church', *Manorhamilton Parish Church* (1983).

Gentles, I., 'The civil wars in England' in J. Kenyon and J. Ohlmeyer (eds), *The civil wars: a military history of England, Scotland and Ireland, 1638–1660* (Oxford, 1998).

Gillespie, R., 'An army sent from God: Scots at war in Ireland, 1642–9' in Norman Mac Dougall (ed.), *Scotland and war, AD79–1918* (Edinburgh, 1991), pp 113–32.

Gillespie, R., *Seventeenth century Ireland: making Ireland modern* (Dublin, 2006).

Gillespie, R., 'The murder of Arthur Champion and the 1641 Rising in Fermanagh', *Clogher Record*, 14:3 (1993), 52–66.

Greenwood, R., 'Colonel Alexander Master of Forbes' two Forbes regiments raised in 1631', unpublished compendium of events (2007).

Greenwood, R., 'Colonel William "Blowface" Forbes: a Scot who fought for parliament in Yorkshire during the first English Civil War' (unpublished paper, 2005).

Grimble, I., *Chief of Mackay* (London, 1965).

Grosjean, A., *An unofficial alliance: Scotland and Sweden, 1569–1654* (Leiden, 2003).

Grosjean, A., and S. Murdoch, 'Irish participation in Scandinavian armies during the Thirty Years War', *Irish Sword*, 24:97 (2005), 277–87.

Grosjean, A., and S. Murdoch, *SSNE Database* hosted by University of St Andrews www.st-andrews.ac.uk/history/ssne.

Gurrin, B., *Pre-census sources for Irish demography* (Dublin, 2002).

Guthrie, W., *Battles of the Thirty Years War from White Mountain to Nördlingen, 1618–1635* (Westport, CT, 2002).

Haire, R., *Wesley's one-and-twenty visits to Ireland* (London, 1947).

Hamilton, E., *Hamilton memoirs* (2nd ed., Dundalk, 1920).

Hamilton, Lord E.W., *The Irish rebellion of 1641* (London, 1920).

Hamilton, G., *The house of Hamilton* (Edinburgh, 1933).

Haslette, O., 'The market house Manorhamilton', *Leitrim Guardian 1983*, 95–7.

Hayes, R.J., *Manuscript sources for the history of Irish civilisation* (11 vols, Boston, 1965).

Hill, Revd G., *An historical account of the plantation in Ulster at the commencement of the seventeenth century, 1608–1620* (Belfast, 1877).

Hunter, R.J., 'Plantation in Donegal' in W. Nolan, L. Ronayne and M. Dunlevy (eds), *Donegal: history and society* (Dublin, 1995), pp 283–324.

Hunter, R.J., 'Sir William Cole and plantation Enniskillen, 1607–41', *Clogher Record*, 9:3 (1978), 336–50.

Hunter, R.J., 'Sir William Cole, the town of Enniskillen and plantation County Fermanagh' in E.M. Murphy and W.J. Roulston (eds), *Fermanagh, history and society* (Dublin, 2005), pp 105–45.

Jennings, B. (ed.), *Wild geese in Spanish Flanders, 1582–1700* (Dublin, 1964).

Johnston, G.H., *The heraldry of the Hamiltons* (Edinburgh, 1909).

Jones, W.G., *The Wynnes of Sligo and Leitrim* (Manorhamilton, 1994).

Jope, E.M. (ed.), *Studies in building history* (London, 1961).

Kearney, H., *Strafford in Ireland, 1633–41: a study of absolutism* (Cambridge, 1959).

Kelly, L., *A flame now quenched: rebels and Frenchmen in Leitrim, 1793–1798* (Dublin, 1998).

Kenyon, J., and J. Ohlmeyer (eds), *The civil wars: a military history of England, Scotland and Ireland, 1638–1660* (Oxford, 1998).

Kerrigan, P., *Castles and fortifications in Ireland, 1485–1945* (Cork, 1995).

Knowles, P., 'The Parish church', *Manorhamilton Parish Church* (1983).

Lacy, B., *Siege city: the story of Derry and Londonderry* (Belfast, 1990).

Leask, H.G., *Irish castles and castellated houses* (second ed., Dundalk, 1944).

Lees, J.C., *The abbey of Paisley, 1163–1878* (Paisley, 1878)

Lees, J.C., *The county histories of Scotland: Inverness (mainland)* (Edinburgh, 1897).

Lewis, S., *Topographical dictionary of Ireland* (2 vols, London, 1837), ii.

Lynch, M. (ed.), *The Oxford companion to Scottish history* (Oxford, 2001).

Livingstone, P., *The Fermanagh story* (Enniskillen, 1969).

Lodge, J., *The peerage of Ireland, or a genealogical history of the present nobility of that kingdom ...* (rev. ed. M. Archdall, 7 vols, Dublin, 1789).

Loeber, R., 'A biographical dictionary of engineers in Ireland, 1600–1730', *Irish Sword*, 13:53 (1979), 283–314.

Logan, J., 'Tadhg Ó Roddy and two surveys of Co. Leitrim', *Breifne*, 4:14 (1971), 318.

Mac an Ghalloglaigh, D., 'Sir Frederick Hamilton', *Breifne*, 3:9 (1966), 55–99.

Mac an Ghalloglaigh, D., 'Brian Oge O'Rourke and the Nine Years War', *Breifne*, 2:6 (1963), 171–203.

Mac an Ghalloglaigh, D., '1641 rebellion in Leitrim', *Breifne*, 2:8 (1965), 441–54.

Mac an Ghalloglaigh, D., 'Leitrim, 1600–1641', *Breifne*, 4:14 (1971), 225–54.

MacAtasney, G., *Leitrim and the Croppies, 1776–1804* (Carrick-on-Shannon, 1998).

McCalmont, R.E., *Memoirs of the Binghams* (London, 1915).

MacCarthy Morrogh, M., *The Munster Plantation: English migration to southern Ireland, 1583–1641* (Oxford, 1986).

Mac Cuarta, B. (ed.), *Ulster 1641: aspects of the rising* (Belfast, 1993).

Mac Cuarta, B., 'The plantation of Leitrim, 1620–1641', *IHS*, 32:127 (2001), 297–320.

Mac Dermot, B., *O Ruairc of Breifne* (Manorhamilton, 1990).

McCracken, E., 'Charcoal-burning ironworks in seventeenth and eighteenth-century Ireland', *Ulster Journal of Archaeology*, 20 (1957), 123–38.

McCracken, E., 'Supplementary list of Irish charcoal-burning ironworks', *Ulster Journal of Archaeology*, 28 (1965), 132–6.

McGrath, B., 'A biographical dictionary of the membership of the Irish House of Commons, 1640–1641' (PhD, University of Dublin, 1997).

McGrath, B., 'The membership of the Irish House of Commons, 1613–1615' (MA, University of Dublin, 1985).

McKenney, K.J., 'British settler society in Donegal, c.1625–1685' in W. Nolan, L. Ronayne and M. Dunlevy (eds), *Donegal, history and society* (Dublin, 1995), pp 325–56.

McKenney, K.J., *The Laggan army in Ireland, 1640–1685* (Dublin, 2005).

Mc Neill, T., *Castles in Ireland: feudal power in a Gaelic world* (London, 1997).

MacMahon, M., *Portumna Castle and its lords* (Portumna, 1983).

McParlan, J., *Statistical survey of County Leitrim* (Dublin, 1802).

Macinnes, A., *The British revolution, 1629–1660* (Basingstoke and New York, 2005).

Matthew, H.C.G., and B. Harrison, *Oxford dictionary of national biography* (60 vols, Oxford, 2004).

Maxwell, Sir H., *A history of the house of Douglas* (2 vols, London, 1902).

Meehan, C.P., *The Confederation of Kilkenny* (Dublin, 1882).

Meehan, C.P., *The rise and fall of the Irish Franciscan monasteries* (London, 1872).

Millett, B., *The Irish Franciscans, 1651–1665* (Rome, 1964).

Moody, T.W., F.X. Martin and F.J. Byrne (eds), *A new history of Ireland, iii: early modern Ireland, 1534–1691* (Oxford, 1978).

Moody, T.W., F.X. Martin and F.J. Byrne (eds), *A new history of Ireland, viii: a chronology of Irish history to 1976* (Oxford, 1982).

Moody, T.W., F.X. Martin and F.J. Byrne (eds), *A new history of Ireland, ix: maps, genealogies, lists* (Oxford, 1984).

Mooney, C., 'The Franciscan friary of Jamestown', *Ardagh and Clonmacnoise Antiquarian Society Journal*, 2 (1946), 3–25.

Moore, M.J. (comp.), *Archaeological inventory of County Leitrim* (Dublin, 2003).

Murdoch, S., 'James VI and the formation of a Scottish-British military identity' in S. Murdoch and A. Mackillop (eds), *Fighting for identity: Scottish military experience, c.1550–1900* (Leiden, 2002), pp 3–31.

Murdoch, S. (ed.), *Scotland and the Thirty Years War, 1618–1648* (Leiden, 2001).

Murdoch, S., 'The Scots and Ulster in the seventeenth century: a Scandinavian perspective' in W. Kelly and J.R. Young (eds), *Ulster and Scotland, 1600–2000: history, language and identity* (Dublin, 2004), pp 85–104.

O'Connell, D., *A memoir on Ireland, native and Saxon* (New York, 1843).

O'Dowd, M., 'Landownership in the Sligo area, 1585–1641' (PhD, UCD, 1979).

O'Dowd, M., *Power, politics and land: early modern Sligo, 1568–1688* (Belfast, 1991).

Ó Duigneáin, P., *North Leitrim in Famine times, 1840–1850* (Manorhamilton, 1986).

Ó Duigneáin, P., *North Leitrim in Land League times, 1880–1884* (Manorhamilton, 1987).

Ó Duigneáin, P., *North Leitrim: the Land War and the fall of Parnell* (Manorhamilton, 1988).

O'Flanagan, M. (ed.), *Letters containing information relative to the antiquities of the counties of Cavan and Leitrim (Breifny) collected during the progress of the ordnance survey in 1836* (Bray, 1929).

Ó Gallachair, P., 'The 1641 war in Clogher', *Clogher Record*, 4:3 (1962), 135–47.

Ó Gallachair, P., 'Tirconnell in 1641' in Revd T. O'Donnell OFM (ed.), *Fr John Colgan OFM* (Dublin, 1959), pp 70–110.

Ó Gallachair, P., *Where Erne and Drowes meet the sea* (Ballyshannon, 1961).

O'Grady, H., *Strafford and Ireland* (2 vols, Dublin, 1923).

Ollard, R., *The image of the king: Charles I and Charles II* (London, 1979).

Ó Mordha, S.P., 'Heber MacMahon, soldier bishop of the Confederation of Kilkenny', *Clogher Record Album* (1975), 41–62.

O'Rorke, T., *The history of Sligo: town and county* (2 vols, Dublin, 1889).

O'Rourke, Sr E., *Dúnta Uí Ruairc: O'Rourke strongholds of West Breifne* (Sligo, 1995).

Ó Rúnaí, L., *From Rosclogher to Rooskey: the Leitrim story* (Ros Inbhir, 1996).

Ó Siochrú, M., *God's executioner: Oliver Cromwell and the conquest of Ireland* (London, 2008).

Parker, G. (ed.), *The Thirty Years War* (second ed., Abingdon, 1997).

Perceval-Maxwell, M., *The outbreak of the Irish Rebellion of 1641* (Dublin, 1994).

Perceval-Maxwell, M., *The Scottish migration to Ulster in the reign of James I* (Belfast, 1999).

Perceval-Maxwell, M., 'Strafford, the Ulster-Scots and the covenanters', *IHS*, 18 (1972–3), 524–51.

Philips, W.A. (ed.), *History of the Church of Ireland: from the earliest times to the present day* (3 vols, Oxford, 1933).

Pyle, H., *The Sligo–Leitrim world of Kate Cullen, 1832–1913* (Dublin, 1997).

Reid, J.S., *History of the Presbyterian Church in Ireland* (3 vols, Belfast, 1867), i.

Reid, S., *Auldearn 1645: the marquess of Montrose's Scottish campaign* (Edinburgh, 2003).

Reid, S., *Scots armies of the seventeenth century – 1: the Army of the Covenant, 1639–51* (Nottingham, 2001).

Robinson, P., 'The Ulster Plantation and its impact on the settlement pattern of Co. Tyrone' in C. Dillon and H.A. Jefferies (eds), *Tyrone: history and society* (Dublin, 2000), pp 223–66.

Rogers, N., *Ballymote: aspects through time* (Sligo, 1994).

Rooney, D., '18th-century military barracks in Manorhamilton and Lurganboy', *Leitrim Guardian 2003*.

Rooney, D., 'Mid-19th-century watercolours of Manorhamilton', *Leitrim Guardian 2005*.

Rooney, D., 'The history of Manorhamilton post office', *Leitrim Guardian 2011*.

Rooney, D., '250 years of maps of Manorhamilton', *Leitrim Guardian 1996*.

Rooney, D., 'Count Owen O'Rourke (1670–1742) of Castletown, Manorhamilton', *Leitrim Guardian 2012*.

Roulston, W., 'The Ulster Plantation in the manor of Dunnalong, 1610–70' in C. Dillon and H.A. Jeffries (eds), *Tyrone: history and society* (Dublin, 2000), pp 267–89.

Ryder, I., *An English army for Ireland* (Leigh-on-Sea, 1987).

Salter, M., *Castles and stronghouses of Ireland* (Worcester, 1993).

Schama, S., *A history of Britain: the British wars, 1603–1776* (London, 2001).

Schlegel, D.M., 'A Clogher chronology: October 1641 to July 1642', *Clogher Record*, 16:1 (1997), 79–94.

Slevin, F., *By hereditary virtues: a history of Lough Rynn* (published privately, 2006).

Scott, D., *Politics and war in the Three Stuart Kingdoms, 1637–49* (Basingstoke and New York, 2004).

Simpson, R., *The annals of Derry* (Londonderry, 1847).

Smith, D.L., *A history of the modern British Isles, 1603–1707* (Oxford, 1998).

Smith, P.G., *The Wild Rose of Lough Gill* (Dublin, 1883).

Sprinks, N., *Sligo, Leitrim and northern counties railway* (Leicester, 2001).

Stalley, R. (ed.), *Daniel Grose (c.1766–1838): the antiquities of Ireland* (Dublin, 1991).

Starkey, D. (ed.), *The English court: from the Wars of the Roses to the Civil War* (Harlow, 1987).

Stevenson, D., *Revolution and counter revolution, 1644–51* (Edinburgh, 2003).

Stevenson, D., *Scottish covenanters and Irish Confederates* (Belfast, 1981).

Stevenson, D., *The Scottish Revolution, 1637–44* (Edinburgh, 2003).

Stone, G.C., *A glossary of the construction, decoration and use of arms and armour –
in all countries and in all times* (New York, 1961).

Sweetman, D., *Medieval castles of Ireland* (Cork, 1999).

Tayler, A. & H., *The house of Forbes* (Aberdeen, 1937).

Townend, P. (ed.), *Burke's peerage and boronetage* (London, 1970).

Treadwell, V., *Buckingham and Ireland, 1616–1628: a study in Anglo-Irish politics*
(Dublin, 1998).

Trimble, W.C., *The history of Enniskillen* (3 vols, Enniskillen, 1919), i.

Warrand, D. (ed.), *More Culloden papers* (5 vols, Inverness, 1923), i.

Wauchope, P., *Patrick Sarsfield and the Williamite War* (Dublin, 1992).

Wedgwood, C.V., *The king's peace, 1637–41* (London, 1955).

Wedgwood, C.V., *The king's war, 1641–7* (London, 1958).

Wedgwood, C.V., *The Thirty Years War* (London, 1938).

Wheeler, J.S., *The Irish and British wars, 1637–1654* (London, 2002).

Wood-Martin, W.G., *History of Sligo, county and town* (3 vols, Dublin, 1882–92).

www.landedestates.ie Connacht landed estates, *c.*1700–1914 database.

Yeats, W.B., *The secret rose* (London, 1897).

Young, A., *Three hundred years in Innishowen* (Belfast, 1929).

Index